Unmanned Aerial Vehicles for Internet of Things (IoT)

Scrivener Publishing
100 Cummings Center, Suite 541J
Beverly, MA 01915-6106

Publishers at Scrivener
Martin Scrivener (martin@scrivenerpublishing.com)
Phillip Carmical (pcarmical@scrivenerpublishing.com)

Unmanned Aerial Vehicles for Internet of Things (IoT)

Concepts, Techniques, and Applications

Edited by

Vandana Mohindru, Yashwant Singh, Ravindara Bhatt and Anuj Kumar Gupta

Scrivener Publishing

WILEY

This edition first published 2021 by John Wiley & Sons, Inc., 111 River Street, Hoboken, NJ 07030, USA and Scrivener Publishing LLC, 100 Cummings Center, Suite 541J, Beverly, MA 01915, USA

For more information about Scrivener publications please visit www.scrivenerpublishing.com.

Wiley Global Headquarters
111 River Street, Hoboken, NJ 07030, USA

For details of our global editorial offices, customer services, and more information about Wiley products visit us at www.wiley.com.

Library of Congress Cataloging-in-Publication Data

ISBN 978-1-119-76882-1

Cover image: Pixabay.Com
Cover design by Russell Richardson

Set in size of 11pt and Minion Pro by Manila Typesetting Company, Makati, Philippines

Contents

Preface

Unmanned aerial vehicles (UAVs) have become one of the rapidly growing areas of technology, with widespread applications covering various domains. UAVs play a very important role in delivering Internet of Things (IoT) services in small and low-power devices such as sensors, cameras, GPS receivers, etc. These devices are energy-constrained and are unable to communicate over long distances. The UAVs work dynamically for IoT applications in which they collect data and transmit it to other devices that are out of the communication range. Furthermore, the benefits of the UAV include deployment at remote locations, the ability to carry flexible payloads, reprogrammability during tasks, and the ability to sense for anything from anywhere. Using IoT technologies, a UAV may be observed as a terminal device connected in the ubiquitous network, where many other UAVs are communicating, navigating, controlling, and surveilling in real time and beyond line-of-sight.

However, many significant research challenges should be addressed before bringing such UAV capabilities into practice. The aim of this book is to explore the theoretical as well as technical research outcomes of all aspects of UAVs. The UAV has drastically altered the perspectives of users, practitioners, and researchers in many fields of application such as disaster management, structural inspection, goods delivery, transportation, localization, mapping, pollution and radiation monitoring, search and rescue, farming, etc. The advancements introduced by UAVs are countless and have led the way for the full integration of UAVs as intelligent objects in the IoT.

This book helps to realize the full potential of the UAV for the IoT by addressing its numerous concepts, issues and challenges, and develops conceptual and technological solutions for handling them. It is comprised of 15 chapters authored by various renowned experts in the UAV and IoT fields. The book is organized as follows:

Chapter 1 presents a comprehensive survey of UAVs. The communication standards, workings, and various technologies of UAV are presented.

Also, platforms of different types of drones in various categories, their working, types, sizes, and other technology employed in making them are explored. Furthermore, the latest ongoing technology used in drones and their recent advancements are discussed.

Chapter 2 highlights the state-of-the-art, challenges encountered and the open research issues in designing UAV-aided wireless communication networks. A few of the challenges identified and presented include the best methods of 3D deployment of drones, allocation of resources, optimization of the flight time and trajectory of UAVs, handover management, channel modeling of highly dynamic UAV channels in various scenarios of UAV-assisted networks, interference management, effects of higher Doppler shifts in mmWave networks, on-board energy availability of UAV devices, etc.

Chapter 3 focuses on the techniques available for effective battery and energy management in UAV-based communication networks. The mechanisms for the optimal utilization of energy resources by UAVs to maximize their lifespan or deployment in a network are critically examined. This helps to significantly reduce the usage of network energy that results in a prolonged network lifetime. Furthermore, potentially promising areas for future research in energy management are also explored.

Chapter 4 emphasizes the most used communication techniques in UAVs. The state-of-the-art literature regarding UAV communication techniques and a summary of the same in the form of challenges and issues that arise when developing communication methods for UAVs are presented. A comprehensive performance comparison of UAV communication techniques is provided at the end of this chapter.

Chapter 5 discusses different challenges and threats posed by UAVs such as hijacking, privacy, cybersecurity, and physical safety. Also discussed are different solutions for avoiding these issues with current technologies.

Chapter 6 bridges the landscape between the IoT and the UAV by identifying the technical and nontechnical issues facing integration. Also presented are various applications, architecture, and technologies of the UAV-enabled IoT. This chapter answers the question regarding the proximity between IoT and UAV by exploiting the mobility of UAVs.

Chapter 7 introduces the practice of using UAVs for security and intelligence and also relates how drones are employed in different domains and for different purposes, including mischievous ones. Also, new experiments are presented related to security, safety, and privacy concerns when UAV drones are engaged in dangerous activities.

Chapter 8 explores blockchain-based solutions for various security issues in UAV-enabled IoT. Though the fusion of UAVs and IoT proves disruptive, it is needed to address increased security issues. Identity management, authentication, UAV hijacking, secured and trustworthy data sharing in intra-UAV communications, and UAV signal jamming are explored in this chapter. Since blockchain is a decentralized technology, a distributed ledger offers solutions to some of these UAV issues presented here.

Chapter 9 introduces the efficient energy management systems in UAV-based IoT networks. The major constraint envisaged is the limited battery capacity of UAVs, proving them to be energy-constrained devices. The methods described here either harvest energy from RF signals or mmWaves, charge wirelessly from the charging station, or change the flight conditions for efficient energy utilization.

Chapter 10 contains an inclusive survey on the challenges and opportunities of IoE-enabled UAVs. There is a review of technologies enabling these opportunities, such as battery constraint, security issues, computing, and coverage constraints; and there is also an overview of UAVs. Finally, IoE-enabled UAV technology is presented that uses UAV deployment and mobility with IoE's intelligence, scalability, and diversity.

Chapter 11 provides a comprehensive survey of research for exploring applications of AI in UAV-enabled IoT systems with a specific focus on the research being conducted in the field of convergence of three disruptive technologies—namely, AI, UAVs, and the IoT—for improving the quality of life. The importance of AI in realizing an autonomous and intelligent flying IoT is emphasized.

Chapter 12 aims to follow a modular design approach to provide better functionality and a wide range of applications in all sorts of fields. It also incorporates the IoT in the UAV with all the sensor data of the surrounding environment with a UAV position that can be transmitted to a remote server and analyzed in real time.

Chapter 13 focuses on a mind-controlled UAV using brain-computer interface (BCI), which is a connection between the human brain and computers. The scope of this chapter is concentrated on the development boards which permit wireless communications.

Chapter 14 analyzes the new era farming system and the role of UAV technologies which help to improve the agricultural area to enable farmers to make cost-effective decisions while also preserving the ecosystem and changing how food is generated.

Chapter 15 explores the IoT-based UAV platform revolutionizing smart healthcare. The mobile phone industry and the IoT networks that are making robust data collection possible are rapidly being used in medical tools and software. This chapter discusses healthcare IoT technologies and their advantages for society.

In closing, we would like to thank our contributing authors for their valuable work, without which it would have been impossible to complete this book. We would also like to express our deepest appreciation to our reviewers for submitting their valuable comments in a timely manner. Last but not least, we thank GOD for giving us the strength and wisdom to carry out this work successfully even during tough circumstances due to the COVID-19 pandemic.

We hope that the quality research work published in the 15 chapters of this book will serve the needs of those in the academic, research, science and technology communities along with all of humanity.

Dr. Vandana Mohindru
Assistant Professor, Chandigarh Group of Colleges, Mohali, Punjab, India
Dr. Yashwant Singh
Associate Professor & Head, Department of Computer Science and IT, Central University of Jammu, J&K, India
Dr. Ravindara Bhatt
Assistant Professor (Senior Grade), Jaypee University of Information Technology, Solan, H.P., India
Dr. Anuj Kumar Gupta
Professor, Chandigarh Group of Colleges, Mohali, Punjab, India

1

Unmanned Aerial Vehicle (UAV): A Comprehensive Survey

Rohit Chaurasia and Vandana Mohindru*

Department of Computer Science & Engineering, Chandigarh Group of Colleges, Mohali, India

Abstract

Research on Unmanned Aircraft Vehicle (UAV) or unmanned aircraft system (UAS) are increasingly becoming popular in recent times and are widely used for various commercial purposes like photogrammetry, surveying, remote sensing for mapping, rescuing as well as for military purposes and so on. This chapter presents a wider explanation of UAV in terms of working, communication, various types along with various technologies, starting from the various platforms of different types of drones to various categories, its working, types, sizes, and various other technologies employed in making of it. The communication aspect of a UAV is critical from both security and safety points of view and it is discussed in a separate section thoroughly. UAVs have tremendous applications in various fields and therefore their recent advancement has also raised concern for their misuse in a certain activity. Still, UAVs have a lot of limitations to overcome to properly meet the demand of the market in the 21st century. It also discusses the latest on-going technology used in drones and their recent advancement that will likely be the wave of the future.

Keywords: UAV types, radio communication, tactical & strategic drones, military drones, photogrammetry, UAV application, mapping

**Corresponding author*: vandanamohindru@gmail.com

Vandana Mohindru, Yashwant Singh, Ravindara Bhatt and Anuj Kumar Gupta (eds.) Unmanned Aerial Vehicles for Internet of Things (IoT): Concepts, Techniques, and Applications, (1–28) © 2021 Scrivener Publishing LLC

1.1 Introduction

An Unmanned Aerial Vehicle or UAV (also known as a drone) is an aircraft without a human pilot on-board and can be piloted remotely or can fly autonomously with predefined paths [1]. UAV is a component of an unmanned aircraft system (UAS) which further includes a remote control station and a system of communication between the two. UAV is a term mostly referenced to be used in military use cases while in civil it is "drone". A drone is a general term used to refer to the UAVs [2].

UAVs are becoming increasingly famous because of their numerous good applications in various fields and scopes. E.g. Disaster monitoring, assessment and management, aerial mapping, Asset Inspection & Videography, Mapping & Surveying, Aerial Photography, Real estate photography [3], Crop spraying & monitoring, Agriculture, Payload carrying, different applications requiring Multispectral/thermal/NIR cameras, Mining, Search and Rescue, Disaster-zone mapping, Live-streaming events, Marine Rescue, Forensics, Disaster Relief, Emergency Response, Monitoring Poachers, Roof inspections, Firefighting, Product Delivery, Meteorology, Aviation, etc. and with further advancement in technology UAV can survive extreme weather condition which makes them a perfect fit for it [4, 16].

1.2 Related Work

According to the research, it is found that UAVs have powerful applications in both civil as well as in the military. With their mobility, low-cost, safety & reliability, now UAVs can replace a manned-aerial vehicle in similar tasks as well as outperform them in many curriculums. However, several usage challenges have to be overcome first and one of these challenges is the avoidance of collision with the other objects. For proper use and advancement, UAVs must have the feature of avoiding collision with both static and moving obstacles. It is quite similar to that of mobile robots & air traffics. UAVs have unique characteristics that make them considerable and interesting research ground. Vision-based UAV navigation is a slight modification of this because UAVs are unable to perceive their surrounding environment clearly and therefore they act accordingly due to limitations in the perception ability of their sensors and in communication [5]. A considerable amount of work is done to improve this weakness. However, a still effective and systematic method is needed to be developed. Hence, high-performance robust autonomous navigation is of immense importance.

Apart from this, there is also one significant aspect of drone and i.e. photogrammetry and mapping which is the concept of acquiring imagery for any useful purpose, it can be for disaster research and management, automatic forest fire monitoring, detection & fighting, mapping the terrain or for any commercial purpose. Due to such a wide variety of applications, it not only becomes the most engaging but also a vital area of research and development. In this case, UAV photogrammetry & mapping proves a much viable and economical option than traditional methods like satellite imagery [6]. The main contribution of our work is to give a brief overview and introduction of various terms, techniques, latest technologies, and their implementation in modern UAVs through a holistic approach.

1.3 UAV Technology

1.3.1 UAV Platforms

Given the great diversity of UAVs, there are varying numbers of UAV platforms and they can be classified broadly in terms of their sizes, design, usage, how high, and how long a UAV can fly. Nevertheless, the most basic categorization is determined by the weight of the drone. Here are some classifications done on various features.

Classification based on the weight of UA (Unmanned Aircraft) as follows [16]:

- Micro: Less than two kilograms (<2 kg).
- Mini: Greater than 2 kg and less than 20 kg.
- Small: Greater than 20 kg and less than 150 kg.
- Large: Greater than 150 kg.

Classification based on the aerial platform according to which there are four types of drones [7, 8]:

1. Fixed-wing drones
2. Multirotor drones
3. Single-rotor helicopter
4. Fixed-wing hybrid VTOL (Vertical Take-Off & Landing).

1.3.1.1 Fixed-Wing Drones

Fixed-wing type of drone is the type of drone that uses a 'wing' like the normal airplanes out there. They never use their energy to stay afloat rather they cruise in the air. They move forward as remotely controlled by a human or they could be made autonomous through guided GPS coordinates. Most fixed-wing drones have a couple of hours of average flying time as shown in Figure 1.1. Liquid fuel or gas-powered drones have high endurance and can fly up to 10 h or longer [9]. Fixed-wing is ideal for long-distance operations such as surveillance or mapping owing to their flight time and fuel efficiency. Still, they can be handy when aerial-photography involves loitering over a particular area for a longer duration of time. Also, there are some other downsides which include the higher cost and skill required for flying. It is not easy to put this type of drone in the air. One either needs a 'runway' or a catapult for the launch and the same goes for the landing you either need a runway or a parachute or a net to land them back in the ground safely.

1.3.1.2 Multi-Rotor Drones

Multi-rotor drones are the most heavily used drones by the professional or hobbyist for various activities and operations mainly for aerial-photography and surveillance etc. They are further classified based on the number of rotors in a platform. There is a *Quadcopter* having four-rotors, a *Hexacopter* with six-rotors, *Bicopter* with two-rotors, an *Octocopter* with eight-rotors, and *Tricopter* with three-rotors. Among these, Quadcopter is the heavily used variant.

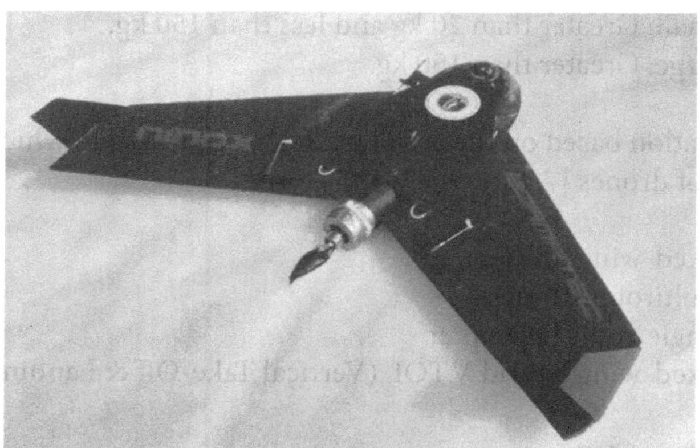

Figure 1.1 Fixed-wing UAVs [33].

It is easy to manufacture and having capabilities like vertical take-off, loiter makes it suitable for many applications but like others, it also has some downsides too. The prominent ones being are its speed, limited endurance, and flying time. They are not much suitable for large-scale projects like surveillance or long-distance aerial mapping [9]. The major problem with this type of drone is that majority of their energy is spent in stabilizing themselves in the air and defying gravity. At present, most of the multi-rotor drones are powered from battery sources and are capable of 20–30 min of flying time with some exceptional cases going to 50 min. often with a payload of a lightweight camera.

1.3.1.3 Single-Rotor Drones

Single-rotor is indistinguishable in terms of design and structure from an actual helicopter. The single-rotor consists of one big-sized rotor with a smaller one on the tail of the drone to control the heading as shown in Figure 1.2. However, in terms of efficiency, they are much more efficient than multi-rotor drones. They usually have higher flying times & with gasoline or gas-powered engine, it can be increased significantly as shown in Figure 1.3. As a general rule of thumb, lower the count of rotors, lesser would be the spin of an object i.e. why quads are much stable than octocopters. In the same sense, a single rotor will be much more stable than Multirotor. However, they also have some complexity and operational risk. Their high cost and large-size blades often pose a risk of injuries, if mishandled and even involve accidents. On the other hand, multi-rotor having small blades is unlikely to cause an accident or injury although a scar is likely is mishandled but that can also be avoided with ducts which

Figure 1.2 Single rotor drone [35].

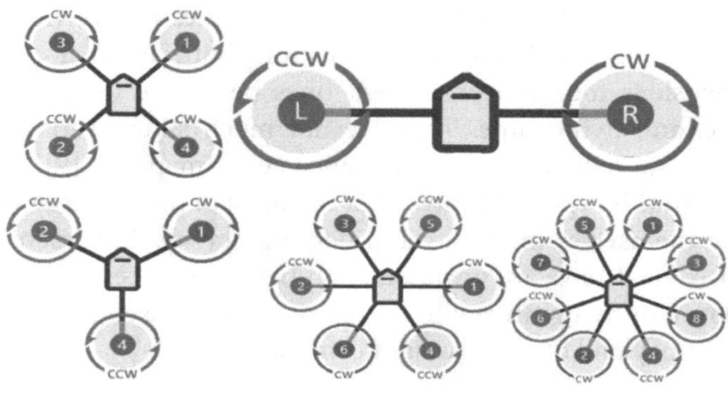

Figure 1.3 Types of multi-rotor drones [34].

also have an extra-added advantage. Single-rotor drones also require much training and skill to fly them in the air properly.

1.3.1.4 Fixed-Wing Hybrid VTOL

This type of drone has the best of both features from rotor-based & fixed-wing design. In the fix-wing hybrid, it will have a couple of rotors which will be attached at the end of wings or in the middle of wings given the wings must rotate accordingly to perform VTOL (Vertical Take-off & Landing). For e.g., the rotor will be perpendicular during take-off and attains to parallel while cruising.

These types of drones are formed from the type of aircraft that dates back to the 50s and 60s. However, implementing this type of technology to real-life was considerably difficult, and they were largely helved before they came as drones. These types of units are still in the experimental or trial stage and are less commercially available than the fixed-wing, multi-rotor, and single rotor counterparts. They are still in the military while several companies are developing them, and they may well be the wave of the future.

1.3.2 Categories of the Military Drones

UAVs in the military are classified according to their speed, range, weight & on the basis of their special capabilities. In general, drones tend to come in different shapes and sizes depending on the type of functions they serve and because military drones are top-class military tech as shown in Figure 1.4.

Figure 1.4 V-22 osprey military helicopter [36].

Therefore, it is quite interesting to examine them and their various types. NATO (North Atlantic Treaty Organization) troops have different classification of drones which is as shown below [10, 16]:

(i) CLASS-I (<150 kg): Mini, small or micro drones

There are various types of class-I drone which are used to execute many informational, Communicational, command, control, and computerized solutions. These types of drones are of immense importance as they provide ISTAR (Intelligence, Surveillance, Target Acquisition, and Reconnaissance). It also includes micro, mini, or small drones. Also, Flapping wing platform types drones are used here also called "Ornithopter".

(ii) CLASS-II (150–600 kg): Tactical drones

Tactical Unmanned aircraft (UA) or drones are designed explicitly to be used in Special Forces or at the battalion level. These types of UAVs have greater advantages for medium-range surveillance. They fill the space between the range of the function of the short-range micro & strategic UAVs, which is comprised of HALE (High-Altitude Long Endurance) & MALE [11] (medium-altitude Long Endurance). They have a combination of flexibility, ruggedness as well as endurance. They offer an intermediate function between that of small and strategic drones as shown in Figure 1.5. They are used in awareness and situational-analysis to offer surveillance and protection, target acquisition, and also in the evaluation of damage based on a particular given force. E.g. MQ-9 Reaper (Predator B)—Tactical Drone.

Figure 1.5 RQ-11B Raven Small UAS (SUAS) [3, 37].

One of the most polished and elegant tactical ISTAR system around the world is Watchkeeper which is developed by Thales and it is the largest UAS program in the whole of Europe and it is one of the largest UAVs in Europe which is authorized to fly even in civilian airspace including urban areas.

(iii) CLASS-III (>600 kg): Strategic Drones
This class of drones comprises of MALE and HALE systems. MALE is good for reconnaissance as well as surveillance in a non-threatening area. They have a tremendous range of application, which includes determining the movement of a certain population which are not in conflict or position of the enemy. They have state of the art infrastructure & technology and are also used to accumulate the lists of targets.

Some globally acclaimed MALEs are Reaper/Predator, Anka, and Heron family of drones. Some of the few HALEs available right now are the global hawk family & triton [12].

1.3.3 How Drones Work

What is a drone and how do drones work can be understood through the technologies employed in it. UAV drone technology is constantly evolving

Figure 1.6 RQ-4 Global Hawk—Heavy Strategic Military Drone [38].

as innovation and heavy investment brings more advanced drones to the market every few months. Mostly UAV drones have similar incorporated systems.

UAV technologies cover everything from the aerodynamics of the drone, materials used in the manufacture of the physical UAV, to the circuit boards, chipset, and software, which are the brains of the drone. The fast pace of UAV technology is tremendous.

UA is made of light composite material for increased maneuverability and reduced weight. This allows the military drones to cruise at extremely high altitudes. These materials are highly-complex composites, lightweight, strong, durable at the same time and they help in the absorption of vibration and reduces the sound produced. They are also equipped with the state-of-the-art technology such as precise and accurate GPS, laser, infrared cameras, etc as shown in Figure 1.6. Drones are controlled remotely by remote ground control also referred to as a ground cockpit.

1.3.3.1 Firmware—Platform Construction and Design

A firmware platform construction and design for small-scale UAV research is important. As open-source autopilot systems with much reliability (e.g. ArduPilot) were not publicly available until 2009. Most of the researchers' groups have to start from scratch to build a reliable UAV firmware platform as shown in Figure 1.7. Fixed-wing and rotor types are conventional,

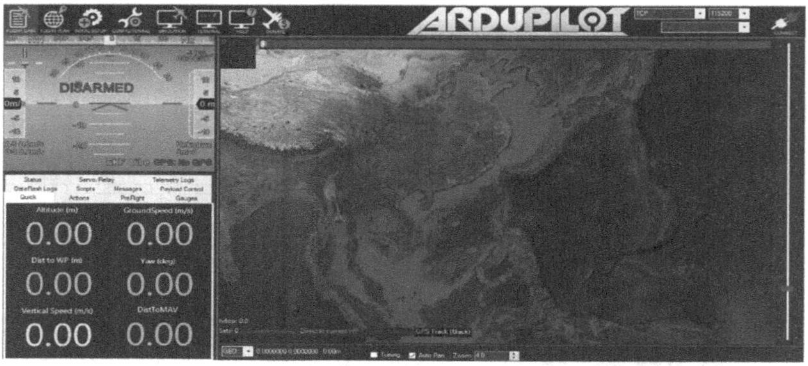

Figure 1.7 Representation of GUI configuration of ArduPilot open-source platform.

therefore the Flight control System (FCS) in this firmware mainly consists of the above platforms [3].

1.3.4 Comparison of Various Technologies

1.3.4.1 Drone Types & Sizes

UAVs have a much wider variety of sizes and vary according to the need. The largest one is being used for military purposes such as the MQ-4 Triton, built by Northrop Grumman, Raytheon and L3 Comm, the MQ-4 is 47.6 feet long with a wingspan of 130.9 feet, giving it a span wider than a Boeing 737 airliner. The next in size is unmanned aircraft, which have fixed wings and require short runways or sometimes catapult. These are generally used to cover a larger area of land, for geographical mapping, surveying, or to combat wildlife poaching and numerous other examples. These are mainly used for commercial or civil purposes. VTOL drones on the other hand have the endurance of fixed-wing type and vertical take-off quality like quadcopter which makes it more suitable for a job where there is not much space for landing e.g., in hilly areas.

1.3.4.2 Radar Positioning and Return to Home

Most drones are equipped with GPS but now the latest drones have dual Global Navigation Satellite Systems (GNSS) [13] such as GPS [14] and GLONASS [3] (Global Orbiting Navigation Satellite System, Russian). Drones can fly in both non-satellite mode and GNSS mode. For example, DJI drones can fly in P-Mode (GPS and GLONASS) or ATTI mode, which don't use GPS. Highly accurate drone navigation is important while flying, as it has immense importance in drone applications such as surveying the landscape, SAR (Search and Rescue) missions, and creating 3D maps.

When the quadcopter is switched on its navigation satellite searches and detects GNSS satellite. High-end GNSS systems use satellite Constellation Technology. A satellite constellation is a group of satellites working together in near proximity and sync with one another giving coordinated coverage. This is done in such a way that these satellites overlap an area and is well in coverage. Here, pass or coverage is referred to as the period in which a satellite is visible above the local horizon.

1.3.4.3 GNSS on Ground Control Station

RADAR displays the below data on the remote control display:

1. Signals that adequate GNSS satellite signals are detected and the drone is ready to fly.
2. Displays the current location and position or orientation of a drone in accordance with the controller.
3. Records the home-point for the 'Return to Home' safety feature.

The return-to-home safety feature can be pilot initiated by pressing the button on the remote controller or in an application/software, also it can be automatically triggered when the battery is low as a failsafe whenever there is a loss of contact between remote controller and UAV, then UAV will fly back automatically to its home point. The latest technology drone has obstacle avoidance technology while returning home.

1.3.4.4 Collision Avoidance Technology and Obstacle Detection

Modern drones are now equipped with a collision-avoidance system. They use sensors/cameras or scanners to scan their surroundings, while SLAM (Simultaneous Localization & Mapping) technology produces 3D maps from real-time images allowing them to involve in real-time to sense and avoid. SLAM is an extremely important technology when it comes to drones, robots and cars in detecting and avoiding obstacles. Through the combined feedback of the sensors the drone's sense and avoid, there are:

1. Monocular Vision
2. Vision Sensor

3. Ultrasonic Sensor
4. Time-of-Flight (ToF)
5. Infrared
6. LIDAR.

Drones these days have obstacle avoidance sensors on all six sides. They use both infrared and vision sensors which are then fused into the vision system and this technique is known as Omni-directional obstacle sensing [3]. It senses an object then flies around the obstacle, avoiding any collision and can also do the same when flying in the opposite direction. Also, it can hover if it isn't possible to pass the obstacle. This technology is known as APAS (Advanced Pilot Assistance System).

1.3.4.5 Gyroscopic Stabilization, Flight Controllers and IMU

Gyroscopic stabilization technology gives the UAV drone its smooth flying capabilities. The gyroscope works almost instantly to the forces moving against the drone, keeping it flying or hovering smoothly. It provides essential navigational information to the flight controller.

The IMU (Inertial Measurement Unit) detects the current rate of acceleration using one or more accelerometers. The IMU detects the changes in rotational attributes like pitch, yaw, and roll using one or more gyroscopes. Sometimes a magnetometer is also used with the IMU to assist with calibration against orientation drift. Gyroscope is a component of IMU and IMU is an essential component of the Flight controller which is the central brain of the drone.

1.3.4.6 UAV Drone Propulsion System

The propulsion system with which drones fly in any direction or hover includes BLDC motors (Brushless DC motor), ESC (Electronic Speed Controller), and propellers. It varies according to the different types of platforms. In a quadcopter, the motor and propellers work in pairs with two motors & propellers placed alternatively one pair rotating clockwise (CW propellers), the other two motors rotate counter-clockwise (CCW Propellers). Similarly, in Hex three motors/propellers pair and in Oct four motors/propellers pair. These BLDC motors receive the electric signal from ESC which receives the signal from the flight controller which in turn receives the signal from the radio transmitter. Together they signal motor speed, braking, monitoring, and fault tolerance.

Apart, from this combustion-derived propulsion is also used in UAV mostly in a fixed-wing platform where some of them use a mini Turbojet engine to cruise at a higher speed. These fast jet mini UAVs have achieved speed as high as 700 km/h and even more. It uses ECU (Engine Control Unit) which comes along with actuators and some sensors and is directly connected to the fuel supply line of the combustion chamber to control the speed of the Turbojet engine.

1.3.4.6.1 Proposed Technology

With advancement and improvement in propulsion system technology, it could be possible in the future that drone would be propelled by ion thruster without brushless motor, while drones with turbojet engine traveling very far distance have already become possible but still achieving heights as high as that of satellites with much higher speed is still a future tech. However, this type of drone will have less application for commercial purposes and will be more for research & military tech, and would be costly [15].

1.3.4.7 Flight Parameters Through Telemetry

Nearly all drones have a Ground Station Controller (GSC), allowing the remote controller to fly the drone and keep track of the current flight telemetry. Telemetry data on the remote controller may include remaining battery power, warnings, speed, height, UAV range, GNSS strength, and video.

1.3.4.8 Drone Security & Hacking

UAV in many ways is a kind of flying computer with an operating system, flight controllers, and other boards with programmable codes, they can also be hacked into. There are Drones that have been developed to fly around seeking other drones and hacking into the drone wireless network, which then disconnects the owner and takes over that drone. However, there are some ways to protect your drone from hackers [17, 18].

1.3.4.9 3D Maps and Models With Drone Sensors

Multispectral, LIDAR & Photogrammetry sensors are used to build 3D models of landscapes and buildings. Thermal vision and low light night vision sensors are used by drones to scan landscapes, building to assist in agriculture, search & rescue, firefighting, and so on.

A technology called Sensor Fusion can be used in drones in which drones carry different sensors with software combining the data together for better results. These systems automatically combine input data from several different sensors such as regular RGB camera, thermal camera for the purpose of improving system performance or application. Combining data from multiple sensors reduces and corrects the errors as compared to using individual sensors to calculate the accurate position and orientation information. For e.g. Multi-Spectral sensors in drones can create Digital Elevation Maps (DEMS) of land areas to provide precise data on flowers, shrubs, trees, fauna, and on the health of crops or more.

Drones with Time-of-Flight (ToF) sensors came to the market in 2016. ToF is also called Flash Lidar which can be used on its own or can be combined with RGB and regular LIDAR sensors to provide economical solutions across various sectors. ToF depth ranging camera sensors can be used for 3D photography, tracking objects, measure volumes, object scanning, obstacle avoidance, indoor navigation, gesture recognition, gesture recognition, augmented reality games, and much more. These Flash LIDAR ToF cameras have a huge advantage as it can measure distances to objects within a complete scene in a single shot. In photogrammetry and lidar mapping, the UAV is programmed to fly over an area autonomously, using waypoint navigation [19]. The camera on the drone will take photographs at a continuous interval like every 0.5 or 1 s then these photos will be stitched together using specialized photogrammetry software to create 3D images as shown in Figure 1.8.

DroneDeploy is a widely used 3D mapping software. It's a mobile app and a live map is being used in various sectors for creating 3D models and

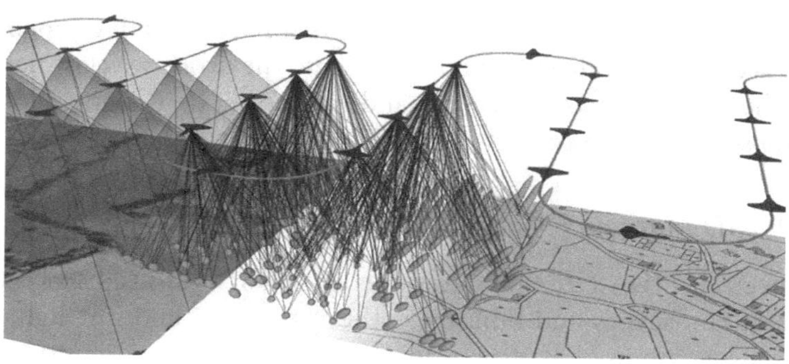

Figure 1.8 Visual representation of a fixed-Wing platform taking photographs at its designated points [39].

maps. Their specific software solution for the agricultural sector and others work with most of the latest drones.

Capturing high-resolution images on a drone that is stabilized is important and using top photogrammetry software to process them into real maps and models is just as important. Some of the top drone mapping softwares are as follows:

- Autodesk ReCap Photogrammetry Software.
- Pix4D-Mapper Photo-grammetry Soft.
- Drone-Deploy 3D Mapping Solutions.

1.3.5 UAV Communication Network

The unmanned aircraft system (UAS) or UAV is facing enormous growth from capital as well as the technological point of view. The number of drones in operation is increasing in gigantic number, with several million produced annually in recent years. The scale and mass of drones vary from micro-drones weighing a few grams to heavy gigantic machines as big as the size of almost a commercial aircraft.

According to ICAO (International Civil Aviation Organization), UAS has been classified broadly into two categories:

- *Remotely-piloted Aircraft systems*: It consists of various elements which include unmanned aircraft, ground control & some necessary command and control links, or any other element which is configurable together and is required for flight operation.
- *Autonomous aircraft*: It is an unmanned aircraft which don't require pilot involvement in the controlling or management of the flying aircraft [20].

Communication is a key aspect of the UAS system due to the presence of a human in a remote place. Therefore, the operation of UAS depends upon communication which enables safe UAS operation in non-segregated airspaces.

1.3.5.1 Classification on the Basis of Spectrum Perspective

International Telecommunication Union (ITU) classifies unmanned aircraft broadly in three categories on the spectrum perspective. It is highly dependent on the range, cruise speed, and altitude of the unmanned aircraft. The Table 1.1 depicts the same classification [21]:

Table 1.1 UA categories on the basis of spectrum perspective.

Category of unmanned aircraft (UA)	Weight (kg)	Maxim height/ altitude (m)	Cruise speed (km/h)	Endurance (h)	Maximum range (km)
Small	<25 kg	<300 m	<111 km/h	<5 h	Visual LoS <3 km
Medium	25–2,000 kg	300–5,500 m	111–185 km/h	5–30 h	RF LoS 150–250 km
Large	>2,000 kg	>5,500 m	>185 km/h	>30 h	Beyond RF LoS

1.3.5.2 Various Types of Radiocommunication Links

For the safe operation of unmanned aircraft under Beyond LoS (Line-of-Sight) and Line of sight (LoS), three types of radio communication between UA & ground control are required, which is as follow [22]:

1. Radiocommunication for the air traffic control relay.
2. Radiocommunication for command and control.
3. Radiocommunication for the sense and avoid function.

After this, it is left to the UA system designer to combine the links accordingly as per the needs of these three radiocommunications into a common physical link.

1.3.5.2.1 Radio-Communications for the Air-Traffic Control

In non-segregated airspace, the link between ATC (air traffic control) and UACS via Unmanned Aircraft (UA) is called ATC relay and it will be required to relay ATC and air-to-air communications received and transmitted by the UA. For communication with ATC, the UA uses the same equipment as that of the manned aircraft. There are two types of communication between UACS and UA via ATC i.e. the downlink bringing the ATC information from the UA to the UACS (Unmanned Combat Aircraft System) and the uplink from the UACS to the UA allowing the UACS to communicate with ATC. This type of communication is critical from the point of view of the safety of the controlled airspaces, especially in areas with a high density of aircraft and terminal in approach. In this case, Future ICAO standards are of immense importance for these kinds of communication.

1.3.5.2.2 Radio-Communications for Command and Control

Command & control is the typical link between the Control station and the unmanned aircraft. The following are two ways of communications:

The uplink: For sending telecommands to the aircraft for flight and navigation equipment control.

The downlink: To send telemetry (e.g. cruise speed, flight status) from the UA to the UACS. It is expected that in some flight conditions or in specific airspaces it could be necessary to downlink video streams.

This consideration is of higher importance for the work of the ITU-R related to Resolution 421 (WRC-07) and it must also be considered with the similar requirement that may come from the support of sense and avoid function and a requirement like these could lead to data rates of several hundreds of kbit/s per UA. In areas under the responsibility of the aeronautical authorities, it is expected that the command and control communications will have to be compliant with ICAO standards to be further specified on this function. However, in the periods where the UA will follow a fully autonomous flight, the up and downlinks could have very low data rates.

1.3.5.2.3 Radio-Communications for the Sense and Avoid Function

Sense and avoid (S&A) corresponds to the piloting principle "see and avoid" used in all air space volumes where the pilot is responsible for ensuring separation from nearby aircraft, terrain, and obstacles (e.g. weather). To determine appropriate spectrum requirements related to the S&A function, two aspects must be considered:

Firstly, all the RF equipment designed to collect raw data related to the "sense" function will have specific requirements depending on the ITU-R services involved. For example, the evaluation of the close proximity of the UA using radar equipment will operate in radio determination service bands. It should be studied if this functionality can be developed by using existing systems such as radar, ACAS, ADS-B, and UAT. The data derived by the sensors could either directly be processed inside the UA or be transmitted to the UACS.

Secondly, the control of the proper operation of this S&A function will be permanently or regularly checked at the UACS. If necessary, S&A parameters may be modified by the UACS, depending upon the area of flight, the weather conditions, or the level of autonomy assigned to the UA. In these bi-directional communications between the UACS and the UA for the S&A function, two different information streams must be considered:

The S&A data uplink will allow the UACS to control the operation of this function according to the conditions of the flight. Identical to the Control uplink, it is expected that such communication will not require high bit rates.

The S&A data downlink from the UA to the UACS indicates that the S&A function operates as desired. Similar to the Control downlink requirement, the need to send video streams under this S&A function must be considered avoiding duplication between Command and Control and S&A video downlinks.

Similar to the command and control considerations, it is expected that the "S&A data" RF communication requirements will have to be compliant with future ICAO standards for the safe flight of the UA in areas under the responsibility of the aviation authorities.

1.3.5.3 VLOS (Visual Line-of-Sight) and BLOS (Beyond Line-of-Sight) Communication in Unmanned Aircraft System

Figure 1.9 depicts the links in VLoS deployment scenario of UAS [23]. Figure 1.10 depicts the links in the BLoS deployment scenario of UAS.

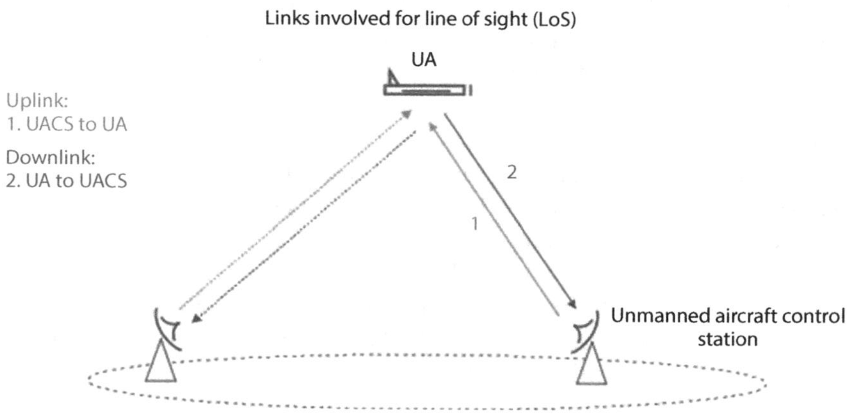

Figure 1.9 VLoS deployment scenario for UAS [40].

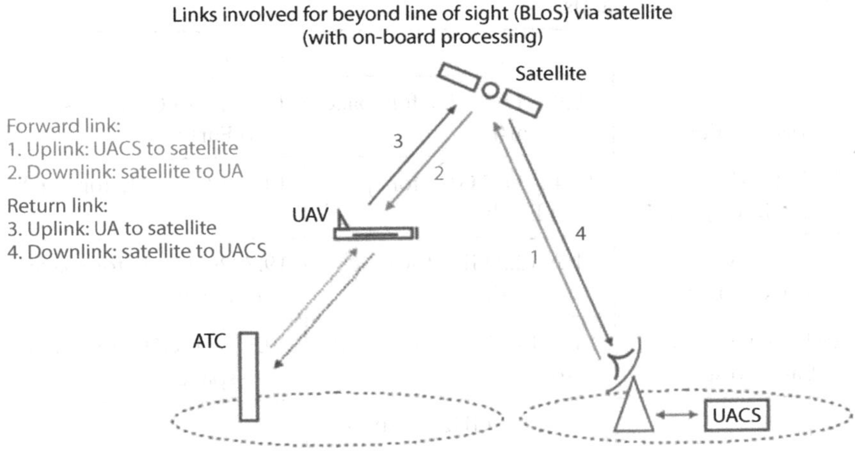

Figure 1.10 BLoS deployment scenario for UAS [40].

1.3.5.4 Frequency Bands for the Operation of UAS

The category of small UAS generally, uses the unlicensed band of 2.4 GHz, 5.8 GHz unlicensed 900 MHz, and UHF (Ultra-High Frequency) bands for communication. The UAS has to comply with the national regulations applicable for the operation of other technologies in these bands. WRC-12 allocated the frequency band 5,030–5,091 MHz to be used for the terrestrial RPAS control links. Subsequently, WRC-15 identified the following spectrum to be used by satellite systems controlling drones. However, it was also noted that ICAO is to develop the relevant SARPS before the spectrum can be used and there will be a progress report to WRC-19 and WRC-23 will review the effectiveness of the allocation. There are power limits associated with some of these frequency bands as given in Table 1.2 [20, 24].

- → Africa, Europe, and some parts of the Middle-East are covered in region 1.
- → America is covered in region 2.
- → Asia and the Pacific are covered in region 3.

1.3.5.5 Cellular Technology for UAS Operation

Cellular-tech. like emerging 5G technology & LTE are likely to be a candidate for UAS development. It ensures [25]:

Table 1.2 Frequency bands.

Region 1	**Region 2**	**Region 3**
12.5–12.75 GHz for space to Earth	10.95–11.2 GHz for space to Earth	12.2–12.75 GHz for space to Earth
14.0–14.47 GHz for Earth to space	11.45–11.7 GHz for space to Earth	14.0–14.47 GHz for Earth to space
19.7–20.2 GHz for space to Earth	11.7–12.2 GHz for space to Earth	19.7–20.2 GHz for space to Earth
29.5–30.0 GHz for Earth to space	14.0–14.47 GHz for Earth to space	29.5–30.0 GHz for Earth to space
	19.7–20.2 GHz for space to Earth	
	29.5–30.0 GHz for Earth to space	

- High mobility
- Increased reliability & quality of services
- Ubiquitous coverage
- Robust security Radio Division.

Numerous telecom companies are conducting trials for UAS operation in cellular LTE network and consequently, the problems faced are [26]:

- Optimization of the cellular requirement for drones: Cellular networks are needed to be distinguished from the one which is currently in use by worldwide users for optimal operation (e.g. Noise avoidance) of UAs in cellular networks.
- Handover optimization: While in operation it is obvious UAs are going to receive signals from multiple base stations. Therefore, handover will be frequent which will lead to heavy signaling overheads.
- Interference mitigation: When airborne UA will receive signals from multiple base stations hence there will be interference.

1.4 Application of UAV

UAVs have an immense possibility to be used widely in both military and civil applications because of economic viability, safety benefits, and high mobility. Recent technological advancements in UAVs have made it more compatible for replacing the manned aerial vehicles and even outperforming them in many tasks and at the same time proving its worth in the commercial market is also commending.

1.4.1 In Military

Nikola Tesla, in 1898, first developed which was arguably the first remote-controlled unmanned vehicle, also called 'Teleautomation', a boat controlled by radiofrequency. From those humble times, unmanned systems have undoubtedly achieved a huge milestone. In today, UAVs accomplish many missions and roles in the service of the military as well as in other sectors. Military are currently the principal operators of UAVs employing the paramount technologies including stealth features. Primary military drones include services like ISR (Intelligence, Surveillance, and Reconnaissance) or light attack functions. They range from small or medium tactical drones to high-altitude, the long-endurance once. Combat-enabled drones, like the armed version of reaper or predator, can carry out light attacks or against light-ground targets which are also widely reported in Libya and Afghanistan [27].

UAV can be used for military missions "Dangerous, Dull, dirty" as there is no loss of life asset. Also, robots don't mind circling a particular area for a dozen hours and can be operated in military and civil environments. They are also used to carry notorious missions of surveillance, security, and attack. In today's world, the term 'Unmanned Aerial' has gained so much acceptance, and when these things are combined with a ground control station and a communication channel (or data link) they constitute UAS. Nowadays, UAS are cheaper to operate, procure, and maintain when compared to manned aircraft with some limitations. As they eliminate the risk of a pilot's life while in operation and their capabilities like endurance aren't constrained by human limitations [28]. However, in the future, they could be used for air-refueling, resupply, air combat, and search and rescue operations. The remote operation of UAS has been made more practical because of the availability of advanced navigation and satellite communication technology. The capability of UAV to loiter, search & strike the targets while minimizing the collateral damage, makes this thing an indispensable weapon. Its features are further enhanced by using multispectral thermal and night vision state of the art cameras and better remote control allows the UAS to take on more reconnaissance roles. Today's UAV can remain on a mission for 30–40 h, far beyond the capabilities of any human crew. Research into ultra-efficient solar power and in-flight refueling could help in increasing the range of UAVs, limited primarily by maintenance needs.

1.4.2 In Geomorphological Mapping and Other Similar Sectors

Topographic surveys are important from the point of view of the study of earth surface dynamics and processes. These types of surveys are often required for huge (>11 km^2) areas at a relatively higher temporal resolution which can be used in monitoring the ecological change, hazard monitoring, or any kind of detailed process studies [6].

The geomorphic study includes the study of landforms, their classification, origin, development, and history which can be done through acquiring high-resolution topographic data which holds the key to many studies and discoveries in Earth sciences including that of earth surface processes and dynamics. For mapping, studies that require data at high temporal (hourly or daily basis), and large spatial (>10 km^2) scales, these traditional surveying methods are often time-intensive and costly. However, recent development and changes in technology have seen a rise in digital photo-grammetry as a viable means of obtaining high-resolution topographic data [6].

Such advancement in technologies and increase in affordability of UAVs makes it a novel platform for low-level aerial photography which can be done whenever needed for such photogrammetry in geomorphological studies where traditional methods like satellite imagery might not work. Moreover, it has also various applications where a similar type of work is involved like in filmmaking, scientific research, surveying, mining, cargo transport, forestry and agriculture, journalism, aerial surveillance, etc.

1.4.3 In Agriculture

Farmers can use the agricultural drone to spray pesticides, fertilizers, and other chemicals. Special cameras and sensors can be used to spot problems in the crops. Diseased parts of the crop can be spotted early. Different types of data related to the farm, crop, land, and atmospheric conditions can be collected. This data is used to ensure healthy crops and successful harvest [29].

1.5 UAV Challenges

UAVs are of significant use for various novel activities. However, when it comes to the regulation of flying small drones it becomes a challenge. There are thousands of small drones that are sold worldwide. A small drone can be built even by a novice using parts available from the internet. A small drone can also pose a high safety risk to large planes, fuel depots. Losing control by drone operators is an occasional instance. There isn't any severe accident so far reported but there are some criminal reports in which drone is used to supply illegal and banned items into prisons or targeted area. Even the insurance aspect is not fully defined or developed. There is also the risk of privacy as drones can be used to spy over someone without his/her knowledge, look inside a home through windows, can fly high and record visible parts of the property. However, government authorities have been trying to reduce the challenges of imposing proper rules and regulations for UAV ownership and operations. Law enforcement always tries to make significant efforts to stop rogue UAVs by signal jamming as well as by attacking and capturing them [30, 31].

Following are some technological limitation for UAV which also include top-notch military drones as well as commercial drones:

Loss of Contact: If contact is lost with the ground control station, the vehicle may be lost.

Less Versatile: UAVs are designed for a specific mission and type of need. These machines are not as versatile as a modern generation multi-role combat aircraft.

Limited Range: UAVs have much higher complex machinery and light body design. Therefore, they may not be able to carry as much fuel as manned aircraft and may have a shorter range. It is a limitation that is now being overcome.

Limitations of Payload: UAVs are typically smaller except few than a manned plane, they cannot carry as much as manned aircraft, and there is also a risk of losing balance easily in case of high wind or any unavoidable circumstance in which manned aircraft are much better. However, as compared to manned aircraft, their payload to total weight is higher.

Programming Limitations: There is a high possibility that UAVs might not be able to compensate for the changing battlefield environment such as attacking a new more desirable target that appeared after the aircraft was launched or changing course to avoid enemies.

However, technological advancement is overcoming the drawbacks of UAV/UAS making it suitable for many operations, uses, and needs.

1.6 Conclusion and Future Scope

A fairly comprehensive overview is presented of various platforms of UAVs according to different classifications with a brief introduction of the latest technologies used in UAVs along with the communication and application. UAVs were being used for decades by the world's military forces. Today, with the advancement of technology, it has become easier to produce and control drones. In today's era, if UAVs are combined with smartphone technology then together along it will bring heavy commercialization and secure, reliable tools and features can be made.

As far as military drones are considered, certain doom-mongers are predicting a dystopia where automated 'killer drones' escort in the era of robotic warfare, without humans. UAVs give us both the opportunities to take advantage and bring betterment as well as challenges that are needed to confront head-on. There is a clear need for ethical and legal questioning for the increasing use of drones which must be answered satisfactorily. Debates are of crucial importance to achieve a possible accord. This will surely take time and will involve questions, sharing of experiences and views, and not wait until a technological fait accomplish make this thing obsolete [32].

The advancement of UAVs has given a clean slate for its commercialization. UAVs are already being utilized in the agricultural industry to monitor farmland, analyze soil samples, and even herd cattle. It could expand more in the future required the demand is ever increasing. UAVs are also used in search and rescue to save people from life-threatening situations and every time this technology proves its usefulness more than ever. In near future, it is of no surprise that UAVs or drone will have their application in retail, transportation, entertainment, home security, and even in construction using 3D printers. The future scope for UAVs is immense and market share is also expected in the favour of this technology.

References

1. Guilmartin, John F. Unmanned aerial vehicle. *Encyclopedia Britannica*, 15 July 2020, https://www.britannica.com/technology/unmanned-aerial-vehicle. Accessed 31 March 2021.

2. Sharma, A., Basnayaka, C.M.W., Jayakody, D.N.K., Communication and networking technologies for UAVs: A survey. *J. Netw. Comput. Appl.*, 168, 102739, May 2020.
3. Drones Importance and Usage in Real Estate. https://www.ifsec.events/india/visit/news-and-updates/drones-importance-and-usage-real-estate. Accessed 31 March 2021.
4. Cai, G., Dias, J., Seneviratne, L., A Survey of Small-Scale Unmanned Aerial Vehicles: Recent Advances and Future Development Trends. *Unmanned Syst.*, 2, 2, 175–199, 2014.
5. Pham, H., Smolka, S.A., Stoller, S.D., Phan, D., Yang, J., A survey on unmanned aerial vehicle collision avoidance systems. *CoRR*, abs/1508.07723, 2015.
6. Hackney, C. and Alexander, C., 2.1.7. Unmanned Aerial Vehicles (UAVs) and their application in geomorphic mapping. In, *Geomorphological Techniques*. L. Clarke, and J. M. Nield, (Eds.), British Society for Geomorphology, London, GB, 2015.
7. Types of Drones – Explore the Different Models of UAV's. Circuit Today. https://www.circuitstoday.com/types-of-drones. Accessed on 31 March 2021.
8. Types of Drones, https://www.aircraftcompare.com/blog/types-of-drones/ Accessed on 31 March 2021.
9. Drone types: multi-rotor vs fixed-wing vs single rotor vs hybrid VTOL. https://www.auav.com.au/articles/drone-types/ Accessed on 31 March 2021.
10. Types of military drones: The best technology available today, By Jack Brown. https://www.mydronelab.com/blog/types-of-military-drones.html Accessed on 31 March 2021.
11. Weibel, R.E., *Safety Considerations for Operation of Different Classes of Unmanned Aerial Vehicles in the National Airspace System (PDF)*, p. 15, 38, 39, 43, 77, Massachusetts Institute of Technology, 2002, https://www.leonardocompany.com/en/products/falco-xplorer.
12. Pomerleau, M., Future of unmanned capabilities: Male vs Hale. MAY 27, 2015. https://defensesystems.com/articles/2015/05/27/uas-male-vs-hale-debate.aspx Accessed on 31 March 2021.
13. Sanz Subirana, J., Juan Zornoza, J.M., Hernandez-Pajares, M., University of Catalunia, Spain. GNSS signal, 2011. https://gssc.esa.int/navipedia/index.php/GNSS_signal
14. Global positioning system wide area augmentation system (WAAS) performance standard, 31 October 2008. https://www.gps.gov/technical/ps/2008-WAAS-performance-standard.pdf Accessed on 31 March 2021.
15. Andrei, I., Niculescu, M., Pricop, M., Cernat, A., Study of the turbojet engines as propulsion systems for the unmanned aerial vehicles. *Sci. Res. Educ. Air Force*, 18, 115–126, 2016.
16. Gupta, S.G., Ghonge, M.M., and Jawandhiya, P.M., Review of Unmanned Aircraft System (UAS). *Int. J. Adv. Res. Comput. Eng. Techol. (IJARCET)*, 2, 4, 1646–1658, April 2013.

17. Security and drones — what you need to know. *Kaspersky*. https://www.kaspersky.co.in/resource-center/threats/can-drones-be-hacked. Accessed on 31 March 2021.
18. Rodday, N., Hacking a Professional Drone, Black Hat Asia, 2016. https://www.blackhat.com/docs/asia-16/materials/asia-16-Rodday-Hacking-A-Professional-Drone.pdf. Accessed on 31 March 2021.
19. Corrigan, F., *How do drones work and what is drone technology*, October 1, 2020. https://www.dronezon.com/learn-about-drones-quadcopters/what-is-drone-technology-or-how-does-drone-technology-work/. Accessed on 31 March 2021.
20. Remotely Piloted Aircraft System (RPAS) Concept of operations (CONOPS) for International IFR Operations. ICAO. https://www.icao.int/safety/UA/Documents/ICAO%20RPAS%20Concept%20of%20Operations.pdf. Accessed on 31 March 2021.
21. Report ITU-R M.2171, Characteristics of unmanned aircraft systems and spectrum requirements to support their safe operation in non-segregated airspace, p. 48, International Telecommunication Union (ITU), 12/2009.
22. Report ITU-R M.2171, Characteristics of unmanned aircraft systems and spectrum requirements to support their safe operation in non-segregated airspace, p. 3, 4, International Telecommunication Union (ITU), 12/2009.
23. Report ITU-R M.2171, Characteristics of unmanned aircraft systems and spectrum requirements to support their safe operation in non-segregated airspace, p. 10,11, International Telecommunication Union (ITU), 12/2009.
24. Drozd, A.L., *Spectrum-Secure Communications for Autonomous UAS/UAV Platforms*, ANDRO, Computational Solutions, LLC Advanced Applied Technology Division Rome, NY.
25. *The Road to 5G: Drivers, Applications, Requirements and Technical Development*, Huawei. https://www.huawei.com/minisite/5g/img/GSA_the_Road_to_5G.pdf, November 2015. Accessed 31 March 2021.
26. Mishra, D., *A Survey on cellular-connected UAVs: Design Challenges, Enabling 5G/B5G Innovations, and Experimental Advancements*, Enrico Natalizio Université de Lorraine, CNRS, LORIA, France.
27. *NATO Parliamentary Assembly, Unmanned Aerial Vehicles: Opportunities and Challenges for the Alliance*, p. 2,3,8, Special Report, Pierre Claude Nolin (Canada), Special Rapporteur, International Secretariat, November 2012.
28. *NATO Parliamentary Assembly, Unmanned Aerial Vehicles: Opportunities and Challenges for the Alliance*, p. 8, Special Report, Pierre Claude Nolin (Canada), Special Rapporteur, International Secretariat, November 2012.
29. Sylvester, G. *E-Agriculture in action: Drones for Agriculture*, p. 112, Food and Agriculture Organization of the United Nations and International Telecommunication Union, Bangkok, 2018.
30. 10 Major Pros & Cons of Unmanned Aerial Vehicle (UAV) Drones. https://www.equinoxsdrones.com/blog/10-major-pros-cons-of-unmanned-aerial-vehicle-uav-drones. Accessed on 31 March 2021.

31. Yaacoub, J.P., Noura, H., Salman, O., Chehab, A., Security analysis of drones systems: Attacks, limitations, and recommendations. *Internet of Things*, 11, 100218. https://doi.org/10.1016/j.iot.2020.100218
32. *NATO Parliamentary Assembly, Unmanned Aerial Vehicles: Opportunities and Challenges for the Alliance*, p. 11, 12, Special Report, Pierre Claude Nolin (Canada), Special Rapporteur, International Secretariat, November 2012.
33. Pfeifer, C., Barbosa, A., Osama M., Hans-Ulrich, P., Marie-Charlott, R., and Alexander B. Using Fixed-Wing UAV for Detecting and Mapping the Distribution and Abundance of Penguins on the South Shetlands Islands, Antarctica. *Drones*, 3, 2, 39, 2019. https://doi.org/10.3390/drones3020039.
34. Connect ESCs and Motors. https://ardupilot.org/copter/docs/connect-escs-and-motors.html Accessed on 31 March 2021.
35. Yinka-Banjo, C. and Ajayi, O., Sky-Farmers: Applications of Unmanned Aerial Vehicles (UAV) in Agriculture, *Autonomous Vehicles*, 2019.
36. V-22-osprey-fleet-tops-40000-flight-hours. 19 Dec. 2017. *www.helicopter-industry.com*, 19 Dec'2017, www.helicopter-industry.com/2017/12/19/v-22-osprey-fleet-tops-40000-flight-hours/.
37. RQ-11B Raven Small Unmanned Aircraft Systems (SUAS). *U.S. Army*, November 4, 2014. https://www.army.mil/article/137604/rq_11b_raven_small_unmanned_aircraft_systems_suas Accessed on 31 March 2021.
38. Saldivar, J., *Grand Forks AFB Airmen welcome Global Hawk. Af.mil*, U.S Air Force, www.af.mil/News/Photos/igphoto/2000250415/, 26 May 2011.
39. Sakharkar, A., New software for improved and accurate drone mapping. 22 May 2020, https://www.techexplorist.com/new-software-improved-accurate-drone-mapping/32444/
40. Characteristics of unmanned aircraft systems and spectrum requirements to support their safe operation in non-segregated airspace, Report ITU-R M.2171 (12/2009). https://www.itu.int/en/ITU-R/space/snl/Documents/R-REP-M.2171-2009-PDF-E.pdf. Accessed on 31 March 2021.

2

Unmanned Aerial Vehicles: State-of-the-Art, Challenges and Future Scope

Jolly Parikh* **and Anuradha Basu**

ECE Department, Bharati Vidyapeeth's College of Engineering, GGSIP University, New Delhi, India

Abstract

Unmanned aerial vehicles (UAVs) form an important part of the wireless communication systems. Compared to the terrestrial communication systems, these on-demand UAV networks need to be critically designed. The article highlights, the state of art, challenges encountered and the open research issues in designing UAV-aided wireless communication networks. The dense heterogenous wireless network scenarios of the present era, poses various challenges to the deployment of UAV-assisted communication networks. Few of the challenges identified here include best method of 3D deployment of drones, allocation of resources (computational and wireless), optimization of the flight time and trajectory of UAV, handover management, channel modelling of highly dynamic UAV channels in various scenarios of UAV-assisted networks, interference management, effects of higher doppler shifts in mmWave networks, on-board energy availability of UAV devicies, etc. The article also aims to give an insight to the future scopes in the designing of UAV-assisted networks. The budding researchers will be able to identify the open research area of their interest in further development of this technology and thereby contribute to the advancement of wireless communication systems.

Keywords: Unmanned aerial vehicles, UAV, channel modeling of UAV, trajectory optimization, cellular assisted UAV, UAV mmWave communication

**Corresponding author*: jolly.parikh@gmail.com

Vandana Mohindru, Yashwant Singh, Ravindara Bhatt and Anuj Kumar Gupta (eds.) Unmanned Aerial Vehicles for Internet of Things (IoT): Concepts, Techniques, and Applications, (29–42) © 2021 Scrivener Publishing LLC

2.1 Introduction

On account of their high mobility and their capability of being deployed easily, on-demand UAVs have been used in a wide range of applications like in the military, telecommunication, surveillance and monitoring, rescue operations, and so on [1, 2]. They have played a vital role in numerous applications spanning over various areas of human life. UAVs have been envisioned to support various applications in 5G wireless networks [3–5]. Over the past 40 years, UAV-centric research has focused on a wide range of issues in UAV assisted wireless networks. Work is still continuing and new applications with their own challenges and solutions are being explored daily. Compared to the terrestrial communication systems, these on-demand UAV networks have to be critically designed considering the non-stationary channels, high mobility of the UAV-user equipment, and the UAV-base station, energy and altitude constraints, and the various environmental factors affecting system performance. UAV-assisted wireless communication is a promising application for the next generation networks which are looking forward to the Internet of Things (IoT) era. As we move towards a heterogeneous communication network, the complexity in designing such networks is increasing by leaps and bounds. Here, in this article, effort has been made to bring forth the state of art and the challenges posed in designing UAV-assisted networks. Some of the open research areas identified are channel modeling of A2G links considering the communication over water bodies and highy urban scenarios, effects of higher doppler shifts in A2A links of UAV-mmWaves network, better effective interference mitigation techniques to deal with UAV-BS channel in UAV-cellular network, efficient spectrum sharing schemes for increasing network throughput and spectral efficiency of UAV-mmWave communication network, trajectory optimization, on-board energy requirements of UAVs and multidimensional UAV channel modeling. Need arises to explore more areas of this cutting edge technology of next generation communication networks. As work progresses in this area, researchers will come across more challenges to deal with.

2.2 Technical Challenges

While using UAVs in the Drone-Base Station scenario, we need to consider the network performance characterization, best method of 3D deployment of drones, allocation of both wireless as well as computational resources, optimization of flight time, and planning of UAV network. Operation in Drone-UE scenario should take into consideration issues like channel modeling, handover management, low latency control, interference management and 3D localization. To use UAVs for specific applications of wireless communication networks, factors like capability of UAV, flight constraints of UAV, energy constraints of UAV, the flying altitudes of UAV must be taken into account. Since UAV communication has distinctive channel characteristics of its own, accurate channel characterization is essential for optimum performance and efficient designing. The propagation characteristics of the highly dynamic UAV channels have not yet been properly explored, in terms of the spatial and temporal variations induced in the non-stationary channels of UAV networks. Designing of a generic channel model for UAV air to ground communications (A2G), demands for simulations and measurements to be carried out comprehensively in various environments, taking into consideration the altitudes at which the UAV is flying, it's antenna movements, shadowing caused by UAV's body, etc. Airframe shadowing caused due to structural design and maneuvering of small rotary UAVs is yet to be explored in detail, though preliminary studies were carried out by Sun *et al.* in 2017. Figure 2.1 depicts the design issues faced in the UAV-assisted communication networks.

The rest of the chapter discusses in detail the above mentioned design issues encountered in deployment of UAV-assisted communication networks,

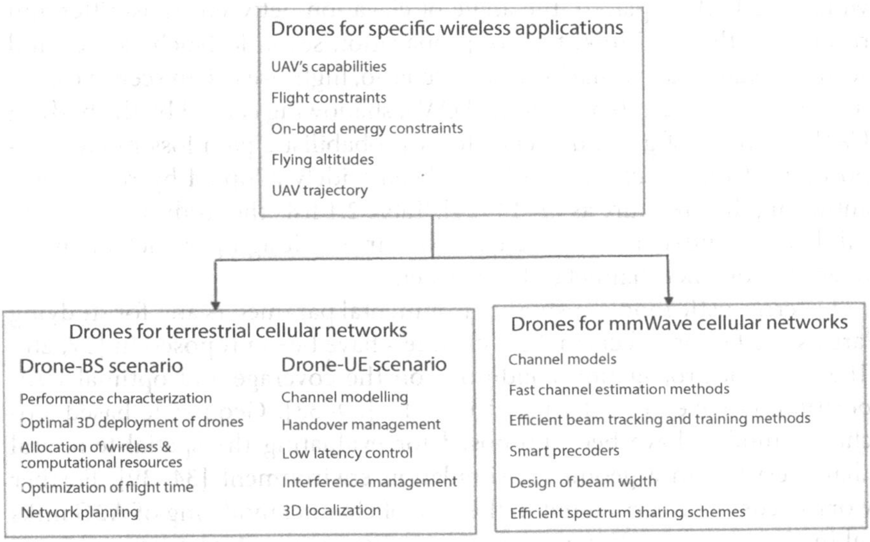

Figure 2.1 Design issues of UAV-assisted communication networks.

the solutions proposed till date and the open research areas that need to be worked upon for optimizing the performance of the UAV systems. Designing of UAV-assisted communication networks is a great challenge in itself.

2.2.1 Variations in Channel Characteristics

The control signaling and data signaling in UAV communication need two types of channels—UAV-ground and UAV–UAV channel. Both types of channels exhibit several unique characteristics.

a) Air to Ground Channel Modeling

Due to complexity in the operating environments, systematic measurements and modeling of UAV-ground channels needs to be carried out as in Refs. [6, 7]. Problems to be considered are link blockage due to obstacles like terrain, buildings, shadowing during aircraft maneuvering in critical operations, multipath links due to reflections, scatterings, diffractions, from different physical contours like mountains, ground surface, foliage, water bodies, desert, etc.

Compared to the characteristics of terrestrial communication channels, the A2G channel characteristics differ in terms of coverage and capacity [8–12]. This demands for optimal designing and deployment of A2G channel models for various applications like cellular-connected UAV-UE and IoT communication. We need to consider the type of UAV, the altitude at which the UAV is placed, the angle of elevation between transmitter and receiver in the A2G link, type of propagation scenario (such as the rural scenario, suburban scenario, urban scenario, high rise urban scenario), the movements of the antennas at the UAVs, shadowing caused by the body of UAV, locations of ground users, etc. A probabilistic path loss model proposed by Hourani *et al.* [9, 13] has been widely adopted by researchers authoring the literature as in [14–24]. Table 2.1 lists the studies carried out till date for understanding the effect of various design parameters on the operation of A2G channel in UAV systems.

Deterministic models using environmental parameters and for studying large scale fading effects in A2G channels have been proposed in [27, 28]. The effect of propagation conditions on the coverage and optimal UAV positioning have been discussed in Refs. [29–33]. Geometric based stochastic models have been proposed for evaluating the spatial-temporal characteristics in a geometric simulation environment [34–39]. Further work needs to be carried out in the area of channel modeling of A2G links taking into consideration the communication over water bodies and communication in highly urban scenarios.

Table 2.1 Parameters determining the performance of A2G channel.

Parameter worked upon	Reference
Effect of environment on path loss, delay spread, fading	[25]
Effect of high altitude of platform	[10, 11]
Effect on signal strength due to path loss and shadowing on account of various propagation scenarios and high elevation angle between transmitter and receiver.	[10]
Effect of low altitude UAV in suburban environments	[12]
Effect of angle of elevation and building height in urban environment	[26]

b) Air to Air Channel Modeling

A dominant LoS (Line of Sight) component is preferred for the air to air (A2A) communication channels of UAV communication. A2A propagation channel is useful in multi hop UAV networks for sensing and coordination applications. In case of emergency situations, it can replace the existing communication systems and provide a backhaul wireless connectivity. Large scale fading statistics in A2A propagation channels have been discussed in Refs. [40–45]. But the impact of antenna orientation, gain from UAV-MIMO system and Doppler spectrum of the A2A channel are yet to be worked upon. The major challenge encountered by these channels is the higher Doppler frequency shifts which occur due to higher relative velocity between UAVs. In 5G networks, if millimeter waves are used for backhauling than it would result in wider spectrum allocations, higher data rates, reduced latency in A2A channels. But the drawback is higher Doppler shifts. Hence we need to work out suitable techniques to be used in A2A links.

Various empirical and analytical channel models characterizing A2A and A2G propagation channels have been discussed in Ref. [46]. Multi-dimensional UAV channel modeling is yet to be explored thoroughly.

2.2.2 UAV-Assisted Cellular Network Planning and Provisioning

Network planning is more challenging in the case of UAV assisted cellular network. Parameters such as mobility, line of sight interference, energy constraints, and wireless backhaul connectivity have to be considered while planning such networks. The network needs to be planned taking into consideration the LoS interference between numbers of UAV-UE in the uplink connections. The BS in UAV assisted networks should be able to offer 3D communication coverage as the UAV-UEs are located at heights greater than the conventional BS antenna heights. The types of antennas at the ground stations involved in the UAV-UE in downlink communication need to be redesigned to provide wider coverage over the sky. The characteristics of the channel between UAV and BS are different from the channels of conventional terrestrial systems, as strong LoS links exist in this scenario. Such strong communications links result in efficient communication between UAV and the associated BS but also poses the threat of inter-cell interference from adjacent but non-associated BSs, in scenarios having both aerial and terrestrial UEs [47]. One also needs to consider the signaling and overhead involved in such networks due to the mobility feature of the UAVs. Studies carried out by researchers and presented in Refs. [18, 20, 48–50] focuses on problems like user association, backhaul connectivity, optimization of the number of UAVs that should be deployed in a network, placement of UAVs etc. Researchers have thrived to prove that optimal planning of UAV assisted cellular networks would require exhaustive work to be carried out to achieve an enhancement in throughput, reduction in delay, reduction of signaling overheads, reduction in interference in case of multiple UAV scenarios, less operational cost, reduced energy consumption, better effective interference mitigation techniques to deal with UAV-BS channel, techniques for supporting asymmetric UAV traffic requirements and so on.

2.2.3 Millimeter Wave Cellular Connected UAVs

The challenges encountered by cellular networks operating at mmWaves (Millimeter Waves) can be enumerated as, high attenuation, reduced transmission range, increased scattering, high penetration losses when encountering objects, frequent signal blockage, etc. These can be overcome to a certain extent by the use of UAV-assisted cellular networks. But such UAV based wireless communication systems operating at mmWaves also face certain issues. The channel characteristics of UAV mmWave communication networks are quite different as compared to those of the traditional UAV communication networks as well as the terrestrial cellular network communication. Channel models incorporating air to air channels, air to ground channel, air to sea channels need to be designed for UAV mmWave communication networks. There is need to carry out both empirical as well as analytical studies for UAV mmWave channels used in dense urban scenarios. Need arises to develop models that would assist in study of effects of weather on performance of UAV assisted mmWave networks, as mmWave propagation and the stability of UAV both get affected by rain and wind. The fast channel estimation methods should be developed to solve the problems due to reduced channel coherence time in high-mobility UAV communication systems. At mmWave frequencies more efficient beam training and tracking methods, which can handle rapid variations of path gain and fast deviations in angle of arrival and departure of beam, are required. Strategies to detect the abrupt changes and designing of smart precoders are required to improve the performance of UAV assisted mmWave communication systems. In UAV to BS mmWave communication, UAV detection and positioning is another critical challenge to be sorted out. In order to solve the interference problems, beam width needs to be designed judiciously. Higher frequencies will give narrow beams but result in heavy training overheads for beam alignment as in UAV-to-BS mmWave communication. On other hand, broader beams will increase interference to other cells. Efficient spectrum sharing schemes for increasing the network throughput and spectral efficiency needs to be designed for UAV mmWave communication.

2.2.4 Deployment of UAV

Another challenging issue in UAV based communication networks is the deployment of the UAVs. Parameters like the geographical area, location of ground users, altitude of the UAV, etc. play a critical role in determining the performance of UAV-based communications Simultaneous deployment of UAVs causes inter system interference. Both distance and Line of sight probability are to be considered while deciding the optimal altitude. Deployment at lower altitudes poses problems of lower coverage and less probabilities of LoS links due to the shadowing effect whereas UAVs at higher altitudes tend to exhibit poor coverage performances on account of higher path losses because of the large distance between transmitter and receiver [51]. Research work of Refs. [15, 16, 20, 52] discusses the algorithms developed to find the optimal placement of LAP's, the maximum number of UAVs required to serve all the users on the ground, the impact of UAV's altitude on the performance of networks, placement of UAV's for maximizing the coverage etc. Optimal deployment of UAVs reduces the average transmit power of the devices in an UAV-IoT communication network [53]. Also, the number of UAV's required in such networks is also determined by the altitude of the UAVs [33]. UAVs with directional antennas and higher antenna beam widths perform well even if deployed at lower altitudes. Another challenge lies in determining the continuous UAV trajectory as it involves a large number of variables. A solution to this has been discussed in Ref. [54].

2.2.5 Trajectory Optimization

The performance of UAV assisted wireless networks can be significantly improved in aspect of throughput as well as coverage by optimizing the trajectory of the UAVs. This optimization depends upon the factors like flight constraints, energy constraints, ground user's demands, collision avoidance, channel variations, mobility of UAV, etc. Table 2.2 lists the work carried out till date for optimizing the performance of the UAV systems by designing the optimum UAV trajectory.

The article by Chen *et al.* [62] proposes autonomous UAV wherein positions of the UAVs are self-optimized based on real time radio measurement.

Table 2.2 State-of-the-art solutions for optimizing the UAV trajectory.

Parameter optimized	Effect on performance of system	Research article
User scheduling and trajectory of UAV	Maximized the minimum average data rate experienced by ground users	[55]
Trajectory of UAV with multiple antennas	Maximized system rate in uplink communication	[56]
Joint optimization of UAV trajectory and source/relay transmit power	Maximized throughput of relay based UAV system	[57]
Path planning algorithm	Minimized total energy consumption of the UAV	[53, 58]
UAV trajectory using mixed integer linear programming	Fuel consumption minimization	[59]
Path planning	Likelihood of target detection	[60]
Trajectory of UAV	Connecting of ad-hoc networks was improved	[61]

2.2.6 On-Board Energy

Another major factor having a crucial impact on the performance of UAV assisted wireless communication networks is the limited available UAV on-board energy. This in turn limits the UAV flight and hovering duration. Over a period of time, research work has been carried out as in Refs. [63–74], where various methods have been proposed for minimizing the energy usage of UAVs in UAV communication. Few solutions proposed to encounter this challenge can be listed as, UAV optimal trajectory determining, efficient scheduling in multiple UAV scenario, dynamically activating only the required number of drones at a particular time, optimization of transmission times, reducing the required transmit power, efficient resource allocation schemes, energy harvesting for operations of small UAVs and many more. Managing the available resources of energy, bandwidth and time plays a crucial role in improving the performance of UAV communication systems [70, 75].

2.3 Conclusion

UAV aided wireless communication networks is yet another important step towards the development of future smart cities of 5G-IoT era. For the past 4 decades UAVs have been occupying the sky and playing a vital role in wireless communication systems. Researchers across the globe have identified various challenges of this technology and have proposed feasible solutions to these problems. Efforts have been made here to highlight few of the challenges to be overcome while designing the optimum UAV-assisted networks, thereby paving a path for the budding researchers to tread upon. Over the past few years many research challenges have been identified and worked upon and this technology is being updated at a tremendous speed. The progress is still ongoing.

References

1. Singhal, G., Bansod, B., Mathew, L., *Unmanned Aerial Vehicle Classification, Applications and Challenges: A Review*, 2018.
2. Shakhatreh, H. *et al.*, Unmanned Aerial Vehicles (UAVs): A Survey on Civil Applications and Key Research Challenges. *IEEE Access*, 7, 48572–48634, 2019.

3. Khawaja, W., Ozdemir, O., Guvenc, I., UAV air-to-ground channel characterization for mmWave systems. *Proc. IEEE VTC Fall Workshops*, Sep. 2017.
4. NTT DOCOMO Inc. and Ericsson, *New SID on Study on enhanced LTE Support for Aerial Vehicles, 3GPP Study Item Description (RP-170742)*, 3GPP, Dubrovnik, Croatia, Mar. 2017.
5. Li, B., Fei, Z., Zhang, Y., UAV Communications for 5G and Beyond: Recent Advances and Future Trends. *IEEE Internet Things J.*, 1, 1, 99, December 2018.
6. Matolak, D.W. and Sun, R., Unmanned Aircraft Systems: Air-Ground Channel Characterization for Future Applications. *IEEE Veh. Technol. Mag.*, 10, 2, 79–85, June 2015.
7. Sun, R. and Matolak, D.W., Initial Results for Airframe Shadowing in L- and C-Band Air-Ground Channels. *Proc. Integrated Commun., Navigation, and Surveillance Conf*, Apr. 2015, pp. 1–8.
8. 3GPP, *Enhanced LTE support for aerial vehicles*, May 2017.
9. Khawaja, G. *et al.*, A Survey of Air-to-Ground Propagation Channel Modeling for Unmanned Aerial Vehicles. *IEEE Commun. Surv. Tutorials*, 21, 3, 2361–2391, December 2019.
10. Zajić, A., *Mobile-to-mobile wireless channels*, Artech House, Boston, London, 2012.
11. Zheng, Y., Wang, Y., Meng, F., Modeling and simulation of pathloss and fading for air-ground link of HAPs within a network simulator, in: *Proc. of IEEE International Conference on Cyber-Enabled Distributed Computing and Knowledge Discovery (CyberC)*, Beijing, China, Oct. 2013.
12. Chu, X., Calvo-Ramirez, C., Briso, C., Yin, X., Low Altitude UAV Air-to-Ground Channel Measurement and Modeling in Semi urban Environments. *Wirel. Commun. Mob. Comput.*, 2017, Article ID 1587412, 11 pages, November 2017.
13. Mozaffari, M., Saad, W., Bennis, M., Debbah, M., Efficient deployment of multiple unmanned aerial vehicles for optimal wireless coverage. *IEEE Commun. Lett.*, 20, 8, 1647–1650, Aug. 2016.
14. Yaliniz, R., El-Keyi, A., Yanikomeroglu, H., Efficient 3-D placement of an aerial base station in next generation cellular networks, in: *Proc. of IEEE International Conference on Communications (ICC)*, Kuala Lumpur, Malaysia, May 2016.
15. Bor-Yaliniz, I. and Yanikomeroglu, H., The new frontier in ran heterogeneity: Multi-tier drone-cells. *IEEE Commun. Mag.*, 54, 11, 48–55, 2016.
16. Hayajneh, A.M., Zaidi, S.A.R., McLernon, D.C., Ghogho, M., Drone empowered small cellular disaster recovery networks for resilient smart cities, in: *Proc. of IEEE International Conference on Sensing, Communication and Networking (SECON Workshops)*, June 2016.
17. Gomez, K., Hourani, A., Goratti, L., Riggio, R., Kandeepan, S., Bucaille, I., Capacity evaluation of aerial LTE base-stations for public safety communications, in: *Proc. IEEE European Conference on Networks and Communications (EuCNC)*, June 2015.

18. Challita, U. and Saad, W., Network formation in the Sky: Unmanned aerial vehicles for multi-hop wireless backhauling, in: *Proc. of IEEE Global Telecommunications Conference (GLOBECOM)*, Singapore, Dec. 2017.
19. Chen, M., Mozaffari, M., Saad, W., Yin, C., Debbah, M., Hong, C.S., Caching in the sky: Proactive deployment of cache-enabled unmanned aerial vehicles for optimized quality-of-experience. *IEEE J. Sel. Areas Commun.*, 35, 5, 1046–1061, May 2017.
20. Kalantari, E., Yanikomeroglu, H., Yongacoglu, A., On the number and 3D placement of drone base stations in wireless cellular networks, in: *Proc. of IEEE Vehicular Technology Conference*, 2016.
21. Shakhatreh, H., Khreishah, A., Chakareski, H., Salameh, B., Khalil, I., On the continuous coverage problem for a swarm of UAVs, in: *Proc. of IEEE 37th Sarnoff Symposium*, Sep. 2016, pp. 130–135.
22. Azari, M.M., Rosas, F., Chen, K.C., Pollin, S., Joint sum-rate and power gain analysis of an aerial base station, in: *Proc. of IEEE GLOBECOM Workshops*, Dec. 2016.
23. Hayajneh, A.M., Zaidi, S.A.R., McLernon, D.C., Ghogho, M., Optimal dimensioning and performance analysis of drone-based wireless communications, in: *Proc. of IEEE GLOBECOM Workshops*, Dec. 2016.
24. Jia, S. and Lin, Z., Modeling unmanned aerial vehicles base station in ground-to-air cooperative networks. *IET Commun.*, 11, 8, 1187–1194, 2017.
25. Matolak, D.W. and Sun, R., Airground channel characterization for unmanned aircraft systems part-I: Methods, measurements, and models for over-water settings. *IEEE Trans. Veh. Technol.*, 66, 1, 26–44, Jan. 2017.
26. Yang, Z., Zhou, L., Zhao, G., Zhou, S., Channel model in the urban environment for unmanned aerial vehicle communications, in *Proc. 12th Eur. Conf. Antennas Propag. (EuCAP)*, London, U.K., p. 719, 2018.
27. Yan, C., Fu, L., Zhang, J., Wang, J., A comprehensive survey on UAV communication channel modeling. *IEEE Access*, 7, 107769–107792, 2019.
28. Zhou, L., Ma, H., Yang, Z., Zhou, S., Zhang, W., Unmanned Aerial Vehicle Communications: Path-Loss Modeling and Evaluation. *IEEE Veh. Technol. Mag.*, 15, 2, 121–128, June 2020.
29. Azari, M.M., Rosas, F., Chen, K., Pollin, S., Optimal UAV Positioning for Terrestrial-Aerial Communication in Presence of Fading. *2016 IEEE Global Communications Conference (GLOBECOM)*, Washington, DC, pp. 1–7, 2016.
30. Abdel-Malek, M.A., Ibrahim, A.S., Mokhtar, M., Optimum UAV positioning for better coverage-connectivity tradeoff. *IEEE 28th Annual International Symposium on Personal, Indoor, and Mobile Radio Communications (PIMRC)*, Montreal, QC, pp. 1–5, 2017.
31. Munaye, Y.Y., Lin, H.P., Adege, A.B., Tarekegn, G.B., UAV Positioning for Throughput Maximization Using Deep Learning Approaches. *Sensors*, 19, 2775, 2019.
32. Al-Hourani, A. *et al.*, Coverage and rate analysis of aerial base stations. *IEEE Trans. Aerosp. Electron. Syst.*, 52, 6, 3077–3081, Dec. 2016.

33. Mozaffari, M., Saad, W., Bennis, M., Debbah, M., Efficient deployment of multiple unmanned aerial vehicles for optimal wireless coverage. *IEEE Commun. Lett.*, 20, 8, 1647–1650, Aug. 2016.
34. Newhall, W.G. and Reed, J.H., A geometric air-to-ground radio channel model, in: *Proc. IEEE Military Commun. Conf. (MILCOM)*, Anaheim, CA, USA, Oct. 2002, pp. 632–636.
35. Wentz, M. and Stojanovic, M., A MIMO radio channel model for low altitude air-to-ground communication systems, in: *Proc. IEEE Veh. Technol. Conf. (VTC-Fall)*, Boston, MA, USA, Sep. 2015, pp. 1–6.
36. Ibrahim, M. and Arslan, H., Air-ground Doppler-delay spread spectrum for dense scattering environments, in: *Proc. IEEE Military Commun. Conf. (MILCOM)*, Tampa, FL, USA, Oct. 2015, pp. 1661–1666.
37. Gulfam, S.M., Syed, J., Patwary, M.N., Abdel-Maguid, M., On the spatial characterization of 3-D air-to-ground radio communication channels, in: *Proc. IEEE Int. Conf. Commun. (ICC)*, London, U.K., Jun. 2015, pp. 2924–2930.
38. Zeng, L., Cheng, X., Wang, C.-X., Yin, X., A 3D geometry-based stochastic channel model for UAV-MIMO channels, in: *Proc. IEEE Wireless Commun. Netw. Conf. (WCNC)*, San Francisco, CA, USA, Mar. 2017, pp. 1–5.
39. Chetlur, V.V. and Dhillon, H.S., Downlink coverage analysis for a finite 3-D wireless network of unmanned aerial vehicles. *IEEE Trans. Commun.*, 65, 10, 4543–4558, Oct. 2017.
40. Zhou, L., Yang, Z., Zhao, G., Zhou, S., Wang, C.-X., Propagation Characteristics of Air-to-Air Channels in Urban Environments, in: *2018 IEEE Global Communications Conference (GLOBECOM) [8647360] (Global Communications Conference (GLOBECOM))*, 2019.
41. Vinogradov, E., Sallouha, H., Bast, S.D., Azari, M.M., Pollin, S., Tutorial on UAV: A blue sky view on wireless communication. *J. Mob. Multimedia*, 14, 4, 395–468, January 2019.
42. Ahmed, N., Kanhere, S.S., Jha, S., On the importance of link characterization for aerial wireless sensor networks. *IEEE Commun. Mag.*, 54, 5, 52–57, May 2016.
43. Goddemeier, N. and Wietfeld, C., Investigation of air-to-air channel characteristics and a UAV specific extension to the rice model, in: *Proc. IEEE Glob. Commun. Conf. (GLOBECOM)*, San Diego, CA, USA, Dec. 2015, pp. 1–5.
44. Yanmaz, E., Kuschnig, R., Bettstetter, C., Channel measurements over 802.11a-based UAV-to-ground links, in: *Proc. IEEE Glob. Commun. Conf. (GLOBECOM)*, Houston, TX, USA, Dec. 2011, pp. 1280–1284.
45. Yanmaz, E., Kuschnig, R., Bettstetter, C., Achieving air–ground communications in 802.11 networks with three-dimensional aerial mobility, in: *Proc. IEEE INFOCOM*, Turin, Italy, Apr. 2013, pp. 120–124.
46. Khawaja, A.A., Chen, Y., Zhao, N., Alouini, M.-S., Dobbins, P., A survey of channel modeling for UAV communications. *IEEE Commun. Surv. Tutor.*, 20, 4, 2804–2821, 4th Quart., 2018.
47. Zeng, Y., Lyu, J., Zhang, R., Cellular-connected UAV: Potentials, challenges and promising technologies. *IEEE Wirel. Commun.*, 26, 1, 120–127, 2019.

48. Sharma, V., Bennis, M., Kumar, R., UAV-assisted heterogeneous networks for capacity enhancement. *IEEE Commun. Lett.*, 20, 6, 1207–1210, 2016.
49. Mozaffari, M., Saad, W., Bennis, M., Debbah, M., Optimal transport theory for power-efficient deployment of unmanned aerial vehicles, in: *Proc. of IEEE International Conference on Communications (ICC)*, May 2016.
50. Galkin, B., Kibiłda, J., DaSilva, L.A., Backhaul for low-altitude UAVs in urban environments, in: *Proc., International Conference on Communications (ICC)*, May 2018, pp. 1–6.
51. Hourani, A., Sithamparanathan, K., Lardner, S., Optimal LAP altitude for maximum coverage. *IEEE Wirel. Commun. Lett.*, 3, 6, 569–572, Dec. 2014.
52. Zhang, X. and Duan, L., Fast deployment of UAV networks for optimal wireless coverage. *IEEE Trans. Mob. Comput.*, 18, 3, 588–601, 2019.
53. Mozaffari, M., Saad, W., Bennis, M., Debbah, M., Mobile unmanned aerial vehicles (UAVs) for energy-efficient Internet of Things communications. *IEEE Trans. Wireless Commun.*, 16, 11, 7574–7589, Nov. 2017.
54. Schouwenaars, T. *et al.*, Mixed Integer Programming for Multi-Vehicle Path Planning. *Proc. Euro. Control Conf*, pp. 2603–08, 2001.
55. Wu, Q., Zeng, Y., Zhang, R., Joint trajectory and communication design for multi-uav enabled wireless networks. *IEEE Trans. Wirel. Commun.*, 17, 3, 2109–2121, 2018.
56. Jiang, F. and Swindlehurst, A.L., Optimization of UAV heading for the ground-to-air uplink. *IEEE J. Sel. Areas Commun.*, 30, 5, 993–1005, June 2012.
57. Zeng, Y., Zhang, R., Lim, T.J., Throughput maximization for UAV enabled mobile relaying systems. *IEEE Trans. Commun.*, 64, 12, 4983–4996, Dec. 2016.
58. Franco, C.D. and Buttazzo, G., Energy-aware coverage path planning of UAVs, in: *Proc. of IEEE International Conference on Autonomous Robot Systems and Competitions (ICARSC)*, Vila Real, Portugal, April 2015, pp. 111–117.
59. Grøtli, E.I. and Johansen, T.A., Path planning for UAVs under communication constraints using splat! and milp. *J. Intell. Robot. Syst.*, 65, 1–4, 265–282, 2012.
60. Tisdale, J., Kim, Z., Hedrick, J.K., Autonomous UAV path planning and estimation. *IEEE Robot. Autom. Mag.*, 16, 2, 35–42, 2009.
61. Han, Z., Swindlehurst, A.L., Liu, K., Optimization of MANET connectivity via smart deployment/movement of unmanned air vehicles. *IEEE Trans. Veh. Technol.*, 58, 7, 3533–3546, Dec. 2009.
62. Chen, J. and Gesbert, D., Optimal Positioning of Flying Relays for Wireless Networks: A LOS Map Approach. *Proc. IEEE Int'l. Conf. Commun. (ICC)*, May, 2017.
63. Zeng, Y. and Zhang, R., Energy-efficient UAV communication with trajectory optimization. *IEEE Trans. Wireless Commun.*, 16, 6, 3747–3760, June 2017.

64. Tran, T.X., Hajisami, A., Pompili, D., Cooperative hierarchical caching in 5G cloud radio access networks. *IEEE Network*, 31, 4, 35–41, July 2017.
65. Zorbas, D., Razafindralambo, T., Guerriero, F. *et al.*, Energy efficient mobile target tracking using flying drones. *Proc. Comput. Sci.*, 19, 80–87, June. 2013.
66. Lyu, J., Zeng, Y., Zhang, R., Cyclical multiple access in UAV aided communications: A throughput-delay tradeoff. *IEEE Wirel. Commun. Lett.*, 5, 6, 600–603, 2016.
67. Song, Q., Jin, S., Zheng, F., Completion Time and Energy Consumption Minimization for UAV-Enabled Multicasting. *IEEE Wireless Commun. Lett.*, 8, 3, 821–824, June 2019.
68. Ceran, E.T., Erkilic, T., Uysal-Biyikoglu, E., Girici, T., Leblebicioglu, K., Optimal energy allocation policies for a high altitude flying wireless access point. *Trans. Emerging Telecommun. Technol.*, 28, 4, e3034, 2017.
69. Chen, M., Saad, W., Yin, C., Liquid state machine learning for resource allocation in a network of cache-enabled LTE-U UAVs, in: *Proc. of Global Communications Conference (GLOBECOM)*, Singapore, Dec. 2017.
70. Mozaffari, M., Saad, W., Bennis, M., Debbah, M., Wireless communication using unmanned aerial vehicles (UAVs): Optimal transport theory for hover time optimization. *IEEE Trans. Wireless Commun.*, 16, 12, 8052–8066, Dec. 2017.
71. Zeng, Y., Xu, J., Zhang, R., Energy minimization for wireless communication with rotary-wing UAV. *IEEE Trans. Wirel. Commun.*, 18, 4, 2329–2345, 2019.
72. Mohindru, V., Bhatt, R., Singh, Y., Reauthentication scheme for mobile wireless sensor networks. *Sustainable Comput.: Inf. Syst.*, 23, 158–166, 2019.
73. Mohindru, V. and Garg, A., Security Attacks in Internet of Things: A Review, in: *The International Conference on Recent Innovations in Computing*, March 2020, Springer, Singapore, pp. 679–693.
74. Mohindru, V., Singh, Y., Bhatt, R., Hybrid cryptography algorithm for securing wireless sensor networks from Node Clone Attack. *Recent Adv. Electr. Electron. Eng. (Formerly Recent Patents Electrical & Electronic Engineering)*, 13, 2, 251–259, 020.
75. Mohindru, V., Singh, Y., Bhatt, R., A Review on Lightweight Node Authentication Algorithms in Wireless Sensor Networks, in: *2018 Fifth International Conference on Parallel, Distributed and Grid Computing (PDGC)*, 2018, December, IEEE, pp. 517–521.

3

Battery and Energy Management in UAV-Based Networks

Santosh Kumar[1]*, Amol Vasudeva[2] and Manu Sood[1]

[1]*Department of Computer Science, Himachal Pradesh University, Shimla, India*
[2]*Department of Computer Science and Engineering, Jaypee University of Information Technology, Waknaghat, Himachal Pradesh, India*

Abstract
Unmanned aerial vehicles (UAVs) technologies are attracting great attention with growing demands for autonomy for commercial, military, and other purposes. UAV-based communication networks play an important role in application presently using UAVs and upcoming potential future applications. Besides the number of pros, there are many challenges like line-of-sight communication, distance from the data receiver, limited access to the communication spectrum, energy constraints, and most concerning limited battery power. The focus of this chapter is on studying the techniques available for effective battery and energy management in UAV-based communication networks. The mechanisms for the optimal utilization of energy resources by UAVs to maximize their lifespan or deployment in a network are critically examined. This helps in a significant reduction in the usage of network energy resulting in a prolonged network lifetime. Further potentially promising areas for future research are also explored.

***Keywords*:** UAV, IoT drone, UAV-based networks, cognitive radio, NOMA, WPT

3.1 Introduction

Wireless networks are powerful technologies that facilitate communication simpler for human beings. The technology's transition has introduced

**Corresponding author*: santosh4103@gmail.com

Vandana Mohindru, Yashwant Singh, Ravindara Bhatt and Anuj Kumar Gupta (eds.) Unmanned Aerial Vehicles for Internet of Things (IoT): Concepts, Techniques, and Applications, (43–72) © 2021 Scrivener Publishing LLC

major improvements to computing and interacting with exciting technologies. The wireless networks provide connectivity for fast communication between applications and nodes. The involvement of UAVs in wireless communication networks leads to many advantages in various applications [1, 2]. Additionally, the transformation of this technology has shown radical improvements in computation and connectivity with innovative services. The UAV-based networks are also low-cost as opposed to the wired as well as wireless networks. The performance of UAV-based communications gets improved from compact transceiver technology and sophisticated signal processing methods that achieve universal coverage and fewer connections to cable [3], several networking models for UAV-based networks were proposed by researchers as listed in Table 3.1. Unmanned aerial vehicle communication networks (UAVCN) [4] consist of a group of UAVs to construct a network that can be implemented in several applications. However, due to their battery power constraints, UAV-based networks are usually unable to communicate over a long distance and for a longer time. To effectively use UAV-based networks for collaboration and communication, several challenges such as optimized positioning, movement and energy-aware deployment of these devices need to be addressed [3, 5]. Traditionally, the research on UAV-based networks usually focused mainly on problems regarding control, navigation, and autonomy. However, recent studies are focused on communication-related issues like power and energy efficiency. The chapter is confined to efficient energy management in UAV-based networks.

Table 3.1 Example of UAV-based networking models.

Sr. no.	Literature	Networking model	Explanation
1	[6]	Flying Ad-Hoc Network	An ad-hoc network between UAVs under restrictive environment (like terrain structures and node movements)
2	[7]	Airborne network/ Airborne Communication Network	Network framed using heterogeneous devices designed to use satellites, low & high altitude UAVs.
3	[8]	Unmanned Aeronautical Ad-Hoc Network	A network consisting of several cooperative UAVs (between 10 and 25).

(*Continued*)

Table 3.1 Example of UAV-based networking models. (*Continued*)

Sr. no.	Literature	Networking model	Explanation
4	[9]	UAV Ad-Hoc Network	UAV ad-hoc network is a highly dynamic network of UAV nodes, where new nodes can join and old nodes can depart the network.
5	[10]	Aerial Communication Network	An airborne base station consisting of low altitude UAVs to facilitate wireless coverage.
6	[11]	Networked Aerial Robots	A group of aerial vehicles to execute a task on a shared basis using wireless communication.
7	[12]	Distributed Aerial Sensor Network	The sensing and communication capabilities of wireless sensor networks are combined with small-scale UAVs to allow the active placing of sensor nodes.

In this study, UAV-based network challenges about energy, factors alleviating the need for efficient energy management, and different solutions to solve critical issues are being considered thoroughly. In the remainder of the chapter, Section 3.2 presents various challenges emphasizing the urgency of battery and energy management in UAV-based networks. Section 3.3 presents an overview of various techniques proposed by researchers to resolve the issues regarding energy management in UAV-based networks. Finally, Section 3.4 concludes the chapter.

3.2 The Need for Energy Management in UAV-Based Communication Networks

The management of energy in UAV-based networks is a relatively less explored and quite promising area. While these networks promise increased capacity and capability, yet it is very challenging to establish

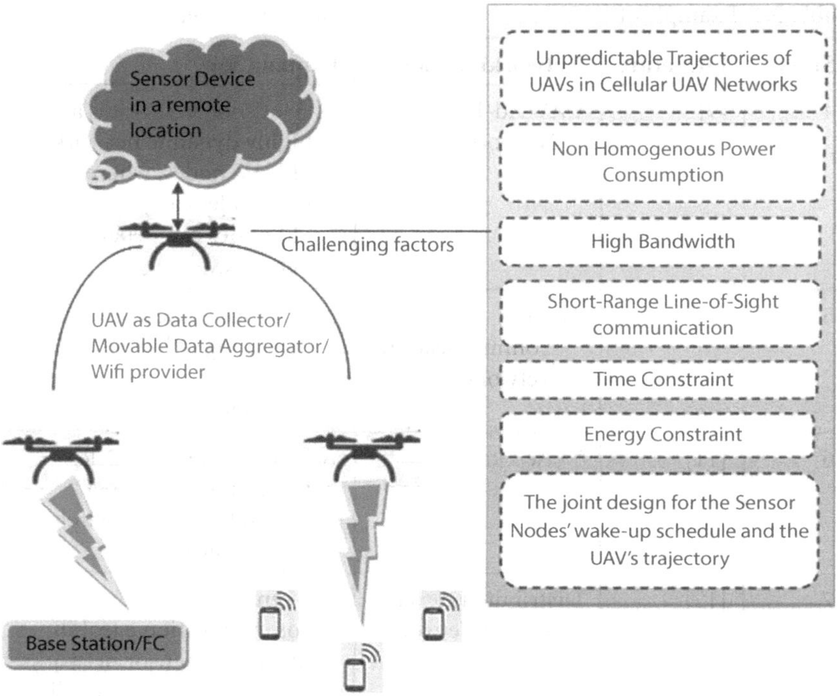

Figure 3.1 Challenges faced by UAVs-based networks.

and maintain effective communications between UAVs [13]. The Travel time and performance of a UAV-based network is primarily limited by the restricted onboard power. The technologies providing Power-storage has improved significantly over time. The dynamic nature of nodes in UAV-based networks would compel the network to change its topology frequently. This contributes to the fact that the network's energy needs to be handled effectively. Figure 3.1 illustrates numerous operations involved in a UAV-based network, emphasizing the need to make effective use of resources to extend the reliability of the UAV network [14]. All these factors responsible for poor energy management are discussed as follows:

3.2.1 Unpredictable Trajectories of UAVs in Cellular UAV Networks

In the upcoming 5G network, using the UAVs for sensing purposes has been of picky interest, owing to their versatile use, highly dynamic nature, and cheap operating cost [15]. UAV-based networks have been passionately applied to perform critical sensing applications like traffic monitoring in UAV based sensing applications [16]. The data related to sensory collected through the mobile UAV nodes must be forwarded to the sink node promptly, which is to be further processed to provide necessary real-time sensing information. In a UAV-based WSN, to sense the required data at a particular remote site and further forward it to the intermediate node(s) or the final aggregator node simultaneously with adequate performance is quite a challenging task. When the task site is far away from the base station, owing to the low uplink communication quality there may be difficulties in the communication of the sensory data along with the risk of getting invalid sensed data. Therefore, when designing their trajectories, the UAVs must consider their sensing precision and signal broadcast quality. This unpredictability of UAV trajectories leads to increased unmanaged power consumption. To allow time-bound sensing applications using UAV the transmission is managed by the cellular network. But the determination of their paths/trajectories in an energy-efficient manner remains a major concern of UAVs.

3.2.2 Non-Homogeneous Power Consumption

The last twenty years have seen dramatic advances in WSN research and development for specific applications. Typically, sensor nodes are cheap and energy-efficient devices that can sense, process, save, and communicate information. Even though sensor nodes usually have limited capacity to sense, process, and transmit, they can work efficiently and reliably in collaboration. WSNs are generally used to estimate unknown parameters (e.g. temperature, pressure, etc.) in a noisy environment. Specifically, each node carries out localized sensing, signal quantization, and then transmits the quantified data to the FC, where the data obtained from sensor devices is processed to generate the final approximation of the unknown parameter [16]. Authors in Ref. [17] observed that the earlier research on distributed computation in WSN is restricted to static Fusion Center at a fixed site. Due to the short distance between sensor nodes and Fusion Center, the transmission power required is less as compared to a movable Fusion Center, resulting in inhomogeneous power consumption and thus a short life span of the UAV-based WSN.

3.2.3 High Bandwidth Requirement/Low Spectrum Availability/Spectrum Scarcity

The low mobility, low cost, and flexible utilization of low altitude UAVs are becoming ever more attractive. In certain cases, UAVs are required to sustain elevated data rate demands such as broadcasting of traffic data from real-time video surveillance and high-resolution images to ground stations, consequently resulting in fast drainage of network energy [18]. Similarly, micro unmanned aerial vehicles (MUAVs) are powered by batteries and their battery consumption is mainly attributed to hovering, traveling, and proving power to other equipment installed on them. This restricts the flight time and transmission range. Hence, most of the MUAV-based applications with data communication requirements are therefore designed to support short connectivity periods with no permanent access to the expensive spectrum. MUAVs typically run on the S&L bands of the IEEE and ISM band [19]. Owing to the speedy development of the upcoming 5G networks, the device-to-device communication technology [20] and many other IoT-based wireless technologies like Bluetooth, cellular networks, and Wi-Fi normally use the common spectrum bands, making them overcrowded. Thus networks based on MUAVs experience the spectrum scarcity problem [21]. Therefore, the optimization of spectrum efficiency (SE) is of great importance [22].

3.2.4 Short-Range Line-of-Sight Communication

UAVs have evolved as a revolutionary trend to provide all-round connectivity from the aerial platform, especially for temporary user devices or disaster-affected areas as Aerial Communication Platforms. Alongside reduced cost and miniaturization, low-altitude UAVs are becoming the first preference for their deployment in the network due to a more swift and flexible nature. The network-based on low-altitude UAVs need redeployment and reconfiguration due to UAVs mobility and affinity to powerful short-range line-of-sight transmission links with the base station. Owing to their energy limitations, these devices usually cannot communicate over a long distance for an extended time duration [5, 23].

3.2.5 Time Constraint (Time-Limited Spectrum Access)

The MUAVs attracted significant interest in many applications. Because of the restricted battery power of these flying units, most MUAV-based network applications require a time-bound spectrum link to do full data transmission. Because of their versatile three-dimensional placement, they can carry out efficient transmissions without affecting the path loss. While other ground transceivers are powered by external power sources, drones rely on batteries. Their power consumption is devoted primarily to hover, travel, and to supply energy to other onboard components. This restricts their travel time and their ability to communicate. Thus, most applications of drones involving data sharing are created for a short communication time-period that does not require stable access to the expensive spectrum [24]. These features are the source of two issues in communications based on MUAV:

1) Managing energy efficiently, and
2) Selective exposure to the spectrum [21].

3.2.6 Energy Constraint

In modern UAV applications such as control and examination of electrical networks [25] and high-power-lines [26], limited battery power is seen as a major technological challenge [27]. The UAV-based monitoring system can save resources, improve access to impenetrable or distant areas, lower inspection costs, and computerize inspection processes. However, a miniature drone's battery power limits its flight distance and life of the mission. Improving the drones' energy supply and overcoming the limited battery capacity issue is crucial to encouraging the use of UAVs for routine inspection and maintenance operations.

Furthermore, the mission length of a standard small-sized drone used to track activity is limited by its battery capacity. While, from the perspective of applications like inspection and monitoring of electric power lines, gas pipelines, the UAV must remain autonomous for the maximum possible time. Furthermore, in emergency cases forwarding a squad of technical persons to carry out the maintenance is infeasible or even impractical due to the dangerous environment or non-accessibility of the target, whereas a UAV offers a viable substitute to perform this mission. There is also an open debate on how to prolong UAV's mission and make UAVs more robust. To increase the flight duration two methods can be applied. The first method is to augment the battery power which seems a very restricted choice in the conditions of currently available battery material technologies. Precisely, the battery may be a bit heavy to run the drone, or the battery's content could be too costly to be feasible for deployment. The second choice is to recharge the battery intermittently from an exterior energy source. It could be approached either using wires or wirelessly. While the techniques with wires are linked with some difficulties, such as inadequate drone movement during charging; wireless alternatives provide far greater movement independence. They can also be applied on-demand, that is, the drone doesn't need to go back to the ground station for charging [28].

3.2.7 The Joint Design for the Sensor Nodes' Wake-Up Schedule and the UAV's Trajectory (Data Collection)

WSNs generally entails a huge number of cheap sensor nodes usually powered by static sources of battery, and are hard to recharge once deployed.

Thus, energy-conserving sensing and computing technologies for sensor nodes are essential for extending the WSN's lifetime. Recently, an increasing interest in using the UAVs as movable data assembler for base sensor nodes in WSN [29]. UAV can collect sensed information from the sensor nodes in an energy-preserving manner by exploiting its high mobility, as it can only visit the sensor nodes sequentially and gather data by moving close enough to each sensor node. Thus, the link distance between UAV and active sensor nodes is substantially reduced, thereby saving all nodes' transmission energy. Short-range line-of-sight transmission links between aircraft and base terminals can be effectively used in various wireless sensor networks by appropriately designing the trajectory of the UAV for performance improvement [30]. Another helpful strategy to reduce the power utilization of sensor nodes is a sleep-wake UAV-enabled WSN [31]. The sensor nodes remain sleeping under this system until they receive a powerful wake-up call from the nearby UAV. After getting the wake-up call, the sensor nodes start transmitting data to the UAV. After transmitting the information, the sensing nodes again switch to a sleeping state. The architecture of UAV-enabled WSNs for data collection poses two major problems. The first is because of the sensor node's limited battery power. Thus, the sensor node's wake-up plan should be accurately designed such that each sensor node can perform its data communication with low energy utilization. The second concern is the mobile nature of wireless medium between the sensor nodes and the UAVs, which are vulnerable to loss of packets [32]. Thus, the UAV's trajectory/path should be appropriately designed to guarantee that any sensor node can pass on data with a low probability of failure while it is in an active state. The issue of crafting the UAV's path and wake-up schedule for energy-proficient data collection together must be considered while designing the techniques for efficient energy management [33].

3.3 Efficient Battery and Energy Management Proposed Techniques in Literature

All possible problems/factors discussed in Section 3.2 lead to poor energy utilization, decreased network life and degraded overall performance. With futuristic advancement and upcoming communication technologies like 5G, these challenges must be taken into consideration. In this section, few potential techniques as illustrated in Figure 3.2 introduced by researchers aiming to provide optimized battery and energy performance in UAV-based Networks are discussed.

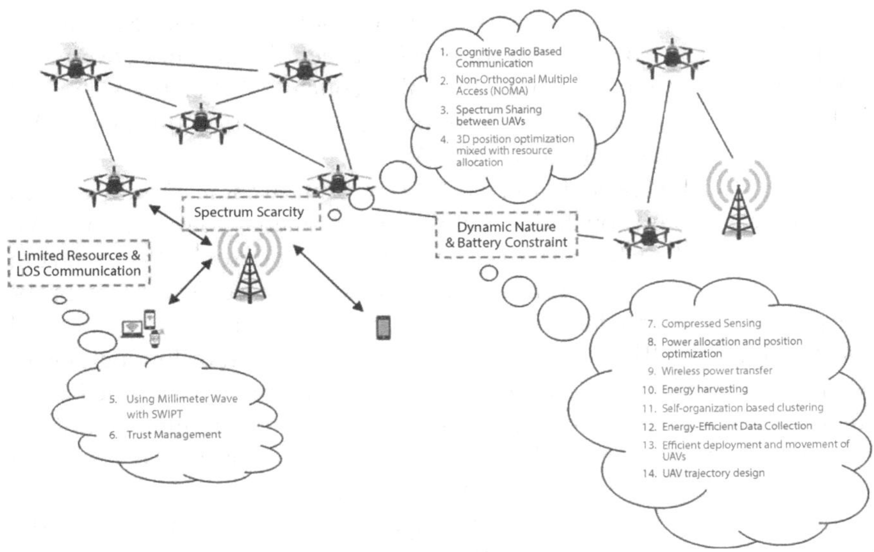

Figure 3.2 Solutions for battery & energy management in UAV-based networks.

3.3.1 Cognitive Radio (CR)-Based UAV Communication to Solve Spectrum Congestion

Cognitive Radio is a new platform where its unlicensed customers (secondary clients) can have the right to use it to the authorized frequency band. In wireless networks based on CR, the communication schemes must be configured in a manner that the involvement of secondary nodes does not impact the throughput of the approved users (primary nodes). These technologies play a very vital role to counter the issue of spectrum scarcity affecting the aviation domain. The UAVs generally function on ISM-band and IEEE S, L-Band. Most other wireless networks (e.g. Wi-Fi and Bluetooth) also operate over the same set of frequencies, which are becoming increasingly overcrowded. Thus, using CR-based UAV transmission is regarded as a possible alternative in UAV applications to the issue of spectrum congestion [34, 35].

To provide efficient energy management in CR-based UAV communication, a convex optimization problem has been framed to attain the best possible power distribution and placement of the UAV as well as its sensing capability so that the highest size of data can be communicated. In a scenario where the UAV moves toward the proposed target, the UAV-based communication system yield a better throughput and sensing performance.

However, the increased throughput is at cost of the extra energy required for its movement. So there is a trade-off between the distance covered by UAV and energy consumption. It is also concluded that the suggested technique can significantly optimize power consumption through UAV's movement and data communication [36].

Authors [37] reviewed the overlay CR technique in context to UAV-based communication and concluded that the overall energy consumed by UAV is reduced and the necessary data rate for the proprietor of the spectrum must be preserved. In Ref. [21], the authors discussed two major problems in MUAV-enabled communication: efficient power management and spectrum scarcity. The authors suggested integrating CR technologies with MUAV and a power-efficient convex optimization problem is framed using underlay mode. To achieve the optimized position of cognitive MUAV as well as transmission energy level a deterministically optimized algorithm inspired by Weber formulation is also proposed. The main objective is to reduce the energy consumed by the flying MUAV without affecting the QoS for the authorized users. The authors implemented the proposed method considering the QoS level and observed that under relaxed QoS criteria, the MUAV working in underlay mode moves to the closest position where it can reduce its energy consumption and increase its output, but must consider its degree of intervention so as not to affect the primary throughput. While in the case of strict QoS, the MUAV is overburdened with the extra responsibility to locate itself at a distant place from the main receiver; this will augment the energy consumption and poor throughput. However, by using an optimal power distribution scheme, the proposed solution may produce better results as it can vary its power to undo the interference effect.

3.3.2 Compressed Sensing

FANET is a shared, decentralized, and reconfigurable UAV-based network. FANET is an evolving technology that has many civil and military implementations such as search and rescue operations, surveillance, analysis, tracking, etc. For these applications, the main necessities are to maintain and preserve connectivity with devices, and to use limited resources such as bandwidth effectively. Furthermore, as the UAVs fly at very high speed, their topology is extremely dynamic, and coordination among them could be weakening. The usage of a novel method known as compressed sensing [38] is suggested to solve this issue. To employ the Compressed Sensing technique, the signal sampling is done at the Sub-Nyquist rate, i.e. the sample rate lesser than that of the Nyquist rate, in its place of sampling by the

Nyquist rate. Using a convex optimization approach, a lesser number of samples are communicated which can be recovered at later stages. There are few UAVs in a FANET. Consequently, a lesser number of frequencies will be occupied relative to the board spectrum available. The authors in Ref. [39], exploited the sparsity of the UAVs deployed in FANET and implemented compressed sensing on information for coordination that is shared among nodes. To co-ordinate these UAVs, an essential exchange of information between them needs to be optimized through effective use of spectrum.

3.3.3 Power Allocation and Position Optimization

In future wireless communication networks, mobile base stations can be made possible by UAVs. The energy consumption for flying and communication can be reduced for MUAVs while combining the 3D position optimization with the power distribution scheme [21]. In Ref. [40], authors considered a relay network based on the UAVs where UAVs acts like a decode and forward relay to expand the basic station coverage area. For a communication link created between a mobile device and a base station, the authors initially calculated the outage probability, and then mutually optimize the UAVs' path/trajectory along with the transmitting power allocated to the mobile devices. The authors also demonstrated that the proposed algorithm shows better energy efficiency and improved performance.

3.3.4 Non-Orthogonal Multiple Access (NOMA)

The rapid development of the IoT paradigm makes it an important component of the upcoming 5G mobile networks. The communication spectrum has to be used efficiently to fulfill the necessity of large IoT connections. NOMA is a popular technology that can increase spectrum efficiency. In Ref. [41], the authors have considered the single input single output (SISO) NOMA device downlink power assignment issue. The aim is to maximize the overall system throughput, thus upholding a strong level of consumer fairness. There are multiple sub-bands of the available network bandwidth and two users are allocated to any sub-band. The grouping of the allocated users is dependent on each individual's performance in terms of efficiency. Two methods have been stated to allocate the power to every sub-band. The first technique divides the potential transmission power into all bands; the second method uses an algorithm name the particle swarm optimization (PSO) to distribute energy to each band to optimize the total device efficiency. The power delegated to each strip is further subdivided into two consumers using multiplexing. The authors compared the proposed method with other schemes of power allocation and observed that the proposed methods significantly improve the overall system performance and user fairness. In Ref. [42], the authors suggested employing a base station based on UAVs to provide services to multiple clients for a NOMA. The objective was to minimize UAV transmission power focusing on the least rate prerequisites that are achievable and to optimize the attainable rate of a certain user under the minimum rates of other users. Owing to the NOMA system, the proposed variables for optimization include the position of the UAV and the transmitting power allocation. Considering the UAV's position decoding order, a globally optimal solution is proposed to achieve the functional objectives; by including all feasible decoding orders. The authors also demonstrated that the proposed combined optimization algorithms produced better results as compared to individual applications of NOMA and the UAV fixed-position NOMA schemes.

In Ref. [43] authors considered a fog wireless UAV network seeking to boost energy performance by granting and transferring resources to sub-channels. For the better utilization of the available spectrum, UAV wireless network is integrated with NOMA, which is widely recognized as an evolving transmission technology. To simplify the sub-channel allocations problem author proposed a double-sided matching and swapping technique based on the current UAV network design and framework for allocating resources. The proposed technique, when implemented on the current UAV infrastructure design and the resource distribution approach will substantially increase the energy performance of UAV wireless networks in fog.

3.3.5 Wireless Charging/Power Transfer (WPT)

In Ref. [28] authors reviewed numerous wireless options for extending the mission duration of UAVs instead of conventional wired changing methods. Some of these methods include installation of gust soaring, wireless charging, laser beaming, solar PV arrays, and fuel cell utilization. Some researchers also propose and advocate UAV charging through a transmission cable [44, 45].

WPT is emerging as an attractive approach to providing a convenient supply of energy to extend the lifetime of IoT devices operating wirelessly whereas conventional sources of energy like wind and solar, which are heavily dependent on environmental conditions [46]. It is a potential way to provide low-power electronic devices with permanent and cost-effective energy supplies and it is expected that there will be ample implementations in future wireless IoT networks [47]. One of the main uses of radio frequency (RF) wireless data transmission is the simultaneous transfer of wireless information and data transmission (SWIPT), which can relay data and provide power to charge the wireless equipment parallelly. In Ref. [48] authors considered a wireless charging station mounted on the ground to power up the UAVs and examine the combined optimization of energy distribution and the location of a base station to make the most of downlink efficiency. Nevertheless, the effect of the UAV location on power management was not studied [46]. A modern WPT in context to multiuser UAV powered devices has been designed. The design takes the advantage of the UAVs versatility to optimize the energy transmitted to energy receivers over a defined charge time by maximizing the trajectory of the UAV under its realistic speed limit. The objective is to maximize the total power received by every energy receiver by exploiting the UAVs path via trajectory design, the proposed solution to this non-convex problem shows that the UAV will float at just one defined position over the entire charge duration.

3.3.6 UAV Trajectory Design Using a Reinforcement Learning Framework in a Decentralized Manner

Recently, UAVs have been commonly utilized over cellular networks in real-time sensing systems, which sense the conditions of the assignments and relay the sensor data to the sink node (BS) in a time-bound fashion [37]. UAV's performance is determined by the efficiency of its capacity to sense and transmit, which are affected by the UAV's trajectory. Nevertheless, planning their trajectories effectively is difficult for UAVs because they operate in a complex setting (unpredictable environment). To deal with this problem, a reinforcement learning model has been applied for decentralized resolution of the UAVs trajectory design problem. To organize several UAVs conducting real-time sensing activities, initially, a sense and send technique is introduced then the probability of efficient accurate data transmission utilizing nested-Markov-chains is analyzed. Authors formulated a decentralized trajectory modeling problem and also proposed an improved multi UAV Q learning technique to resolve this problem, they suggested that the improved multi UAV Q learning technique converges more rapidly and in the real-time task-sensing scenarios achieves higher benefits for the UAV and helps in efficient energy management for networks based on them.

3.3.7 Efficient Deployment and Movement of UAVs

In Ref. [5], the authors have presented a scheme for the efficient placement and movement of several UAVs to gather data from ground IoT devices in an energy-efficient uplink. The scheme involves the estimation of UAVs' positions, system affiliation, and connection power management for the IoT systems to reduce the overall transmitting capacity of the systems under their signal to interference plus noise ratio (SINR) constraints. Besides, the UAVs efficiently travel to capture sensed data in a dynamic IoT network. In this scenario, using the device activation technique, the time-shift instances are derived where UAVs need to change their positions. Moreover, the optimal trajectories are obtained that the UAVs use to efficiently represent the IoT systems with reduced energy consumption. The overall transmission power consumption of the systems decreases dramatically compared with the case of pre-deployed static airborne base stations by smartly shifting and placing the UAVs. In reality, there is a profound balance between the number of changes, the durability of the UAVs, and the transmission capacity of the systems. Particularly a larger number of updates contribute to reduced transmission capacity for IoT devices but all at the cost of higher energy usage of UAVs.

3.3.8 3D Position Optimization Mixed With Resource Allocation to Overcome Spectrum Scarcity and Limited Energy Constraint

In Ref. [24], the authors suggested an optimal approach for spectrum and power conservation by incorporating the cognitive antenna overlay system. The authors used the drone as a minor node and try to define an optimal three-dimensional position and a resource management scheme to complete data transfer and primary communication simultaneously. UAV-based connectivity has two major issues: bandwidth scarcity and energy conservation. To tackle the bandwidth scarcity, an overlay of the cognitive network scheme has been suggested. So, a collaborative design strategy is proposed for drone placement and its resource distribution to reduce the flying node's energy usage. The technique uses a modified algorithm derived from particle swarm optimization (PSO) to optimize the bandwidth and power allocation to ensure successful transmission with minimal power consumption. Furthermore, the location and the assets are modified opportunistically for the positions of the transceivers combined with primary user requirements. In Ref. [24], an optimization problem is framed that minimizes the overall drone energy usage. The goal is to optimize the position of the drone and the distribution of resources in a way that

1) Minimize the travel time,
2) The power consumption for communication is decreased, and

3) Constant data transfer rate shall be retained for the primary transmission.

A jointly optimized solution is projected in Ref. [21] to decide the 3D position of the target to which the UAV has to fly and simultaneously follow an optimal resource allocation scheme the secondary data communication can be completed with priority to the primary communication.

3.3.9 UAV-Enabled WSN: Energy-Efficient Data Collection

The authors [33] introduced a novel approach for capturing the sensed data in an energy-efficient manner in UAV-enabled WSNs. The wake-up cycle of the sensing nodes and the route of UAV were mutually designed to reduce the sensor nodes' overall energy usage thus maintaining accurate data collection in fading networks. A powerful repetitive algorithm is suggested to uncover a sub-optimal result using the sequential convex optimization technique. The empirical findings indicate substantial energy savings as opposed to the standard schemes for the proposed plan. Collaborative networks are gaining more attention these days with the desire for improved access and increased coverage. With battery-powered sensors, WSNs face a critical energy depletion problem while performing network operations. The energy depletion issues can be resolved to a large extent by collaborating WSNs with UAVs. UAVs have help for maneuvering by performing a crucial function as a controller node in certain networks. However, integrating these networks requires an advanced data transmission strategy for efficient utilization of network infrastructure. To provide energy-efficient relaying, authors in Ref. [49] proposed a new approach for data transmission using the affection properties of a firefly optimization algorithm [50]. The solution provides the UAV-managed WSNs with constant communication, longer lifespan, and increased coverage.

3.3.10 Trust Management

A specific level of data trust and peer honesty must be ensured to enable these communication-based applications. Since the life of a UAV is dependent on its battery, it is not recommended to use them for performing highly complex computations. Thus, trust-based management solutions are being adopted in different types of UAV-based networks like MANET and WSN. Trust management is required when participant nodes (UAVs) choose to create a network with an appropriate degree of confidence relationships between themselves, without any prior experiences. Trust administration has broad applicability in numerous decision-making contexts, including prevention of attack, authorization, access protection, key management, separation of mischievous nodes for efficient routing, and other operations [51]. Although the trust-based solution reduces the energy consumed in computation, the energy consumption for the communications interface remains the same. To solve the aforementioned challenge and to get a balanced trade-off between energy consumption and security levels, in Ref. [52], the authors proposed a trust-based network. The suggested methodology incorporates faith measurement and links duration to identify the neighborhood's most trustworthy and secure neighbors. Subsequently, nodes that trust each other should synchronize in a clustered fashion and settle on the monitoring plan for their neighborhood. The approach significantly reduces the energy usage if a node is surrounded by reliable nodes in its neighborhood.

3.3.11 Self-Organization-Based Clustering

The extremely mobile nature of UAVs contributes to regular shifts in topology resulting in link related issues. The solution to these issues is to adopt a suitable clustering method. Clustering is the process of splitting up the network into related subgroups. Usually, a cluster comprises a cluster leader (CH) and its related cluster members. For handling the inter-cluster and intra-cluster communication a CH is elected from the group of sensor nodes using clustering algorithms. The key routing problem in UAV-based networks (FANET or flying WSN) is the regular connection breakage due to their high moving speeds in the air. To overcome the above problem and for better energy management in FANETs, a self-organization clustering scheme (SOCS) based on the glowworm swarm optimization (GSO) algorithm [53] has been proposed [54]. The process of cluster creation and CH selection relies on UAVs' residual energy, luciferin value, and their connectivity with the ground control station. The position of the UAV is used to update the value of luciferin following the GSO algorithm. The route discovery is based on the parameters like UAVs' position, residual energy, and neighbors' range.

Furthermore, as the data packets of varying nature are being exchanged in FANETs, these data packets have to be processed by the UAVs which eventually exhausts the restricted resources of UAVs and thus contributes to network congestion affecting the overall network efficiency. To address the problems and for effective traffic management, some packet scheduling system needs to be built with better support for the energy-efficient routing schemes in FANETs.

3.3.12 Bandwidth/Spectrum-Sharing Between UAVs

Since UAVs are flexible in handling and coverage, they are widely used for the provision of all-round wireless connections with base stations (BSs) mounted on UAVs. The BSs can be applied to alleviate the disparity between the fixed infrastructures and the varied traffic load. Like, the requirement for movable and friendly wireless service is vital for the places already suffering from traffic congestions. In this scenario BSs mounted on UAVs can solve the purpose by transferring the traffic from a congested cellular network to the UAVs. Similarly in the areas affected by disasters, and all existing ground infrastructures got destroyed, the BSs mounted on UAV can provide network coverage.

The UAV based networks and cellular networks are spatially separated, hence there is a scope for spectrum sharing between these two networks. Though many researchers have studied the problem of sharing of spectrum between the networks based on UAVs and other types of wireless networks, limited studies have discussed the problem of spectrum sharing in context to UAV-based networks and cellular networks. A spectrum sharing scheme has been proposed to enhance the capacity of networks based on UAVs by employing air-to-air communications [55]. The author applied, stochastic geometry [56] to evaluate the network coverage probability for users using UAVs' network and ground cellular networks, As a result, the optimum height of drones can be determined by limiting the probability of coverage of ground network users.

3.3.13 Using Millimeter Wave With SWIPT

UAVs must meet high data rate demands, e.g., streaming to ground nodes, in certain cases, with large real-time traffic data monitoring and high-quality images. For promoting high data rates, mmWave communication is a crucial facilitator in its wide usable bandwidth for the UAV-enabled IoT networks. Because, mmWave signals are especially susceptible to blocking, ground communication using them is disrupted if significant barriers, such as hills and large buildings occur. UAVs can quickly switch from one place to another in comparison to the terrestrial systems to avoid blockages and will preserve a great probability of line-of-sight communication and are more suitable for mmWave transmission. To maintain the line-of-sight communication network has to sacrifice its energy in the movement of UAV. To overcome this issue authors in Refs. [18, 57] suggested that the combination of SWIPT UAV-based relay and mmWave is very appealing and has many benefits, such as short-range data transmission and significant gains in the array.

3.3.14 Energy Harvesting

One of the main barriers that hinder the efficiency of a UAV based Network is restricted onboard energy [58]. In the upcoming era of 5G communications, the energy proficient deployment using various energy harvesting techniques can provide an effective solution. The conventional energy harvesting techniques are mostly using wind energy or solar energy, but with technological advancements, the RF energy harvesting technique has received extensive consideration. One way to accomplish power-efficient deployment is to leverage inter-UAV coordination so that only one UAV can abandon its objective to supplement its power reserves at any given moment. In Ref. [59], the authors studied the energy harvesting techniques employing solar energy and vibrations for networks based on MUAVs. Furthermore, new sensor techniques have been developed, which harvest energy from wind and kinetic energy from the environment. The extracted energy is converted to electrical signals that are either immediately absorbed or preserved for future use. Researchers proposed various mechanisms for energy harvesting, in Ref. [60], the authors studied UAV-based amplify and forward relay networks in which the distribution of source and power control is jointly optimized to implement energy harvesting. In Ref. [61], the authors proposed the transmission time optimization during a consumer–UAV-based communication network [62]. Analyzed UAV based decode and forward relay network in which energy is harvested by averaging the symbol fault rate. Meanwhile, Ref. [63] proposed a mechanism to use the harvested energy for uplink transmission in a UAV-based network. Applied the energy harvesting technology to the UAVs, in which the energy received from the ground base station is utilized to provide the transmission power during UAV-assisted relay [64]. The overall system performance can be improved by increasing the span of energy harvesting and efficiency of energy conversion. The authors proposed the use of energy harvesting techniques employing time switching along with power splitting mechanisms to UAV relays during transmission [65]. The optimal transmission signal is obtained via maximizing signal to noise ratio [70].

3.4 Conclusion

The UAV based network is a fresh essence of the ad-hoc mobile network family. However, this has been discussed that UAVCN has a lot of design problems. In this study, major concerns in communication-based on UAV networks responsible for the spectrum dearth and poor power management are pointed out. The factors like the unpredictability of the UAV trajectory, high bandwidth requirements, overcrowded spectrum, dynamic topology, line-of-sight communication, energy and time constraints, and limited battery life are studied in the context of UAV based networks. Power/ Energy efficiency is a critical issue for the UAV nodes in WSNs because the limited energy of battery-powered WSNs is impacting the lifespan and throughput of systems. These issues also hamper the performance of communication networks, resulting in degraded quality of service. Different solutions proposed by researchers as listed in Table 3.2 are also reviewed critically. The cognitive radio-based communication, use of NOMA, and using 3D position optimization with resource allocation scheme can overcome the problem of scarcity and congestion in the spectrum resulting in optimized use of energy. Using combined optimization of UAV trajectory and energy distribution for energy-proficient data collection, spectrum sharing, and trust management schemes can efficiently reduce the network energy consumption by solving the issues like limited resources and poor network coverage. The challenges posed by the dynamic nature of UAVs can be solved by using compressed sensing and self-organization based clustering. Furthermore, wireless power transfer and the combination of Millimeter Wave communication with SWIPT can efficiently alleviate critical issues like limited battery power and short-range line-of-sight transmission problem. The recent technological advancements in energy-efficient deployment with energy harvesting techniques provide an effective solution; the application of these techniques can assist in the sustainable deployment of UAVs in networks and also helps in the efficient management of limited battery and energy resources.

Table 3.2 Solutions projected by researchers for proficient battery and energy management in UAV based networks.

Challenge	Solution	Literature	Major contributions
Spectrum Congestion	Cognitive radio (CR) based UAV communication	[36]	Proposed cognitive radio-based UAV-enabled communication for Optimization of energy usages.
		[37]	Proposed the use of overlay CR approach for communication-based on UAVs.
		[21]	Suggested the integrated use of CR technology with MUAV and framed an optimization problem for the underlay mode.
Dynamic Topology	Compressed Sensing	[39]	Exploited sparsity of the number of UAVs in FANET and implemented compressed sensing.

(*Continued*)

Table 3.2 Solutions projected by researchers for proficient battery and energy management in UAV based networks. (*Continued*)

Challenge	Solution	Literature	Major contributions
Power Consumption	Power allocation and position optimization	[21]	Combined 3D position optimization with the power distribution scheme
		[40]	Proposed a relay network for an unmanned aerial vehicle, where a UAV acts as decode and forward relay to expand the basic station coverage area.
Spectrum scarcity	Non-Orthogonal Multiple Access (NOMA)	[41]	Considered the Single Input Single Output (SISO) NOMA Device Downlink power assignment issue.
		[42]	Proposed employing a base station based on UAVs to provide services to multiple clients.
		[43]	Proposed a Fog Wireless UAV Network.

(*Continued*)

Table 3.2 Solutions projected by researchers for proficient battery and energy management in UAV based networks. (*Continued*)

Challenge	Solution	Literature	Major contributions
Limited Battery Power	Wireless Charging/ power transfer (WPT)	[46]	Studies a modern WPT multiuser UAV powered devices.
Energy efficiency	UAV trajectory design using a reinforcement learning framework in a decentralized manner	[37]	Considered the decentralized trajectory modeling, and proposed an improved multi-UAV Q-learning algorithm.
Energy efficiency	Efficient deployment and movement of UAVs	[5]	Presented a new framework for the efficient placement and movement of group UAVs to gather data from ground IoT devices in an energy-efficient uplink.
Spectrum scarcity	3D position optimization mixed with resource allocation	[24]	Suggested an optimal approach for spectrum and energy conservation by incorporating the cognitive antenna overlay system.

(*Continued*)

Table 3.2 Solutions projected by researchers for proficient battery and energy management in UAV based networks. (*Continued*)

Challenge	Solution	Literature	Major contributions
Energy efficiency	UAV enabled WSN: Energy-Efficient Data Collection	[33]	Introduced a novel approach for capturing sensed data in an energy-efficient manner in UAV-enabled WSNs
Limited Resources	Trust Management	[52]	Proposed a trust-based network for monitoring.
Dynamic Topology	Self-organization based clustering	[54]	Proposed a clustering scheme (SOCS) based on self-organization implemented on FANETs using the behavioral study of the Glowworm Swarm Optimization algorithm.
Network Coverage	Bandwidth/ spectrum sharing between UAVs	[66]	Studied the feasibility of spectrum sharing among the UAV based network and cellular networks.
		[67]	Proposed the optimization of the transmitting power to optimize energy efficiency.

(*Continued*)

Table 3.2 Solutions projected by researchers for proficient battery and energy management in UAV based networks. (*Continued*)

Challenge	Solution	Literature	Major contributions
		[68]	Designed a spectrum sharing technique working orthogonally between UAV and base station.
		[69]	Proposed a routing technique for cognitive radio based aerial networks.
		[55]	Proposed a stochastic geometry-based solution to analyze the coverage possibility of the UAV network.
Short Distance line-of-sight communication	Using Millimeter Wave with SWIPT	[18]	Proposed the use of mmWave UAV-based SWIPT relay networks.
Energy efficiency	Energy harvesting	[65]	Proposed the use of energy harvesting techniques employing time switching along with power splitting mechanisms to UAV relays during transmission.

References

1. Jiang, J., Liu, H., Yuan, B., Wang, X., Liang, B., A new concept of UAV recovering system, in: *International Conference on Intelligent Robotics and Applications*, pp. 327–338, 2019.
2. Bai, G., Li, Y., Fang, Y., Zhang, Y.-A., Tao, J., Network approach for resilience evaluation of a UAV swarm by considering communication limits. *Reliab. Eng. Syst. Saf.*, 193, 106602, 2020.
3. Nawaz, H., Ali, H.M., Laghari, A.A., UAV Communication Networks Issues: A Review. *Arch. Comput. Methods Eng.*, 27, 1–21, 2020.
4. Park, P.-J., Choi, S.-M., Lee, D.-H., Lee, B.-S., Performance of UAV (unmanned aerial vehicle) communication system adapting WiBro with array antenna, in: *2009 11th International Conference on Advanced Communication Technology*, vol. 2, pp. 1233–1237, 2009.
5. Mozaffari, M., Saad, W., Bennis, M., Debbah, M., Mobile unmanned aerial vehicles (UAVs) for energy-efficient Internet of Things communications. *IEEE Trans. Wirel. Commun.*, 16, 11, 7574–7589, 2017.
6. Bekmezci, I., Sahingoz, O.K., Temel, Ş., Flying ad-hoc networks (FANETs): A survey. *Ad Hoc Netw.*, 11, 3, 1254–1270, 2013.
7. Cao, X., Yang, P., Alzenad, M., Xi, X., Wu, D., Yanikomeroglu, H., Airborne communication networks: A survey. *IEEE J. Sel. Areas Commun.*, 36, 9, 1907–1926, 2018.
8. Frew, E.W. and Brown, T.X., Airborne communication networks for small unmanned aircraft systems. *Proc. IEEE*, 96, 12, 2008–2027, 2008.
9. Sun, J. *et al.*, A data authentication scheme for UAV ad hoc network communication. *J. Supercomput.*, 76, 6, 4041–4056, 2020.
10. Chandrasekharan, S. *et al.*, Designing and implementing future aerial communication networks. *IEEE Commun. Mag.*, 54, 5, 26–34, 2016.
11. Aloul, F.A. and Kandasamy, N., Sensor deployment for failure diagnosis in networked aerial robots: A satisfiability-based approach, in: *International Conference on Theory and Applications of Satisfiability Testing*, pp. 369–376, 2007.
12. Quaritsch, M., Kruggl, K., Wischounig-Strucl, D., Bhattacharya, S., Shah, M., Rinner, B., Networked UAVs as aerial sensor network for disaster management applications. *E Elektrotech. Inf.*, 127, 3, 56–63, 2010.
13. Zeng, Y., Zhang, R., Lim, T.J., Wireless communications with unmanned aerial vehicles: Opportunities and challenges. *IEEE Commun. Mag.*, 54, 5, 36–42, 2016.
14. Gupta, L., Jain, R., Vaszkun, G., Survey of important issues in UAV communication networks. *IEEE Commun. Surv. Tutor.*, 18, 2, 1123–1152, 2015.
15. Wang, J., Jiang, C., Han, Z., Ren, Y., Maunder, R.G., Hanzo, L., Taking drones to the next level: Cooperative distributed unmanned-aerial-vehicular networks for small and mini drones. *IEEE Veh. Technol. Mag.*, 12, 3, 73–82, 2017.

16. Sorniotti, A., Gomez, L., Wrona, K., Odorico, L., Secure and trusted in-network data processing in wireless sensor networks: A survey. *J. Inf. Assur. Secur.*, 2, 3, 189–199, 2007.
17. Zhan, C., Zeng, Y., Zhang, R., Trajectory design for distributed estimation in UAV-enabled wireless sensor network. *IEEE Trans. Veh. Technol.*, 67, 10, 10155–10159, 2018.
18. Sun, X., Yang, W., Cai, Y., Ma, R., Tao, L., Physical layer security in millimeter wave SWIPT UAV-based relay networks. *IEEE Access*, 7, 35851–35862, 2019.
19. Jain, R. and Templin, F., Requirements, challenges and analysis of alternatives for wireless datalinks for unmanned aircraft systems. *IEEE J. Sel. Areas Commun.*, 30, 5, 852–860, 2012.
20. Sultana, A., Zhao, L., Fernando, X., Energy-efficient power allocation in underlay and overlay cognitive device-to-device communications. *IET Commun.*, 13, 2, 162–170, 2018.
21. Ghazzai, H., Ghorbel, M.B., Kadri, A., Hossain, M.J., Menouar, H., Energy-efficient management of unmanned aerial vehicles for underlay cognitive radio systems. *IEEE Trans. Green Commun. Netw.*, 1, 4, 434–443, 2017.
22. Zhang, H., Da, X., Hu, H., Ni, L., Pan, Y., Spectrum efficiency optimization for UAV-based cognitive radio network. *Math. Probl. Eng.*, 2020, 2020.
23. Bouaziz, M., Rachedi, A., Belghith, A., EKF-MRPL: Advanced mobility support routing protocol for Internet of Mobile Things: Movement prediction approach. *Future Gener. Comput. Syst.*, 93, 822–832, 2019.
24. Ghorbel, M.B., Ghazzai, H., Kadri, A., Hossain, M.J., Menouar, H., An energy efficient overlay cognitive radio approach in UAV-based communication, in: *2018 IEEE Global Communications Conference (GLOBECOM)*, pp. 1–6, 2018.
25. Fernandes, R.A., Monitoring system for power lines and right-of-way using remotely piloted drone, US Patent 4,818,990, Apr. 04, 1989.
26. Luque-Vega, L.F., Castillo-Toledo, B., Loukianov, A., Gonzalez-Jimenez, L.E., Power line inspection via an unmanned aerial system based on the quadrotor helicopter, in: *MELECON 2014-2014 17th IEEE Mediterranean Electrotechnical Conference*, pp. 393–397, 2014.
27. Naqvi, S.A.R., Hassan, S.A., Pervaiz, H., Ni, Q., Drone-aided communication as a key enabler for 5G and resilient public safety networks. *IEEE Commun. Mag.*, 56, 1, 36–42, 2018.
28. Lu, M., Bagheri, M., James, A.P., Phung, T., Wireless charging techniques for UAVs: A review, reconceptualization, and extension. *IEEE Access*, 6, 29865–29884, 2018.
29. Abdulla, A.E., Fadlullah, Z.M., Nishiyama, H., Kato, N., Ono, F., Miura, R., An optimal data collection technique for improved utility in UAS-aided networks, in: *IEEE INFOCOM 2014-IEEE Conference on Computer Communications*, pp. 736–744, 2014.
30. Zeng, Y., Zhang, R., Lim, T.J., Throughput maximization for mobile relaying systems, in: *2016 IEEE Globecom Workshops (GC Wkshps)*, pp. 1–6, 2016.

31. Say, S., Inata, H., Liu, J., Shimamoto, S., Priority-based data gathering framework in UAV-assisted wireless sensor networks. *IEEE Sens. J.*, 16, 14, 5785–5794, 2016.
32. Ahmed, N., Kanhere, S.S., Jha, S., On the importance of link characterization for aerial wireless sensor networks. *IEEE Commun. Mag.*, 54, 5, 52–57, 2016.
33. Zhan, C., Zeng, Y., Zhang, R., Energy-efficient data collection in UAV enabled wireless sensor network. *IEEE Wireless Commun. Lett.*, 7, 3, 328–331, 2017.
34. Haykin, S., Cognitive radio: Brain-empowered wireless communications. *IEEE J. Sel. Areas Commun.*, 23, 2, 201–220, 2005.
35. Jacob, P., Sirigina, R.P., Madhukumar, A.S., Prasad, V.A., Cognitive radio for aeronautical communications: A survey. *IEEE Access*, 4, 3417–3443, 2016.
36. Hu, H., Huang, Y., Da, X., Zhang, H., Ni, L., Pan, Y., Optimization of energy management for UAV-enabled cognitive radio. *IEEE Wireless Commun. Lett.*, 9, 9, 1505–1508, 2020.
37. Hu, J., Zhang, H., Song, L., Reinforcement learning for decentralized trajectory design in cellular UAV networks with sense-and-send protocol. *IEEE Internet Things J.*, 6, 4, 6177–6189, 2018.
38. Donoho, D.L., Compressed sensing. *IEEE Trans. Inf. Theory*, 52, 4, 1289–1306, 2006.
39. Parab, L.S. and Vinayakray-Jani, P., Compressed sensing for optimising connectivity in FANET architecture, in: *2016 Second International Conference on Research in Computational Intelligence and Communication Networks (ICRCICN)*, pp. 100–105, 2016.
40. Zeng, S., Zhang, H., Bian, K., Song, L., UAV relaying: Power allocation and trajectory optimization using decode-and-forward protocol, in: *2018 IEEE International Conference on Communications Workshops (ICC Workshops)*, pp. 1–6, 2018.
41. Pliatsios, D. and Sarigiannidis, P., Power allocation in downlink non-orthogonal multiple access IoT-enabled Systems: A particle swarm optimization approach, in: *2019 15th International Conference on Distributed Computing in Sensor Systems (DCOSS)*, pp. 416–422, 2019.
42. Hu, D., Zhang, Q., Li, Q., Qin, J., Joint position, decoding order, and power allocation optimization in UAV-based NOMA downlink communications. *IEEE Syst. J.*, 14, 2, 2949–2960, 2019.
43. Li, Y., Zhang, H., Long, K., Choi, S., Nallanathan, A., Resource allocation for optimizing energy efficiency in NOMA-based fog UAV wireless networks. *IEEE Netw.*, 34, 2, 158–163, 2019.
44. Moore, J. and Tedrake, R., Powerline perching with a fixed-wing UAV, in: *AIAA Infotech@ Aerospace Conference and AIAA Unmanned... Unlimited Conference*, p. 1959, 2009.
45. Moore, J. and Tedrake, R., Magnetic localization for perching UAVs on powerlines. ZN. *2011 IEEE/RSJ International Conference on Intelligent Robots and Systems*, pp. 2700–2707, 2011.

46. Xu, J., Zeng, Y., Zhang, R., UAV-enabled wireless power transfer: Trajectory design and energy optimization. *IEEE Trans. Wireless Commun.*, 17, 8, 5092–5106, 2018.
47. Yin, S., Zhao, Y., Li, L., Resource allocation and basestation placement in cellular networks with wireless powered UAVs. *IEEE Trans. Veh. Technol.*, 68, 1, 1050–1055, 2018.
48. Zeng, Y., Clerckx, B., Zhang, R., Communications and signals design for wireless power transmission. *IEEE Trans. Commun.*, 65, 5, 2264–2290, 2017.
49. Sharma, V., You, I., Kumar, R., Energy efficient data dissemination in multi-UAV coordinated wireless sensor networks. *Mob. Inf. Syst.*, 2016, 2016.
50. Yang, X.-S., Firefly algorithms for multimodal optimization, in: *International Symposium on Stochastic Algorithms*, pp. 169–178, 2009.
51. Mohammed, F., Jawhar, I., Mohamed, N., Idries, A., Towards trusted and efficient UAV-based communication, in: *2016 IEEE 2nd International Conference on Big Data Security on Cloud (BigDataSecurity), IEEE International Conference on High Performance and Smart Computing (HPSC), and IEEE International Conference on Intelligent Data and Security (IDS)*, pp. 388–393, 2016.
52. Kerrache, C.A., Barka, E., Lagraa, N., Lakas, A., Reputation-aware energy-efficient solution for FANET monitoring, in: *2017 10th IFIP Wireless and Mobile Networking Conference (WMNC)*, pp. 1–6, 2017.
53. Marinaki, M. and Marinakis, Y., A glowworm swarm optimization algorithm for the vehicle routing problem with stochastic demands. *Expert Syst. Appl.*, 46, 145–163, 2016.
54. Khan, A., Aftab, F., Zhang, Z., Self-organization based clustering scheme for FANETs using Glowworm Swarm Optimization. *Phys. Commun.*, 36, 100769, 2019.
55. Wei, Z. *et al.*, Spectrum sharing between UAV-based wireless mesh networks and ground networks, in: *2018 10th International Conference on Wireless Communications and Signal Processing (WCSP)*, pp. 1–6, 2018.
56. Lee, C.-H., Shih, C.-Y., Chen, Y.-S., Stochastic geometry based models for modeling cellular networks in urban areas. *Wirel. Netw.*, 19, 6, 1063–1072, 2013.
57. Kong, L., Khan, M.K., Wu, F., Chen, G., Zeng, P., Millimeter-wave wireless communications for IoT-cloud supported autonomous vehicles: Overview, design, and challenges. *IEEE Commun. Mag.*, 55, 1, 62–68, 2017.
58. Khan, M.A., Qureshi, I.M., Khanzada, F., A hybrid communication scheme for efficient and low-cost deployment of future flying ad-hoc network (FANET). *Drones*, 3, 1, 16, 2019.
59. Anton, S.R. and Inman, D.J., Performance modeling of unmanned aerial vehicles with on-board energy harvesting, in: *Active and Passive Smart Structures and Integrated Systems 2011*, vol. 7977, p. 79771H, 2011.

60. Ding, Z., Perlaza, S.M., Esnaola, I., Poor, H.V., Power allocation strategies in energy harvesting wireless cooperative networks. *IEEE Trans. Wireless Commun.*, 13, 2, 846–860, 2014.
61. Lyu, J., Zeng, Y., Zhang, R., Cyclical multiple access in UAV-aided communications: A throughput-delay tradeoff. *IEEE Wireless Commun. Lett.*, 5, 6, 600–603, 2016.
62. Cvetkovic, A., Blagojevic, V., Ivaniš, P., Performance analysis of nonlinear energy-Harvesting DF relay system in interference-limited Nakagami-m fading environment. *ETRI J.*, 39, 6, 803–812, 2017.
63. Xie, L., Xu, J., Zhang, R., Throughput maximization for UAV-enabled wireless powered communication networks. *IEEE Internet Things J.*, 6, 2, 1690–1703, 2018.
64. Yang, L., Chen, J., Hasna, M.O., Yang, H.-C., Outage performance of UAV-assisted relaying systems with RF energy harvesting. *IEEE Commun. Lett.*, 22, 12, 2471–2474, 2018.
65. Ji, B., Li, Y., Zhou, B., Li, C., Song, K., Wen, H., Performance analysis of UAV relay assisted IoT communication network enhanced with energy harvesting. *IEEE Access*, 7, 38738–38747, 2019.
66. Zhang, C. and Zhang, W., Spectrum sharing for drone networks. *IEEE J. Sel. Areas Commun.*, 35, 1, 136–144, 2016.
67. Sboui, L., Ghazzai, H., Rezki, Z., Alouini, M.-S., Energy-efficient power allocation for UAV cognitive radio systems, in: *2017 IEEE 86th Vehicular Technology Conference (VTC-Fall)*, pp. 1–5, 2017.
68. Lyu, J., Zeng, Y., Zhang, R., Spectrum sharing and cyclical multiple access in UAV-aided cellular offloading, in: *GLOBECOM 2017-2017 IEEE Global Communications Conference*, pp. 1–6, 2017.
69. Huang, X.-L., Wang, G., Hu, F., Kumar, S., Stability-capacity-adaptive routing for high-mobility multihop cognitive radio networks. *IEEE Trans. Veh. Technol.*, 60, 6, 2714–2729, 2011.
70. Mohindru, V., Bhatt, R., Singh, Y., Reauthentication scheme for mobile wireless sensor networks. *Sustainable Comput.: Inf. Syst.*, 23, 158–166, 2019.

4

Energy Efficient Communication Methods for Unmanned Ariel Vehicles (UAVs): Last Five Years' Study

Nagesh Kumar

Shoolini University of Biotechnology and Management Sciences, Solan, India

Abstract

Small sized drones and devices which can fly and collect or deliver data from parts of area under consideration are referred to as unmanned aerial vehicles. These devices are now a days emerging into multiple defense and civil applications like surveillance, crop monitoring etc. UAV devices communicate with each other as well as with source and destination with help of certain communication methods. These communication techniques must be energy efficient as most of these devices are battery powered and have multiple operations to perform in flight. This article focuses on mostly used communication techniques in UAVs. The aim is to present a literature and summarize the same in form of challenges and issues arise when developing communication methods for UAVs. The performance comparison has been made at the end of literature study. This article may help new researchers to cope up with existing challenges and issues in UAV communication protocols.

Keywords: Unmanned aerial vehicle, Internet of Things, fog computing, communication protocols

4.1 Introduction

Drone technologies are emerging as Unmanned Ariel Vehicles (UAVs) nowadays and have numerous of applications in almost every domain for making human life better. UAV technologies are having potentials in defense,

Email: engg.nagesh2@gmail.com

Vandana Mohindru, Yashwant Singh, Ravindara Bhatt and Anuj Kumar Gupta (eds.) Unmanned Aerial Vehicles for Internet of Things (IoT): Concepts, Techniques, and Applications, (73–88) © 2021 Scrivener Publishing LLC

civil and other public applications like in defense applications surveillance systems, intrusion detection systems, exploration and area monitoring etc. are important. Civil and public sector applications include UAVs as forest fire monitoring and control, manufacturing site surveillance and carrying essential supplies to remote areas etc. In most of the applications UAVs are equipped with Internet of Things (IoT) devices, helping these to maintain connectivity with owner servers. Internet of things devices and UAV, both are battery operated and require low cost communication technologies. Unlike in MANETs and VANETs, study of energy consumption by UAVs for motor rotation and operating preinstalled IoT devices is an important research area [1]. The lifetime of UAVs is very limited depending on the battery capacity (typically less than 30 min), which is a major drawback to be used in long-term operations required in critical applications. Most of the applications required multi-UAV systems which are more reliable and have the abilities to perform multiple tasks in parallel. As compared to single UAV systems, these are more efficient, scalable and have fault tolerance as well [2].

Although multi-UAV systems may be used for enhancing application lifetime, but at the same time there are more challenges in deployment and communication. Communication between multiple UAVs is a challenging task as it requires path finding algorithms to be processed on controllers of the devices. Ad-hoc communication protocols may play a vital role in UAV technology because of the mobility and thin deployment of UAVs. As UAVs are battery powered, energy efficiency is an important factor to be considered while developing any communication protocol. Therefore, this paper try to focus and discuss the present scenario of energy efficient communication protocols or algorithms proposed for UAV technologies. Upcoming subsection give a brief introduction about UAV and applications. Also basic communication techniques are covered in the remaining of this section. Section 4.2 will discuss the process followed to prepare an extensive literature and research questions this paper tries to answer. Section 4.3 will discuss actual literature studied and gist of various researches carried out in this field. Section 4.4 discusses the answers to research questions from Section 4.2 based on literature survey carried out in Section 4.3. Then paper concludes the arguments and questions in Section 4.5.

4.1.1 Introduction to UAV

Flying drones or a military aircraft operating autonomously or by a remote control, is generally referred to as an Unmanned Ariel Vehicle (UAV) [2, 3]. Unfettered by squad, equipment of life-support, and the strategy for protection necessities of manned air-vehicle, UAVs may be extraordinarily effective, contributing significantly better range and durability than corresponding human operated systems. UAVs era started somewhere around World War II with radio-controlled aircrafts for military uses or personal usage. But in last four to five years a range of applications started using UAVs like in agriculture, good governance and industry monitoring etc. UAVs are helping more in remote-sensing field by providing high resolution images of the area under consideration. For most of the applications, single flight UAVs are having certain demerits like large area coverage is not possible in single flight due to battery constraint. Also, the flight of an UAV is permitted to low heights, typically around 200 m (mostly below clouds) [4, 5]. UAVs are therefore more often suitable for small scale farming and industries.

UAV devices are composed of hardware parts, similar to traditional drones including battery, controller/processor, sensors and actuators etc. Also, software include, operating system, firmware, middleware, autopilot and communication protocols etc. Sensors are basically used for measuring distance from objects and other application specific parameters. Operating system for UAV systems handle the tasks of management of processes like control of flight, navigation control and handling other decisions. A global positioning system (GPS) is also recommended to locate the device or it may help autopilot program to get back to the origin of the device [5]. Apart of these all functionalities software and hardware also required for controlling take-off, landing, throttling and shifting altitudes etc. The future applications of UAV technologies depends on the evolution in hardware and software technologies for UAVs. Also, as the use of multi-UAV systems is evolving, there is need of developing new communication technologies and considering battery/fuel constraints, energy efficiency must be considered as an important parameter.

4.1.2 Communication in UAV

The most important part of any kind of networking is transfer of data packets from one part of the network to other part. Routing algorithms are utilized for efficient communicating inside or outside of a network. The routing mechanisms include certain common strategies like broadcasting, unicasting and multicasting. In broadcasting all the data transmitted by one node can also be received by all other nodes in the range of that node. In unicasting the data is intended for only one node and only that node can receive the same. While, multicasting is a communication technique in which the packets are transmitted to a dedicated group of nodes. In order to transmit data packets efficiently there is requirement of good routing strategies which are based on most important parameters utilized in development of a routing metric. As UAVs are wireless systems, there is a need of wireless routing protocols like used in MANETs, VANETs and wireless sensor networks. Most of the UAV networks are self-organized networks, which means UAVs will setup their own network, when these devices comes in the vicinity of each other. This self-organized network is called as UAV ad-hoc network [5], which is having most of the similar features as compared to MANETs and VANETs. But as already discussed above the limited resources and mobility are major constraints in UAV networks, one cannot directly use ad hoc routing protocols for communication in UAV. Most of the UAV devices take flight in high speed due to which the communication protocols should not introduce high delays like most of ad hoc routing protocols do.

The researchers focusing on UAV communication protocols have proposed many such protocols which introduced optimal resource utilization and low delays [4]. Based on the operation of UAVs the communication techniques are divided into two classifications i.e. single and multi-hop communication [5]. The UAV devices are capable of transferring data packets from one location to another due to mobility and this makes one device to carry packets toward intended destination. This communication method is referred to as singe-hop communication method as only one relay node is used to carry packets from source to destination. On the other hand, multi-hop communication utilizes more than one UAV devices as relay nodes. In this method a swarm of such devices makes communication with each other to deliver packet at destination node. In single-hop routing method the important scenario is path construction for single relay node in the flight, which should be efficient and less time consuming.

In the later type, selection of next-hop is very important as multiple relay nodes are used for data transmission. There may be different next-hop selection strategies to be utilized. Based on these strategies multi-hop communication methods for UAV are further been classified as location-based and topology-centered communication methods. The location-based communication techniques depends on GPS and always require to calculate distance to next-hop, based on coordinates of multiple neighbor devices. Real-time device locations are used and packets will be transmitted accordingly towards destination. Most of the protocols proposed in this category introduced high cost of communication as it require GPS to be switched on every second. Another category is topology-centered communication methods, which require UAV devices to organize themselves in an arrangement where each device can establish a connection to every other device directly or indirectly. This type of communication methods may be treated as a hybrid communication methods as topology-centered communication techniques introduce single-hop and multi-hop in a single network. In upcoming sections a detailed review of such protocols is presented and a discussion will be carried out about best parameter and topology selection for UAVs.

4.2 Literature Survey Process

This literature study was carried out on communication methods for UAV include various research and review papers from last five years. Papers beyond last five years are only considered, where it seems to be extreme requirement to include those. Before starting literature research questions were formulated and study was carried out based on these questions only.

4.2.1 Research Questions

The chapter focused to answer following question after the completion of literature survey. These question are focused towards energy efficient communication mechanisms in UAVs.

RQ1. What are various challenges introduced during communication of data in UAV?
RQ2. What are various focused parameters and metrics utilized in communication methods for UAV during last five years?
RQ3. What are various issues and challenges researchers may face, when they try to develop new communication methods for UAV?

4.2.2 Information Source

For a successful literature survey to be carried out it was required that only quality papers must be included in this chapter. Hence, to fulfill this requirement, different research databases was extracted for existing work on communication methods in UAVs. In this chapter mainly five databases are extracted, to generate the state of the art in energy efficient routing for UAVs. These databases are

1. IEEE Xplore (www.ieeexplore.ieee.org)
2. ACM digital library (dl.acm.org)
3. Science direct (www.sciencedirect.com)
4. Google Scholar (www.scholar.google.com)

5. Springer (www.springer.com)
6. Taylor & Francis Online (https://tandfonline.com/).

The articles considered for the analysis in this chapter are only from high impact research journals and conferences. These articles are indexed in SCI, Scopus and Web of Sciences databases. The searching keywords or phrases were related to UAV, UAV communication techniques, routing in UAV, energy efficiency in UAV, energy efficient routing for UAVs and other related phrases.

4.3 Routing in UAV

This paper is apprehensive to research work carried out by different researchers around the world in the field of UAV communication technologies. This section will introduce summary of papers in this area of study and discuss the challenges and issues in upcoming sections. The literature review covers communication technologies in UAV, energy efficient routing in UAV and parameters and metrics of consideration during communication method development.

4.3.1 Communication Methods in UAV

As discussed earlier, the communication protocols proposed for ad-hoc networks cannot directly be applicable to UAVs. The challenges in UAV includes high mobility and changing topologies within fraction of seconds. The routing protocols studied for this review are divided into two classifications i.e. single-hop communication (Figure 4.1) [22] and multi-hop communication (Figure 4.2) [22].

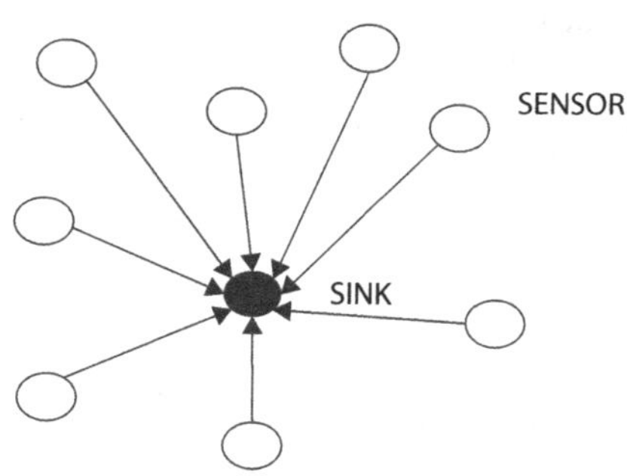

Figure 4.1 Single hop communication.

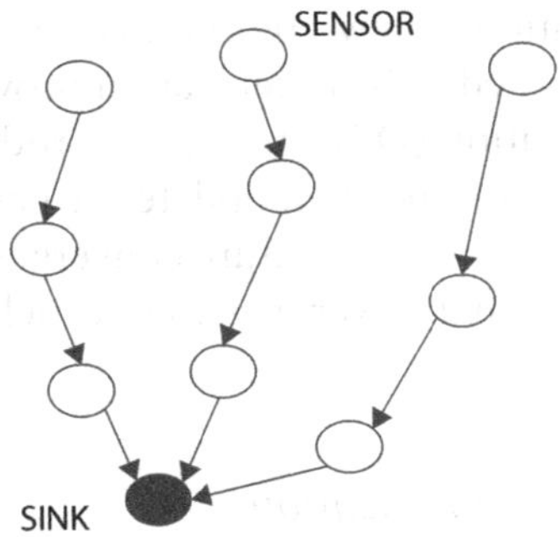

Figure 4.2 Multi-hop communication.

4.3.1.1 Single-Hop Communication

The simplest type of communication technique is single-hop communication in which the decision of path planning remains static. The UAV devices are used as data packet transporters which basically pick up packets from source and deliver directly to destination. Although it is easy to construct such communication methods, but as the topology and rules are fixed the fault tolerant capability is very low. This makes these protocols not to be used in dynamic environments.

There are very few examples of research on single hop communication in UAVs and most of the researchers have shifted to multi-hop communication systems because of abundance of advantages and technology advancements. A well know single-hop communication protocol is load carry and deliver (LCAD) [6] which consider the deployment of UAV device (may be one or more) for carrying data packets from one location to other. In this protocol only a single UAV carry data and do not pass data to any other relay in between the source and destination. The packets was delivered on radio frequency links and hence enables highly reliable packet delivery by avoiding collisions and other environment problems. But there are certain limitations of this communication system like time of flight should be lesser, energy consumption in flight should be optimized and fault tolerant capability is not present. Another protocol proposed in this category is differential evolution with quantum-behaved particle swarm optimization (DEQPSO) [7]. It is basically a hybrid communication system combining the functionalities of differentials and particle swarm optimization algorithms. Performance of this communication scheme was high as compared with other single-hop communication systems. This protocol was used by many applications like defense systems and other industry applications [7, 8]. To solve the problems of low global convergence and optimal speed of operation a new communication system was proposed in Ref. [9]. Authors named this system as improved quantum-behaved pigeon-inspired optimization (QPIO), which introduced logistic mapping method for starting purpose and then update the path metrics accordingly to balance the local optima and premature convergence. The results shown the performance improvement over existing particle swarm optimization methods.

4.3.1.2 Multi-Hop Communication

As the name suggests multi-hop communication transmits packets through multiple relays. In UAV multiple devices are used to transmit data packets, during their flight, from source to destination. Similar to that of wireless ad-hoc networks it will be important to plan an efficient path between source and destination. Based on this problem, multiple routing metric and communication protocols were proposed by various researchers. Based on this study multi-hop communication can further be divided into topology-centered, location based and cluster based communication systems.

Topology-Centered Multi-hop Communication: Topology-centered communication methods can also be divided into two categories, depending on the formation of topologies by UAV devices. The first class is called as proactive methods in which the path planning data is stored inside the devices before deployment. This will decrease the packet and route processing time as the routes are already available inside the devices. These protocols are seems to be reliable and easy to build and deploy, but not recommended many times for high mobility networks formed by UAVs. This is because in UAV networks, topology changes occur very frequently and a static information like in proactive communication methods will not be suitable. However few researchers worked in this field and proposed some proactive communication systems.

Topology broadcast based on reverse path forwarding (TBRPF) [10] is one of the example in which predefined path is selected for packet transmissions. The path selection is made statically based on finding the minimum number of hops from source to destination. Although as in case UAV minimum hop path may not be the optimal one and there may be more energy consumption involved. Another problem arise over here is selection of weak links which in turn increase packet drops. Another well know protocol based on optimized link state routing is proposed in Ref. [11] and known as directional optimized link state routing (DOLSR). DOLSR try to reduce the overhead of communication by introduction of directional antennas. Another version of this protocol is proposed in Ref. [12] called as predictive-OLSR (POLSR) which utilizes GPS information to transmit data packets.

Another type in topology-centered category are reactive communication methods, which are also refer to as passive communication protocols. These protocols are basically on-demand protocol which operates only when there is a requirement of sending data packets. Reactive protocols effectively reduce the control packet requirements and thus reducing overhead of central topology control. Famous protocols like dynamic source routing (DSR) and ad hoc on demand distance vector (AODV) are the examples of reactive communication protocols. For UAV networks reactive-greedy-reactive (RGR) [13] protocol was proposed which was based on AODV methodology. The difference is that the paths with fewest hop count are considered first for data transmission. Some other researchers have also worked in the same direction and proposed modified-RGR [14] and UAV-assisted routing [15].

Location-Based Communication Methods: Dynamic characteristics of UAV networks do not allow the use of static communication methods. Therefore, in multi-hop communication knowledge of geographic location of UAV devices can help in better path planning toward destination nodes. Such communication protocols which are making the path planning decisions based on location information are referred to as geographic communication protocols [16]. Most of these type of communication systems utilized greedy approach for path discovery which consider closest hop as next relay. Some of the popular communication protocols in this category are greedy distributed spanning tree routing-3D (GDSTR) [17], greedy-hull-greedy [18] and greedy-random-greedy [19]. These protocols utilizes location information to find out local minimum distance and forward packets accordingly. In Ref. [17] 3D location coordinates are utilized, while in Refs. [18] and [19] 2D coordinates of a node are utilized to calculate position of next-hop nodes.

Energy Efficient Hierarchical Communication: UAV networks are most of the time are utilized for enhancement of area coverage which in turn lead to packet distribution and collection in remote places. In this case, UAV networks can be thought of as similar to wireless sensor networks [20, 21]. Developing cluster based communication systems proved to be a benchmark in wireless networks as single reliable node takes the responsibility of data collection and data forwarding. Also these cluster based protocols proved to be efficient and effective for wireless sensor networks as well [22].

Cluster head selection is an important criterion to be decided in these type of protocols. Also the performance of communication protocols depends on how frequently the cluster heads are changing from one node to another [23]. Most popular protocols for UAVs are hybrid routing based on clustering (HCR) [24], mobility prediction clustering algorithm (MPCA) [25] and temporarily ordered routing algorithm (TORA) [26]. Some other communication systems proposed recently are single mobile data collector-assisted (SDCA) [27] and IMRL [28].

4.4 Challenges and Issues

The analysis of various communication protocols studied in this article is presented in Table 4.1. From the literature study it is clear that each kind of communication method have certain advantages or disadvantages. By keeping this fact in view below are major challenges which a researcher may face while making new communication method for UAVs.

4.4.1 Energy Consumption

Developing power aware protocols, which will help in optimizing the energy consumption is a major challenge. As already discussed in previous sections, that UAVs are battery powered devices and utilized this limited amount of power to perform multiple operations like flight, communication, path discovery, data processing and collection etc. Hence, energy efficiency parameters must be considered while developing new communication mechanisms for UAVs [22].

4.4.2 Mobility of Devices

Mobile devices in flight are major challenge as in this case speed of the device must also be considered while designing new communication methods. In case of MANETs and VANETs nodes are little slow as compared to UAVs. Various researchers have developed such UAVs, which are having speeds ranging between 30 and 460 km/h [29].

4.4.3 Density of UAVs

When UAVs are deployed in groups then density comes into the picture. Such UAV network impose more challenging tasks for the communication protocols. The only good news in UAVs is that one can simple not

Table 4.1 Analysis of existing communication protocols.

Communication protocol	Class	Communication basis	Path discovery	Route updation	Energy efficiency	Communication metric
LCAD [6]	Single-hop	Unicast	Static	No update	No	No metric
DEQPSO [7]	Single-hop	Unicast	Static	No update	No	No metric
QPIO [9]	Single-hop	Unicast	Static	No update	No	Minimum Cost path
TBRPF [10]	Topology-centered	Broadcast	Static	No update	No	Minimum Cost path
DOLSR [11]	Topology-centered	Broadcast	Static	Yes, periodical	No	Optimized Link
POLSR [12]	Topology-centered	Broadcast	Static	Yes, periodical	No	Optimized Link
RGR [13]	Topology-centered	Multicast	Dynamic	Yes, periodical	No	Minimum Distance
Modified-RGR [14]	Topology-centered	Multicast	Dynamic	Yes, periodical	No	Minimum Distance
UAV-assisted routing [15]	Topology-centered	Multicast	Dynamic	Yes, periodical	No	Minimum Distance

(Continued)

Table 4.1 Analysis of existing communication protocols. *(Continued)*

Communication protocol	Class	Communication basis	Path discovery	Route updation	Energy efficiency	Communication metric
GDSTR [17]	Location-based	Unicast	Dynamic	On-demand	No	Nearest active neighbor
GHG [18]	Location-based	Unicast	Dynamic	On-demand	No	Nearest active neighbor
GRG [19]	Location-based	Unicast	Dynamic	On-demand	No	Nearest active neighbor
HCR [24]	Hierarchical	Multicast	Dynamic	On-demand	Yes	No metric
MPCA [25]	Hierarchical	Unicast	Dynamic	Hybrid	Yes	Fast path
TORA [26]	Hierarchical	Unicast	Dynamic	Hybrid	Yes	Optimized Link
SDCA [27]	Hierarchical	Broadcast	Dynamic	Hybrid	Yes	Cluster selection
IMRL [28]	Hierarchical	Broadcast	Dynamic	On-demand	Yes	Cluster selection

allowed to increase the density of devices because of speed limits and other flying license problems [30, 31].

4.4.4 Changes in Topology

Frequent changes in topology is also a big challenge and issue as well for most of the UAV networks. Self-organization and high speed mobility give arise to these problems. Developing communication method for such type of networks is a very tedious task.

4.4.5 Propagation Models

Surrounding environment of UAVs may affect the communication capabilities of UAV devices. UAVs communication techniques mostly support line-of sight methods as these devices are far away from ground [29]. The only challenge to overcome is flying these devices in such a manner that they do not interfere each other.

4.4.6 Security in Routing

Like any other network, researchers must think of security issues like breaching of data packets, theft of data packets, injecting false messages and node cloning attacks etc. developers of communication protocols for UAVs must think about energy efficient techniques to cope up with security issues. Some of the energy efficient methods were proposed for wireless sensor networks recently [32–34].

Apart of these challenges networking such devices is still a tedious process and require extra efforts from researchers. High speeds of UAV devices provide no guarantee of data packet delivery and also traditional efficient protocols cannot be utilized in UAVs.

4.5 Conclusion

UAVs are emerging to be new exciting area of research, but routing is a tedious task and attracting many researchers in past four to five years. This article was an attempt to list out the summary of majorly used communication methods for UAVs by looking at merits and demerits. Also Table 4.1 stated various tasks involved inside each and every communication method discussed in this chapter. Later challenges and issues are discussed out of which the major challenge is building new energy efficient and high performance communication method for UAVs. The article summarizes major classifications of communication methods for UAVs. The future of UAVs is bright and may be used in many application as most of the applications now a days require autonomous operations of devices.

References

1. Gupta, L., Jain, R., Vaszkun, G., Survey of important issues in UAV communication networks. *IEEE Commun. Surv. Tutor.*, 18, 2, 1123–1152, 2015.
2. Erdelj, M., Natalizio, E., Chowdhury, K.R., Akyildiz, I.F., Help from the sky: Leveraging UAVs for disaster management. *IEEE Pervasive Comput.*, 16, 1, 24–32, 2017.
3. Naqvi, S.A.R., Hassan, S.A., Pervaiz, H., Ni, Q., Drone-aided communication as a key enabler for 5g and resilient public safety networks. *IEEE Commun. Mag.*, 56, 1, 36–42, 2018.
4. Sikeridis, D., Tsiropoulou, E.E., Devetsikiotis, M., Papavassiliou, S., Wireless powered public safety IoT: A UAV-assisted adaptive-learning approach towards energy efficiency. *J. Netw. Comput. Appl.*, 123, 69–79, 2018.
5. Jiang, J. and Han, G., Routing protocols for unmanned aerial vehicles. *IEEE Commun. Mag.*, 56, 1, 58–63, 2018.
6. Cheng, C., Hsiao, P., Kung, H.T., Vlah, D., Maximizing throughput of UAV-relaying networks with the load-carry-and-deliver paradigm, in: *IEEE Wireless Communications and Networking Conference*, March 2007, pp. 4417–4424.
7. Roberge, V., Tarbouchi, M., Labonté, G., Fast genetic algorithm path planner for fixedwing military UAV using GPU. *IEEE Trans. Aerosp. Electron. Syst.*, 54, 5, 2105–2117, 2018.
8. Fu, Y., Ding, M., Zhou, C., Hu, H., Route planning for unmanned aerial vehicle (UAV) on the sea using hybrid differential evolution and quantum-behaved particle swarm optimization. *IEEE Trans. Syst. Man Cybern. Syst.*, 43, 6, 1451–1465, 2013.
9. Hu, C., Xia, Y., Zhang, J., Adaptive Operator Quantum-Behaved Pigeon-Inspired Optimization Algorithm with Application to UAV Path Planning. *Algorithms*, 12, 3, 2019, https://doi.org/10.3390/a12010003.
10. Bellur, B.R., Lewis, M.G., Templin, F.L., An Ad-Hoc Network for Teams of Autonomous Vehicles. *Proc. 1st Annual Symp. Autonomic Intell. Net. Sys.*, Los Angeles, CA, pp. 1–6, 2002.
11. Alshabtat, A. and Dang, L., Low Latency Routing Algorithm for Unmanned Aerial Vehicles Ad-Hoc Networks. *World Acad. Sci. Eng. Technol.*, 80, 705–11, 2011.
12. Rosati, S. *et al.*, Speed-Aware Routing for UAV Ad-Hoc Networks. *IEEE GLOBECOM*, pp. 1367–73, 2013.

13. Forsmann, J.H., A Time-Slotted On-Demand Routing Protocol for Mobile Ad Hoc Unmanned Vehicle Systems. *Proc. SPIE*, 6561, 1–11, 2 May 2007.
14. Biomo, J., Kunz, T., St-Hilaire, M., Routing in Unmanned Aerial Ad Hoc Networks: Introducing a Route Reliability Criterion. *WMNC*, pp. 1–7, 2014.
15. Oubbati, O.S. *et al.*, Intelligent UAV-Assisted Routing Protocol for Urban VANETs. *Comput. Commun.*, 107, 93–111, 2017.
16. Lam, S.S. and Qian, C., Geographic routing in d-dimensional spaces with guaranteed delivery and low stretch, in: *Proceedings of the ACM SIGMETRICS Joint International Conference on Measurement and Modeling of Computer Systems, SIGMETRICS '11*, ACM, New York, NY, USA, pp. 257–268, 2011.
17. Zhou, J., Chen, Y., Leong, B., Sundaramoorthy, P.S., Practical 3D geographic routing for wireless sensor networks, in: *Proceedings of the 8th ACM Conference on Embedded Networked Sensor Systems, SenSys '10*, ACM, New York, NY, USA, pp. 337–350, 2010.
18. Liu, C. and Wu, J., Efficient geometric routing in three dimensional ad hoc networks, in: *IEEE INFOCOM*, pp. 2751–2755, 2009.
19. Flury, R. and Wattenhofer, R., Randomized 3D geographic routing, in: *IEEE INFOCOM 2008—The 27th Conference on Computer Communications*, April 2008, pp. 834–842.
20. Wu, J., Zou, L., Zhao, L., Al-Dubai, A., Mackenzie, L., Min, G., A multi-UAV clustering strategy for reducing insecure communication range. *Comput. Netw.*, 158, 132–142, 2019.
21. Wang, G., Lee, B., Ahn, J., Cho, G., A UAV-assisted CH election framework for secure data collection in wireless sensor networks. *Future Gener. Comput. Syst.*, 102, 152–162, 2020.
22. Kumar, N. and Singh, Y., Routing protocols in wireless sensor networks, in: *Handbook of Research on Advanced Wireless Sensor Network Applications, Protocols, and Architectures*, pp. 86–128, IGI Global, USA, 2017.
23. Doddapaneni, K., Omondi, F.A., Ever, E., Shah, P., Gemikonakli, O., Gagliardi, R., Deployment challenges and developments in wireless sensor networks clustering, in: *2014 28th International Conference on Advanced Information Networking and Applications Workshops*, May 2014, pp. 227–232.
24. Liu, K., Zhang, J., Zhang, T., The Clustering Algorithm of UAV Networking in Near-Space. *Proc. ISAPE*, pp. 1550–53, 2008.
25. Zang, C. and Zang, S., Mobility Prediction Clustering Algorithm for UAV Networking. *IEEE GLOBECOM*, pp. 1158–61, 2012.
26. Zhai, Z., Du, J., Ren, Y., The Application and Improvement of Temporally Ordered Routing Algorithm in Swarm Network with Unmanned Aerial Vehicle Nodes. *9th ICWMC*, pp. 7–12, 2013.
27. Wu, Q., Peng, S., Azzedine, B., Unmanned aerial vehicle-assisted energy-efficient data collection scheme for sustainable wireless sensor networks. *Comput. Networks*, 165, 106927, 2019.

28. Khelifi, F., Bradai, A., Singh, K., Atri, M., Localization and energy-efficient data routing for unmanned aerial vehicles: Fuzzy-logic-based approach. *IEEE Commun. Mag.*, *56*, 4, 129–133, 2018.
29. Clapper, J., Young, J., Cartwright, J., Grimes, J., *Unmanned systems roadmap*, pp. 2007–2032, Tech. rep., Department of Defense, United States, 2007.
30. Mukherjee, A., Dey, N., Kausar, N., Ashour, A.S., Taiar, R., Hassanien, A.E., A disaster management specific mobility model for flying ad-hoc network. *Int. J. Rough Sets Data Anal. (IJRSDA)*, 3, 72–103, 2016.
31. Bouachir, O., Abrassart, A., Garcia, F., Larrieu, N., A mobility model for UAV ad hoc network, in: *2014 International Conference on Unmanned Aircraft Systems (ICUAS)*, IEEE, pp. 383–388, 2014.
32. Mohindru, V. and Singh, Y., Node authentication algorithm for securing static wireless sensor networks from node clone attack. *Int. J. Inf. Comput. Secur.*, 10, 2–3, 129–148, 2018.
33. Mohindru, V., Bhatt, R., Singh, Y., Reauthentication scheme for mobile wireless sensor networks. *Sustain. Comput.: Inf. Syst.*, 23, 158–166, 2019.
34. Mohindru, V., Singh, Y., Bhatt, R., Securing wireless sensor networks from node clone attack: A lightweight message authentication algorithm. *Int. J. Inf. Comput. Secur.*, 12, 2–3, 217–233, 2020.

5

A Review on Challenges and Threats to Unmanned Aerial Vehicles (UAVs)

Shaik Johny Basha* **and Jagan Mohan Reddy Danda**

Department of CSE, Lakireddy Bali Reddy College of Engineering (A), Mylavaram, India

Abstract

Unmanned Aerial Vehicles (UAVs) are the most common applications used by many organizations in the present situation. Like every application, there are different issues and challenges with these UAVs also. One of the main cyber threats to UAVs is hijacking, which can be easy with small IoT devices. Also, they lack the privacy of the data which was captured by the UAVs, such as Images, Audio, and Video. This chapter discusses different challenges and threats that cause the tricky to Unmanned Aerial Vehicles, such as hijacking, privacy, cyber-security, and physical safety. The different solutions for avoiding those issues with current technologies are also discussed.

Keywords: Unmanned aerial vehicle (UAV), hijacking, IoT devices, data privacy, cyber security, physical safety

5.1 Introduction

Artificial Intelligence is becoming a boom in various fields, such as Automation, Robotics, Machines, etc. Along with these, Artificial Intelligence has entered the field of Aircraft as On-Board Pilotless Crafts with the name called 'Unmanned Aerial Vehicles (UAVs)' or 'Flying Robots.' Humans can manage UAVs with the help of the Ground Control Station. These are divided into categories as Heavier UAVs, Miniature UAVs, and Micro UAVs

**Corresponding author*: shaikhjanibasha@gmail.com

Vandana Mohindru, Yashwant Singh, Ravindara Bhatt and Anuj Kumar Gupta (eds.) Unmanned Aerial Vehicles for Internet of Things (IoT): Concepts, Techniques, and Applications, (89–104) © 2021 Scrivener Publishing LLC

according to their weight and working nature [1]. In the starting days, these UAVs are mainly developed for the military purpose to get rid of the attacks from the opposite teams. Due to the ease in usage, these UAVs expand their applicability ranging from Commercial and Civilian Applications like Drones. These drones are using for photography, agriculture, delivery of goods (logistics), rescue operations, 3D-mapping [2], searching and distributions, etc., and in military applications to track the movement of trespassers, object movements, human movements, combing operations, etc.

These are mainly useful in the toughest situations or places like land surveillance of agriculture (where humans cannot move and monitor) and hazardous places such as nuclear reactors, border security forces monitoring [3]. The rise in usage of these UAVs in various sectors shows how demanded and useful they are. Their use was approximately $250 Million in 2013, $19,300 Million in 2019, and expected to reach $45,000 Million in 2025 [4].

5.2 Applications of UAVs and Their Market Opportunity

As we have discussed in Section 5.1, UAVs are used over the various scenarios, as shown in Figure 5.1. In this regard, we are giving different UAV applications such as:

i. Aerospace
ii. Military—Reconnaissance, Attacks
iii. Demining
iv. Civil—Archaeology, Cargo, Conservation, Healthcare, Filmmaking, Journalism, Agriculture, Search, Surveillance, etc.

5.2.1 Applications

Aerospace:
UAVs can be used in Aerospace for various purposes like maintenance, repair, and flight operations. In 2016, one of the leading flight manufacturers named Airbus demonstrated how they are using the UAVs to visualize the aircraft [5].

Military:
Military Forces of different countries like the USA, UK, India, China, and others use UAVs for monitoring, surveillance, object movement, tracking

of people, etc. Some of the important UAVs used by different militaries are AeroVironment RQ-11 Raven, IAI Heron, TAI Anka, Hydra Technologies Ehécatl, Lipan M3, Predator, and DRDO Nishant. Not only in the military, but some of the terrorist groups are also using these UAVs for reconnaissance and dropping bombs on geographical positions. One example for this category is the ISIS announcement [6] of a UAV named "Unmanned Aircraft of the Mujahideen" in 2017.

Demining:
Many scientists are trying to develop UAVs with advanced imaging technology, which is cheaper and effective to map the mining fields. Some of the important UAVs developed for demining are the Dutch Mine Kafon project, Mine Kafon Drone [7], and more.

Civil:
Civil Applications of UAVs are not limited to a single source. But they are involved in various activities such as survey works by Archaeological Department, medicine delivery by DHL, goods delivery by Amazon [8], prehospital emergency care and expediting laboratory testing [9], aerial cinematography [10] by directors, monitoring animals and soil variation monitoring, water access, weeds and insects [11] in agriculture.

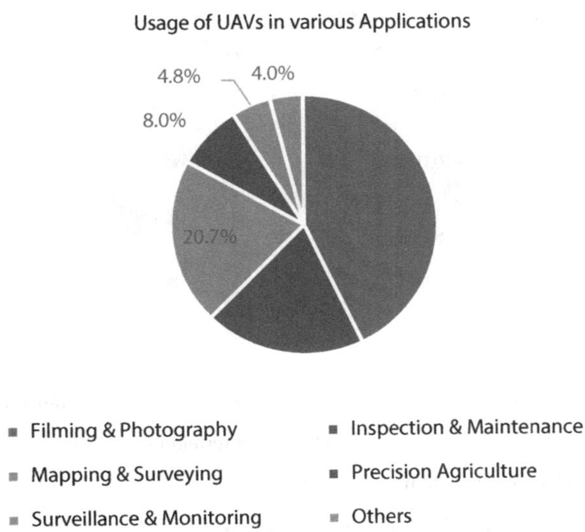

Figure 5.1 UAVs usage in various applications [12].

5.2.2 Market Opportunity

UAVs are raising their importance in the fields of manufacturing, investors, and business service providers. According to the report given by the PwC [13], the predicted value of the UAVs in various industries will reach a view of $127.3bn. While in the report given by the PwC, the infrastructure is going to be a key industry in using the UAVs with an addressable market value of $45.2bn. Then the agriculture is turning UAVs into different aspects and raising the market value to $32.4bn in the future. Transport takes a share of $13bn in the market. Security will gain an addressable market of $10bn, Media and Entertainment with $8.8bn, Insurance and other commodities will take an addressable market of $17.9bn. All the above-said market opportunities are shown in Figure 5.2, which will be occupied in the future.

5.3 Attacks and Solutions to Unmanned Aerial Vehicles (UAVs)

With the help of Sections 5.1 and 5.2, we realized that UAVs are simply a pilotless craft operated by humans from the ground. While these crafts

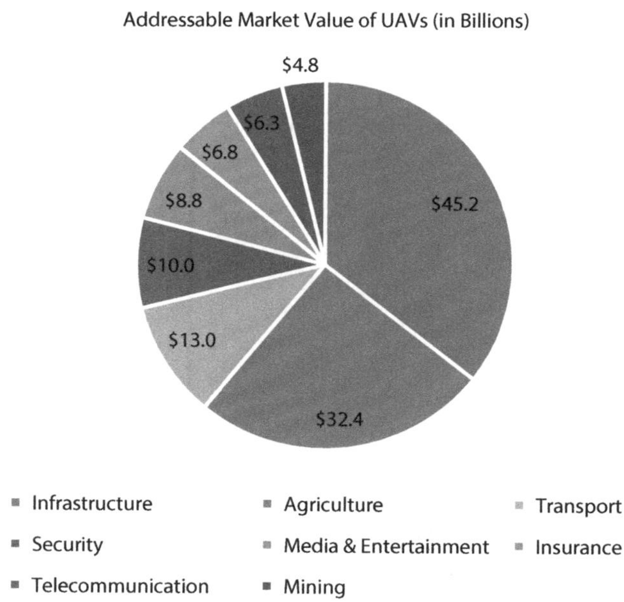

Figure 5.2 Addressable market value of UAVs (in billions).

are autonomous and fly with a connection to the network, they may come across different challenges and lead to threats. Important types of challenges and threats faced by the UAVs such as Access Control Attack, Wi-Fi Attack, Fabrication of Authentication, Linking Attacks, Sybil Attack, Data Fabrication/Modification, Data Duplication/Redundancy, Denial-of-Service Attack, Jamming, Session Hijacking, and Appending Attack. Most of the above-said attacks are related to network-based, but some are related to privacy concerns.

Attacks on UAVs or UAV networks are classified into different categories [18] based on their threat levels. They are:

i. Confidentiality Attacks
ii. Integrity Attacks
iii. Availability Attacks
iv. Authenticity Attacks.

5.3.1 Confidentiality Attacks

These attacks will happen on the security of the communication links among the network communication components through Session Hijacking, Cross-Layer Attacks, Eavesdropping, Packet Sniffing, Wiretapping, Man-in-the-Middle Attack, and Identity Spoofing.

Session Hijacking:

Threat: One of the dangerous network security attacks is Session Hijacking. A UAV is mainly dependent on the Global Positioning System (GPS) to move from one place to another. So, the attackers will consider this an advantage and perform GPS-Spoofing to gain access [19] over the UAV and perform illegal activities like terrorist attacks.

Solution: Authors [19] developed a technique that will use the UAV's gyroscope to detect whether it is hijacked or not. In their development, they have used the GPS's data and the different angular velocities detected by the gyroscopes to accelerate the UAV.

Cross-Layer Attacks:

Threat: Cross-Layer is intendedly developed to raise the network efficiency by information exchange among different layers. But the attackers are using this as an advantage and making attacks on the different layers of UAVs to gain network access and make the control to be with them.

Solution: Authors [20] proposed a framework named BlueBox, retrofitted with UAV's original system. BlueBox consists of a computing unit with both hardware and software components. This will be used to gain access and information from the original system. If an attack has happened, BlueBox will automatically stop the attacked component and land the UAV on to the ground.

Eavesdropping:

Threat: An Eavesdropping Attack is also called a Sniffing or Snooping Attack. This attack is a theft of information from the network. At the same time, it is transmitted over the network, which will take advantage of unsecured network communication for accessing data [21] while it is sent or received from UAV to the user. These attacks cannot be detected normally due to their working nature, i.e., the transmission in the network will appear normal.

Solution: Authors [22] built different predictive models with K-Means Clustering and One-Class Support Vector Machine (OC-SVM). In their approach, they have presented a framework for creating relevant features and performing training and testing. They have suggested that OC-SVM will be better for identifying stability in the network based on those results. In contrast, K-Means is better when Eavesdropper uses high power consumption to transmit data over the network. This means that there will be high power consumption in the transmission when there is an Eavesdropper Attack in the network.

Sharma *et al.* [23] proposed a new DMM Schema that can solve hierarchical security issues in the network layout and guarantees less energy consumption while the transmission is over the network with fully distributed security requirements. This approach is based on Blockchain, which takes advantage of the latency and communication overheads.

Man-in-the-Middle Attack:

Threat: Altering the communication between the user and the UAV is known as the Man-in-the-Middle Attack. It is also the best example of the active eavesdropper attack where the attacker establishes a connection with the victims independently. Then starts sending messages between the user and UAV to think that both are communicating themselves. But the fact is the attacker truly controls communication.

Solution: Authors [30] proposed a technique that maintains the security among the UAV networks by verifying information about the events from different sources. In their model, they have used secure asymmetric encryption with the already available list of official UAVs. So, this technique removes the man-in-the-middle attacks among the networks.

5.3.2 Integrity Attacks

Integrity means whether the data transmitted through the network is consistent, not corrupted, and accurate. The data which is transmitted should be accessed or modified only by authorized users. The attacks that will happen on the data transmitted through the network by UAV to the user or user to the UAV with the help of the malware, viruses, and trojans are known as Integrity Attacks. Attacks such as Data Modification and Data Duplication/Redundancy comes under Integrity Attacks.

Data Modification/Data Fabrication:

Threat: When the data is in transmission, some hackers or intruders try to access the network through malware or bots. Then the data in the transit will be modified or fabricated by the attacker as per their need. So, the transmitted data to the user or a UAV does not provide the information's integrity.

Solution: Authors [24] proposed a Blockchain-based scheme to solve the privacy issues that are happening in the networks. Their proposal consists of a system model with five modules, viz. content providers, user communities, miners, blockchain ledgers, and storage in the cloud [14]. Their proposal implementation has established a mutual trust between the sender and the receiver, which helps catch up on the modified or fabricated data.

Xueping *et al.* [25] proposed a solution to secure the transit data using Blockchain and traditional cloud servers. Their proposal linked the hashed data records and blockchain network. It then generated a receipt of blockchain for each record stored in the cloud—their proposal results in the assurance of data and scalability for many UAVs.

Data Duplication:

Threat: The name itself represents that duplication or redundancy means the irrelevant and unwanted data present in the network during transmission. This duplication or redundancy of data decreases the network throughput and causes data inconsistency.

Solution: Motivated by the Data Duplication issue, Roberto *et al.* [24] suggested that the UAV must decide whether the data is authentic. It is not altered by sending the data through a security system on Blockchain, known as Hash. Hash will allow the data and then determines whether the obtained information is distinct or redundant.

5.3.3 Availability Attacks

Availability refers to the ease and access of data or information [25] all over time without failure. Ensuring availability all the time is the biggest task in UAVs and complex tasks also. These attacks in UAVs mainly affect service and asset availability. Availability Attacks include Denial-of-Service Attack, Jamming Attack, Appending Attack, and many more.

Denial-of-Service Attack:

Threat: In this attack, the resources and services will not be available [25] to the users, and it affects the performance of the system. DoS Attack will cause the system to be overloaded and fails to be reloaded. This type of attack will be done from a single source and can be eradicated using different mechanisms such as firewalls and intrusion detections. Different examples of the DoS Attack are Ping Flood, Smurf Attack, SYN Attack, and Buffer Overflow.

Solution: Authors [26] have discussed Blockchain and its applications in the network systems for security. In their discussion, they have given that Blockchain will be considered superior by removing all the obstacles like single-point-of-failures. Using the Blockchain technique, the security will be most effective because it works on the Blockchain ledger, distributed among all the participating members. So, the Blockchain ledger makes the use of this technique and makes the resources and services available to all the users at any point in time.

Jamming Attack:

Threat: Jamming Attack refers to the subset of Denial-of-Service attacks. In this type of attack, an interference signal will be emitted to block the communication among the user at the ground and the UAV [27]. When the communication is blocked, it will cause the UAV to disrupt the normal operation and cause performance issues. Sometimes these attacks will cause the UAV to stop flying and damage the control system also. These attacks will be performed at the physical layer of the network.

Solution: Sliti *et al.* [28] presented their assumptions on detecting the Jamming Attack in UAV using the MCR decoding method and the transmitted signal recovery in the UAV network. In their assumptions, the MIMO/FSO (Multiple-Input Multiple-Output/Free Space Optics) transmitters will start every beam by sending it to the nearest known beam so that the channel coefficient will be calculated based on the transmitted and received beams. Whenever there is a blockage between the nearest beams' communication, it can be reported as a jamming attack.

Menaka Pushpa Arthur [29] proposed a new Intrusion Detection System (IDS) named Self-Taught Learning with a multiclass SVM. Her proposal gives the highest positive rate of the IDS, including at the unidentified territories also. A deep reinforcement learning was used in her proposal to dynamic route learning to return the UAV to its source at the time of the attack.

5.3.4 Authenticity Attacks

Authentication is important in a UAV network to keep control between the user and the UAV safe and secure from the attackers. Different methods have been coming into existence to obtain authenticity, such as two-factor authentication, high-security passwords, key generations, etc. Still, the attacks are happening on the authenticity of the network. These attacks include Access Control Attack, Wi-Fi Attack, and Fabrication of Authentication Attack.

Access Control Attack:

Threat: One of UAVs' main challenges is Access Control, which will view and access computing resources. With this method's help, we can prevent the UAV networks from hackers or unknown persons or unauthorized users to control the data available at remote or UAVs connected to a network. Access Control may have happened as physical, restricted to a limited area, or logical, consisting of multiple connections and data [15].

Solution: To protect the UAVs from access controlled by others, a Blockchain-based authentication framework was proposed by Ref. [16]. Their proposal consists of a scheme named Blockchain-based anonymous access (BAA), which will address the network authentication with a 3-way agreement between the manufacturer, user, and the operator. With this framework, it will reduce the cost of the operations and disbursement of the network.

Authors [17] designed a method that will make the decisions independently to coordinate communication protocols. Their design consists of a Distributed and Decentralized Ethereum Blockchain Framework and IPFS. As we know that, Blockchain can track the changes on its own without any third-party mechanism, so the access control and user identification can be made by the locally generated cryptographic keys which are committed in a network.

Wi-Fi Attack:

Threat: In this attack, the attacker tries to take control of the UAV by forcing the user to the cloned Wi-Fi network, and the data sent over this network will be intercepted [31]. This is also a type of Man-in-the-Middle Attack that gains access to the UAV system and the network's data packets.

Solution: To solve this issue, authors [32] have examined different cybersecurity issues of such networks. Their examination discussed the scalability problem that can be handled by Attribute-Based Encryption (ABE). With this ABE, the data will be encrypted with features decrypted by the authenticated users only. This method supports efficient broadcast key distribution and allows Wi-Fi authorization using some of the key features.

Fabrication of Authentication Attack:

Threat: Fabrication Attack comprises a duplicate message embedded into the attacker's network as a valid user [33]. This attack is mainly used to redirect the authentication checks by fabricating the information in the network.

Solution: As we know that UAV is also an IoT device that can be controlled through Blockchain. Authors [34] proposed that with the RSA Algorithm's help, the IoT devices can be controlled and configured without any fabrication. Their proposal has managed the keys using the RSA Public Key Cryptosystem, where Ethereum is used for storing public keys, and the device's private keys are stored in the devices only. With that technique, they claim that consensus algorithms will eradicate or stop the devices' fabrication attacks.

5.4 Research Challenges

As UAVs are increasing day-by-day and occupying a major market portion by the year 2025, there are still many challenges in developing and controlling the UAVs. In this section, we will discuss the different research challenges facing by scientists and well-reputed researchers.

5.4.1 Security Concerns

As the UAVs are smaller in size, it gives the biggest advantage to the criminals and youth to make use of this. Also, the terrorists are taking advantage [34] of this and started using UAVs for terror attacks, mainly due to the less prone to detection. UAVs can be used to carry weapons and deadly chemicals or can be fit with high explosives to make a blast of buildings or structures. Military analysts are worrying about espionage purposes like spying and gathering political and military-related information. This will cause the nation's security issues and any organization, and still, the research is going on about the security and structure of the UAVs.

5.4.2 Safety Concerns

Safety is not always the same as Security and vice-versa. Not only in the military, but UAVs are also used by the civilians who are crashing into the nearby houses, creating a disturbance to the property [35], recording video unauthorizedly, and making human injuries also. One of London's worst incidents is that a woman died in a car crash when a police UAV (drone) is followed by her vehicle near Wandsworth Prison [36]. A baby of an 18-month old lost his eye in Worcestershire, London when a UAV lost its control from the ground control and hit the baby eye [37]. As per the sources [38], in January 2019, UAVs have made a UK airport to shut down for over an hour. All these are the various safety issues causing the UAVs' safety for the humans and their surroundings.

Different safety concerns related to UAVs based on the above incidents are [39]:

i. Design issues in the UAVs
ii. Technological and Operational Standards
iii. Distortion of Signals—Jamming and Hijacking
iv. Government Regulations and Awareness.

5.4.3 Privacy Concerns

A huge amount of data is being collected by the UAVs in images, videos, and mapping coordinates. The data will be transmitted to the user from UAVs through the network. While the transmission or storage, there might be some privacy concerns or issues that will arise, such as location privacy, linking attacks, man-in-the-middle attack, eavesdropping attack, and many more. As the authors said in Refs. [22–25, 30], there are many solutions available for data privacy in UAVs; still, the attackers perform various attacks on the UAVs to steal the data.

5.4.4 Scalability Issues

When the UAVs are in communication as a Group or a Swarm, the information movement should be done with an atomic and required speed. Scientists and researchers have developed different techniques to make communication scalable. But those are limited to a small group of UAVs only. When the group is getting bigger than the normal size, the new developments such as the Blockchain platform are also not suitable for getting the communication scalable. Different platforms are developed to improve the communication or transmission speed using consensus algorithms; still, they are not supported for the UAV swarms [3] as UAVs are getting bigger day-by-day, mainly in smart cities.

5.4.5 Limited Resources

UAVs will consume low-power due to their light-weight structure. When the Blockchain and consensus algorithms are used to transmit data from UAV to other resources, then the high computation power is needed to do all this. In this regard, researchers are finding ways to get maximum operation time from the limited resources such as low-energy by developing a processor for UAVs [40–43] where the transmission and computation should be done on that low-energy only.

5.5 Conclusion

This chapter presented a comprehensive review of challenges, threats, and solutions in the Unmanned Aerial Vehicles (UAVs). Initially, we discussed UAV's basics and its applications & market opportunities in the future by 2025. In later sections, we have gone through a brief discussion on different attacks. In that section, we have discussed different threats to UAVs, and the solutions given by different authors are also discussed. After having the solutions to different attacks in the UAVs, still, UAVs are facing a lot of issues such as security, scalability, safety, privacy, limited resources, and data storage. Then we have discussed research challenges facing by the researchers for the features of UAVs. We plan to extend this work by going through different attacks that are causing harm to UAVs and their respective networks in Blockchain and cloud-related areas. Finally, this chapter gives an overview of UAVs and different threats & solutions to the UAVs and research areas.

References

1. Nikhil Chand, B., Mahalakshmi, P., Naidu, V.P.S., Sense and Avoid Technology in Unmanned Aerial Vehicles: A Review. *2017 International Conference on Electrical, Electronics, Communication, Computer and Optimization Techniques (ICEECCOT)*, pp. 512–517, 2017.
2. Choudhary, G., Sharma, V., Gupta, T., Kim, J., You, I., Internet of Drones (IoD): Threats, Vulnerability, and Security Perspectives. *The 3rd International Symposium on Mobile Internet Security (MobiSec'18)*, Cebu, Philippines, vol. 37, pp. 1–13, 2018.
3. Mehta, P., Gupta, R., Tanwar, S., Blockchain envisioned UAV networks: Challenges, solutions, and comparisons. *Comput. Commun.*, 151, 518–538, 2020.
4. MarketsAndMarkets, *Unmanned Aerial Vehicle (UAV) Market by Vertical, Class, System, Industry (Defense & Security, Agriculture, Construction & Mining, Media & Entertainment), Type, Mode of Operation, Range, Point of Sale, MTOW and Region—Global Forecast to 2025*, https://www.marketsandmarkets.com/Market-Reports/unmanned-aerialvehicles-uav-market-662.html, 2019.
5. AIRBUS, *Airbus demonstrates aircraft inspection by drone at Farnborough*, https://www.airbus.com/newsroom/press-releases/en/2016/07/airbus-demonstrates-aircraft-inspection-by-drone-at-farnborough.html, 2016.
6. Warrick, J., The Washington Post, *Use of weaponized drones by ISIS spurs terrorism fears*, https://www.washingtonpost.com/world/national-security/

use-of-weaponized-drones-by-isis-spurs-terrorism-fears/2017/02/21/9d-83d51e-f382-11e6-8d72-263470bf0401_story.html, 2017.

7. Hassani, M., Kickstarter, *Mine Kafon Drone*, https://www.kickstarter.com/projects/massoudhassani/mine-kafon-drone, 2020.
8. Lee, D., BBC News, *Amazon to deliver by drone 'within months'*, https://www.bbc.com/news/technology-48536319, 2019.
9. Ganapathy, K., Asian Hospital & Healthcare Management, *Drones in Healthcare*, https://www.asianhhm.com/healthcare-management/drones-in-healthcare, 2019.
10. Karakostas, I., Mademlis, I., Nikolaidis, N., Pitas, I., Shot type constraints in UAV cinematography for autonomous target tracking, *Information Sciences*, 506, 273–294, ISSN 0020-0255, 2020. https://doi.org/10.1016/j.ins.2019.08.011
11. Yinka-Banjo, C. and Ajayi, O., Sky-Farmers: Applications of Unmanned Aerial Vehicles (UAV) in Agriculture. IntechOpen, https://www.intechopen.com/books/autonomous-vehicles/sky-farmers-applications-of-unmanned-aerial-vehicles-uav-in-agriculture, 2019.
12. Joshi, D., Business Insider India, *Drone technology uses and applications for commercial, industrial and military drones in 2020 and the future*, https://www.businessinsider.in/tech/news/drone-technology-uses-and-applications-for-commercial-industrial-and-military-drones-in-2020-and-the-future/articleshow/72874958.cms, 2019.
13. PwC, *Global market for commercial applications of drone technology valued at over $127bn*, https://pwc.blogs.com/press_room/2016/05/global-market-for-commercial-applications-of-drone-technology-valued-at-over-127bn.html, 2016.
14. Rahman, M.A., Hossain, M.S., Loukas, G., Hassanain, E., Rahman, S.S., Alhamid, M.F., Guizani, M., Blockchain-based mobile edge computing framework for secure therapy applications. *IEEE Access*, 6, 72469–72478, 2018.
15. Rouse, M., TechTarget, *Access Control*, https://searchsecurity.techtarget.com/definition/access-control, 2018.
16. Yang, H., Zheng, H., Zhang, J., Wu, Y., Lee, Y., Ji, Y., Blockchain-based trusted authentication in cloud radio over fiber network for 5G. *2017 16th International Conference on Optical Communications and Networks*, ICOCN, pp. 1–3, 2017.
17. Kapitonov, A., Lonshakov, S., Krupenkin, A., Berman, I., Blockchain-based protocol of autonomous business activity for multi-agent systems consisting of UAVs. *2017 Workshop on Research, Education and Development of Unmanned Aerial Systems (RED-UAS)*, Linkoping, pp. 84–89, 2017.
18. He, D., Chan, S., Guizani, M., Drone-Assisted Public Safety Networks: The Security Aspect. *IEEE Commun. Mag.*, 55, 8, 218–223, 2017.
19. Feng, Z., Guan, N., Lv, M., Liu, W., Deng, Q., Liu, X., Yi, W., An Efficient UAV Hijacking Detection Method Using Onboard Inertial Measurement

Unit. *ACM Trans. Embedded Comput. Syst.*, 17, 6, Article 96, 19 pages, 2019.

20. Fei, F. *et al.*, Cross-Layer Retrofitting of UAVs Against Cyber-Physical Attacks. *2018 IEEE International Conference on Robotics and Automation (ICRA)*, Brisbane, QLD, pp. 550–557, 2018.
21. Jake, Investopedia, *Eavesdropping Attack*, https://www.investopedia.com/terms/e/eavesdropping-attack.asp, Updated on Apr 10, 2020.
22. Hoang, T.M., Nguyen, N.M., Duong, T.Q., Detection of Eavesdropping Attack in UAV-Aided Wireless Systems: Unsupervised Learning With One-Class SVM and K-Means Clustering. *IEEE Wireless Commun. Lett.*, 9, 2, 139–142, 2020.
23. Sharma, V., You, I., Palmieri, F., Jayakody, D.N.K., Li, J., Secure and Energy-Efficient Handover in Fog Networks Using Blockchain-Based DMM. *IEEE Commun. Mag.*, 56, 5, 22–31, 2018.
24. Ferro, R., Bernal, Y., Tapicha, J., *Technical Development of a Security Platform for IoT Based on Blockchain, Knowledge Management in Organizations*, pp. 625–633, Springer International Publishing, Cham, 2018.
25. Hack2Secure, *Common Attacks Against Availability*, https://www.hack2secure.com/blogs/common-attacks-against-availability, 2018.
26. Bozic, N., Pujolle, G., Secci, S., A tutorial on blockchain and applications to secure network control-planes. *2016 3rd Smart Cloud Networks & Systems (SCNS)*, Dubai, pp. 1–8, 2016.
27. IFAC Blog, International Federation of Automatic Control, *Jamming attacks: A major threat to controlling over wireless channels*, http://blog.ifac-control.org/technology/jamming-attack/jamming-attacks-a-major-threat-to-controlling-over-wireless-channels/, 2019.
28. Sliti, M., Abdallah, W., Boudriga, N., Jamming Attack Detection in Optical UAV Networks. *2018 20th International Conference on Transparent Optical Networks (ICTON)*, Bucharest, pp. 1–5, 2018.
29. Arthur, M.P., Detecting Signal Spoofing and Jamming Attacks in UAV Networks using a Lightweight IDS. *2019 International Conference on Computer, Information and Telecommunication Systems (CITS)*, Beijing, China, 2019.
30. García-Magariño, I. *et al.*, Security in networks of unmanned aerial vehicles for surveillance with an agent-based approach inspired by the principles of blockchain. *Ad Hoc Networks*, 86, 72–82, ISSN 1570-8705, 2019. https://doi.org/10.1016/j.adhoc.2018.11.010
31. TitanHQ, TitanHQ WebTitan, *Most Common Wireless Network Attacks*, https://www.webtitan.com/blog/most-common-wireless-network-attacks/, 2018.
32. He, D., Chan, S., Guizani, M., Drone-Assisted Public Safety Networks: The Security Aspect. *IEEE Commun. Mag.*, 55, 8, 218–223, 2017.
33. UKEssays, *Interruption Interception Modification and Fabrication Attacks Computer Science Essay*, https://www.ukessays.com/essays/

computer-science/interruption-interception-modification-and-fabrication-attacks-computer-science-essay.php?vref=1, 2018.
34. Hudson, B., The Washington Post, *Drone attacks are essentially terrorism by joystick*, https://www.washingtonpost.com/opinions/drone-attacks-are-essentially-terrorism-by-joystick/2018/08/05/f93ec18a-98d5-11e8-843b-36e177f3081c_story.html, 2018.
35. Finn, R.L. and Wright, D., Unmanned aircraft systems: surveillance, ethics, and privacy in civil applications. *Comput. Law Secur. Rev.*, 28, 2, 184–194, 2012.
36. Lusher, A., Independent, *London woman dies in possibly the first drone-related accidental death*, https://www.independent.co.uk/news/uk/home-news/drones-fatal-road-accident-first-non-military-drone-death-accident-car-crash-surveillance-safety-a7180576.html, 2016.
37. Ng, K., Independent, *Drone propeller slices Worcestershire toddler's eyeball in half*, https://www.independent.co.uk/news/uk/home-news/drone-propeller-slices-worcestershire-toddlers-eyeball-in-half-a6750981.html, 2015.
38. Chris, NewScientist, *Drones are causing airport chaos—Why can't we stop them?*, https://www.newscientist.com/article/2190096-drones-are-causing-airport-chaos-why-cant-we-stop-them/, 2019.
39. Du, H. and Heldeweg, M.A., *Responsible Design of Drones and Drone Services Legal Perspective Synthetic Report*, pp. 11–45, October 2, 2017. Available at SSRN: https://ssrn.com/abstract=3096573 or http://dx.doi.org/10.2139/ssrn.3096573
40. Li, B., Fei, Z., Zhang, Y., UAV Communications for 5G and Beyond: Recent Advances and Future Trends. *IEEE Internet Things J.*, 6, 2, 2241–2263, 2019.
41. Mohindru, V., Bhatt, R., Singh, Y., Reauthentication scheme for mobile wireless sensor networks. *Sustainable Comput.: Inf. Syst.*, 23, 158–166, 2019.
42. Mohindru, V. and Singh, Y., Node authentication algorithm for securing static wireless sensor networks from node clone attack. *Int. J. Inf. Comput. Secur.*, 10, 2–3, 129–148, 2018.
43. Mohindru, V., Singh, Y., Bhatt, R., Hybrid cryptography algorithm for securing wireless sensor networks from Node Clone Attack. *Recent Adv. Electr. Electron. Eng. (Formerly Recent Patents Electrical & Electronic Engineering)*, 13, 2, 251–259, 2020.

6

Internet of Things and UAV: An Interoperability Perspective

Bharti Rana* **and Yashwant Singh**†

Department of Computer Science & Information Technology, Central University of Jammu, Jammu, India

Abstract

The technological leap in Information and Communications Technology (ICT), brings a new paradigm of the Internet of Things (IoT) as an "intelligent connection of things". Moreover, the IoT technology is extended beyond to provide connectivity between people, data, processes, and things that constitutes the Internet of Everything (IoE). In the meantime, IoT encounters several challenges due to the constrained nature of network and devices by memory, power, processing, and link speed. Recently, the concept of Unmanned Aerial Vehicles (UAVs) has elevated to potentially conquer the challenges faced by IoT. However, the assimilation of UAV into IoT poses many scientific and technical challenges during integration. The purpose of this study is to bridge the landscape between IoT and UAV by identifying the technical and non-technical issues facing integration. Also, the study discusses the applications, architecture, and technologies of UAV enabled Internet of Things. The study definitely answers the question regarding the proximity between IoT and UAV by exploiting the mobility of UAVs. The UAV-enabled IoT solution can greatly help to improve the scalability, heterogeneity, and network coverage constraint of IoT.

Keywords: Internet of Things (IoT), Internet of Everything (IoE), Unmanned Aerial Vehicles (UAVs), Unmanned Aerial System, interoperability, UAV-enabled IoT, ubiquitous computing, UAV mobility

**Corresponding author*: rana9bharti@gmail.com

†*Corresponding author*: yashwant.csit@cujammu.ac.in

Vandana Mohindru, Yashwant Singh, Ravindara Bhatt and Anuj Kumar Gupta (eds.) Unmanned Aerial Vehicles for Internet of Things (IoT): Concepts, Techniques, and Applications, (105–128) © 2021 Scrivener Publishing LLC

6.1 Introduction

With the tremendous advancement in information and communication technology (ICT), catalyzed the integration of diverse technologies and smart devices to achieve ubiquitous networking. IoT is such an emerging technology that is a blend of multiple intelligent technologies and smart devices. UAVs are intelligent devices that come the way in IoT. With the miniaturization in embedded and sensor technologies, headed towards the progression in UAV technology. Miniaturization in technologies efficiently collects and transmits data from end terminals that interact with the physical world via IoT applications. The innovations in intelligent technologies along with big data processing brought a lot of opportunities to realize intelligent decision making, intelligent monitoring, and intelligent discovery of objects. Because of the innovations in technology, traditional IoT is evolved as the Internet of Everything (IoE) that supports the omnipotent connection of things thereby provides ubiquitous connections. IoT networks are constrained in memory, power, and processing capabilities. Moreover, the growing scalability of IoT linked devices is a great matter of concern. Existing wireless communication technologies like WSN, cellular networks, and LPWAN are used to enable scalability in IoT. In addition to this, cutting edge technologies like cloud computing, edge computing, and fog computing facilitates intelligence in IoT. High maneuverability of UAVs supports diverse applications of IoT by extending the network coverage to various geographical and spatial regions. The different aspects of IoT technology like scalability, intelligence, and heterogeneity are taken into account in our proposed UAV based IoT architecture.

UAVs have an enormous potential to provide a pragmatic solution to overcome the limitations of terrestrial IoT networks. The integration of terrestrial IoT with UAV is currently attracting significant attention from the research point of view to improve network coverage, surveillance [1], monitoring, and disaster management in smart cities. UAV network is controlled by a ground controller to provide wireless interconnection between UAVs to control the upstream [2] flow of messages and downstream flow of sensor data and telemetry. Multiple unmanned vehicles collaborate to perform complex aerial tasks. A reliable and stable network is necessary to carry out the tasks by UAVs. UAV network exchanges crucial information by sending commands between ground controllers and aerial vehicles [3]. UAVs in IoT network can work as gateways [4] to collect the data from IoT sensors and send to the authorised users that are linked via 5G network. Depending upon the distribution of sensors over a specified area, the position of UAVs is arbitrarily set to extend the network coverage. Moreover, UAVs act as an intermediate node for the passage of information thereby providing multiple IoT solutions. UAV-based IoT can be broadly utilized for automation, smart cities, remote surveillance, package delivery applications, transport, and logistics, etc. The use cases of UAV-based IoT are discussed in Table 6.1.

The study extensively covers the limitations and opportunities brought by the UAV-based IoT network. Accordingly, the study stressed upon challenges encountered during the integration of UAV and IoT commonly referred to as interoperability challenges. The integration challenges include standardization, security, and technical challenges. Real-life applications of UAV-based IoT are explored to examine the beneficence in day to day activities. For instance, UAV based IoT is commonly used in military operations for surveillance purposes on the battlefield and to launch attacks in case of emergency. Terrestrial satellite links are used to capture images and videos to track the movement of the enemy's troops. For example, satellite-terrestrial links are used to capture the images on the India-China border to track the actions of the army. Therefore, unmanned military operations reduce the man force and large infrastructure deployment.

Table 6.1 Use cases of UAV-based IoT.

Use cases	Description
Network Coverage	Incorporating UAV in IoT enhances the network coverage in 5G heterogeneous IoT networks.
Aerial Communication	UAV-based IoT networks provide fast, reliable, and flexible wireless communication to expand security.
Connectivity	UAV in IoT enhances the network connectivity and support terrestrial network by disseminating information.
Data Aggregation	By increasing the cellular network coverage, UAV in IoT collects the vast amount of data in smart cities from wide areas to get business insights.
Energy Efficiency	UAV offers reliable, flexible, and energy-efficient [5] IoT uplink connections.
Large-Scale Deployment	UAV drones are deployed over large areas to enable multiple inputs, multiple output massive networks, 3D networks, and millimeter-wave communications.

The rest of the chapter is organized as follows: The background section provides the evolution of IoT and UAV. The various controversies, issues, and problems are also highlighted in the background section. The next section provides the concepts of IoT and IoE. The various opportunities offered by UAV are also discussed in the background section. Then, the UAV-based IoT applications are explored in detail. In the following section, various research challenges related to UAV-based IoT are identified and reported. Subsequently, a high-level UAV-based IoT architecture is proposed keeping in account the various IoT challenges. The last section emphasizes on the interoperability challenges in UAV-based IoT communicative network.

6.2 Background

IoT is an interconnection of a huge number of smart devices that interact among each other without human intervention. The term "IoT" was first proposed by Kevin Ashton in 1999. The number of IoT linked devices increases from 15.41 billion to 23.14 billion from the year 2015 to 2018. And this number would increase to 75.44 billion by the year 2025 [6]. IoT is used in various sectors like smart home automation, logistics, transportation, e-health, and environmental monitoring. The era of IoT evolved from the advancements in the industrial revolutions. Industry 1.0 happened in the eighteenth century in which machines worked via water and stream. Industry 2.0 occurred in the 20th-century deals with the use of electronics for bulk production. Industry 3.0 in the early 1970s makes use of information and communication technology. Industry 4.0 is happening at present to provide connectivity between intelligent devices and sensors known as IoT [2]. And the upcoming Industry 5.0 integrates humans and robots to work as coordinates instead of a competitor. On the other hand, UAVs have been in existence since 1849. Abraham Karem is known as the "drone father" of UAV technology. Karem built his first drone "Albatros" for the Israel Air force. For instance, the first use of UAV was recorded on August 22, 1849 [7] by the Australian forces. Australian forces use UAVs loaded with balloons that are filled with bombs to attack Venice city [8]. Unmanned Aerial Vehicles (UAVs) or Unmanned Aerial Systems (UASs) encompasses the aircraft or Unmanned Aerial Vehicles and the ground controllers/machines operated by persons. The system of interconnection between the two is known as "Drones" [9]. UAVs consist of both remotely piloted drones and autonomous vehicles. Enormous research has been carried out by researchers to integrate UAV and IoT technology to overcome the limitations of IoT. UAV-based IoT is already used in diverse applications to provide multiple IoT solutions.

6.2.1 Issues, Controversies, and Problems

IoT and UAV come with their own weaknesses and strengths. The integration of UAV with IoT will potentially mitigate some of the challenges that arise from IoT. The scalability of devices in IoT is a matter of concern as the number of linked devices increases exponentially. Identification, perseverance, connectivity, and locating devices in an IoT network are still difficult to manage. Connecting IoT devices on a large scale brings heterogeneity issues to the fore. IoT devices are not interoperable because of the different protocols and communication technologies supported by different devices. Another reason for heterogeneity is that the company owners do not want to lose the market edge over their customers. Manufacturers and developers must take into account the heterogeneity concern while the inception of devices so the overall performance of the network is not compromised. Provisions should be made on what type of data is available to what type of applications. Imposing laws on data sharing preserves the privacy and authenticity of data. IoT lacks universal standards and regulations at the protocol and architectural level that introduce a "Babel Tower Effect". Every developed device must prevent the Babel Tower Effect that forms a disjoint set of devices thereby gives rise to heterogeneous technologies. The next most important challenge is related to the security responsible for the proper functioning of the system. Security [10] is the most important factor for any technology or device to get customer's satisfaction and to be accepted by the public. Moreover, data processing on the cloud also brings certain challenges such as real-time processing of data, supporting multiple users, high latency, low throughput, etc.

UAVs have great potential to mitigate the scalability issue of IoT by increasing the network coverage particularly areas with poor network infrastructures and weak internet connectivity by supporting Low power wide area networks (LPWAN), wireless local area network (WLAN) and satellite networks. Weak connectivity is the result of variations in the geographical environment due to the harsh or unfavorable conditions. Mostly urban construction sites, transportation areas, forest areas, disaster sites have obstructions that result in the interruption of wireless connection via access points. UAVs can avoid this limitation by acting as intermediate relay nodes, gateways, and base stations to link to the IoT nodes. Moreover, aerial to aerial and aerial to ground links of UAVs can avoid the obstacles that lie in between the line-of-sight. Also, UAV performs the execution of the lightweight intelligent algorithms to provide intelligent services on edge, fog, and the cloud of the IoT network. The intelligent algorithms make it possible to take real-time decisions and to get actionable insights from data. Object identification, real-time processing, data management on the remote cloud are done via intelligent algorithms in UAV-enabled IoT networks. UAV technologies are utilized to achieve stereoscopic and geographic diversity. Stereoscopic diversity is based on spatial locations and geographical diversity [11] is based on diverse geographical locations. High mobility of UAV covers diverse regions to support different applications.

6.3 Internet of Things (IoT) and UAV

The term IoT connects digital and electronic components with varying sizes and demands. Cisco refers to the term IoT for representing the connection of "things". On the other hand, the Internet of Everything (IoE) evolved from the IoT extends the capabilities of IoE. IoT and IoE are used interchangeably but there is a slight difference between the two. Cisco's definition of IoE is based on "four pillars" pertains to connecting people, data, processes, and things. IoE represents an augmented interconnection of things and people-centric processes (intelligent machines/devices). IoE goes beyond the IoT competency to not just only connect physical machines (pure machines and devices). IoE stems from the extended capability of machines through big data processing, ubiquitous internet, and artificial intelligence. In the meantime, the idea of IoE is discussed so many times. But the potential challenges posed by IoE bring complexity in the actualization of IoE. Therefore, IoE is still in fantasy somewhere.

IoE is a future internet in which everything is connected to the internet to offer any kind of intelligent services to anyone at any point of time to facilitate decision making. In the past few decades, emerging innovations in Information and communication technology (ICT) instigates the notion of IoE. Advancements in sensor technologies and embedded technologies make IoT nodes more energy-efficient and portable. Thereafter, the usage of low-power wide-area technologies makes possible the ubiquitous network of low power IoT nodes. Finally, the use of Artificial Intelligence and a massive amount of IoT data generated has driven a whole new discipline of intelligent "IoE".

IoE is more perceptive thereby enriching the lives of people with automated industrial and non-industrial processes. For the proper realization of IoT and IoE, it must satisfy three expectations [11]:

- *Scalability:* Deals with scalable network architecture with ubiquitous coverage.
- *Intelligent Connections:* Intelligent decision making and events for internet-connected devices in IoT.
- *Diversity:* Supportability for diverse applications, protocols, and technologies in IoT.

However, some intrinsic factors are restricting IoT from achieving the above expectations. IoT is constrained in power, memory, and network coverage. Moreover, security and privacy vulnerabilities in IoT also hinder the progress of IoT. Due to the network coverage constraint in IoT, achieving ubiquitous networking in IoT also becomes difficult. However, battery constrained nature of IoT leads to the exhaustion of battery life and loss of network connection. Moreover, an increase in the security vulnerabilities in IoT because of the utilization of simplified protocols like NB-IoT, LPWAN causes information loss due to the malicious attacks and eavesdropping [12] of information. A flexible and efficient deployment mechanism must be required to conquer limited battery constraint, network coverage, and for achieving better quality response time.

Because of the high flexibility, mobility and on-demand deployment, Unmanned Aerial Vehicles (UAVs) have an enormous potential to provide better solutions to address the emerging challenges of IoE. UAVs extend the network coverage of IoT due to the high mobility of UAVs. Myriad IoT applications, flexible deployment, and extended network coverage are possible through UAVs. The various opportunities brought by UAVs are depicted in Figure 6.1.

i. *Ubiquitous Network Coverage:* Sensors in IoT are placed in unattended harsh environments for a long time. To make communication possible sensors must be in the line of sight. This is a great matter of concern to achieve reliable and effective communication. UAV's network of communication assists IoT to increase the network coverage thereby providing a ubiquitous network. Ubiquitous connections play a prominent role to cover each and every node anywhere at any time. UAVs extend the network coverage with weak internet connections and poor network infrastructures by using multi UAV Adhoc networks. Multi UAV networks are self-configured autonomous networks that support mobile connections. Multi UAV networks offer connectivity during emergency operations, aerial operations, and in sensor-actuator networks.

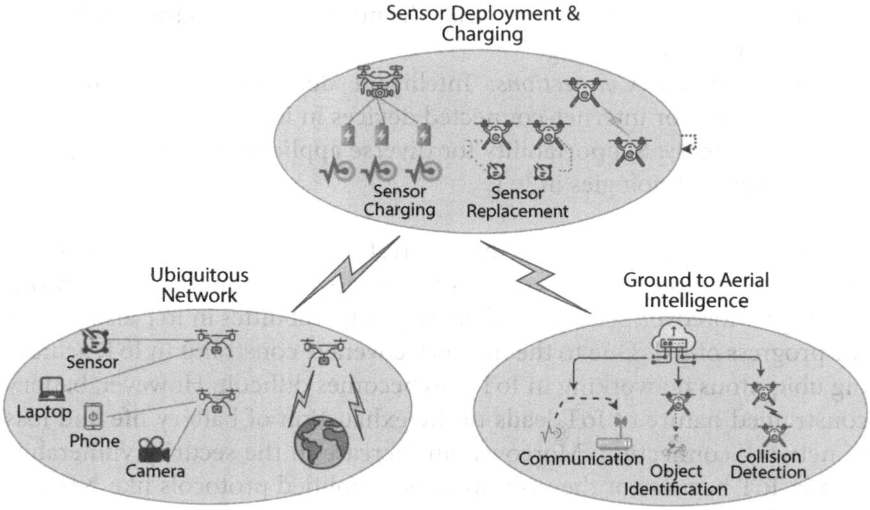

Figure 6.1 UAV opportunities for IoT [11].

ii. *Ground to Aerial Intelligence:* UAVs offer ground to aerial intelligence by implementing several intelligent algorithms onboard. UAVs collect the data from distributed sensors over a specific area. UAVs make use of intelligent algorithms to discover the optimal path, collision detection and avoidance, and object identification. UAVs are utilised for various intelligent aerial applications. The most found application of UAV is the identification of mobile objects. UAVs facilitate to make intelligent decision making in constrained IoT networks.

iii. *Sensor Deployment and Charging:* High reconfigurability of UAVs assists the IoT to maintain its sustainability. UAVs can be used to power and recycle the IoT nodes. IoT nodes are battery operated. Sensing and transmitting data by a node decays its battery life within a short time. This process is not only time consuming but also increases the pollution and cost to replace sensor nodes. UAVs make use of wireless power transfer (WPT) technologies to charge sensor nodes. Also, UAVs transfer the information and power simultaneously. UAVs recover the malfunctioned nodes by replacing them with new nodes.

6.4 Applications of UAV-Enabled IoT

In the past few years, UAVs show an exceptional surge in the IoT market. Nowadays, employing a swarm of UAVs for IoT services has become a reality. The integration of UAVs with IoT would be a great assistance for IoT applications dealing with security and privacy of public, mitigation of pollution, smart transportation and logistics, weather forecasting, and disaster management. Table 6.2 depicts the UAV-enabled IoT applications.

Table 6.2 UAV-aided IoT applications.

Applications	**Description**
Meteorological Weather Forecasting [10]	UAVs equipped with IoT sensors gather the information regarding the wind flow, tsunami, flood, temperature, moisture level to predict the upcoming weather conditions. The gathered data once sensed is send to the central server.
Smart Traffic Monitoring [13]	UAVs fused with IoT technology is deployed over transport areas to determine the traffic patterns, road congestion, and fatalities to reduce the time of drivers. Drivers get the information about the shortest route in real-time. Drivers can reroute according to their convenience at any time.
Aerial Surveillance [14]	UAVs incorporated with cameras act as "security agents" to detect abnormal situations. For surveillance purposes, UAVs are mostly utilized in big events like music shows, restaurants, sports tournaments to monitor public crowded places. The drones are used to detect any abnormalities by continuously capturing images and videos. The information is sent to the security guards so that they can physically interfere with the place to ensure proper security and privacy measures.
Environmental Monitoring and Control [10]	UAVs equipped with IoT sensors fly over the affected areas to record important information like pictures, videos, and temperature, etc. This helps the rescue teams to reach on spot to evacuate the persons from affected areas. UAV drones are also used to deliver essential commodities like water, medicines, and food when it becomes difficult to reach the affected areas.

(Continued)

Table 6.2 UAV-aided IoT applications. (*Continued*)

Applications	Description
Military [11]	UAVs along with suitable IoT devices are widely used by US, DARPA, British, and Australian armies. Because of the high mobility of UAVs, UAVs offer troops with 24 × 7 facilities of aerial observation while it is difficult to do so with manned flight. "System to System" approach was unfurled by DARPA in 2015 [14] that includes various low-cost drone's forms a swarm. The aim of the "system to system" approach is to destroy the enemy's target.
Disaster Management [15]	UAVs with IoT cameras are efficiently utilized in case of management of the disaster. In Japan, UAVs detect the images of destroyed reactors of the nuclear power plant in Fukushima Daiichi prefecture for the initiation of construction work.
Agriculture [16]	UAV drones integrated with cameras and sensors are used in agriculture to protect the crop from insects, weeds, and pests. UAV uses a sprayer mechanism to spread fertilizers on the crop. UAVs quadcopter is added with fertilizer to spray uniformly to cover every corner of crop area without manual work. Spraying mechanism prevents farmers to incur extra cost, labor, and time. The spraying mechanism protects farmers from toxic chemicals and pesticides.

6.5 Research Issues in UAV-Enabled IoT

The facts and scenarios outlined above are very interesting though there are several challenges encountered for the complete realisation of UAV-based IoT network. We have identified several research challenges [11] as depicted in Figure 6.2: i) No proper resource allocation methods are used to improve the performance of a resource-constrained network, ii) No legislation is imposed to restrict the illegal use of UAVs, iii) Absence of intelligent light-weight algorithms to enhance the autonomous mobility in UAV, iv) Lack of standardized architecture to support diverse applications, v) Absence of collaborative schemes operated between cloud, edge, and UAVs.

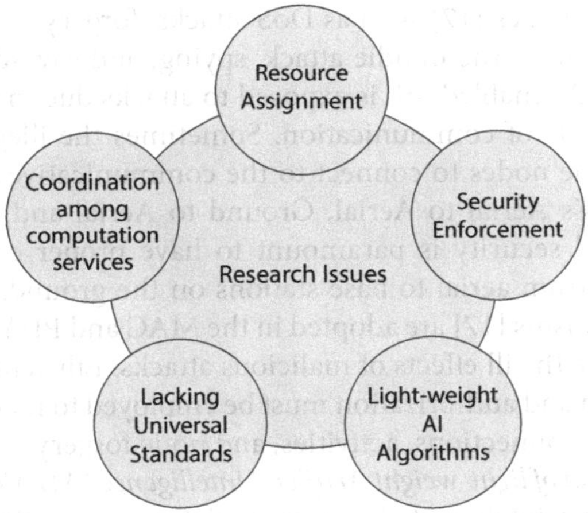

Figure 6.2 Research Issues in UAV-enabled IoT [4].

i. *Resource Assignment:* Resource allocation includes the supply of energy, memory allocation, computation capacity, data storage of every node (end nodes, intermediate nodes, UAV ground stations, Gateways, and Routers). Resource allocation usually occurs locally or globally. Global resource allocation takes into account the total distribution of nodes in IoT. On the other hand, local resource allocation takes into account the hardware specifications of each node locally. Global resource allocation focuses on achieving global maximum efficiency in terms of cost, time, energy, and equipment/devices. In UAV enabled IoE, global efficiency is obtained by employing various types of equipment like fog devices/edge devices and UAVs. Local resource allocation focuses on achieving efficiency in each task dedicated to specific nodes in terms of communication, processing, data storage. For example, in a smart building automation data collection algorithms are viable for improving the data rate at local nodes. In the case of aerial drones, energy management systems are used for improving the efficiency of limited storage. In a nutshell, despite various allocation techniques of resources, there must be a uniform strategy for the optimal utilization of resources at each node.
ii. *Security Enforcement:* With the growing scalability of IoE objects, the ubiquitous computing faces a lot of security and

privacy issues [17] such as DoS attacks, forgery of information, man in the middle attack, spying, and eavesdropping. The UAV-enabled IoE is exposed to attacks due to the wireless mode of communication. Sometimes the illegal UAVs forge the nodes to connect to the communicative network. In UAVs Aerial to Aerial, Ground to Aerial and Aerial to Ground security is paramount to have proper communication from aerial to base stations on the ground. Security mechanisms [17] are adopted in the MAC and PHY layers to mitigate the ill effects of malicious attacks. Efficient authentication and authorization must be employed to identify suspicious connections, activities, and node forgery.

iii. *Inclusion of light-weight Artificial Intelligence (AI) Algorithms:* To make intelligent decisions and for actionable insights taking into account the computing constraints, lightweight AI algorithms are necessary. AI algorithms are executed on the cloud at distributed locations in IoT applications. Mostly AI [18] algorithms are considered while ignoring the computation constraints of IoT. For instance, AI is used to identify the number of cars in a particular traffic area. Similarly, AI is used for the detection of human movement in a specific area. Also, AI [19] detects the boundaries and shapes of various objects [19]. Moreover, the use of AI captures the images of UAVs to identify mobile objects in UAV enabled IoT. In today's scenario, we still lack portable lightweight algorithms/models especially meant for UAVs. There are only a few studies that consider the less complex algorithms for navigation purposes and path discovery in UAVs. The upcoming IoT services require lightweight AI algorithms to provide autonomous solutions with quick data visualization.

iv. *Lacking Universal Standards:* UAV enabled IoT lacks universal standards that can orchestrate multiple information and communication technologies for diverse IoT applications. Inculcating universal standards in IoT minimizes the cost as well as maximises the efficiency. Similar to the OSI (Open System interconnection model) network model, IoE must incorporate common rules and protocols that would operate on each layer of IoT. There must be a universal design of chips for each node, universal standards and protocols [20] in each layer, and computation facilities. However, manufacturers only take into account the hardware configuration of chips with a particular set of protocols. The global standards can be achieved by fusing the edge computing, fog computing, and cloud computing with intelligent approaches. This presents a high-level interface to link computing services among different layers.

v. *Coordination among computation services:* The inevitable communication between cloud services and edge devices provide a wide scope for IoT applications. IoT applications need AI algorithms for batch processing, real-time streaming, data analysis, and real-time responses. Real-time processing of data is required in smart manufacturing, smart e-health, supply chain, and smart transportation. The coordination among services is achieved by scheduling the computational tasks. In a UAV-enabled IoT network scenario, first, the computation requirements are determined then, the task is sent to the remote cloud-based on the type of computation required by the task. Some of the computation is done on the edge or fog devices and some of the computation is shifted to the cloud for historical analysis. These coordinating mechanisms and computing requirements are optimized dynamically to achieve global efficiency in UAV enabled IoT. Thus, the coordination among various computing resources (ranging from IoE nodes, UAVs edge servers to remote cloud servers) is going to be a future research direction.

6.6 High-Level UAV-Based IoT Architecture

The proposed high-level UAV-based IoT architecture targets the scalability, intelligence, and heterogeneity limitations of IoT. The UAV-based IoT architecture is divided into three modules as shown in Figure 6.3. At the lower module, UAV ground controllers are operated. The middle module encompasses all the IoT devices, communication technologies, and diverse applications. The top module represents the multi cooperative UAV drones or vehicles.

6.6.1 UAV Overview

Unmanned Aerial System (UAS) consists of three components: UAV ground controllers, Communication link, and UAVs. UAS manages the

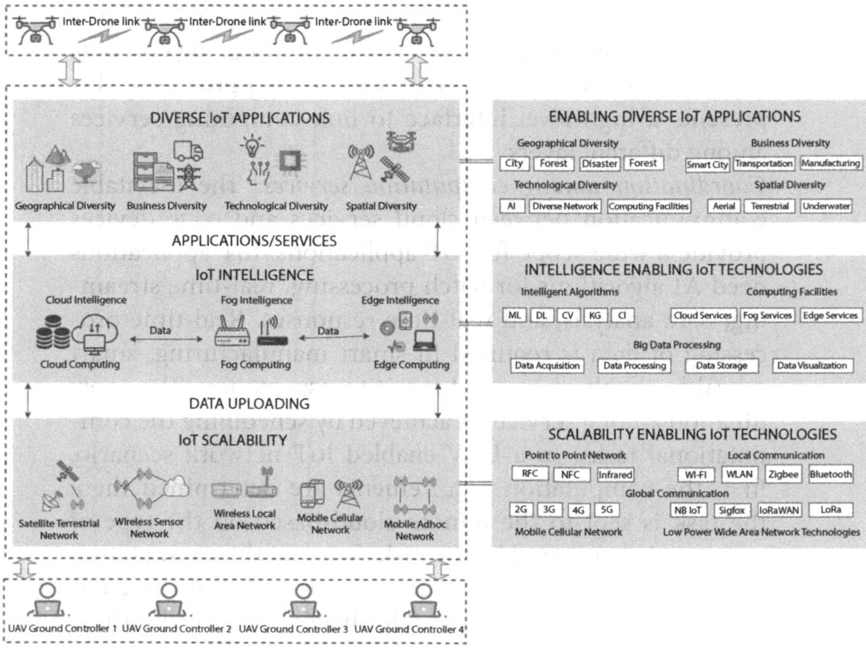

Figure 6.3 High-level UAV-based IoT architecture [23].

overall UAV's flight control and maneuverability. Ground control stations control the UAV's take-off and landing. The flight task of UAV initiates when the UAV reaches a certain altitude [21]. The UAV ground controller is the decision center of UAS. The UAV ground controller manages the communication remotely and tasks scheduling. The UAVs ground station takes into account the wireless communication unit, large storage unit, intelligent onboard decision-making algorithms, remote mechanisms, and recall mechanisms. Wireless communication monitors the communication between the UAVs and the ground controllers. The storage unit manages the data requirements while processing data. Intelligent algorithms are used for trajectory optimization [22], minimized time, and resource optimization. The remote mechanism manages the maneuverability of UAVs. The recall mechanisms are used to abort flight operations in case of an emergency. There are two types of communication links in UAS: Aerial to Ground (A2G)/Ground to aerial (G2A) and Aerial to Aerial (A2A). A2A link provides connectivity among multiple UAVs to perform collaborative flight tasks. G2A links provide connectivity between UAVs and the ground nodes. A2G link focuses on optimising the feedback information from UAV to ground controllers. G2A link controls the signals from ground stations to UAVs. On the other side, A2A set up a link between multiple UAVs in air. The link capacity of A2A depends upon the mobility of UAVs.

6.6.2 Enabling IoT Scalability

Scalability issues in IoT can be tackled by enabling several short-range, medium-range, and long-range communication technologies. The vision of having a ubiquitous network is achieved through collaboration and cooperation among diverse IoT technologies. Communication technologies must have the potential to adapt itself to any kind of network topology. Adaptation and Collaboration between technologies assist to realize the scalable IoT. The enabling technologies are depicted in Figure 6.3 is classified into three types: point to point network, local communication, and global communication.

The point to point network provides point to point connections and low-cost solutions to IoT. Point to point network encompasses the several near field wireless communication (NFWC) technologies such as Radio-frequency identification (RFID), Bluetooth, Near Field Communication (NFC), etc. NFWC is a short-range communication technology having a range of up to a few centimeters that intend devices to act smarter. NFWC helps to make e-payments and object identification easier. Wireless RFID tags and readers are used for real-time monitoring and tracking of objects. NFWC technology is used in myriad applications nowadays such as in logistics, fleet tracking, and real-time object identification.

Local communication is the medium-range communication technology supporting a few meters to 100 m. Local communication network forms a wireless personal area network, mesh networks, wireless sensor networks, wireless body area networks, and wireless local area networks. The local communicative network supports indoor communication such as home automation, Heating Ventilation, and Air Conditioning (HVAC) systems, and industrial processes. Wireless body area network is used to monitor the patient health [23] and fitness in IoT. The most commonly enabling technologies used in the local communicative network is Bluetooth Low Energy (BLE) [24], Zigbee [25], 6LoWPAN [24], Z-WAVE, and 802.11ah variations.

The global communicative network [26] provides a global network to cover everything at any time to enable ubiquitous computing. The global communicative network offers a long-range up to tens of kms or greater. The global communicative network manages the whole process of communication includes data aggregation, transmission, and processing. The most fitting technologies under global networks are cellular technologies

[24] and low power wide area networks (LPWAN) [25]. Cellular technologies [25] include 2G, 3G, 4G/LTE, and 5G. LPWA technologies such as LoWPAN, LoRa, and Sigfox works with resource constrained IoT nodes.

6.6.3 Enabling IoT Intelligence

Intelligent algorithms consist of traditional programming and artificial intelligence. Traditional techniques include dynamic programming and operation research programming used in mechanical and industrial processes for mass production. Artificial Intelligence has already penetrated its roots in the IoT market successfully. Artificial Intelligence provides automation to processes by learning from ambient data and makes intelligent decisions. Intelligent algorithms include machine learning, deep learning, computer vision, swarm intelligence, reinforcement learning. Different statistical methods like clustering, classification, and decision making are used to train the models. Different storage and computing requirements are needed by different algorithms. Deep learning models use convolutional networks that require excessive computing via GPU server that is infeasible on edge devices. IoT requires lightweight AI algorithms to be executed on edge devices.

In distributed computing, intelligent algorithms are implemented to enable ubiquitous intelligence. AI algorithms are used for descriptive, diagnostic, and predictive analysis of the mass production of data. AI is used to get valuable insights from raw data. Depending on the different storage requirements on the edge, fog, and cloud, different intelligent algorithms are required. Edge and fog computing have limited resources than the cloud. Cloud computing supports extensive data processing tasks to train models via GPU clusters thereby provides cloud intelligence. Fog intelligence is enabled by incorporating lightweight and portable deep learning models. Local intelligence is achieved by collecting data by local nodes and pre-process data locally.

IoT sensors continuously sense and generate data results in IoT big data [27]. The big data results in redundancy, errors, and duplication of data. Real-time processing of data is done on the edge near to where the data is generated. Big data processing includes a sequence of steps like data collection, pre-processing, storage, analysis, and visualization. Data preprocessing includes the filtration of data, compression, and data integration techniques. Hadoop, Hive, Map Reduce, and NoSQL databases [10] are used for big data processing. Big Data analysis includes the diagnostic and statistical analysis of data. The batch data is sent to the cloud [28] for predictive analysis of data remotely. Real-time data analysis demands less latency. Therefore, less time-sensitive data is processed on the edge or fog. Fog [29] includes intermediate devices such as gateways and routers located near to the edge devices.

6.6.4 Enabling Diverse IoT Applications

IoT applications are flourishing in every domain. Accordingly, diverse IoT applications are categorized into four types: geographical, business, technology, and spatial [11]. Geographical applications cover rural, urban [26], forest, deserts, and oceans. Spatial applications include aerial, terrestrial, underwater, and space applications. Business applications are based on diverse sectors like smart cities, transportation [30], logistics, agriculture [31], and military. Technological diversity includes heterogeneous technologies such as artificial intelligence, machine learning, deep learning, sensor technologies, embedded technologies, and data processing technologies. The blending of different technologies assists IoT to actualize the diverse applications. High mobility of UAVs increases the probability to provide network coverage to diverse applications.

6.7 Interoperability Issues in UAV-Based IoT

The introduction of UAV in IoT brought several opportunities. However, it is not an easy road to accomplish the opportunities offered by UAV in the IoT network. Most of the challenges arise because of the integration of UAVs with IoT that operates on diverse technologies, protocols, hardware, and software specifications. Here, the challenges are categorized according to three aspects: technical challenges, security challenges, and standardization challenges as shown in Figure 6.4.

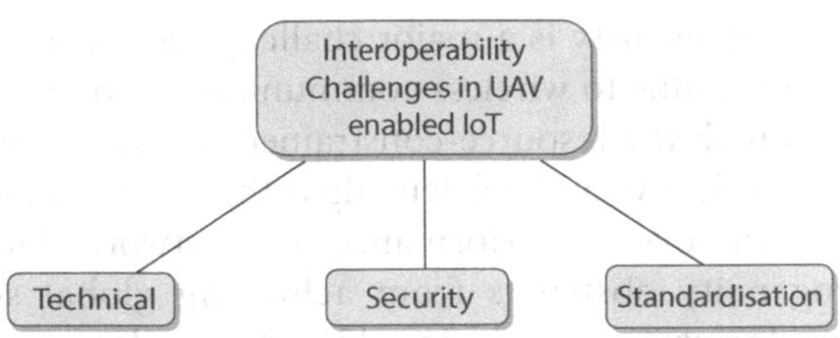

Figure 6.4 Interoperability issues in UAV based IoT [10].

i. *Technical Challenges:* Several technical challenges arise while integrating UAVs with IoT. IoT devices are constrained in memory, power, and processing capabilities. For the realisation of UAV into IoT, energy-efficient algorithms and protocols are necessary. Technical challenges must take into account the proper management of data locally and on remote servers intelligently in case of connection loss. Another aspect of IoT is the incompatibility and interoperability issues because of heterogeneous protocols [32, 33] and communication technologies developed by different manufacturers. The complexity of the IoT network even increases more when vehicular sensors are incorporated in the IoT network as 'things'. In this case, connections have to be established from sensors pertains to different vehicles. The generated data from sensors is also in the diverse form mostly unstructured data that is difficult to manage. Careful planning is required for the distribution, recovery, and aggregation of data to guarantee security and stream processing of data. There is also a rising concern associated with the security of GPS [17, 34]. GPS spoofing [10] is the most common attack that causes the aircraft to lose its control which is a critical issue to be resolved. UAVs are hijacked by these types of attacks that imitates the behavior of the man in the middle attacks.
ii. *Security Challenges:* The data acquired by UAV is an easy target for attackers. Data infringement poses a significant challenge for the acceptance of technology by the public. UAVs store the data in its main memory for anytime access to data which leaves a security loophole. In such a case UAVs control can easily be lost by a third party that is not authorized to the information. However, the storage of data on the cloud would improve security to some extent. But the data distribution in resource-constrained UAV is another challenge.

Till now, security is a major challenge in a communicative network due to wireless communication. In a UAV IoT network with the resource-constrained nature of devices, it demands effective and efficient algorithms that do not compromise the overall performance of a network. Moreover, heterogeneity obstructs from achieving global security policies for connected devices [35]. In wireless communication, safety is the most important concern deals with the authentication of both external and internal components. There must be a provision for data backup in case a device is compromised. Pervading security solutions in architectural layers reduces the breaches and attacks in the communicative network. Another issue encountered is, UAVs have the freedom to take any type of videos, and photos without any legal permission. The videos and photos taken by UAVs are shared online, thereby making it difficult to search the perpetrator. The Govt. must impose laws for UAVs registration to avoid an invasion of privacy.

iii. *Standardization Challenges:* UAVs are not standardized yet. For this reason, UAVs in IoT networks can be used for illegal activities such as physical harm, biological attacks, and drug smuggling, etc. Legislation must be imposed on UAVs to have the proper certification to operate on airspace missions and to block any nefarious activities. Losing control in UAVs may be drastic for people and property. Recently, EASA and FAA take initiatives to regularise the market of UAVs. In the case of IoT, heterogeneous standards are challenging that involves big industrial and government firms. Universal standards are mandatory for enabling effective communication among devices in a network. Standardization assists in preventing the "Babel Tower effect" [10, 36] that specifies devices form a disjoint set from different manufacturers. (For instance, devices developed by the same manufacturer belong to the same subset). From the socio-economic point of view, standardization opens a door for small and medium scale enterprises to compete with the emerging technology.

6.8 Conclusion

The chapter provides deep insight to the readers regarding the integration of UAV with IoT. Firstly, the background section thoroughly covers the evolution of IoT and UAV. Moreover, the background section highlights the issues and controversies in the realization of UAV-based IoT networks. Then, the study discussed the concept of IoT and IoE. Also, challenges faced by IoT and the opportunities provided by UAV to tackle the IoT challenges are discussed. Thereafter, the broad aspect of UAV-based IoT applications is thoroughly covered. The diverse applications include military, traffic management, surveillance, disaster management, and agriculture.

Several research issues related to UAV-based IoT is covered broadly. Based on the challenges faced during the integration of UAV with IoT, we propose a high-level UAV-based IoT architecture. The proposed architecture encompasses the enabling technologies, scalability, intelligence, and supportability for diverse applications of IoT. Diverse technologies include short-range, medium-range, and long-range technologies. Different intelligent techniques are discussed. Applications are based on different factors such as geographic, spatial, technological, and business. At last, interoperability challenges are discussed in detail to identify the complexities during the coordination among UAV and IoT modules.

References

1. Kim, H. and Ben-Othman, J., A Collision-Free Surveillance System Using Smart UAVs in Multi Domain IoT. *IEEE Commun. Lett.*, 22, 12, 2587–2590, Dec. 2018.
2. He, C., Xie, Z., Tian, C., A QoE-oriented uplink allocation for multi-UAV video streaming. *Sensors*, 19, 15, 1–19, 2019, https://doi.org/10.3390/s19153394.
3. Choi, S., Park, J., Kim, J., A Networking Framework for Multiple-Heterogeneous Unmanned Vehicles in FANETs. *2019 Eleventh International Conference on Ubiquitous and Future Networks (ICUFN)*, Zagreb, Croatia, pp. 13–15, 2019.
4. Lagkas, T., Argyriou, V., Bibi, S., Sarigiannidis, P., UAV IoT Framework Views and Challenges: Towards Protecting Drones as "Things". *Sensors*, 18, 11, 1–21, 2018, https://doi.org/10.3390/s18114015.
5. Wang, Z., Liu, R., Liu, Q., Thompson, J.S., Kadoch, M., Energy-Efficient Data Collection and Device Positioning in UAV-Assisted IoT. *IEEE Internet Things J.*, 7, 2, 1122–1139, Feb. 2020.
6. Ul Haq, S. and Singh, Y., On IoT Security Models: Traditional and Block chain. *Int. J. Comput. Sci. Eng.*, 06, 03, 26–31, 2018, https://doi.org/10.26438/ijcse/v6si3.2631.
7. David, D. A Short History of Unmanned Aerial Vehicles (UAV) - Consortiq,. London, UK, 2020, [Online]. Available: https://consortiq.com/short-history-unmanned-aerial-vehicles-uavs/. [Accessed: 22-Aug-2020].
8. Kashyap, V. A Brief History of Drones: The Remote Controlled Unmanned Aerial Vehicles (UAVs), *Interesting Engineering, New America, US, 2020,* [Online]. Available: https://interestingengineering.com/abrief-history-of-drones-the-remote-controlled-unmanned-aerial-vehicles-uavs. [Accessed: 22-Aug-2020].
9. Evolution of Drones, It is the 'Era' of Unmanned Aerial… | by techutzpah |, *The IOT Magazine*, 2018,Pune, Maharashtra [Online]. Available: https://theiotmagazine.com/evolution-of-drones-7216e7e5a9d2. [Accessed: 22-Aug-2020].

10. Rodrigues, M., Pigatto, D.F., Fontes, V.C., UAV Integration Into IoIT: Opportunities and Challenges. *International Conference on Autonomic and Autonomous Systems*, July 2017.
11. Liu, Y., Dai, H., Wang, Q., Shukla, M.K., Imran, M., Unmanned aerial vehicle for internet of everything: Opportunities and challenges. *Comput. Commun.*, 155, 66–83, December 20192020, https://doi.org/10.1016/j.comcom.2020.03.017.
12. Lei, H. *et al.*, Safeguarding UAV IoT Communication Systems Against Randomly Located Eavesdroppers. *IEEE Internet Things J.*, 7, 2, 1230–1244, Feb. 2020.
13. Mohamed, N., Al-jaroodi, J., Jawhar, I., Idries, A., Mohammed, F., Unmanned aerial vehicles applications in future smart cities. *Technological Forecasting and Social Change*, 153, 119–293, 2020, https://doi.org/10.1016/j.techfore.2018.05.004.
14. Marchese, M., Moheddine, A., Patrone, F., IoT and UAV Integration in 5G Hybrid Terrestrial-Satellite Networks. *Sensors*, 19, 3704, Aug 2019.
15. Systems, D., Avanzato, R., Beritelli, F., An Innovative Technique for Identification of Missing Persons in Natural Disaster Based on Drone-Femtocell Systems. *Sensors*, 19, 20, 454, Oct 2019.
16. Vihari, M.M., Nelakuditi, U.R., Teja, M.P., IoT based Unmanned Aerial Vehicle system for Agriculture applications. *2018 International Conference on Smart Systems and Inventive Technology (ICSSIT)*, Tirunelveli, India, pp. 26–28, 2018.
17. Fennelly, L.J. and Perry, M.A., Unmanned Aerial Vehicle (Drone) Usage in the 21st Century, in: *The Professional Protection officer*, 2nd Edition, Practical security Strategies and Emerging Trends, pp. 183–189, 2020, https://doi.org/10.1016/B978-0-12-817748-8.00050-X.
18. He, Y., Zhai, D., Zhang, R., Du, X., Guizan, An Anti-Interference Scheme for UAV Data Links in Air-Ground Integrated Vehicular Networks. *Sensors*, 19, 21, 1–19, 2019, https://doi.org/10.3390/s19214742.
19. Bacco, M. *et al.*, Monitoring Ancient Buildings: Real Deployment of an IoT System Enhanced by UAVs and Virtual Reality. *IEEE Access*, 8, 50131–50148, 2020.
20. Patel, K., Vyas, S., Pandya, V., Saiyed, A., IoT: Leading Challenges, Issues and Explication Using Latest Technologies. *2019 3rd International conference on Electronics, Communication and Aerospace Technology (ICECA)*, Coimbatore, India, pp. 757–762, 2019.
21. Zhang, Q., Jiang, M., Feng, Z., Li, W., Zhang, W., Pan, M., IoT Enabled UAV: Network Architecture and Routing Algorithm. *IEEE Internet Things J.*, 6, 2, 3727–3742, April 2019.
22. Labib, N.S., Danoy, G., Musial, J., Brust, M.R., Internet of Unmanned Aerial Vehicles—A Multilayer Low-Altitude Airspace Model for Distributed UAV. *Sensors*, 19, 21, 4779, Nov 2019, https://doi.org/10.3390/s19214779.

23. Ullah, S. *et al.*, UAV-enabled healthcare architecture: Issues and challenges. *Future Gener. Comput. Syst.*, 97, 425–432, 2019, https://doi.org/10.1016/j.future.2019.01.028.
24. Shafi, U., Mumtaz, R., García-Nieto, J., Hassan, S.A., Precision Agriculture Techniques and Practices: From Considerations to Applications. *Sensors*, 19, 17, 1–25, 2019, https://doi.org/10.3390/s19173796.
25. Al-Turjman, F., Abujubbeh, M., Malekloo, A., Mostarda, L., Malekloo, A., UAVs assessment in software-defined IoT networks: An overview. *Comput. Commun.*, 150, 519–536, 2020.
26. Shaikh, Z., Baidya, S., Levorato, M., Robust Multi-Path Communications for UAVs in the Urban IoT. *2018 IEEE International Conference on Sensing, Communication and Networking (SECON Work*, pp. 1–5, 2018.
27. Kumari, A., Tanwar, S., Tyagi, S., Kumar, N., Parizi, R.M., Choo, K.R., Fog data analytics: A taxonomy and process model. *J. Netw. Comput. Appl.*, 128, 90–104, 2019, https://doi.org/10.1016/j.jnca.2018.12.013.
28. Hanes, D., Salgueiro, G., Grossetete, P., Barton, R., Henry, J., *IoT Fundamentals: Networking Technologies, Protocols and Use Cases for the Internet of Things*, CiscoPress, no. 3491, Indianapolis, IN46240USA, 2017.
29. Azar, J., Makhoul, A., Barhamgi, M., Couturier, R., An energy efficient IoT data compression approach for edge machine learning. *Future Gener. Comput. Syst.*, 96, 168–175, 2019, https://doi.org/10.1016/j.future.2019.02.005.
30. Barmpounakis, E.N., Vlahogianni, E.I., Golias, J.C., Unmanned Aerial Systems for transportation engineering : Current practice and future challenges. *International Journal of Transportation Science and Technology*, 5, 3, 111–122, February 2016, https://doi.org/10.1016/j.ijtst.2017.02.001
31. Al-Turjman, F. and Altiparmak, H., Smart agriculture framework using UAVs in the Internet of Things era, in: *Drones in Smart Cities*, pp. 107–122, 2020, https://doi.org/10.1016/B978-0-12-819972-5.00007-0.
32. Konduru, V.R. and Bharamagoudra, M.R., Challenges and solutions of interoperability on IoT: How far have we come in resolving the IoT interoperability issues. *2017 International Conference On Smart Technologies For Smart Nation (SmartTechCon)*, Bangalore, pp. 572–576, 2017.
33. Mohindru, V. and Garg, A., Security Attacks in Internet of Things: A Review, in: *The International Conference on Recent Innovations in Computing*, 2020, March, Springer, Singapore, pp. 679–693.
34. Mohindru, V. and Singla, S., A Review of Anomaly Detection Techniques Using Computer Vision, in: *The International Conference on Recent Innovations in Computing*, 2020, March, Springer, Singapore, pp. 669–677.
35. Kushawaha, D., De, D., Mohindru, V., Gupta, A.K., Sentiment analysis and mood detection on an Android platform using machine learning integrated with Internet of Things, in: *Proceedings of ICRIC 2019*, Springer, Cham, pp. 223–238, 2020.

36. Mohindru, V., Chitranshi, U., Bhatt, R., Singh, Y., Possibilities of Block Chain in Indian Market and Notably In Advertising Industry, in: *2019 5th International Conference on Signal Processing, Computing and Control (ISPCC)*, IEEE, pp. 84–89, 2019.

7

Practices of Unmanned Aerial Vehicle (UAV) for Security Intelligence

Swarnjeet Kaur[1], Kulwant Singh[1*] and Amanpreet Singh[2]

[1]Department of Electronics and Communication Engineering, College of Engineering and Management Punjabi University Campus, Rampura Phul, Bathinda, India
[2]Department of Computer Science and Engineering, College of Engineering and Management Punjabi University Campus, Rampura Phul, Bathinda, India

Abstract
The term UAV expanded as an unmanned aerial vehicle is a type of flying object without interference of individuals on board. It is often termed as uncrewed aerial vehicle and is commonly termed as a drone. UAVs are the component of Unmanned Aircraft System (UAS). UAVs use sleek forces to provide vehicle lift, fly autonomously and are piloted distantly. The UAVs may operate in defined mode

1. It can be operated through remote control by an individual.
2. It can be operated by onboard computers autonomously.

When comparing to Military aircrafts, UAVs are used for secret missions which is sometimes dangerous for human beings. UAVs are mostly used in military solicitation, so that their use can be expanding to commercial, scientific, agricultural, surveillance, airborne photography, infrastructure, smuggling and drone racing.

UAV includes number of applications and having wide scope. In this chapter the researcher is defining one area of scope with sub points that includes military and security.

***Keywords*:** Unmanned Aerial Vehicle (UAV), military, security

**Corresponding author*: kulwantsingh3003@gmail.com

Vandana Mohindru, Yashwant Singh, Ravindara Bhatt and Anuj Kumar Gupta (eds.) Unmanned Aerial Vehicles for Internet of Things (IoT): Concepts, Techniques, and Applications, (129–142) © 2021 Scrivener Publishing LLC

7.1 Introduction

The Unmanned Aerial Vehicle (UAV) also termed as Drone used in Remote Sensing (RS) areas also for large scale mapping and real time activities [6, 7, 14, 17–19].

The important case studies have been studied with the help of UAV-RS and are discussed as below:

Surveillance of Landslide Affected Area Using UAV
The surveillance of landslide affected area could be done with ease with the help of UAVs with wireless networks [1, 4, 23] which would help the administration to take necessary steps to minimize the loss of life and properties in the affected areas.

Checking Crop Damage Assessment
With the help of UAV flight the crop damage area assessment would be conducted in lesser time and therefore helps the farmers and administration to keep a check on crop damage insects like Brown Plant Hopper insects [21, 22].

The UAV consists of calculating system which calculates the whole process to get the important information in form of images and videos as shown in Figure 7.1 [24]. The images obtained from UAVs helps in many applications like large scale mapping, urbanization, vegetation structure mapping etc [7, 21].

However, there are restrictions in using UAVs which are given below:

- The limitation regarding study area size.
- The restriction in processing of large data volume.
- The obligation of large scale processing and huge storage spaces etc.

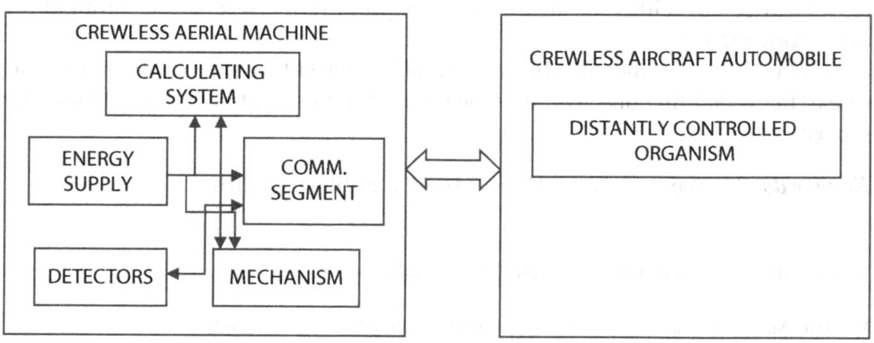

Figure 7.1 Unmanned or crewless aerial vehicle system.

In addition to accessible features capturing and pulling out techniques, there is need to improve high processing UAV data. UAVs can also perform the efficient surveys for tragedy prone or physically unreachable areas, quick damage evaluation of landslides, floods and earthquakes for enabling liberation measures [2, 3, 12, 16].

1. *Aerospace and Inspection*
Aerospace dynamic drone is a perfect solution that offers the inspectors and the officials a professional instrument with three dimensional positioning for viewing difficult accessing areas like floods, earthquakes, tornadoes etc. thereby giving them a harmless and more price efficient way of gaining approach into operation critical procedure. By creating an absolutely automated platform the drone is autonomously deployed and landed with planned missions and applications to collect aerial data view in form of images and videos as the high resolution camera records the data efficiently and therefore providing a clear picture of difficult-to-access system. The Aerospace solution eliminates the use of logistics involved in drone missions to provide consistent, useful airborne data, first-class dispensing and analytical abilities while simplify the inspection process and enable the work to be carried out [8–10]. In UAV classification as shown in Figure

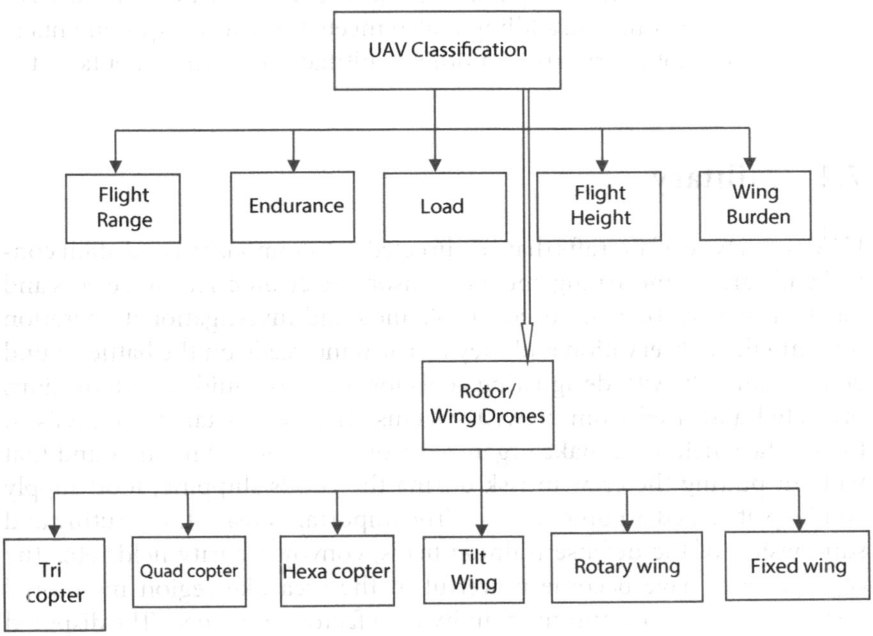

Figure 7.2 Classification of UAV.

7.2 [27, 29] the multi-rotor drone generally use two rotors with stable pitch revolving blades that produce lift. Quad copter is usually used among rotor drones.

In wing drones rotary wing revolves around central mast, which puts impact on air to move towards lower level and generates vertical lift. The fixed wing mainly concentrates on its engine to produce force to move drone and further more pressure generates beneath wings that generates lift.

The tilt wing it is align to rotor and in alteration mode the wings initiates to produce lift for perpendicular or vertical take off [29].

UAV used for inspection consists of antennas, reference real time kinematics (RTK) and smart video cameras all installed onto the UAV. The obligations of the load capacity and aerodynamics include the Telemetry, Tracking, and Control (TT&C) subsystem as it provides the connection between satellites so that they can perform the overall functions correctly. A robust data link which in association with flight control and inspection mission control is required for overall functionality of aerial vehicles. Typical the UAV data link consists of limited data bandwidth where the Universal Flight Information System (UFIS), it is modified to a higher bandwidth and performs flight and inspection information uplink and downlink with real-time capability [11]. The UFIS is not only a UAV platform with avionics straddling it also meets the safety requirements of operating in public airports and other multifaceted environments in the area.

7.2 Military

UAVs are a type of aircrafts that are directed autonomously by a distant control and carry some arrangement of sensors, electronic Transreceivers and nasty ordnance. They are used for planned and investigational operation for battlefield observation and they can also intercede on the battleground either indirectly with designating goals for precision guided ammunitions projected and fired from crewed systems. The instant target of UAVs in the military field is to make organized work in a routine manner and that without putting the crew in risk during the goods shipping, food supply and help at armed argument zones. The important area is the scrutiny and supervision of the defense training fields, convoy security fields etc. The caged drones have become powerful in the area like region monitored during the hours in a minimum individual factor concerned. The disputed zones can be controlled and sensed from a greater area. By carrying these types of drones at the upper of a vehicle is a benefit as it provides a sharp view in a short term of time. The caged drone can be used with different imbursement charges and at any kind of mission for the full 24 h. It is good to see this type of drones across the skies at operational fields [20].

The UAVs drone can also be used for self-directed flights based on pre-programmed flight strategies or through the help of more difficult dynamic automated structures. It is important to realize the cumulative role of Unmanned Aircraft Systems (UAS) in solving the various encounters. Also the implementation of high profile assaults is a very important task for some modern day military organizers [20].

These UAVs can also be categorized based on the definite roles they are intended to play in particular military actions. Based on these statements, the UAVs are as follows:

- *Goal and trap UAVs*—These can be used to deliver ground as well as aerial gunnery at a target and can replicate an enemy mortar or planes.
- *Reconnaissance UAVs*—These can be used to provide intelligence on the battlefields.
- *Warfare UAVs*—These have been used to provide attack proficiency for some dangerous operations.
- *Research and Development UAVs*—These can been used to further advance UAV skills that can be incorporated into UAVs that have been positioned in the field already.
- *Commercial UAVs*—These are the drones that have been planned so that they can be used in civil and commercial applications.

7.3 Attack

The attacks can be conducted by using commercial UAVs for dropping bombs, firing a missile, or crashing on to the destination. The commercial UAVs are equipped with such weapons as guided bombs, mass bombs, combustible devices, missiles marked air to surface, missiles marked air to air, anti-tank directed missiles or other types of guided weapons such as autocannons and machine guns. These unmanned aerial vehicles (UAVs) can also be made as a loaded weapon with dangerous explosives and then crashed into vulnerable targets or exploded on them. These aerial vehicles are also capable of conducting aerial bombing by dropping hand grenades, mortar shell or other improvised explosive directly on the targets. These payloads also include the chemical, radiological or biological hazards [5].

A group of aerial vehicles can also be piloted by specially trained pilots to drop weapons onto enemy forces.

These vehicles (UAV) are well-equipped so as to evade the ground defense forces. The other attacks include the logical attacks by using bogus mobile networks or a rogue Access Points which tips to the interruption of smart receivers traffic by attracting users to connect to a nearby Access Points typically termed as unrestricted Wi-Fi. In this way an attacker can capture user's delicate information like passwords and other bank credentials. These UAVs are also capable of hijacking other drones by connecting the devices on to drone and encoding it to capture and skyjacking other nearby UAVs working as a drones. This turns the mischievous drone into a rogue Access Point for nearby devices and drones thereby injecting the malwares to connected smartphones devices through the intervention and rerouting of user's information traffic. The other method the UAVs can adopt is through phishing (malicious acquaintances, forged advertisement and fabricated updates). In fact, the various UAVs drone attacks including the jamming and spoofing in the network [25, 26].

7.4 Journalism

By the term the drone Journalism we mean the practice of drones or unmanned aircraft systems (UAS) for journalistic tenacities. The use of Journalism drones for material gathering in the journalism industry is new concept. In the past the journalists take the airborne videotape with helicopters and that were rented which increases the expenditure costs. The drone technology allows reporters to take shots of events such as volcanic outbursts and natural calamities. Since the UAVs Journalism drones are operated remotely the journalists can obtain the cost efficient means of video recording and that too especially in highly vulnerable coverage. Journalism is one of the sectors where the use of drones in gathering news and information is helpful any time and in any situation [15].

UAVs drones offer certain explicit benefits common across any domain of use [21, 30, 31]:

- Flexibility—Being trivial and controlled remotely the UAVs drones have the elasticity to reach inaccessible destinations very quickly.

- ➢ Safety—Being above the earth level these unmanned drones are a safer option for collecting the information when the target area is a difficult and dangerous or during an emergency such as earthquake or fire.
- ➢ Budget benefits—The functioning costs are significantly lesser when associated to manned aircrafts. The running expenditures of a drone with high end HD cameras are approximately 2/3rd of that of a manned air plane.
- ➢ Advancement—The advances in drone technology have set them apart from probable substitutions. The use of high end HD cameras the communication and celestial navigation UAVs devices or drones can now effectually multitask.

More precise to Journalism sector the drones can seize and capable of live streaming the video data to ground stations. Now day by day with the exponential rise in online videos, there is a marked shift in distribution and consumption of news and other entertainment sources. The ability to provide customers with exclusive video contents can now prove to be a game changer. The drones can also broaden the possibility of observer explanations thereby accessing places that are challenging or hazardous for human coverage [13]. The use of infrared HD cameras, sensors and LED lightings allows the audio and video footages at night time. The drones have the capability to capture and release the panoramic vision of affected regions during floods, earthquakes and other natural calamities. Real-time data from farm UAVs drones can provide insights on weather forecasting and crop growth thereby giving an aid to the local farming community [30, 31]. The biggest weakness to a wider adoption of drones in journalism is the complex supervisory atmosphere surrounding the use of UAVs drones. The other concerns that have been raised include the drones being used for controlling purposes and security hazards, especially when used in densely populated areas. The flying of drones is synchronized by the aviation authority in concerned country. The guidelines may vary from country to country, making it difficult for the global media groups to scale up their usage of UAVs drones. The Principled contemplations are significant as well with privacy apprehensions high among citizens of every concerned country. By given the improvements in equipment of drones, there are genuine concerns over their influence on people's confidentiality. The civic attitude remains a major obstacle towards a wider acceptance of UAVs drones. The drones, with their HD cameras can easily capture unobstructed sights of people and their property which can consequently be misused by any unauthorized user or the group when hacked. The risks are similar to anxieties over satellite images and have led to promoting in favour of tighter regulations and transparent approval procedures [34, 35].

The other drawbacks include the country restrictions which remains the robust while consents from the higher authorities can be slow. The laws concerning that of UAVs drones are still budding even as journalists continue to familiarize to changing necessities.

7.5 Search and Rescue

The search and rescue UAVs drone is an unmanned aircraft used in crisis amenities such as police officers, fire-fighters and rescue crews for examining over massive regions for lost individuals and crime victims in need of saving in any type of environment.

These Unmanned aerial vehicles (UAVs) can grant real-time photographic evidence and figures in the aftershock of an earthquake or tornado. They can also become an eye in the open atmosphere to locate a lost individual. When a tragedy or event threatens lives and employments, the crisis responders need the evidence and real time images in order to make improved decisions. The UAVs can provide evidential alertness over a large area quickly thereby tumbling the time and the number of searchers required to trace and rescue an injured or lost individual and therefore reducing the charge and risks of search and rescue operations [9]. The Alligator drones are planned to provide price effective real time facts day or night in tough conditions and without risk to any individuals or public property and aiding in the search for lost individuals by using thermal imaging camera that can sense individual body temperature. This competence significantly raises the capability to find individuals at night that may get concealed during day time actions [30, 31].

The applications for search and rescue include:

- Search for accused and missing individuals.
- Crime scene examination.
- Search and revival operations.
- Calamity & emergency investigation.

Many agencies concerned in search and rescue processes have turned to UAVs drones to develop their life saving capabilities. A drone can be positioned within minutes of arrival on a sight thereby saving time and cost in deployment of manned air plane. A drone flying at elevation is equipped with a high firmness camera for daylight and a heat infrared sensor for night time search operations. It will significantly increase the probability of objective detection. Further assisting in the search for lost individuals UAVs use the infrared sensors and camera, easily fitted to a drone. The Law administration has been using infrared cameras fixed to manned air plane to assist in chasing and locating accused for years. By the use of drone these endeavors far safer, the imaging technology can also be seized with a drone in a quicker and in price effective manner. The Fire organizations benefit from the same capabilities. The thermal gadzets provide vision through smoke and can quickly recognize individuals in need of rescue in burning structures. This makes the drones so striking to searchers and rescuers to define their ability to fly into dangerous and hard to reach destinations without putting pilots and air crew in risk. In addition to safety remuneration, there is also an added advantage is that the drones can execute these types of missions at a fraction of the cost linked with a traditional chopper. The drones can also replace manned airplanes for deliveries of medical kits and other materials to areas that are potentially quarantined or unreachable to rescuers thus provides the immediate help to keep people safe until the full help arrives [8].

In accordance with survey the drone benefits almost fully in urban areas depends on environmental conditions with traffic control, drones pace or speed and the coverage area. If the environmental conditions are good drones gives the maximum coverage as a survey research for data as shown in the Figure 7.3 [28].

In a few minutes these drones bring the observer to the top of the event, hovering over sudden, unreachable distant and dangerous zones for the

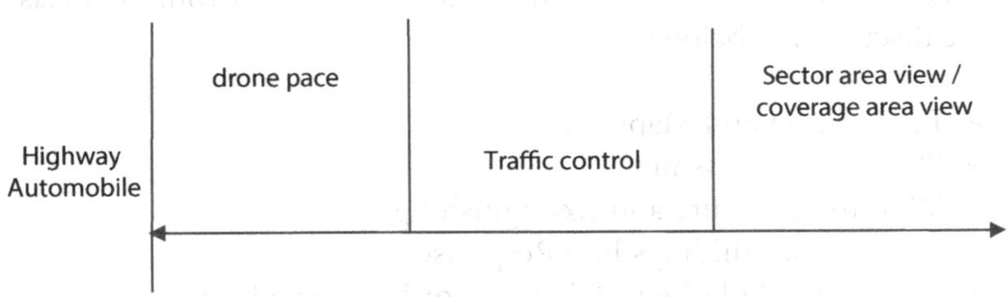

Figure 7.3 Survey by drone.

individuals. Once a victim has been identified optical zoom cameras can be used to check on their well being to detect the severity of the rescue and make sure that the rescue teams have the necessary tools to get their goals.

7.6 Disaster Relief

Whenever an environmental disasters strikes, then first 2–3 days are very critical. As relief staff works to save the lives of individuals and also to diminish the damage they rely on precise terrestrial to synchronize the missions. The more the officials know about impacted areas, the more effective is their response. Since the drones can be rapidly deployed over disaster areas, acceptors are using them to generate 3D maps, scan for fatalities and assess smashed road and rail network [32, 33].

The Acceptors use drones to:

- ➢ Grant quick situational attentiveness with mapping skills.
- ➢ Help firefighters to identify main affected area and evaluate property damage.
- ➢ Capture images for communications and news reporting
- ➢ Search for individuals.
- ➢ Evaluate utility and road and rail network damage.

When a tornado damaged dozens of homes and injured individuals in particular area, then management granted permission to these drones over the damaged areas to assist with disaster assistance efforts. They helped by providing airborne views of the consequences and using the high resolution images to position the individuals belongings of those whose home have been damaged. The images and the video collected by UAV drones have become a proof that shared both the story of the tornado demolition and the aid of the drones provided afterwards [13].

The report outlines some of the most capable uses for drones in disaster relief are discussed as below:

- ➢ Exploration and Mapping
- ➢ Structural Assessment
- ➢ Wildfire Exposure and Extinguishing
- ➢ Apartment Buildings Fire Response
- ➢ Biological, Radiological, Nuclear or Explosive Event
- ➢ Investigate and Rescue Operations
- ➢ Indemnity Claims Response and Risk Evaluation.

7.7 Conclusion

In summary, the use of UAV drones can be useful into the various fields. As explained above in this chapter, the menace of Drones as UAVs is extremely alarming and taking place at a growing rate with the rising terrorist and criminal use to conduct malicious activities. As stated in this chapter, drones are employed in different domains for tremendous purposes but it is used for mischievous ones also. Accordingly, the new experiments are done related to several securities, safety and privacy concerns when the UAVs drone are engaged for dangerous activities.

References

1. Kalantari, E., Shakir, M.Z., Yanikomeroglu, H., Yongacoglu, A., Backhaul-aware robust 3D drone placement in 5G+ wireless networks. *2017 IEEE International Conference on Communications Workshops (ICC Workshops)*, pp. 109–114, 2017.
2. Tuna, G., Gungor, V.C., Gulez, K., An autonomous wireless sensor network deployment system using mobile robots for human existence detection in case of disasters. *Ad Hoc Networks, 13*, 54–68, 2014.
3. Nakamura, H. and Kajikawa, Y., Regulation and innovation: How should small unmanned aerial vehicles be regulated? *Technol. Forecasting Soc. Change, 128*, 262–274, 2018.
4. Ueyama, J., Freitas, H., Faical, B.S., Filho, G.P., Fini, P., Pessin, G., Villas, L.A., Exploiting the use of unmanned aerial vehicles to provide resilience in wireless sensor networks. *IEEE Commun. Mag., 52*, 12, 81–87, 2014.
5. Alzenad, M., El-Keyi, A., Yanikomeroglu, H., 3-D Placement of an Unmanned Aerial Vehicle Base Station for Maximum Coverage of Users With Different QoS Requirements. *IEEE Wireless Commun. Lett., 7*, 1, 38–41, 2018.
6. Felice, M.D., Trotta, A., Bedogni, L., Chowdhury, K.R., Bononi, L., Self-organizing aerial mesh networks for emergency communication. *2014 IEEE 25th Annual International Symposium on Personal, Indoor, and Mobile Radio Communication (PIMRC)*, 2014.
7. Motlagh, N.H., Bagaa, M., Taleb, T., UAV-Based IoT Platform: A Crowd Surveillance Use Case. *IEEE Commun. Mag., 55*, 2, 128–134, 2017.
8. Sutheerakul, C., Kronprasert, N., Kaewmoracharoen, M., Pichayapan, P., Application of Unmanned Aerial Vehicles to Pedestrian Traffic Monitoring and Management for Shopping Streets. *Transp. Res. Proc., 25*, 1717–1734, 2017. Jones, T., *International Commercial Drone Regulation and Drone Delivery Services*, 2017.

9. Robinson, W.H. and Lauf, A.P., Aerial MANETs: Developing a Resilient and Efficient Platform for Search and Rescue Applications. *J. Commun.* Vol. 8, No. 4, April 2013.
10. Sun, Y., Ng, D.W., Xu, D., Dai, L., Schober, R., Resource Allocation for Solar Powered UAV Communication Systems. *2018 IEEE 19th International Workshop on Signal Processing Advances in Wireless Communications (SPAWC)*, 2018.
11. Sturdivant, R.L. and Chong, E.K., Systems Engineering Baseline Concept of a Multispectral Drone Detection Solution for Airports. *IEEE Access, 5*, 7123–7138, 2017.
12. Shi, X., Yang, C., Xie, W., Liang, C., Shi, Z., Chen, J., Anti-Drone System with Multiple Surveillance Technologies: Architecture, Implementation, and Challenges. *IEEE Commun. Mag., 56*, 4, 68–74, 2018.
13. Vattapparamban, E., Guvenc, I., Yurekli, A.I., Akkaya, K., Uluagac, S., Drones for smart cities: Issues in cybersecurity, privacy, and public safety. *2016 International Wireless Communications and Mobile Computing Conference (IWCMC)*, 2016.
14. Dalamagkidis, K., Aviation History and UAS, in: *On Integrating Unmanned Aircraft Systems into the National Airspace System*, pp. 9–28, 2012.
15. Cress, J.J., Sloan, J.L., Hutt, M.E., Implementation of unmanned aircraft systems by the U.S. Geological Survey. *Geocarto Int., 26*, 2, 133–140, 2011.
16. Park, J., Kim, S., Suh, K., A Comparative Analysis of the Environmental Benefits of Drone-Based Delivery Services in Urban and Rural Areas. *Sustainability, 10*, 3, 888, 2018.
17. Stocker, C., Bennett, R., Nex, F., Gerke, M., Zevenbergen, J., Review of the Current State of UAV Regulations. *Remote Sens., 9*, 5, 459, 2017.
18. Jones, T., *International Commercial Drone Regulation and Drone Delivery Services*, Rand Corporation, USA, 2017.
19. Kurt Barnhart, R., Marshall, D.M., Shappee, E., Thomas, M., *Introduction to Unmanned Aircraft Systems*, pp. 83–105, 2016.
20. Griffin, C., Operation Barkhane and Boko Haram: French Counterterrorism and Military Cooperation in the Sahel. *Small Wars Insur., 27*, 5, 896–913, 2016.
21. Alvear, O., Zema, N.R., Natalizio, E., Calafate, C.T., Using UAV-Based Systems to Monitor Air Pollution in Areas with Poor Accessibility. *J. Adv. Transp., 2017*, 1–14, 2017.
22. Krishna, K.R., *Agricultural Drones: A peaceful pursuit*, CRC Press, USA, 2018.
23. Yang, L., Qi, J., Xiao, J., Yong, X., A literature review of UAV 3D path planning. *Proceeding of the 11th World Congress on Intelligent Control and Automation*, 2014.
24. https://en.wikipedia.org/wiki/File:UAV_physical_and_hardware.jpg
25. Yaacoub, J.A., Noura, M., Noura, H.N., Salman, O., Yaacoub, E., Couturier, R., Chehab, A., Securing internet of medical things systems: Limitations,

issues and recommendations. *Future Gener. Comput. Syst.*, *105*, 581–606, 2020.

26. Yao, H., Qin, R., Chen, X., Unmanned Aerial Vehicle for Remote Sensing Applications—A Review. 1-22, 2019.
27. Singhal, G., Bansod, B., Mathew, L., Unmanned Aerial Vehicle Classification, Applications and Challenges: A Review, 2018.
28. Https://www.unmannedsystemstechnology.com.
29. Https://www.unmannedsystemstechnology.com.
30. Mohindru, V. and Singh, Y., Efficient approach for securing message communication in wireless sensor networks from node clone attack. *Indian J. Sci. Technol.*, 9, 32, 1–7, 2016.
31. Mohindru, V., Singh, Y., Bhatt, R., Hybrid cryptography algorithm for securing wireless sensor networks from Node Clone Attack. *Recent Adv. Electr. Electron. Eng. (Formerly Recent Patents Electrical & Electronic Engineering)*, 13, 2, 251–259, 2020.
32. Mohindru, V., Singh, Y., Bhatt, R., A Review on Lightweight Node Authentication Algorithms in Wireless Sensor Networks, in: *2018 Fifth International Conference on Parallel, Distributed and Grid Computing (PDGC)*, 2018, December, IEEE, pp. 517–521.
33. Mohindru, V. and Garg, A., Security Attacks in Internet of Things: A Review, in: *The International Conference on Recent Innovations in Computing*, 2020, March, Springer, Singapore, pp. 679–693.
34. Mohindru, V., Singh, Y., Bhatt, R., Securing wireless sensor networks from node clone attack: a lightweight message authentication algorithm. *Int. J. Inf. Comput. Secur.*, 12, 2–3, 217–233, 2020.
35. Mohindru, V., Bhatt, R., Singh, Y., Reauthentication scheme for mobile wireless sensor networks. *Sustainable Comput.: Inf. Syst.*, 23, 158–166, 2019.

8

Blockchain-Based Solutions for Various Security Issues in UAV-Enabled IoT

Madhuri S. Wakode* **and Rajesh B. Ingle**

Department of Computer Engineering, Pune Institute of Computer Technology, Pune, India

Abstract

Unmanned Aerial Vehicles (UAVs) enabled Internet of Things (IoT) systems are evolving as effective solutions to critical application including surveillance, agriculture, healthcare, supply chain managements, smart cities, rescue operations and more. Remotely controllable sensors mounted on UAVs are solving issues related to reaching out physically inaccessible areas or remote locations being monitored or controlled by IoT applications. Though fusion of UAVs and IoT proves disruptive, it needs to address increased security issues. Identity management, authentication, UAV hijacking, secured and trustworthy data sharing in intra-UAV communications, UAV signal jamming are few in the series. Blockchain being a decentralized technology and a distributed ledger offers solutions to some of these issues. Blockchain assures secure intra-UAV communications through encryption and hashing. In case of UAV signal jamming, UAV can use blockchain to prepare the flying schedule. Consensus mechanism of blockchain can detect the internal attacks or malicious insider UAV. Blockchain technology provides transparency and trust in trust-less environments involving third parties or multiple parties collaborating to provide UAV based IoT applications and services. Blockchain promises immutability of transactions thereby providing opportunity to thwart out many cyber-physical systems attacks on UAV based IoT systems. In this work we explore the blockchain-based solutions for various security issues in UAV-enabled IoT.

Keywords: UAV, IoT, blockchain, security

**Corresponding author*: mswakode@pict.edu

Vandana Mohindru, Yashwant Singh, Ravindara Bhatt and Anuj Kumar Gupta (eds.) Unmanned Aerial Vehicles for Internet of Things (IoT): Concepts, Techniques, and Applications, (143–158) © 2021 Scrivener Publishing LLC

8.1 Introduction

UAV and IoT are among the most prominent technologies being deployed for civilian and industrial applications and supporting Industry 4.0. UAV is an autonomous vehicle without a human pilot and can be operated remotely. Although UAVs were initially deployed for military applications, the popularity and the advancements in the technology cites the opportunities of using UAVs in civilian and industrial applications [1, 2]. IoT is enabling an enormous number and range of connected devices thereby opening the opportunities for remote monitoring and controlling various operations [3]. Smart homes or home automation, smart cities, security and surveillance applications, remote patient monitoring, precision agriculture are some of the IoT use cases [4–6]. Integration of these two technologies (UAV and IoT) broadens the range of applications for betterment of human-life. Data collection tasks in UAV-based applications can benefit from the well deployed Internet-of-Things. Whereas UAVs can facilitate the data collection for IoT applications from physically inaccessible locations, use of sensor-equipped UAVs in civil and industrial applications is boosting the power of IoT. Literature survey reveals many interesting and effective applications of UAV-enabled IoT systems. Smart cities, agriculture, healthcare, disaster management, rescue operations, supply chains, geoscience are among the few of the target domains for applications for UAV and IoT integration [7–10].

Along with the opportunities, UAV and IoT integration opens many technical and regulatory challenges too. Air traffic management, collision avoidance, preserving integrity of flight schedules and paths, adoption of various communication models, data collection through sensors, real time or near-to-real time processing and delivery of data, lightweight cryptographic algorithms to align with low on-board resources are few to mention. Authors in Refs. [11–13] discuss challenges in collaboration of UAVs with IoT. Security and privacy issues among others are crucial. Some of the security challenges are authentication, UAV hijacking, eavesdropping, spoofing, malicious nodes, distributed denial of service (DDoS) attacks. Authors in Refs. [14, 15] discuss some of the issues in detail; few have proposed the counter measures for these issues. The security challenges such as authentication can be effectively handled with decentralized solutions. Blockchain being a decentralized ledger technology can be explored in this regard. Authors in Ref. [16] present a blockchain-based authentication scheme for IoT. Authors in Ref. [17] present a comprehensive survey of blockchain applications in various domains. Authors in Refs. [18, 19]

focus on the use of blockchain to address some of the security issues in UAV. In Refs. [20–22] authors present role of blockchain to address other issues along with security issues in IoT. We can further extend the use of blockchain to tackle the security risks posed by integration of UAV with IoT. Authors in Refs. [23–25] proposed the blockchain supported security measures to avoid some of the risks for the systems using UAVs and IoT. Exploring the application of blockchain technology to address the security issues in UAV-enabled IoT is thus important and is the topic of discussion for our work.

8.1.1 Organization of the Work

Initially, we introduce UAV, IoT, blockchain technology and the integration of UAV and IoT. We discuss the various security issues posed in the UAV envisioned IoT. We continue the discussion with a survey of solutions to these problems. We further present the blockchain offerings to solve some of the security issues in UAV-enabled IoT systems. We propose the lightweight solutions in this regard. We discuss the research directions in exploiting blockchain principles in the domain of UAV and IoT. Finally, we conclude the work along with the future directions.

8.2 Introduction to UAV and IoT

In this section we introduce UAV, IoT, the integration of these two, and blockchain technology.

8.2.1 UAV

UAVs are autonomous flying vehicles with no human pilot. Initially deployed for military applications. However, the UAV characteristics such as self-configuring, flying autonomy, dynamic operations, make them a suitable choice for civilian, commercial, and industrial applications [1]. Figure 8.1 depicts some of the candidate applications for UAV.

There are various types of UAVs depending on different parameters. UAVs are classified according to their gross weight, payload they can carry, flying mechanism, range and altitude, speed and flight time, power supply. The data collection, data processing, data delivery, communication infrastructure availability and other requirements of the application contribute to the selection of suitable type of UAV.

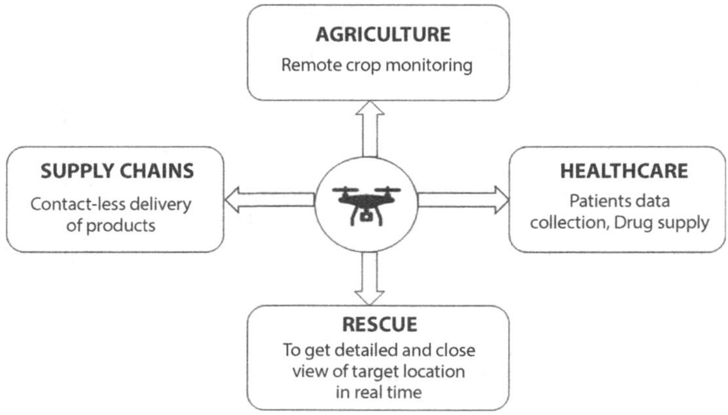

Figure 8.1 Some of the civil applications of UAV.

8.2.2 IoT

Internet of Things is a disruptive technology making physical objects smart and connected to the Internet. Billions of things are already connected, and the number is ever increasing. IoT consists of uniquely identifiable things connected to the Internet. Sensing nodes, communication links and software applications form the basis of IoT systems. The basic property of IoT to allow anytime access to anything from anywhere, makes it a perfect choice for applications that demand remote monitoring and control of devices or processes. Last decade witnessed the widespread use of IoT in the field of consumer electronics, industrial automation, healthcare, agriculture, civilian applications and many more. Figure 8.2 depicts some of the application domains for IoT.

IoT is a layered architecture with perception (sensing and actuation) layer, communication (connect) layer and application (manage) layer. Figure 8.3 shows the layered architecture of IoT.

Perception layer also called as physical layer consists of IoT nodes equipped with various sensors. These nodes collect the sensor data, can perform some local processing, and send data to cloud services for storage and further analysis. Communication layer includes heterogeneous communication models to provide connectivity to IoT nodes. Application layer provides the interface to the IoT devices. Including custom applications, this layer is responsible to manage and provide services to the business applications. It is the layer where sensor's data is used. Characteristics of IoT can be listed as: interoperability among wide range of devices as well as different types of communication models, self-configuration: for example software upgrades, dynamic and self-adapting: to cope up with the

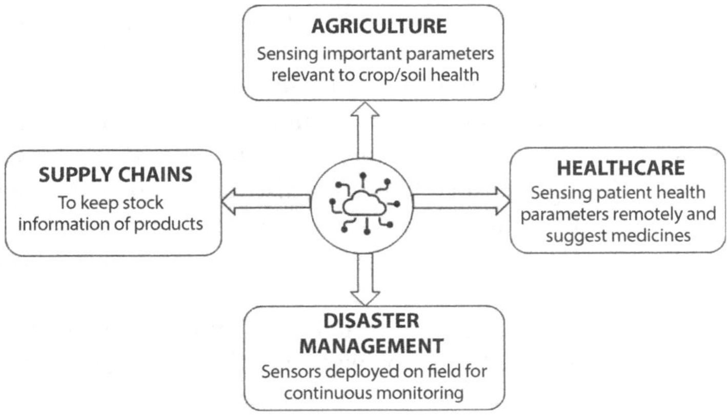

Figure 8.2 Some of the applications of IoT.

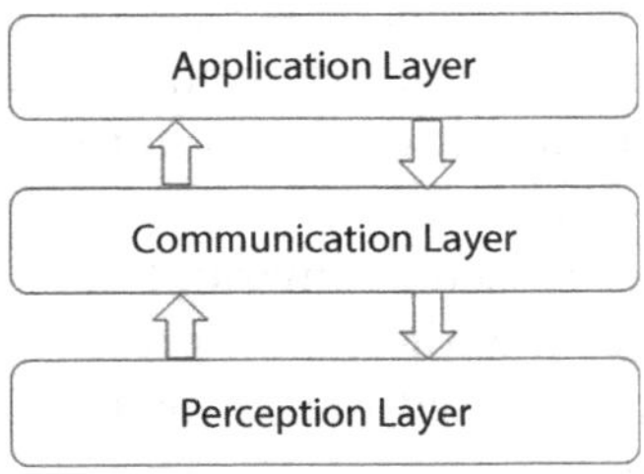

Figure 8.3 Layered architecture of IoT.

changing contexts, Unique identities to IoT devices. The IoT devices are resource constrained in nature and some network segments are Low Power Lossy Networks (LLNs). These constraints put restrictions on implementing contemporary security mechanism in IoT systems. Lightweight security solutions are thus essential for effectively securing the IoT applications. Further, authentication of the devices, access control, establishing the trust in such type of heterogeneous systems is crucial. Blockchain extends the security of IoT systems by addressing some of these issues [16, 21, 22].

8.2.3 UAV-Enabled IoT

UAVs characteristics of self-configuration, dynamic operations, reaching out physically in-accessible regions can be exploited to provide IoT services in many sectors. UAVs with mounted sensors can fly over these regions, collect data, deliver data/process data. They can scan larger regions can get the data on-demand instead of deploying sensors permanently in those locations thus reducing the cost and maintenance efforts. For example, to determine the air quality in some region where network infrastructure is not available. UAVs equipped with sensors to measure air pollutants and other air components can fly over these regions and collect air data through sensors. UAVs can also aid in sensor deployments, sensor recharge (Powering up), IoT nodes replacement in physically inaccessible areas. Figure 8.4 depicts some of the candidate applications for UAV-enabled IoT.

UAVs offer many opportunities to IoT applications namely ubiquitous connectivity, increased scalability by widening the coverage to areas without network infrastructure or with weak connections [31]. It also supports redeployment of damaged IoT nodes/sensors, self-configuring communication networks, powering up the battery-run IoT devices. UAVs can offer protection to IoT nodes by creating demilitarized zone (DMZ) around nodes through jamming (via alteration of SNR) of malicious communications. Convergence of UAV and IoT opens many challenges. Authors in Ref. [34] presented an in-depth discussion of the challenges of UAVs in cyber physical applications.

Authors in Ref. [11], proposed an envisioned architecture for UAV-based integrative IoT. In this paper authors have presented the high-level view of architecture where they proposed the concept of UAV clusters in heterogeneous communication networks. UAVs in a cluster collaborate to fulfil a particular task and are equipped with sensors and camera. Authors have discussed different use-cases of UAV-enabled IoT platform and the relevant issues to be considered. UAVs can have various on-board or mounted

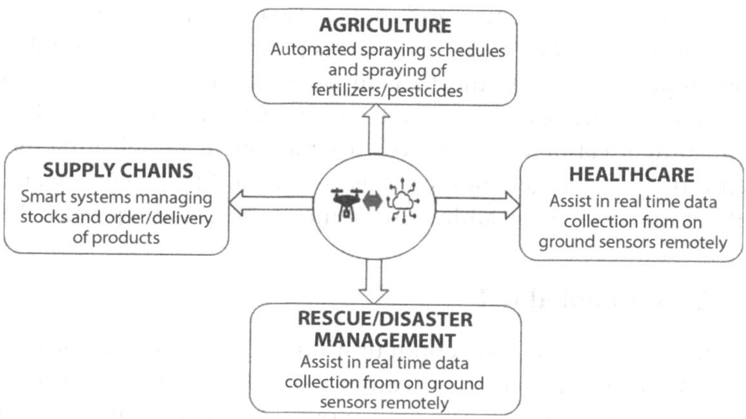

Figure 8.4 Some of the applications of UAV-enabled IoT.

sensors to collect data, capture images. UAV clusters consist of multiple UAVs deployed for some task, for example, to measure air pollution levels in large areas, to forecast the natural disaster risks such as floods. Some UAVs in a cluster may be in air (flying state), some may be in ready to fly state and can fly on receiving commands. Figure 8.5 presents a high-level view of UAV-enabled IoT system. The ground sensor network comprises of IoT nodes deployed in physical region. IoT nodes are equipped with sensors and/or actuators pertaining to the application of interest. The data collected from sensors is further sent to cloud storage through core network for further processing and analysis. UAVs can collaborate with ground sensor network for data collection. They provide extended coverage to larger regions through aerial scans and collect the data on-demand. To support this kind of applications, UAVs need to have mounted sensors, on-board resources, and ability to communicate among themselves, with ground sensor networks and core network too.

In UAV-enabled system designs we need to consider designs of components as:

UAV design:

Hardware: size, weight, payload etc.
Software: autonomy, intelligence etc.

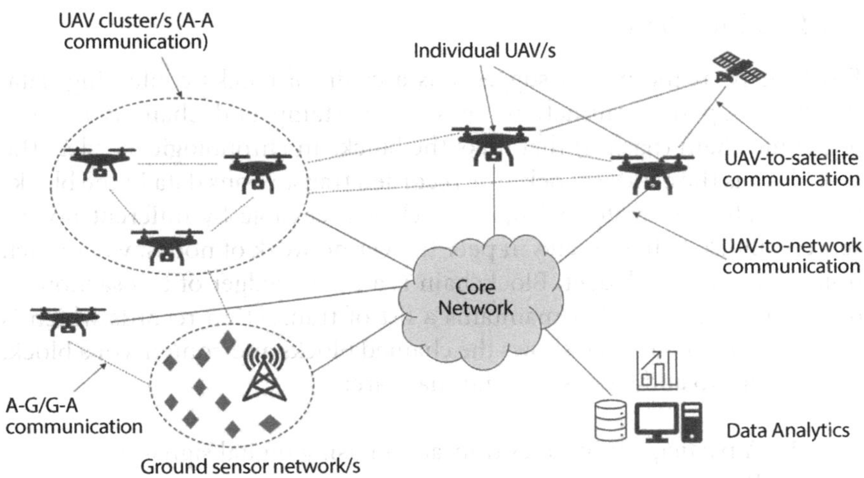

Figure 8.5 Architecture: High level view of UAV-enabled IoT system with heterogeneous components.

Communication links:

Arial-to-Ground (A–G)/(G–A) links design. It is on insecure channels(open as in wireless) so is vulnerable to attacks.
Arial-to-Arial (A–A) communications links for communication between multiple UAVs.
UAV-to-networks
UAV-to-satellite.

Ground station's design:

Communication models
Storage models
Remote monitoring and data processing
Decision making/business logic.

UAVs can communicate to ground sensor networks for collaboration of data collection tasks, for example.

Authors in Refs. [25, 31, 34, 35] discussed the opportunities and challenges of integrating UAVs with IoT. Due to the variety of communication models involved the cyber-attack space becomes larger for UAV-enabled IoT systems. Use of blockchain technology can help reduce some of the security threats.

8.2.4 Blockchain

Blockchain, as the names suggests, is a chain of blocks containing data. Blocks group the transactions, has a timestamp and chain is a cryptographic chain (hashes) that links the blocks in chronological order. The first block is the genesis block. The recorded transactions data in the blocks is immutable. It creates a ledger which is accessible by different nodes/servers. Blockchain operates in peer to peer network of nodes, where each node has a copy of ledger. Blockchain is a public ledger of transactions, a distributed database that maintains a list of transaction records which is tamper-proof. Figure 8.6 shows the chained blocks and contents of a block.

The steps to add blocks into the chain are:

1. A participant initiates transaction using digital signature
2. Participant broadcasts transactions
3. Nodes start validation of broadcasted transactions
4. Aggregate/group transactions into a block

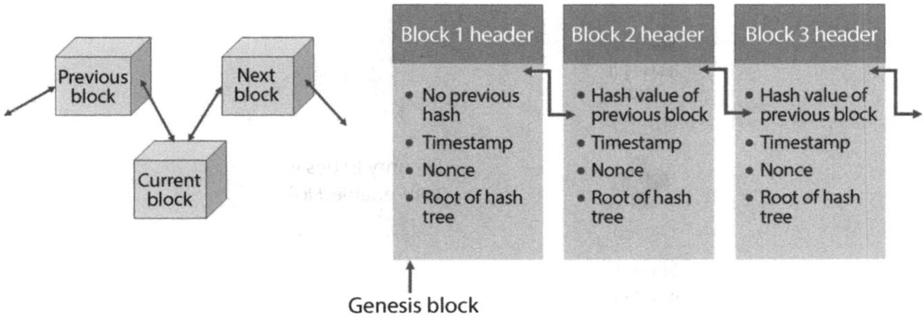

Figure 8.6 Chain of blocks and block details in blockchain.

5. Nodes broadcast blocks to each other
6. Consensus protocol is used to reach the consensus
7. The valid block gets added to the blockchain.

All these steps can be implemented through smart contracts. The blockchain can be of public, permissioned or consortium/federated type depending on permissions and management of pear to pear networks. In public blockchains anyone can join as a new user or miner. Every participant can perform create transactions or execute smart contracts. In permissioned blockchain a set of allowed users can perform the operations on blockchain. A federated blockchain is a combination of public and permissioned blockchains.

The concept of blockchain as a distributed ledger technology over peer to peer network was proposed by Satoshi Nakamoto in 2008. Authors in Ref. [17] provided the systematic review of applications of blockchain. Authors in Refs. [10, 18] discussed the integration of blockchain with UAV. Authors in Refs. [33, 36] discussed the integration of blockchain with IoT. Authors proposed a blockchain-based IoT system to address issues in IoT such as data heterogeneity, interoperability, decentralization, network complexity, security risks.

8.3 Security and Privacy Issues in UAV-Enabled IoT

Authors in Refs. [14, 26] have discussed security and privacy issues in UAV, specifically drones. Authors have classified security attacks according multiple parameters such as active/passive attacks, physical/logical attacks, affected security aspects and others. Researchers have proposed the need for lightweight cryptographic algorithms for authentication,

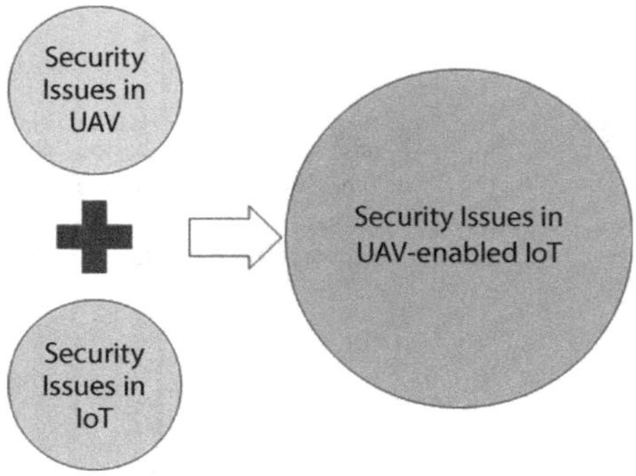

Figure 8.7 Enlarged attack space of UAV and IoT integration.

encryption-decryption considering the resource constrained nature of UAVs. Authors in Ref. [32] proposed a lightweight authentication scheme for UAVs based on the concept of temporal credentials and symmetric keys. Authors in Refs. [3, 21, 22] have discussed security issues in IoT including routing attacks, DDoS, sink hole attacks, replay, malicious code injection and other issues. Authors in Refs. [26, 27, 37] have discussed security issues

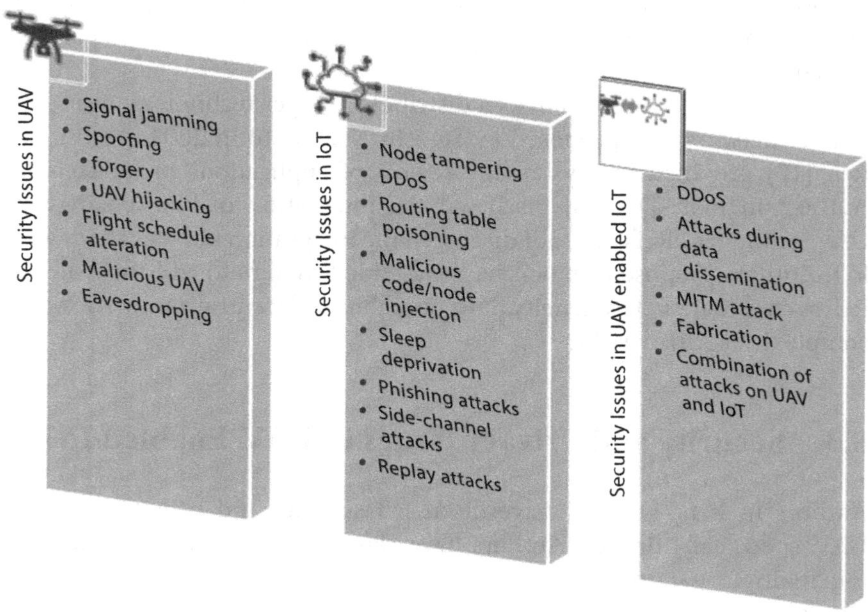

Figure 8.8 Security issues in UAV-enabled IoT.

in UAV-enabled IoT which among other includes DDoS attacks, penetration attacks, UAV hijack, signal jamming. Authors in Refs. [10, 18, 25, 26, 28–30] have discussed the blockchain based solutions to some of these issues.

We further explore the opportunities of blockchain to address security issues in UAV-enabled IoT systems. As shown in Figure 8.7, the attack-space for UAV-enabled IoT systems is obviously larger as it inherits vulnerabilities from the two technologies. Additionally, it has the vulnerabilities arising from the integration of UAV and IoT.

Figure 8.8 lists down the security threats and attacks on UAV, IoT and UAV-enabled IoT systems.

Security issues are observed in various components in the architecture shown in Figure 8.5.

8.4 Blockchain-Based Solutions to Various Security Issues

The decentralization, immutable transactions and use of public-cryptography keys in blockchain thwarts many security issues. In general, systems or applications involving more than one UAVs or multi-UAV swarm systems can get benefited by afore mentioned blockchain characteristics. In such systems, blockchain helps provide transparent and secure intra-UAV data exchange and develop trust among the multiple UAVs in the network. Blockchain based architectures can help to withstand the issues such as UAV signal jamming, hijacking, collisions of UAV in mid-air, data dissemination, secure data communication, trust, data integrity, securing data type, IDS, cyber-physical attacks. Authors in Ref. [27] proposed blockchain based drone delivery system. They discussed the six attacks and proposed privacy preservation through hash and short signatures. Authors in Ref. [28] proposed a blockchain-based access-control scheme for IoT driven drones for A–A and A–G/G–A communications. Authors in Ref. [29] presented the UAV assisted IoT framework for secure healthcare system. Authors have provided the security analysis of the framework and proposed use of blockchain to thwart some of the security attacks including Man-in-the-Middle, replay, unauthorized access, and data tampering. Authors in Refs. [30, 38, 39] have explored the use of blockchain, UAVs and RFID to automate inventory tasks and traceability for Industry 4.0 warehouses. Authors have developed a framework for inventory automation which provides transparency, data integrity and trust among the entities involved.

We propose use of blockchain technology in UAV-enabled IoT systems, to address following:

Data integrity: data stored in the blockchain (transactions) cannot be tampered because of immutable ledger of blockchain. Attempts to tamper the data results in changed hashes. This ensures the data integrity.

DoS/DDoS attack: as the data is available with all peers/nodes, even if DoS attacks make one or more nodes inaccessible, data can be accessed from other nodes. Thus, availability is increased.

Transparency: public blockchain provide transparency as every node contains the identical copy of blockchain.

Authentication: the sender/creator of the transaction is authenticated using public keys generated by blockchain. The sender uses his private key to encrypt the data and receiver uses the senders public key to decrypt it. This assures the authenticity of the sender.

Trust: using immutable transactions, hashes, public keys makes it to create trust among the unknown pears.

We focus on the need of developing blockchain enabled lightweight security solutions for resource constrained environment of UAVs and IoT [40].

8.5 Research Directions

To effectively implement blockchain for securing UAV enabled IoT applications we identify the need for:

Lightweight consensus algorithms for IoT, UAVs.

Developing blockchain-trust models for UAV enabled IoT systems.

Faster rate of transaction validations to support real time applications, which is one of the inherent causes of deploying UAV enabled IoT systems.

Analysis of blockchain security: Blockchain technology is itself vulnerable to attacks such as 51% attack, hard-forks, and problem of double-spending.

Simulators to simulate the working of UAV enabled IoT environments, modeling attacks and experimenting the solutions.

These are the major areas among others where researchers can focus and contribute.

8.6 Conclusion

In this chapter we have explored the opportunity of using blockchain technology to enhance the security of UAV enabled IoT systems. We proposed the use of blockchain-based solutions to thwart the security attacks on UAV, IoT and the integration of these two disruptive technologies. We find the scope of using blockchain to address data integrity issues, DDoS attacks, authentication, injection of malicious UAVs or IoT nodes in the system, among others. The heterogeneous nature of the end-nodes, communications and applications poses many vulnerabilities in such system and importantly establishment of the trust in trust-less environment need to be addressed. We find that the core properties of blockchain, which are decentralization, immutable ledgers and use of public-keys for encryptions, hold it right for establishing trust in parties and components involved in UAV-enabled IoT systems. We conclude that development of blockchain-based frameworks for UAV-enabled IoT systems for specific applications provides prevention of many security risks.

8.7 Future Work

We propose to provide the proof-of-concept (PoC) for most of the ideas presented in this work. The performance evaluation and security analysis of the blockchain-based solutions will be the extension of this work.

References

1. Shakhatreh, H. *et al.*, Unmanned Aerial Vehicles (UAVs): A Survey on Civil Applications and Key Research Challenges. *IEEE Access*, 7, 48572, 2019.
2. Menouar, H., Guvenc, I., Akkaya, K., Uluagac, A.S., Kadri, A., Tuncer, A., UAV-Enabled Intelligent Transportation Systems for the Smart City: Applications and Challenges. *IEEE Commun. Mag.*, 55, 22, 2017.
3. Gubbi, J., Buyya, R., Marusic, S., Palaniswami, M., Internet of Things (IoT): A vision architectural elements and future directions. *Future Gener. Comput. Syst.*, 29, 1645, 2013.
4. Gope, P. and Hwang, T., BSN-Care: A Secure IoT-Based Modern Healthcare System Using Body Sensor Network. *IEEE Sens. J.*, 16, 1368, 2016.
5. Arasteh, H. *et al.*, Iot-based smart cities: A survey. *IEEE 16th International Conference on Environment and Electrical Engineering (EEEIC)*, Florence, pp. 1–6, 2016.
6. Khanna, A. and Kaur, S., Evolution of Internet of Things (IoT) and its significant impact in the field of Precision Agriculture. *Comput. Electron. Agric.*, 157, 218, 2019.
7. Ejaz, W., Azam, M.A., Saadat, S., Iqbal, F., Hanan, A., Unmanned aerial vehicles enabled IoT platform for disaster management. *Energies*, 12, 2706, 2019.

8. Boursianis, A.D., Papadopoulou, M.S., Diamantoulakis, P., Liopa-Tsakalidi, A., Barouchas, P., Salahas, G., Karagiannidis, G., Wan, S., Goudos, S.K., Internet of Things (IoT) and Agricultural Unmanned Aerial Vehicles (UAVs) in smart farming: A comprehensive review. *Internet Things*, 2020, 100187.
9. Erdelj, M., Uk, B., Konam, D., Natalizio, E., From the Eye of the Storm: An IoT Ecosystem Made of Sensors, Smartphones and UAVs. *Sensors*, 18, 3814, 2018.
10. Motlagh, N.H., Bagaa, M., Taleb, T., UAV-Based IoT Platform: A Crowd Surveillance Use Case. *IEEE Commun. Mag.*, 55, 128, 2017.
11. Motlagh, N.H., Taleb, T., Arouk, O., Low-Altitude Unmanned Aerial Vehicles-Based Internet of Things Services: Comprehensive Survey and Future Perspectives. *IEEE Internet Things J.*, 3, 899, 2016.
12. Rodrigues, M., Pigatto, D.F., Fontes, J.V.C., Pinto, A.S.R., Diguet, J.P., Branco, K.R.L.J.C., UAV integration into IoIT: Opportunities and challenges. *International Conference on Autonomic and Autonomous (ICAS)*, Barcelona, pp. 86–91, 2017.
13. Alsamhi, S.H., Ma, O., Ansari, M.S., Almalki, F.A., Survey on Collaborative Smart Drones and Internet of Things for Improving Smartness of Smart Cities. *IEEE Access*, 7, 128125, 2019.
14. Lin, C., He, D., Kumar, N., Choo, K.R., Vinel, A., Huang, X., Security and Privacy for the Internet of Drones: Challenges and Solutions. *IEEE Commun. Mag.*, 56, 64, 2018.
15. Lagkas, T., Argyriou, V., Bibi, S., Sarigiannidis, P., UAV IoT framework views and challenges: Towards protecting drones as Things. *Sensors*, 18, 4015, 2018.
16. Hammi, M.T., Hammi, B., Bellot, P., Serhrouchni, A., Bubbles of Trust: A decentralized Blockchain-based authentication system for IoT. *Comput. Secur.*, 78, 126, 2018.
17. Casino, F., Dasaklis, T.K., Patsakis, C., A systematic literature review of blockchain-based applications: Current status, classification and open issues. *Telemat. Inform.*, 36, 55, 2019.
18. Alladi, T., Chamola, V., Sahu, N., Guizani, M., Applications of blockchain in unmanned aerial vehicles: A review. *Veh. Commun.*, 23, 100249, 2020.
19. Kuzmin, A. and Znak, E., Blockchain-base structures for a secure and operate network of semi-autonomous Unmanned Aerial Vehicles. *IEEE International Conference on Service Operations and Logistics, and Informatics (SOLI)*, Singapore, pp. 32–37, 2018.
20. Reyna, A., Martín, C., Chen, J., Soler, E., Díaz, M., On blockchain and its integration with IoT. Challenges and opportunities. *Future Gener. Comput. Syst.*, 88, 173, 2018.
21. Khan, M.A. and Salah, K., IoT security: Review, blockchain solutions, and open challenges. *Future Gener. Comput. Syst.*, 82, 395, 2018.
22. Dorri, A., Kanhere, S.S., Jurdak, R., Gauravaram, P., Blockchain for IoT security and privacy: The case study of a smart home. *IEEE International*

Conference on Pervasive Computing and Communications Workshops (PerCom Workshops), Kona, HI, pp. 618–623, 2017.
23. Ge, C., Ma, X., Liu, Z., A semi-autonomous distributed blockchain-based framework for UAVs system. *J. Syst. Archit.*, 107, 101728, 2020.
24. Islam, A. and Shin, S.Y., BUAV: A blockchain based secure UAV-assisted data acquisition scheme in Internet of Things. *J. Commun. Networks*, 21, 491, 2019.
25. Yazdinejad, A., Parizi, R.M., Dehghantanha, A., Karimipour, H., Srivastava, G., Aledhari, M., Enabling Drones in the Internet of Things with Decentralized Blockchain-based Security. *IEEE Internet Things*, 2327, 2020.
26. Yaacoub, J., Noura, H., Salman, O., Chehab, A., Security analysis of drones systems: Attacks, limitations, and recommendations. *Internet Things*, 11, 100218, 2020.
27. Ferrag, M.A. and Maglaras, L., DeliveryCoin: An IDS and Blockchain-Based Delivery Framework for Drone-Delivered Services. *Computers*, 8, 58, 2019.
28. Bera, B., Chattaraj, D., Das, A.K., Designing secure blockchain-based access control scheme in IoT-enabled Internet of Drones deployment. *Comput. Commun.*, 153, 229, 2020.
29. Lei, K., Zhang, Q., Lou, J., Bai, B., Xu, K., Securing ICN-Based UAV Ad Hoc Networks with Blockchain. *IEEE Commun. Mag.*, 57, 26, 2019.
30. Fernández-Caramés, T.M., Blanco-Novoa, O., Froiz-Míguez, I., Fraga-Lamas, P., Towards an Autonomous Industry 4.0 Warehouse: A UAV and Blockchain-Based System for Inventory and Traceability Applications in Big Data-Driven Supply Chain Management. *Sensors*, 19, 2394, 2019.
31. Liu, Y., Dai, H., Wang, Q., Shukla, M.K., Imran, M., Unmanned aerial vehicle for Internet of Everything: Opportunities and challenges. *Comput. Commun.*, 155, 66, 2020.
32. Ali, Z., Chaudhry, S.A., Ramzan, M.S., Al-Turjman, F., Securing Smart City Surveillance: A Lightweight Authentication Mechanism for Unmanned Vehicles. *IEEE Access*, 8, 43711, 2020.
33. Dai, H., Zheng, Z., Zhang, Y., Blockchain for Internet of Things: A Survey. *IEEE Internet Things*, 6, 8076, 2019.
34. Shakeri, R. *et al.*, Design Challenges of Multi-UAV Systems in Cyber-Physical Applications: A Comprehensive Survey and Future Directions. *IEEE Commun. Surv. Tut.*, 21, 3340, 2019.
35. Mohindru, V. and Singh, Y., Node authentication algorithm for securing static wireless sensor networks from node clone attack. *Int. J. Inf. Comput. Secur.*, 10, 2–3, 129–148, 2018.
36. Mohindru, V. and Singh, Y., Performance analysis of message authentication algorithms in wireless sensor networks, in: *2017 4th International Conference on Signal Processing, Computing and Control (ISPCC)*, 2017, September, IEEE, pp. 468–472.
37. Mohindru, V., Bhatt, R., Singh, Y., Reauthentication scheme for mobile wireless sensor networks. *Sustainable Comput.: Inf. Syst.*, 23, 158–166, 2019.

38. Mohindru, V., Singh, Y., Bhatt, R., Securing wireless sensor networks from node clone attack: A lightweight message authentication algorithm. *Int. J. Inf. Comput. Secur.*, 12, 2–3, 217–233, 2020.
39. Mohindru, V., Singh, Y., Bhatt, R., Hybrid cryptography algorithm for securing wireless sensor networks from Node Clone Attack. *Recent Adv. Electr. Electron. Eng. (Formerly Recent Patents Electrical & Electronic Engineering)*, 13, 2, 251–259, 2020.
40. Mohindru, V., Singh, Y., Bhatt, R., A Review on Lightweight Node Authentication Algorithms in Wireless Sensor Networks, in: *2018 Fifth International Conference on Parallel, Distributed and Grid Computing (PDGC)*, 2018, December, IEEE, pp. 517–521.

9

Efficient Energy Management Systems in UAV-Based IoT Networks

V. Mounika Reddy[1], Neelima K.[2]* and G. Naresh[2]

[1]*Department of ECE, Center for Communication and Signal Processing, Sree Vidyanikethan Engineering College, Tirupati, India*
[2]*Department of ECE, Center for VLSI and Embedded Systems, Sree Vidyanikethan Engineering College, Tirupati, India*

Abstract

The Unmanned Aerial Vehicles (UAVs) assistance in IoT has gained a lot of attention in recent intelligent systems. The limited battery capacity of UAVs proves them to be energy constrained devices. The energy of the device can be either conserved or new mechanisms can be developed for increasing its efficiency. This brief details about both of those techniques like a multiple-period charging process, the combination of Markov decision process and Random Serial Dictatorship matching algorithm. To minimize the packet loss in IoT networks, optimal data collection and microwave power transfer during flight trajectory of UAV, the onboard double Q-learning scheduling algorithm is used. To ensure effective routing and scheduling in UAVs, deep reinforcement learning based channel and power allocation framework is used for decision making tasks to accomplish accurate mission, collision free navigation and efficient energy management. The UAVs are assisted with token free energy supply from the charging station with a facility to repay back with interest or late fees. An UAV-assisted emergency management system can have a secure wireless links incorporated with easy-to-use mobile user interface which can promptly switch the system between "system-efficient mode" and "energy-efficient mode" based on cloud dependent deep learning cognitive algorithms. By cognitive algorithms that provide strategies for tasks to be performed along with flying control when the drone visits each location without knowing the future enable efficient energy management. The performance metrics used for comparison are system throughput, energy efficiency, latency, etc.

**Corresponding author*: koppala.neelima@yahoo.com

Vandana Mohindru, Yashwant Singh, Ravindara Bhatt and Anuj Kumar Gupta (eds.) Unmanned Aerial Vehicles for Internet of Things (IoT): Concepts, Techniques, and Applications, (159–172) © 2021 Scrivener Publishing LLC

***Keywords*:** Collision avoidance, dynamic matching, energy-constrained IoT device, energy efficiency, energy trading, flying control, Markov decision process, scheduling, task allocation, trajectory planning, wireless charging

9.1 Introduction

The intelligent systems like Unmanned aerial vehicles (UAVs) can provide wireless connectivity to remote locations by using IoT Systems. The UAV assisted architecture as shown in Figure 9.1 [3], is a four-layer network architecture for UAV-assisted IoT architecture comprising of sensing, access, infrastructure and application layered devices being connected using either wired channel or wireless channel to provide the IoT networks with UAVs used as mobile sinks. The Sensing layer senses and collects data from massive IoT information acquisition devices like sensors, cameras, GPS devices, etc.

The Access Layer allows wireless access to the data processing services relating the core networks. It is divided into two sublayers, i.e., Convergence and Mobile Sink sublayers. The Infrastructure Layer receives collected data from access layer and uploads it for processing and storing in application layer. The user sub-layer of application layer supports various user applications (APPs) and optimizes the path plan for UAV and CP node. The decision sub-layer processes information and analyses the data by using big data techniques.

The IoT end devices are powered by batteries especially UAVs. If any device is inactive or dead, then it may yield fault routes leading to disruptive topology. Hence, scheduling must be done with different priorities for both the computing and communication resources.

Also the UAVs in smart sensing applications usually operate as a mobile Energy Provider and Data Gateways where by hovering in 3D space, they exchange data and energy between the network components like relays. Hence, the data traffic requires to be reduced by using cost effective routing schemes. But the limited battery capacity constraints their capabilities. As human intervention is very less in harsh or restricted environments, it becomes unrealistic to charge the device by changing the battery or recharging it using wired connection. This restriction created a way path to recharge the energy or harvest the energy and develop new mechanisms to use the battery in an efficient manner [26, 28]. There exist many methods to overcome this problem in literature. Among them some of the essential and practically are discussed here.

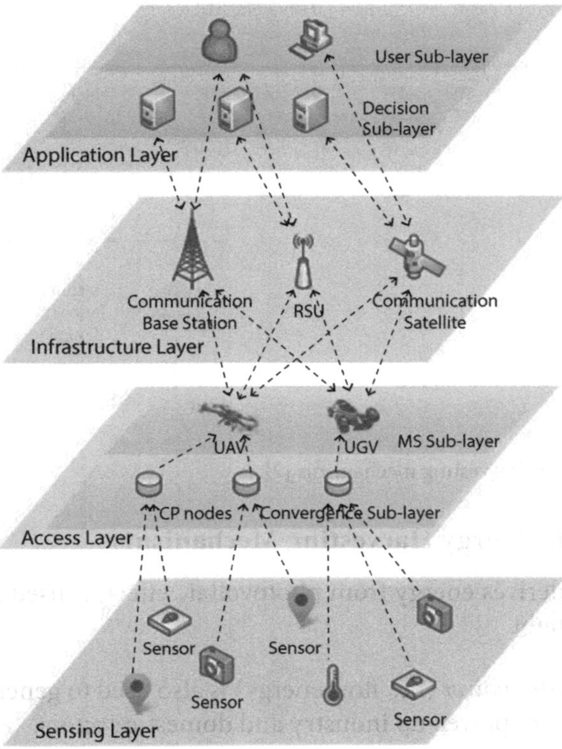

Figure 9.1 UAV-assisted IoT architecture [5].

9.2 Energy Harvesting Methods

Energy Harvesting [27, 28] is the process of exploiting any natural or man-made resource to produce electricity and the energy is stocked without any supervision. This is used for wide area networks. From Figure 9.2, basically energy harvesting can be categorized as

1. Mechanical EH
2. Thermal EH
3. Fluid flow EH
4. Radiant EH and
5. Wireless EH.

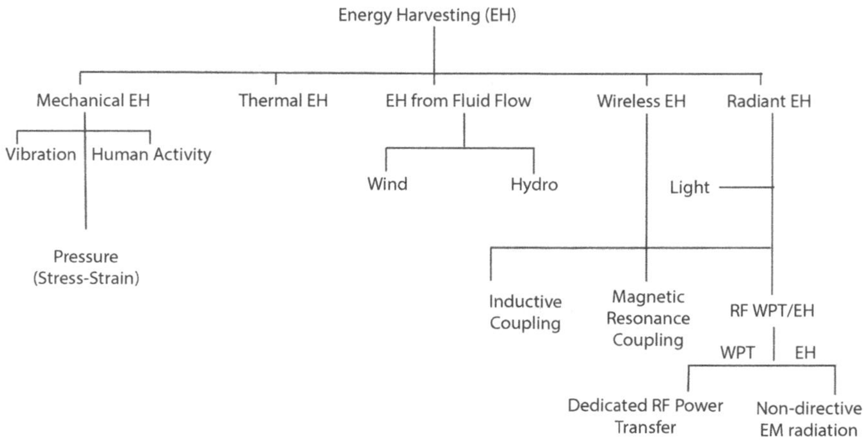

Figure 9.2 Energy harvesting mechanisms [2].

9.2.1 Basic Energy Harvesting Mechanisms

Solar power derives energy from photovoltaic effect, is used in rural areas for artificial light.

Wind and Hydro power (i.e., flow energy) is also used to generate energy in a massive way to power-up industry and domestic sectors.

The mechanical movements like vibration, pressure variation can be used for energy generation by using the property of piezoelectric materials. The temperature gradients can enable smart building services and battery-less wearable devices by using thermoelectric generators. But in urban areas, Radio frequency Energy Harvesting is used to enable self-sufficient communications which is typically low and depends on harvester efficiency, deployment location, etc.

Wireless Power Transfer can be anyone of inductive coupling, magnetic resonance coupling, and RF power delivery [4]. For near field energy transfer, Inductive Coupling is used for within a range of a few centimeters. It works based on the principle of induction between two coils with magnetic field for mutual energy transfer [5]. Its efficiency can reach a maximum of 87% as it depends on factors like tightness of coupling, quality factor of coils, etc. To overcome this, Magnetic Resonance Coupling can be used up to few meters as it offers higher efficiency with a trade-off with the flexibility and cost complexity [4, 10].

Radio Frequency Power Delivery is an electromagnetic (EM) radiation which has low efficiency (typically <40%), but offers advantages like effective energy multi-casting, small form factors, etc. [4]. Often, it requires the devices to meet the standards set for effective isotropic radiated power (EIRP) for selective frequencies by regulatory organizations such as the Federal Communications Commission (FCC) for human safety i.e., say at 2.4 GHz band being 36 dBm (4 W).

According to the signal source characteristics, the types of remote power delivery can be radiative or directive. Radiative power delivery is used for densely populated networks to mitigate interference by using an antenna to receive EM waves from any direction. Here the energy is harvested from any source with omnidirectional EM radiation and can sustain low power devices. In directive or dedicated power transfer, more power is transferred by a controllable/directive source using simultaneous data and power transfer technique, called SWIPT [11] using same waveform, for improving bandwidth utilization efficiency.

9.2.2 Markov Decision Process-Based Energy Harvesting Mechanisms

Many other solutions are like only one-shot charging process, energy harvesting from UAV and charging by using D2D Communication, etc. In energy harvesting, the entire time is classified as phases like energy harvesting and data transmission phases. To overcome the problem of limited energy consumption in information phase, the dynamic resource allocation [6, 9, 14, 15] is used which usually focuses on the trajectory design. As the UAVs can be devised for single purpose or multipurpose by one time or periodic utilization, one-shot allocation remains a critical problem.

As the UAV uses multiple stage dynamic matching [1] that will be obtained from the entire process of charging [8], which is a history-dependent, a Markov Decision Process is formulated for the multi-period matching problem. Here the Markov property based charging process is considered as the current state and the corresponding action has effect on the next period state along with energy constraints imposed on wireless power chargers of UAVs. To overcome this, the house allocation model and the bipartite matching with one-sided preferences are considered by using the evaluation function based on Bellman equation that can maximize the charging amount by considering both current and future rewards.

For higher charging amount of ECDs, the following steps are used

1. The Local Markov Decision Processes are set up for each and every ECD to predict the future reward.
2. The random serial dictatorship matching algorithm is proposed for using the current state.
3. The Joint Markov Decision Process is obtained from the results of steps 1 and 2.
4. The reward is estimated from Bellman equation and evaluated to obtain the optimal branch.

The performance of this mechanism is evaluated by parameters like actual charging amount, energy usage efficiency, etc. The observations made when compared to Genie aided upper bound and myopic greedy algorithms are: (i) The higher charging amount can be obtained when the UAV's velocity is larger as sufficient time is available for charging. (ii) The energy usage efficiency is same when compared with the Genie-aided upper bound and a worst case energy efficiency for myopic greedy algorithm.

9.2.3 mm Wave Energy Harvesting Mechanism

Recently Hybrid Access Point (HAP) [13] connected to a power grid for wireless energy sharing is used for the radio energy harvesting in device-to-device communication system. As path losses are induced by oxygen molecules and vapor, millimeter wave (mmWave) [21] can be used to wirelessly charge. The Ginibre Determinant Point Process (Gin-DPP) is used for dense access system where the EH capability is independent of off-grid configured nodes. A time division orthogonal multi-access protocol that modifies the energy harvesting phase to enhance sustainability in energy consumption by power grid and battery. The Machine Type Communication Devices can either depend on initial energy level of battery or derive the conditional analytic conclusions. Also the UAV-AP service time can be extended by adopting the method of tethering to link UAV and ground power grid system.

Also in the low-power IoT networks, the data collection from the sensors can be regulated by providing a stable energy using a hybrid access point (HAP) [5]. Still, it difficulty lies in supplying energy to sensors from fixed HAP, so more number of HAPs are set-up in the target area which is a cost intensive due to the sparsity of sensors. Hence, the UAV-mounted access point (AP) prove to have deployment flexibility and cost-effective for both energy harvesting and data collection.

9.2.4 Full Duplex Wireless Energy Harvesting Mechanism

The UAV assisted full-duplex IoT networks [16], where a number of sensors are supported. Here, the energy harvest time of each sensor is the data collection time of the last active sensor, so the coupling time modeling proves to be more challenging. Practically there exist two problems, i.e.,

(i). Sum-throughput maximization (STM), is achieved by optimizing constraints of mutual coupling between the UAV-assisted IoT networks to maximize the total throughput [17] with respect to total hover time constant T.
(ii). Total-hover time minimization (THTM), exploits the properties of coupled constraints for UAV-assisted full-duplex IoT networks by using the minimum amount of data sent back to minimize the total hover time of the UAV [18].

The results were evaluated for the line of sight (LoS) channel and the block-fading channel, where this optimal time allocation scheme proved to be a better choice than the equal time allocation scheme.

9.3 Energy Recharge Methods

For critical applications, usually a distributed framework is used for energy trading between Charging Stations [12] and UAVs. Due to weight limitations of UAVs, the battery size cannot be increased beyond certain limit as large weight infuses difficulty in flight at high altitudes for a long duration enabling them to use time to time recharging. To overcome this, they can utilize the services of intermediate charging stations which are usually standalone. But UAVs need energy within a minimum specified time and for minimum possible cost by having a stronger communication between the charging stations and the UAVs [15] as shown in Figure 9.3. The DLT (Distributed Ledger Technology) of block chain [8] allows multiple entities from different geographical locations with secure peer to peer transactions for UAV to UAV communication. It suffers from drawbacks like delay in transaction confirmation, limitations of scalability, and the very power hungry probabilistic nature of consensus algorithms. Due to high Processing fees for each and every transaction for the constrained size of the block, it is suitable only for small transactions in a large number. Other algorithms like Proof of Burn (POB), Proof of Stake (POS), and Proof of

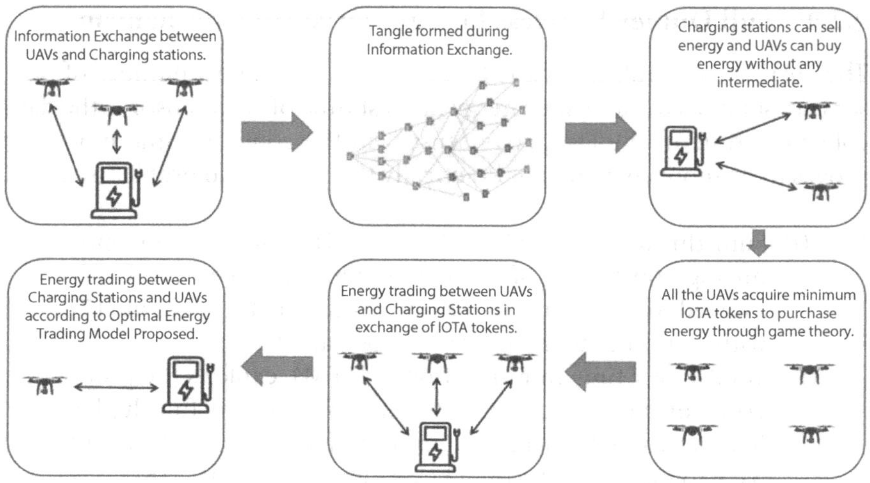

Figure 9.3 Energy trading mechanism.

Elapsed Time (POET) can also be used to avoid the limitations of the basic block chain.

IoTA is a secure and distributed DLT which uses tangle type data structure to store the transactions of UAVs by consuming less power with lower latency. Also it allows transactions without fee, micro-transactions. It also enables borrowing of tokens from charging stations when UAV has insufficient tokens to buy the energy and encourages repaying back with some interest or late fees. This game-theoretic model [30, 31] enhances revenue and utility of the UAVs and the charging stations making them suitable for health care applications [22].

9.4 Efficient Energy Utilization Methods

Usually the data collection of IoT is limited by battery drain of IoT nodes. The communication devices used in UAVs are used as base stations or access points to increase the IoT network life time with an added feature of effective data uploading [4]. These are basically software algorithms that usually modify the path or transit time of the UAV.

9.4.1 GLRM Method

If a virtual grid elects the forwarding nodes depending on the number of packets, energy of the IoT nodes and the Euclidean distance of grid, then this method is called as grid-based load-balanced routing method (GLRM) [7]. But this lacks real-time path planning as the packets travel through a pre-set path. To overcome this, the combination of weighted rendezvous planning (WRP) along with travelling salesman problem (TSP) algorithms are used to find the shortest path traversing of the RP nodes to reduce the transmission delay.

9.4.2 DRL Mechanism

Deep reinforcement learning (DRL) [3, 29, 32] is widely adopted for satisfying the delay constraints by using minimal power for mobility of UAV. The system uses dynamic decision optimization that includes usage of the concepts like duelling DQN [5] and grid-based method. The results proved to reduce computational complexity for the given state space.

In UAV-BS, allocation of proper channels with appropriate uplink power for IoT nodes to increase efficiency of energy [7, 24]. In machine-to-machine communications, the literature reviews the power control optimization and the joint channel allocation problems. Due to the flight of UAV, the distance changes rapidly for UAV-BS and the specified IoT node resulting in dynamic channel gain. Hence, the DRL technique, in which the agent under the UAV-BS deployment can use the changed patterns of the environment by continuous interaction with areas like caching and interference alignment, dynamic spectrum access, etc. [20]. The DRL based framework deploys UAV-BS to obtain information for channel and energy allocation, which proved to achieve optimal max-min energy efficiency [4, 23, 33].

The algorithm is

Step-1: In 0th time slot, Each Node is initially allocated with a random channel with minimum uplink power for transmission.

Step-2: The UAV-BS initializes randomly the critic and actor networks.

Step-3: The UAV-BS starts the trajectory with minimum power consumption by updating time, coordinates and network parameters. Based on Loss Function and Stochastic Gradient Descent Algorithm, the angle of path is updated.

Step-4: Once the path is traversed, the trajectory buffer is cleared by UAV-BS and convergence is evaluated between the critic and actor networks.

Step-5: After the critic network is closed, the UAV-BS decides the channel and power allocation for actor network.

9.4.3 Onboard Double Q-Learning Mechanism

The IoT nodes far away from Microwave Power Transfer (MPT) transmitter usually suffer with low energy transfer efficiency. Then UAVs (drones) can be equipped with MPT capability for wireless power harvesting. In a time switching MPT technique, hardware cost is reduced by using a single RF chain for each IoT node. As the UAV never knows the original network, the Markov Decision Process is used to optimize the power allocation during target tracking by collision-free trajectory [10, 19]. But as the IoT nodes increase, it destabilizes the Q-learning process leading to large packet loss approximation errors under persistent low battery levels, poor channel conditions, errors in approximations, etc. To avoid packet loss approximation errors and stabilize learning with convergence, an onboard double Q-learning based scheduling algorithm [2, 34] is used. It has two phases i.e., the first Q-learning process finds an optimal scheduling strategy based on backlogs of queue and battery levels. Then the second Q-learning generates a virtual scheduling process, which selects the remaining nodes to ensure the decrease of network packet loss rate by nearly 30%.

9.4.4 Collision-Free Scheduling Mechanism

The major problems associated with the usage of drones are battery management, collision avoidance routing and failure of multitasking. To minimize the coverage time of fixed wing drones having image sensors [25], the graphical based MILP modeling approach [6, 35] is used by ignoring battery limitation problem. MILP aka mixed integer linear program is responsible for event scheduling and assignment in every iteration and a simple Dijkstra algorithm helps in finding the shortest trajectory path of each vehicle. The designed framework accepts many events accruing at different time instants and lasts for some period within the time horizon. Assume the discretized time slots are happening a k = 1,..., k with different lengths. Apart from this, charging station is used to recharge UAV batteries.

The Daily instructions like leaving time, arrival time, and trajectory can be provided to UAVs to avoid collision risk or drained batteries as shown in Figure 9.4.

Let D denotes number of drones flying at same fixed altitude or height (h_e,) with a limited battery capacity B_d and an average speed V_d, where d = 1,..., D. E denotes no. of events in 3 different locations (l_{one}, l_{ate}, h_e), with duration P_e, and starting time instants Te where e = 1,..., E and E + 1 is the event of charging station which makes the fleet of drones to charge their powers to P^{ch}. Let the drone executes the event with P_s^d and power

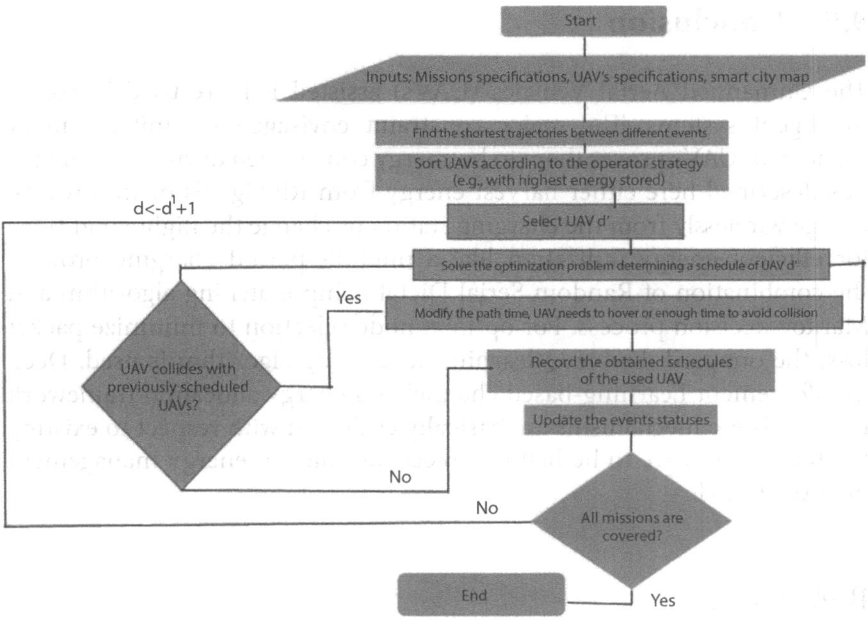

Figure 9.4 Flowchart for CFS mechanism.

consumed by the drone during waiting time to avoid collision is P_W^d. The detailed flowchart summarizes all the procedure of the discussed iterative algorithm by employing the technique of dimensional reduction and safe navigation procedure as follows:

1. The algorithm starts by applying Dijkstra algorithm to the location map to find the shortest path trajectory.
2. In the first iteration, Drones are Assigned to particular Task or event based on the constraints like battery level, distance of coverage and speed.
3. Optimization algorithm MILP to maximize the coverage times and minimize the energy consumption of events.
4. Similarly, the second drone will be assigned from remaining events and employs the same optimization technique.
5. In the next step algorithm compares task scheduling time of both drones and checks for collision. If it predicts that both drones will collide at time T_C sec, then solver automatically hover the lower priority event drone for H_d sec and their new flying times are updated in the data base.

9.5 Conclusion

The Unmanned Aerial Vehicles (UAVs) assisted IoT are used in recent intelligent systems. The major constraint envisaged is limited battery capacity of UAVs proves them to be energy constrained devices. The methods described here either harvest energy from RF Signals or mm waves, charge wirelessly from the charging station or change the flight conditions for efficient energy utilization like a multiple-period charging process, the combination of Random Serial Dictatorship matching algorithm and Markov decision process. For optimal node selection to minimize packet loss, the onboard double Q-learning scheduling algorithm is used. Deep Reinforcement Learning-based channel and energy allocation framework is used. These mechanisms are basically evaluated with respect to existing methods and prove to be better choices for efficient energy management of UAVs in IoT.

References

1. Su, C., Ye, F., Wang, L.-C., Wang, L., Tian, Y., Han, Z., UAV-Assisted Wireless Charging for Energy-Constrained IoT Devices Using Dynamic Matching. *IEEE*, 2327–4662, (c), 1–12, 2019.
2. Li, K., Ni, W., Wei, B., Tovar, E., Onboard Double Q-learning for Airborne Data Capture in Wireless Powered IoT Networks. *IEEE*, 2576–3156, (c), 1–5, 2020.
3. Cao, Y., Zhang, L., Liang, Y.-C., Deep Reinforcement Learning for Channel and Power Allocation in UAV-enabled IoT Systems. *IEEE*, ©2019.
4. Lin, X., Su, G., Chen, B., Wang, H., Dai, M., Striking a Balance Between System Throughput and Energy Efficiency for UAV-IoT Systems. *IEEE Internet Things J.*, 6, 6, 10519–10533, December 2019.
5. Liu, W., Si, P., Sun, E., Li, M., Fang, C., Zhang, Y., Green Mobility Management in UAV-Assisted IoT Based on Dueling DQN. *IEEE*, ©2019.
6. Abedin, S.F., Alam, M.G.R., Kazmi, S.A., Tran, N.H., Niyato, D., Hong, C.S., Resource allocation for ultra-reliable and enhanced mobile broadband IoT applications in fog network. *IEEE Trans. Commun.*, 67, 1, 489–502, January 2019.
7. Cui, L., Xu, C., Yang, S., Huang, J.Z., Li, J., Wang, X., Ming, Z., Lu, N., Joint optimization of energy consumption and latency in mobile edge computing for Internet of Things. *IEEE Internet Things J.*, 6, 3, 4791–4803, June 2019.
8. Li, L., Xu, Y., Zhang, Z., Yin, J., Chen, W., Han, Z., A prediction based charging policy and interference mitigation approach in the wireless powered Internet of Things. *IEEE J. Sel. Areas Commun.*, 37, 2, 439–451, February 2019.

9. Ramezani, P., Zeng, Y., Jamalipour, A., Optimal resource allocation for multi-user Internet of Things network with single wireless-powered relay. *IEEE Internet Things J.*, 6, 2, 3132–3142, April 2019.
10. Zeng, Y. and Zhang, R., Energy-Efficient UAV Communication With Trajectory Optimization. *IEEE Trans. Wireless Commun.*, 16, 6, 3747–3760, 2017.
11. Cetinkaya, O., Balsamo, D., Merrett, G.V., Internet of MIMO Things: UAV-Assisted Wireless-Powered Networks for Future Smart Cities. *IEEE Internet Things Mag.*, 8–13, March 2020.
12. Hassija, V., Chamola, V., Nanda Gopala Krishna, D., Guizani, M., A Distributed Framework for Energy Trading Between UAVs and Charging Stations for Critical Applications. *IEEE*, pp. 1–12, 2019, 0018-9545 (c).
13. Tan, Z., Qu, H., Ren, G., Wang, W., UAV-aided Sustainable Communication in Cellular IoT System with Hybrid Energy Harvesting. *2019 4th International Conference on Smart and Sustainable Technologies (SpliTech)*, Split, Croatia, pp. 1–6, 2019.
14. Luo, Y., Hong, P., Su, R., Xue, K., Resource Allocation for Energy Harvesting-Powered D2D Communication Underlaying Cellular Networks. *IEEE Trans. Veh. Technol.*, 66, 11, 10486–10498, November 2017.
15. Wang, L., Chen, S., Pedram, M., Power Management of Cache Enabled Cooperative Base Stations Towards Zero Grid Energy. *2018 IEEE International Conference on Communications (ICC)*, Kansas City, MO, pp. 1–6, 2018.
16. Ye, H.-T., Kang, X., Liang, Y.-C., Joung, J., Full-Duplex Wireless-Powered IoT Networks With Unmanned Aerial Vehicle. *ICTC*, IEEE, pp. 124–129, 2018.
17. Park, J., Lee, H., Eom, S., Lee, I., Minimum throughput maximization in UAV-aided wireless powered communication networks, arXiv preprint arXiv:1801.02781, January 2018.
18. Xie, L., Xu, J., Zhang, R., Throughput Maximization for UAV-Enabled Wireless Powered Communication Networks. *IEEE Internet Things J.*, 6, 2, 1690–1703, April 2019.
19. Xu, J., Zeng, Y., Zhang, R., UAV-Enabled Wireless Power Transfer: Trajectory Design and Energy Region Characterization. *2017 IEEE Globecom Workshops (GC Wkshps)*, Singapore, December 2017, pp. 1–7.
20. Kang, X., Liang, Y., Yang, J., Riding on the Primary: A New Spectrum Sharing Paradigm for Wireless-Powered IoT Devices. *IEEE Trans. Wireless Commun.*, 17, 9, 6335–6347, Sept. 2018.
21. Zhang, H., Huang, S., Jiang, C., Long, K., Leung, V.C.M., Poor, H.V., Energy Efficient User Association and Power Allocation in Millimeter-Wave-Based Ultra Dense Networks with Energy Harvesting Base Stations. *IEEE J. Sel. Areas Commun.*, 35, 9, 1936–1947, September 2017.

22. Song, Q., Jin, S., Zheng, F., Completion Time and Energy Consumption Minimization for UAV-Enabled Multicasting. *IEEE Wireless Commun. Lett.*, 8, 3, 821–824, June 2019.
23. Zeng, Y. and Zhang, R., Energy-Efficient UAV Communication with Trajectory Optimization. *IEEE Trans. Wireless Commun.*, 16, 6, 3747–3760, June 2017.
24. Mozaffari, M., Saad, W., Bennis, M., Debbah, M., Mobile Unmanned Aerial Vehicles (UAVs) for Energy-Efficient Internet of Things Communications. *IEEE Trans. Wireless Commun.*, 16, 11, 7574–7589, November 2017.
25. Cetinkaya, O. and Merrett, G.V., Efficient Deployment of UAV-Powered Sensors for Optimal Coverage and Connectivity. *Proceedings of IEEE Wireless Communication and Networks Conference*, April 2020.
26. Cetinkaya, O., Dinc, E., Koca, C., Merrett, G.V., Akan, O.B., Energy-Neutral Wireless-Powered Networks. *IEEE Wireless Commun. Lett.*, 8, 5, 1373–1376, October 2019.
27. Zhao, N., Zhang, S., Yu, F.R., Chen, Y., Nallanathan, A., Leung, V.C.M., Exploiting Interference for Energy Harvesting: A Survey, Research Issues, and Challenges. *IEEE Access*, 5, 10403–10421, 2017.
28. Long, T., Ozger, M., Cetinkaya, O., Akan, O.B., Energy Neutral Internet of Drones. *IEEE Commun. Mag.*, 56, 1, 22–28, January 2018.
29. Tang, F., Kawamoto, Y., Kato, N., Liu, J., Future Intelligent and Secure Vehicular Network Toward 6G: Machine-Learning Approaches. *Proc. IEEE*, 108, 2, 292–307, February 2020.
30. Hassija, V., Saxena, V., Chamola, V., Scheduling drone charging for multi-drone network based on consensus time-stamp and game theory. *Comput. Commun.*, 149, 51–61, 2020, https://doi.org/10.1016/j.comcom.2019.09.021.
31. Mohindru, V. and Singh, Y., Node authentication algorithm for securing static wireless sensor networks from node clone attack. *Int. J. Inf. Comput. Secur.*, 10, 2–3, 129–148, 2018.
32. Mohindru, V. and Singh, Y., Performance analysis of message authentication algorithms in wireless sensor networks, in: *2017 4th International Conference on Signal Processing, Computing and Control (ISPCC)*, 2017, September, IEEE, pp. 468–472.
33. Mohindru, V., Bhatt, R., Singh, Y., Reauthentication scheme for mobile wireless sensor networks. *Sustainable Comput.: Inf. Syst.*, 23, 158–166, 2019.
34. Mohindru, V., Singh, Y., Bhatt, R., Securing wireless sensor networks from node clone attack: A lightweight message authentication algorithm. *Int. J. Inf. Comput. Secur.*, 12, 2–3, 217–233, 2020.
35. Mohindru, V., Singh, Y., Bhatt, R., Hybrid cryptography algorithm for securing wireless sensor networks from Node Clone Attack. *Recent Adv. Electr. Electron. Eng. (Formerly Recent Patents Electrical & Electronic Engineering)*, 13, 2, 251–259, 2020.

10

A Survey on IoE-Enabled Unmanned Aerial Vehicles

K. Siddharthraju†, R. Dhivyadevi*†, M. Supriya, B. Jaishankar and Shanmugaraja T.

Department of Electronics and Communication Engineering, KPR Institute of Engineering and Technology, Coimbatore, India

Abstract

The new developments in communication technologies have expanded the Internet of Things to the Internet of Everything (IoE), with many captivating possibilities for the future, where every 'thing' is connected to the internet providing intelligent decision making and enhanced services. The IoE is an inclusive network of people, data, process, and IoT. The main challenges faced by IoE are the limited network resources and network coverage constraints. The implementation of IoE includes technical innovations in multi-disciplinary domains like low power communication, data analytics, sensor-based embedded systems and data storage technologies. In recent decades, the advanced technological innovations open the way for the building the required optimum technologies in implementing IoE. Similarly, a significant technology drift in Unmanned Aerial Vehicles (UAVs) with low cost, high mobility and flexible deployments has capabilities to conquer the challenges faced in IoE. This article presents an inclusive survey on challenges and opportunities of IoE enabled UAVs. The review of technologies enabling this opportunities such as battery constraint, security issues, computing and coverage constraints are addressed with an overview of UAVs. Finally the IoE enabled UAV technology is studied by UAVs' deployment and mobility with IoE's intelligence, scalability and diversity.

**Corresponding author*: dhivyadevi.r@kpriet.ac.in
†*Equal contribution as first author*

Vandana Mohindru, Yashwant Singh, Ravindara Bhatt and Anuj Kumar Gupta (eds.) Unmanned Aerial Vehicles for Internet of Things (IoT): Concepts, Techniques, and Applications, (173–192) © 2021 Scrivener Publishing LLC

***Keywords*:** Internet of Things, Internet of Everything, unmanned aerial vehicles, multi-UAV ad hoc networks, edge intelligence

10.1 Introduction

The Internet of All (IoE) links the internet with a smart service and assists with decision-making. The realization of IoE depends on the adaptability of the low power consumption techniques [1], selection of smart sensors, embedded technologies and data analytics with reliability. The new innovations and ground breaking technologies in recent decades strengthened the infrastructure required to implement IoE in all sectors. Initially, the advance research in sensor technology and in smart embedded systems leads to low power consuming sensor nodes and with more portability. The Low Power Wide Area Network (LPWAN) opened the doors for the Low Power IoT (LP-IoT) nodes. Further emergence of AI and huge data leads to intelligent IoT which find its applications in various sectors such as, smart agriculture, intelligent transportation system, smart factories, and intelligent environment monitoring systems [28]. As envisioned by Cisco technologies, the IoT is the future of internet and it depends on four pillars such as people, data, process and things.

In comparison, IoT includes only the 'stuff' pillar. Obviously, IoE increases IoT's connection power to support automatic and human-driven processes. IoE is more informative in contrast to IoT, which means that it improves people's lives by allowing streamlined and informed business and market processes.

To that end, IoE is dedicated to three prior principles: 1) scalability to create flexible network infrastructure with omnipresent coverage; 2) intelligency to facilitate good decisions and activities for all IoE devices; 3) diversity to be enabled in a range of applications. Consequently, IoE's implementation depends fundamentally on satisfying these three expectations. Eventually, the recent advancements of ICT technologies leads to enhanced WSNs with self-organized network topologies, 4G–5G [30] mobile networks which supports M2M(machine to Machine) communications, and Low power WANs (LP-WAN) in power constraint sensor networks. These technology shifts in the IoT networks, enhanced the data generation of the smart networks leading to huge collection of data, which in collaboration with AI address wide variety of applications such as, intelligent recognition, intelligent management and intelligent decision. Thus, the traditional IoT technology is extended as IoE which powers intelligent systems such as, smart grid, smart meter, intelligent traffic scheduling, smart agriculture, smart factories, etc. The IoE technology is highly scalable and the wireless communication networks such as LPWAN, WSN and 5G mobile communication networks can be realized using this technology. The IoE network intelligence can be improved by artificial Intelligence and big data analysis. Although IoE is implemented in a wide range of applications, IoE technology has few limitations which limit its application in various sectors such as privacy and security threats, network coverage limitations and Battery power constraints of the IoE sensor nodes. Initially the low computation capable sensor networks are prone to potential security threats such as forging malicious relay sensor nodes or eavesdropping of the nodes. Secondly, the network infrastructures with restricted deployment leads to coverage constrained scenarios due to remote and harsh geographical areas. Thus an efficient IoE network cannot be established. Further, IoE powered nodes faces portability and power backup considerations due to limited cost constraints. These nodes may lead to frequent disconnections since they may get exhaust due to limited battery power. Even though the IoE-enabled nodes suffer from network coverage in remote areas, they perform efficiently in local sensor data computation. Further, the protocols such as LPWAN and NB-IoT access protocols are exposes to security threats like malicious relay nodes forging or eavesdropping network information due to simplification. Inorder to address these problems, IoE nodes requires an elastic deployment and flexible coverage.

The industrial and academic communities started experimenting Unmanned Aerial Vehicles (UAVs) in addressing the IoE short comes due to their high mobility, flexible and elastic services. The UAVs can extend the deployment constrains and the can improve the coverage hurdles faced in IoE networks. Further these low-altitude UAVs enable quick deployment, extended network coverage due to reconfiguration flexibility and capacity makes its superior compared to satellite communication and other terrestrial network communications. These UAVs opened various IoE applications due their high mobility, flexible deployments and extended coverage such as military medical evacuation, marine mammals monitoring and agriculture management. These applications also pose new challenges such as precise control, flexible network topology, light weight intelligent algorithms and dynamic network connection. Further these challenges should be addressed using dedicated communication protocol design, UAVs trajectory optimization techniques [27, 31, 32], flexible and quick resource allocation systems, and scalable intelligent algorithms for IoE networks.

Extensive surveys expose the inadequate research in three major aspects of the IoE networks such as scalability, intelligence and diversity. This limited research is the motivation behind the exploration of IoE enabled technologies and its potential applications powered by UAVs. This chapter discusses three main contributions of the surveys for the proposed Ue-IoE networks such as, i) summarizing and reviewing the enabling technologies based on the key expectations of IoE which includes scalability, intelligence, and diversity, ii) exploring the UAV enabled IoE applications and its enabling technologies, and iii) adaptability of UAVs technology in the present IoE powered technologies.

10.2 Overview of Internet of Everything

The key IoE assumptions in Section 10.2.2 of this section are explored in Section 10.2.3 and the future technologies for meeting expectations, and the problems raised by IoE networks are discussed in Section 10.2.4.

10.2.1 Emergence of IoE

The rise of IoT is without a doubt a critical incitement to create the IoE concepts. The term IoT, implies interfacing electrical or electronic gadgets with changing sizes and abilities to the World Wide Web. Lately, fundamentally concentrating on the communications associated with M2M, IoT technology has quickly evolved in an expansive range of varied interfacing protocols, network and its applications. Such empowering IoT environments pose a strong establishment for the IoE's networks with ubiquitous connection and broad coverage.

Further, the real concepts behind the IoE [16] emergence are the automated machines powered by ubiquitous Internet, artificial intelligence and big data processing. By 2012, CISCO introduced four columns such as individuals, information, cycle, and things. This view demonstrates that IoE considers an extensive interconnection of "things" yet in addition "automated and people based cycle" (i.e., smart devices/machines). This concept goes a long ways past the IoT's classification of simple interconnection of "things" (i.e., actual pure machines/gadgets).

Moreover, the proliferation of big data and artificial intelligence invites new bricks for IoE's development. Recent research exhibits the IoE's ability to exploit AI technologies in collecting big data from internet and empower the pure machines/device with automation (Intelligence) abilities. Further, these IoE-enabled devices have the ability to collect real-time data from millions of connected devices to enable automated intelligence through intelligent proactive decision making ability. However the realization of IoE is in its initial stage of development. Although there was a huge challenge in IoE realization, the alluring vision of IoE will never keep us from executing IoE.

10.2.2 Expectation of IoE

IoE's core agenda is to interconnect omnipresent, Internet-based mobile devices that are used as terminal nodes in order to gather and interpret massive data to provide ground-breaking, insightful applications. This vision of IoE can be realized by fulfilling three key expectations of IoE such as, 1) Scalability—highly scalable network architecture for uninterrupted coverage; 2) Intelligence—to deliver intelligent decisions with global computation facility; and 3) Diversity—to act as an enabling platform to design diverse real-time applications.

The three expectations of IoE and its relative technologies are illustrated in Figure 10.1. These three IoE expectations are discussed as follows.

10.2.2.1 Scalability

It represents a scalable network which covers everything at everywhere elastically. IoE with the given scalability can satisfy various geographical scenarios such as rural, urban, aerial, underwater and space. This level of scalability can be achieved through massive access, wide network coverage and ubiquitous connection of the IoE networks. Further to achieve these scalable networks, several communication technologies and network topologies are integrated. The scalable IoE networks enhance data

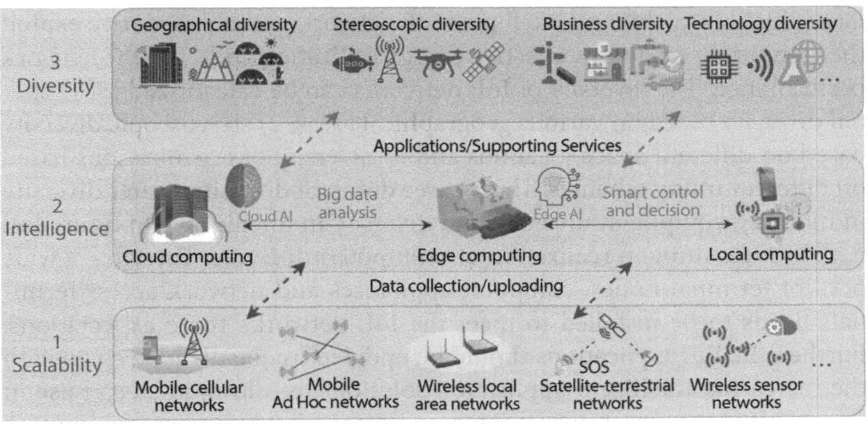

Figure 10.1 Three expectations of IoE.

collection at physical layer and acts as source of big data for intelligent analytics [23–25]. The communication networks lies underneath includes, Wireless Local Area Networks (WLAN), Mobile communication networks, WSNs, Mobile Adhoc Networks and Satellite networks.

10.2.2.2 Intelligence

It represents imparting intelligence in data prediction, analysis [16], decision and the actions performed on all the connected IoE devices that lie at the top of the highly scalable distributed computing facility. To be precise, the IoE networks should be capable of collecting huge data from its wide and large scalable connected devices and extract the potential information from the data collected and use them for generating intelligent control or action on everything and everywhere. These collected IoE data are stored in distributed databases and in various storage systems where the processing algorithms extract valuable information. The data processing algorithms at the storage and distributed databases includes, descriptive, predictive, diagnostic and prescriptive analytical models, essential to cater different IoE intelligent applications. Further, with the distributed computing facility, there are various categories of intelligence are considered in an IoE applications such as local (terminal nodes) network intelligence, edge intelligence and cloud (remote storage) intelligence to cater global intelligence.

10.2.2.3 Diversity

It represents the IoE applications that enable "automated and people-based processes". In order to realize the IoE diverse applications, it is essential to have a highly scalable and intelligent IoE network to enable security, exploit the computing capability, effective energy utilization and cater the network performance. The diversity of IoE networks can be categorized as: 1) spatial diversity based on various geographical areas, 2) stereoscopic diversity based on different space locations and 3) diversity of organizations based on different utility schemes. These three different diversities cater diversity in mobility, equipment diversity and diversity in intelligence in future IoE networks resulting in realization of omnipotent IoE role. Therefore a wide pool of terminal nodes, computer appliances and network access terminals needs to be installed to meet the IoE network's three expectations. Further, the IoE applications should be updated frequently to keep up with the increasing intelligent application solutions, resulting in steep raise in the resource consumptions (storage, energy and battery power, computing capability) to establish a diverse IoE services.

10.2.3 Possible Technologies

10.2.3.1 Enabling Scalability

The technologies which enable the three expectations of the IoE can be classified into three types as follows, Backbone communication (Global), Limb communication (Local) and Capillary communication (Point-to-point) as shown in Figure 10.2.

The backbone of IoE embraces long-distance wireless technology that stretch the network's reach for decades. The communication technologies which enable the requirements are Low Power Wide Area Networks (LP-WANs) and Mobile Communication Networks (MCN). In order to access the backbone network, IoE terminal nodes use MCN networking technologies, including 2G, 3G, 4G-LTE and 5G-beyond [20, 33]. In comparison, LPWAN networking systems support low power solutions for broad-based IoE networks. Hence, the MCN supports IoE terminal with sufficient power back up and LPWANs supports IoE nodes with limited battery backup deployed in a wide area. This two communication technologies, complement each other and establish an efficient backbone communication technology for IoE.

The Limb communication technologies on the other hand support dynamic local networks with coverage ranging from few hundred meters. The enabling communication technologies are LP Bluetooth, Zigbee,

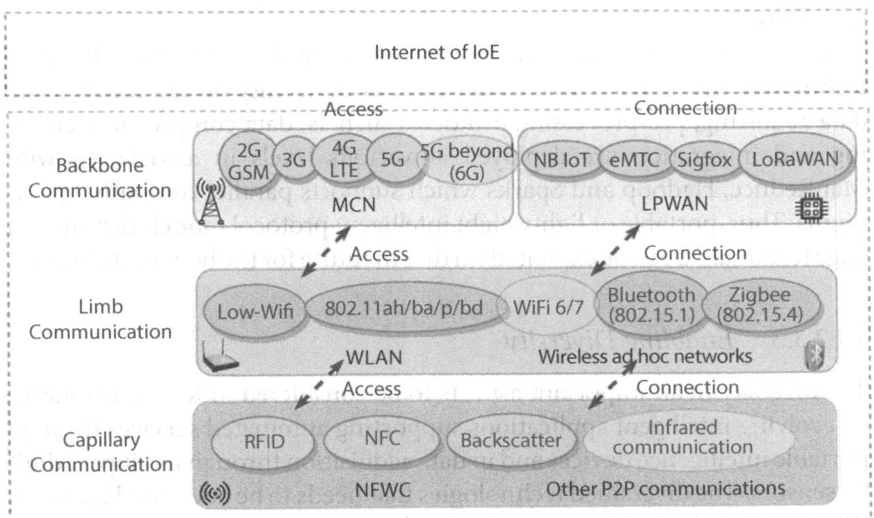

Figure 10.2 IoE scalability enhancing communication technologies.

WLAN, Z-wave, 802.11ah and 6LoWPAN [15, 19]. These technologies are used widely in Wireless Body Area Networks (WBAN), Wireless Sensor Networks (WSNs) and Wireless PANs deployed in industrial process monitoring, medical health monitoring, indoor localization, etc.

The third communication technologies which supports low cost point to point connection in IoE terminal is Capillary communication. The capillary communication technologies are supported by Near Field Wireless Communication technologies (NFWC) which includes, Radio Frequency Identification (RFID), Back Scattering, and NFC. The communication takes places between small tags to readers fixed at points to collect the data to be transmitted to the server.

10.2.3.2 Enabling Intelligence

Several intelligent protocol models and data treatment algorithms in the distributed computing facility are introduced in order to provide information in IoE. The computational facility includes, local IoT terminals, Edge servers, and cloud (remote) servers, where these facilities are inter connected through the backbone, limb and capillary communication technologies. The IoE global intelligence can be achieved through cloud servers which supports massive storage and data having computations. The edge servers support less computational tasks which include encryption, data preprocessing and compression techniques. The IoE local nodes supports limited computing and storage tasks such as local privacy sensitive tasks and context aware data processing.

To bridge the gap between the intelligence and computation, big data techniques play a major role in the computing facility on the IoE. During data acquiring, pre-processing protocols such as, data compression, cleaning and integration are deployed at various levels in association with MapReduce, Hadoop and Sparks which supports parallel computing paradigms. Thus, portable or lightweight intelligent protocol models deployed at edge terminals are to be exploited further in future for the better intelligence.

10.2.3.3 Enabling Diversity

The diversity in an important aspects to be considered in IoE which inhibits evolving intelligent applications supporting automated services through portable intelligence devices and in data acquisition through intelligent digital sensors. The diversified technologies that needs to be addressed includes, sensing technologies, computing technologies, embedded devices, communication networks, AI algorithms and data preprocessing algorithms.

10.2.4 Challenges of IoE

The three technological capabilities expand the IoE to include scalability, intelligence and diversity, but also pose a range of future obstacles in real time. The four major aspects that pose challenge to the IoE implementation are, Network coverage, battery constraint, computing capability and security threats [10–12, 34].

10.2.4.1 Coverage Constraint

To establish a ubiquitous connectivity with coverage in harsh and rural geographical areas is a difficult task. These areas in general are referred to as coverage-constrained areas. The demand for data communication in these areas are low and hence investing advanced and sophisticated systems is of no use and will not be a cost effective. Therefore, an efficient flexible and low cost system should be deployed for this dynamic on-demand network particularly for these coverage-constraint areas.

10.2.4.2 Battery Constraint

The battery constraint is a major tradeoff in IoE efficiency. These IoE terminals/nodes are power limited due to their limited battery backup. The reason for limited battery back is to keep the cost low and to reduce the overall node weight to support portability. In general, the IoE terminals have limited battery or with no power terminals in pushing the data to the IoE network infrastructure. The major challenge is to handle the terminals in a coverage-constraint areas where a lot of connection lost problem arise. These nodes get drained often and get disconnected from the IoE infrastructure leading to data loses. Therefore, it is necessary to identify a sustainable source of energy for these battery constraint IoE terminals/nodes.

10.2.4.3 Computing Constraint

This limitation happens when local terminal nodes are not able to measure smart local algorithms. These low computational nodes usually transit the local data to the remote cloud servers [1, 3] which computes intelligence centrally for processing big data. This leads to latency in data processing and transmission and post a severe threat for the latency-sensitive applications in future. This data processing also adds burden to the cloud servers and leading to congestion in the backbone communication network posing data privacy threats. Inorder to mitigate this computation constraint, the local and edge resources [13, 35] should be utilized fullest to enable intelligent.

10.2.4.4 Security Constraint

The IoE terminals handle large data locally and transmit to the remote server for computation and pose a series security threats since it employs simple security protocols to avoid network cost. To reduce the security threats in network, an effective and easy to deploy security mechanism should be modeled to avoid forging and eavesdropping attacks and to protect the IoE communications.

Therefore inorder to overcome these challenges, the following measure are to be considered for an effective IoE communication,

1. Enhance extended network coverage, flexible and dynamic recoverable networks should be modeled.
2. Enhance the battery power to keep the IoE terminals/nodes active for a long duration, an appropriate sustainable energy source should be identified.
3. Improve the computing capability at the local and edge nodes by utilizing the network resources and schedule the computational tasks accordingly.
4. Model a robust and easy security algorithm to protect the data from malicious attacks.

These challenges can be optimized by UAV technology [2], which is capable of providing optimum solutions for the challenges faced by the IoE networks. The UAVs with enormous on-demand deployment, flexibility and diversity can support edge intelligence, sustainable power, physical security and extended coverage to the IoE network.

10.3 Overview of Unmanned Aerial Vehicle (UAV)

The UAV technology with its enormous intelligent services gained momentum in both industry and academia in recent decades. This boundless application of UAVs relies on the maneuverability technologies. The maneuverability techniques such as obstacle avoiding and flight trajectory optimization are employed to control the UAVs. The following section discusses the UAS—Section 10.3.1 of the Unmanned Aircraft System and UAV communications—Section 10.3.2.

10.3.1 Unmanned Aircraft System (UAS)

The UAS supports several UAV applications with cooperated control services which includes, tasks scheduling, information processing and fight control, etc. A typical UAS has three major units, i) unmanned Aerial Vehicles, ii) a control station/ground based controller and iii) communication link between UAVs and the ground station. The UAVs flight controlling mechanism and its task allocation is managed by the UAS. The ground control station plays a crucial role in takeoff and landing of the large UAVs. The ground control system is integrated onboard on a autonomous flight mode with a onboard task allocation in UAVs and thus the UAS is considered to be the whole autonomous UAV in this case. The ground station tracks the flight and the mission assignment for small UAVs and therefore its flight portfolio is limited to the contact spectrum between the ground and UAV stations. Relevant software such as automated monitoring [14] and automatic surveillance [18] as well as video surveillance [5–7, 17], etc. are planned for the UAVs and their corresponding UAS. There are three aspects that should be considered in designing a UAS system, which includes UAVs design, design of the ground station and design of the communication links.

10.3.2 UAV Communication Networks

The UAVs mobility and the range of operation depend on the communication network which offers stable communication link between a UAV and the ground station or between UAVs. There are two major classifications of communication networks utilized in the UAVs: Ad Hoc Multi-UAV networks and UAV-aided communication networks.

10.3.2.1 Ad Hoc Multi-UAV Networks

The Multi-UAV Adhoc network is known for its autonomy and it does not depend on the traditional incumbent mobile networks [2, 4]. The Multi-UAV Adhoc networks primarily support communication link performance of A2A [29] among UAVs, which includes interaction and uninterrupted connectivity. The high mobility of the UAVs leads to an unstable channel quality of A2A communication links and thus demands a dynamic network topology. This dynamic network topology is supported by dynamic routing protocols [21, 22, 36] and optimization of UAVs trajectory.

10.3.2.2 UAV-Aided Communication Networks

UAV-assisted communications networks are infrastructure-based topology that differs from self-organized architecture, relying on (multi UAV ad hoc networks) prior network access points. Also, UAVs with different functions can be implanted at edge nodes for flying base points, relay nodes or terminal nodes. UAV-assisted networking networks seek to provide complex connectivity capabilities in the field of missing links to incumbent communications networks. In this case, the UAVs perform the part of the transmission/terminal nodes, which attach to the dissociated nodes and create connections. However, functional circumstances confront contingent factors like disconnected node locations and multiple communication protocols. All the variables are not defined to maximize the flight path of the UAVs. The optimization needs specialized scenarios to be designed specifically. UAV tracking is allowed as an instance in which UAV flying trajectory needs to satisfy mobile connectivity, such as UAV mobile contact systems A2G/G2A connections. In this case, the objective of UAV's parameter evaluation is to ensure coverage of the task area while preserving network interconnections. UAV-assisted communication networks typically include most studies in optimizing the UAV route.

Two key concerns are discussed in UAV studies: one is the study of the UAS to ensure regulated UAV versatile and one is to analyze UAV communication mechanisms in order to make sure that they are compliant (including A2A contacts and A2G/G2A links compatible). These two issues are related to the common mobility of the UAV research goal (i.e. trajectory optimization). UAVs are providing IoE-enablement possibilities in conjunction with latest Unmanned Aerial Studies. The integration of UAVs and IoE in the next section will be discussed.

10.4 UAV and IoE Integration

UAVs can be utilized to fill in as flying base stations, jammers, screens, edge figuring workers, power providers, and declaimers for IoE. UAVs offer an answer for satisfy three desire for IoE with arrangement of broadened inclusion, adaptable knowledge, and assorted applications. In this area, we initially research the open doors for applying UAVs in IoE.

10.4.1 Possibilities to Carry UAVs

With great speed and adaptability, UAVs can overcome the four IoE constraints in a profound way. UAVs carry in four IoE incentives, i.e. omnipresent links, aerial intelligence, communications self-maintenance, sensor capacity and deployment.

10.4.1.1 *Widespread Connectivity*

Widespread communications are a must for IoE to protect and link all anywhere. Adaptable UAV communication programs can help IoE expand its scope and thus achieve omnipresent connectivity. As defined in Section 10.4.1, UAVs can expand the communication network via UAV aided communications networks to areas with poor connections; Areas without internet services can be improved by multi-UAV ad hoc network connections by UAVs. Accordingly, it can achieve universal relations.

10.4.1.2 *Environmentally Aware*

By gathering the information and then executing intelligent algorithms, UAVs would allow aerial intelligence. Surround data is accessed either from the UAV itself or from a series of antennas. The clever strategies are designed to satisfy many criteria, such as individual alert systems, integrated aero plane leap activity modification and data collection. So UAVs can enable a lot of smart aerial application areas.

10.4.1.3 *Peer-Maintenance of Communications*

UAVs could even individual training maintenance for IoE communication systems. Due to multiple volatile influences either from the city or environmental systems, some IoE modules are rapidly decomposed and even dropped. So IoE is approaching the threat of breaking connections. UAVs can be dispatched to redeploy IoE nodes to fix this problem, in attempt to reestablish the missing connections.

Furthermore, through IoE communications are vulnerable to malware such as checking up and scripting threats. These risks in extremely sensitive interactions can result in massive financial harms, as they can lead to errors in intelligent development or smart networks. UAVs can be used as helpful jammers in this respect to form a defensive shield for IoE's physical contact.

10.4.1.4 *Detector Control and Reusing*

UAVs can be cross-configured to control sensors and re-use them, making IoE more powerful. The small resource IoE nodes are energy-saving and can then be disabled extremely quickly. This influence not only contributes to a great deal of waste but also to high pollution. By paying the energy to IoE nodes, UAVs may cause this waste or smog. UAVs may pay for these nodes with WTP and will at times have the potential to exchange wireless data and electricity particularly, through SWIPT. Furthermore, UAVs may recycle or put degraded nodes or sensors on network devices with disabled feature.

10.4.2 UAV-Enabled IoE

Empowered by the possibilities that UAVs offer to IoE, we should extend UAVs comprehensively to enhance the functionality of IoE. We are dealing with an IoE approach for vehicle detection that satisfies three IoE expectations (in short, Ue IoE within this article). We will typically develop Ue-IoE according to three strategies for the three goals, i.e., IoE scalability enabled by UAV, IoE competence facilitated by UAV, and IoE variability enabled by UAV.

10.4.3 Vehicle Detection Enabled IoE Optimization

UAVs will allow the Scalable IoE to cover and connect anything everywhere by working with established networks I Wireless, MCN, LPWAN, satellite) UAVs. By enhancing the current IoE network into two major types of fields, UAVs will expand IoE's coverage.

10.4.3.1 Weak-Connected Locations

In general, these regions are protected by current networks, such as WLAN, MCN and LPWAN; however, they are still in a poor connectivity state because of a dynamic geological landscape (for example obstacles) and a hostile atmosphere. Four different regions [26] are urban construction sites, urban tragedy areas, city blind spots coverage and road transport. Such regions are riddled with different obstructions, leading in unreliable wireless connections with established APs between the above areas.

A multi-faceted network of UAV-assisted communication networks can help to overcome this problem. UAVs could also hold IoE nodes on demand as relay nodes or connection points or gateways. In addition, the barriers can be removed, especially in complex geographic environments, with lots-like A2G or A2A connections.

10.4.3.2 Regions with Low Network Support

These areas are usually narrow and low in population. Therefore no channel infrastructures in such areas are deployed. Four typical areas are plantations, mountains, forest, and coastlines. Two communication schemes are necessary to cover these regions: 1) creating a separate infrastructure for each particular location, and 2) designing a model which supports the isolated networks to communicate with the existing network.

10.5 Open Research Issues

To realize the UAV enabled IoE, there are several issues to be addressed. There are lot of on research issues in this UAV enabled IoE networks. The most prominent among them includes

1. To optimize the resource allocation and utilization inorder to enhance the network performance
2. UAVs security models and its legal adaptations
3. Modeling an lightweight Artificial Intelligent algorithm to support UAVs autonomy
4. Optimizing a general framework to support Ue–IoE heterogeneous applications
5. Devising a common facility for various computations at cloud servers [8, 9], edge devices and UAVs

Thus these five potential research areas has huge scope in the future [23] of UAV-enabled IoE.

10.6 Discussion

10.6.1 Resource Allocation

All the node (including ground stations, UAVs, terminal nodes) could improve service availability and reduce the cost through fair allocation of resources (allocating resources containing energy supply, data Storage, and computing capacity). In the future, resource distribution rules can be separated into two categories: global resource allotment (i.e. number of nodes and usage or nodes in IoE) and local resource assignment (i.e., each of IoE's dedicated hardware settings). On the one hand, the global division of capital relies on high cost savings of time, electricity and facilities worldwide.

In UAV-enabled IoE, the globally effective use of IoE equipment including edge systems, cloud service and UAV can be streamlined, although the global performance can be increased by networking and video decoding in the optical media transmission scenario at IoE. On the other hand, the distribution of local services stresses the basic utility in each task such as communications, computing and data storage in the form of power, data rate, communication time, data storage and device computation, complexity, communications time and computational functions.

For example an appropriate data collection algorithm can be applied in a local network scenario to increase the local data speed (such as in a smart building). The energy management framework is also invaluable to optimize limited-energy performance for flying terminals—UAVs/drones. In short, the same principle still extends to various resource utilization methods i.e., the principle on call, to satisfy the anticipated criteria and manage resource usage at different nodes.

10.6.2 Universal Standard Design

A universal IoE standard must be built to orchestrate several heterogeneous ICT and various IoE applications. In addition to lowering usage costs, Universalized Ue-IoE also improves serve efficacy. The IoE universal norm should also include the rules for each IoE layer for an Open System Interconnection (OSI) network layer model (i.e., a physical layer, network layer, and application layer). In these three levels, IoE can have three elements in terms of functional generality: Universal end node networking chips, universal protocols for network management and universal processing units.

But existing studies only consider hardware for communications at end nodes, such as NB-IoT, MTC and LoRa-WAN [37]. The hardware is only usable at endnotes. In comparison, SDN integration will accomplish the uniform network protocols, but no overall scheme has been presented. By combining local, edge and cloud computing facilities together you will achieve the universal computing facility. The convergence of the three machine types can be accomplished by creating a high-level GUI to connect the computing resources.

10.6.3 Security Mechanism

The allergic IoE contact is expected to take place against security problems, such as communication (or telephone taping) and node forges, in expectation of the increasing IoE size. Take the standard example of UAV-aided IoE communication; because of the opening of the wireless medium, it is possibly eavesdropping. Furthermore the illicit UAVs are likely to forge IDs to bind to IoE. Despite a number of recent studies evaluating the safety of UAVs, the security risks in Ue-IoE remain a long way off. With the growing number of Ue-IoE implementations, safety measures that can resolve the stated risks are inevitable to be suggested and planned. Study guidelines can boost UAV-based communications protection levels (including A2A and A2G/G2A links). Especially in order to minimize eave-dropping and other malicious practices, protection measures at the physical layer or MAC layer should be taken.

In addition, strengthened security methods are required to discourage unauthorized IoE or UAV links. In addition, counterfeit or counterfeit UAV mechanisms must be used to minimize the problem of node forgery.

10.7 Conclusion

This chapter uses UAV's properties, such as ubiquent coverage, flexible intelligence and diversity, to improve IoE's ability. The realization of UAV enabled IoE with expectations (such as scalability, intelligence and diversity) were limited network coverage, limited battery backup, computational constraint, and security issues. Thus UAVs with boundless mobility, dynamic deployment and coverage will overcome the challenges posed by the IoE networks. The discussions circles around two major factors: the UAS design and the UAV communication Networks. Based on these factors, the UAV enabled IoE covers several opportunities like self-maintenance, sensor recycling, on-demand aerial intelligence, extension to ubiquitous connections and power supply. Thus, a comprehensive discussion on UAV-enabled IoE opportunities and its enabling technologies are presented in this chapter. To sum up, this chapter provides a survey of the UAV-enabled IoE networks' challenges and opportunities.

References

1. Froytlog, A., Foss, T., Bakker, O., Jevne, G., Haglund, M., Li, F., Oller, J., Li, G., Ultra Low Power Wake-up Radio for 5G IoT. *IEEE Commun. Mag.*, 57, 3, 111–117, 2019.
2. Jamalipour, A., Kaleem, Z., Lorenz, P., Choi, W., Special Issue on Amateur Drone and UAV Communications and Networks. *J. Commun. Networks*, 20, 5, 429–433, 2018.
3. Koubaa, A., Qureshi, B., Sriti, M., Allouch, A., Javed, Y., Alajlan, M., Cheikhrouhou, O., Khalgui, M., Tovar, E., Dronemap planner: A service-oriented cloud-based management system for the internet of drones. *Ad Hoc Networks*, 86, 46–62, 2019.

4. Liu, A. and Lau, V.K.N., Optimization of Multi-UAV-Aided Wireless Networking Over a Ray-Tracing Channel Model. *IEEE Trans. Wireless Commun.*, 18, 9, 4518–4530, Sep. 2019.
5. Duan, B., Fang, S., Zhu, R., Wu, X., Wang, S., Gong, Y., Peng, Y., Remote Estimation of Rice Yield With Unmanned Aerial Vehicle (UAV) Data and Spectral Mixture Analysis. *Front. Plant Sci.*, 10, Article 204, 2019.
6. Alexander, C., Korstjens, A., Hankinson, E., Usher, G., Harrison, N., Nowak, M., Abdullah, A., Wich, S., Hill, R., Locating emergent trees in a tropical rainforest using data from an Unmanned Aerial Vehicle (UAV). *Int. J. Appl. Earth Obs. Geoinf.*, 72, 86–90, 2018.
7. Handford, C., Reeves, F., Parker, P., Prospective use of unmanned aerial vehicles for military medical evacuation in future conflicts. *J. R. Army Med. Corps*, 164, 4, 293–296, 2018.
8. Stergiou, C., Psannis, K.E., Plageras, A.P., Ishibashi, Y., Kim, B.-G., Algorithms for efficient digital media transmission over iot and cloud networking. *J. Multimed. Inf. Syst.*, 5, 1, 27–34, 2018.
9. de A. Lima, C.M., da Silva, E.A., Velloso, P.B., Performance evaluation of 802.11 IoT devices for data collection in the forest with drones, in: *2018 IEEE Global Communications Conference (GLOBECOM)*, pp. 1–7, Dec 2018.
10. Javed, F., Afzal, M., Sharif, M., Kim, B., Internet of things (IoT) operating systems support, networking technologies, applications, and challenges: A comparative review. *IEEE Commun. Surv. Tutorials*, 20, 3, 2062–2100, 2018.
11. Dai, H.-N., Wong, R.C.W., Wang, H., Zheng, Z., Vasilakos, A.V., Big data analytics for large-scale wireless networks: Challenges and Opportunities. *ACM Comput. Surv. (CSUR)*, 52, 5, 99, 2019.
12. Dai, H.-N., Wang, H., Xu, G., Wan, J., Imran, M., Big data analytics for manufacturing internet of things: Opportunities, challenges and enabling technologies. *Enterp. Inf. Syst.*, 14, 9–10, 1–25, 2019.
13. Tang, H., Li, D., Wan, J., Imran, M., Shoaib, M., A reconfigurable method for intelligent manufacturing based on industrial cloud and edge intelligence. *IEEE Internet Things J.*, 7, 5, 4248–4259, 2019.
14. Faigl, J., Váňa, P., Pěnička, R., Saska, M., Unsupervised learning based flexible framework for surveillance planning with aerial vehicles. *J. Field Rob.*, 36, 1, 270–301, 2019.
15. Lee, J., Multichannel WPAN protocol for coexistence under densely deployed bluetooth LE in ISM. *IEEE Trans. Veh. Technol.*, 68, 8, 8103–8116, 2019.
16. Holland, J.L. and Lee, S., Internet of everything (IoE): Eye tracking data analysis, in: *Harnessing the Internet of Everything (IoE) for Accelerated Innovation Opportunities*. pp. 215–245, IGI Global, 2019.
17. Jun, K., Jun, B., Lee, H., Kim, S., Tak, W., The study of utilization and precision based on the comparison and analysis of drone-based coastal hazard data and its application in the ocean environment. *J. Coastal Res.*, 85, 811–815, 2018.

18. Siddharthraju, K. and Dhivyadevi, R., Smart Infotainment System For Vehicular Networks. *Int. J. Eng. Adv. Technol. (IEEE Sponsored), ICEAT'18*, 7, 3.27, 368–370, 2018.
19. Mekki, K., Bajic, E., Chaxel, F., Meyer, F., A comparative study of LPWAN technologies for large-scale IoT deployment. *ICT Express*, 5, 1, 1–7, 2019.
20. Zhang, L., Liang, Y.-C., Niyato, D., 6G visions: Mobile ultrabroadband, super internet-of-things, and artificial intelligence. *China Commun.*, 16, 8, 1–14, 2019.
21. Arafat, M. and Moh, S., A survey on cluster-based routing protocols for unmanned aerial vehicle networks. *IEEE Access*, 7, 498–516, 2019.
22. Khan, M., Heurtefeux, K., Mohamed, A., Harras, K., Hassan, M., Mobile Target Coverage and Tracking on Drone-Be-Gone UAV Cyber-Physical Testbed. *IEEE Syst. J.*, 12, 4, 3485–3496, 2018.
23. Miraz, M.H., Ali, M., Excell, P.S., Picking, R., Internet of nano things, things and everything: Future growth trends. *Future Internet*, 10, 8, 68, 2018.
24. Arafat, M.Y. and Moh, S., Localization and Clustering Based on Swarm Intelligence in UAV Networks for Emergency Communications. *IEEE Internet Things J.*, 6, 5, 8958–8976, 2019.
25. Sezer, O., Dogdu, E., Ozbayoglu, A., Context-aware computing, learning, and big data in internet of things: A survey. *IEEE Internet Things J.*, 5, 1, 1–27, 2018.
26. Oubbati, O.S., Chaib, N., Lakas, A., Lorenz, P., Rachedi, A., UAV-assisted supporting services connectivity in urban vanets. *IEEE Trans. Veh. Technol.*, 68, 4, 3944–3951, 2019.
27. Wu, Q., Liu, L., Zhang, R., Fundamental trade-offs in communication and trajectory design for UAV-enabled wireless network. *IEEE Wireless Commun.*, 26, 1, 36–44, 2019.
28. Siddharthraju, K., Karthika, A., Monisha, B., IoT Based Patient Fall Detection. *Int. J. Adv. Sci. Technol.*, 29, 7s, 1496–1505, 2020.
29. Hadiwardoyo, S.A., Hernández-Orallo, E., Calafate, C.T., Cano, J.C., Manzoni, P., Experimental characterization of UAV-to-car communications. *Comput. Networks*, 136, 105–118, 2018.
30. Feng, W., Wang, J., Chen, Y., Wang, X., Ge, N., Lu, J., UAV-Aided MIMO Communications for 5G Internet of Things. *IEEE Internet Things J.*, 6, 2, 1731–1740, April 2019.
31. Liu, X., Liu, Y., Chen, Y., Hanzo, L., Trajectory Design and Power Control for Multi-UAV Assisted Wireless Networks: A Machine Learning Approach. *IEEE Trans. Veh. Technol.*, 68, 8, 7957–7969, Aug 2019.
32. Mohindru, V. and Singh, Y., Node authentication algorithm for securing static wireless sensor networks from node clone attack. *Int. J. Inf. Comput. Secur.*, 10, 2–3, 129–148, 2018.
33. Mohindru, V. and Singh, Y., Performance analysis of message authentication algorithms in wireless sensor networks, in: *2017 4th International*

Conference on Signal Processing, Computing and Control (ISPCC), pp. 468–472, September, IEEE, 2017.

34. Mohindru, V., Bhatt, R., Singh, Y., Reauthentication scheme for mobile wireless sensor networks. *Sustainable Comput.: Inf. Syst.*, 23, 158–166, 2019.
35. Mohindru, V., Singh, Y., Bhatt, R., Securing wireless sensor networks from node clone attack: a lightweight message authentication algorithm. *Int. J. Inf. Comput. Secur.*, 12, 2–3, 217–233, 2020.
36. Mohindru, V., Singh, Y., Bhatt, R., Hybrid cryptography algorithm for securing wireless sensor networks from Node Clone Attack. *Recent Adv. Electr. Electron. Eng. (Formerly Recent Patents Electrical & Electronic Engineering)*, 13, 2, 251–259, 2020.
37. Mohindru, V., Singh, Y., Bhatt, R., A Review on Lightweight Node Authentication Algorithms in Wireless Sensor Networks, in: *2018 Fifth International Conference on Parallel, Distributed and Grid Computing (PDGC)*, pp. 517–521, December, IEEE, 2018.

11

Role of AI and Big Data Analytics in UAV-Enabled IoT Applications for Smart Cities

Madhuri S. Wakode

Department of Computer Engineering, Pune Institute of Computer Technology, Pune, India

Abstract

Unmanned Aerial Vehicles (UAVs) help in increasing the coverage of Internet of Things (IoT) systems in areas with poor accessibility. UAVs offer the benefit of permanent deployment of IoT nodes at remote locations as well as coverage of temporary events by the virtue of their mobility. UAV enabled IoT systems as any other IoT system tend to generate huge amounts of variety of data at very high rate. Efficient use of this unstructured data in the form of text, images, videos, audios etc., is crucial. Crowd surveillance is a typical use case of UAV enabled IoT that requires real time or near to real time big data analytics. The obvious use of artificial intelligence (AI) in such systems is to bring automation and intelligence for faster and efficient big data analytics. Another important use of AI is in the administration and governance of UAV enabled IoT system itself. The advanced AI techniques are important in implementing highly autonomous UAV operations. Few operations are path finding, flight schedules, navigation, authentication etc. AI can further assist in improving security of UAVs. Machine learning (ML) techniques can assure secured transmission of data between IoT devices and UAVs. This work presents a comprehensive survey of research for exploring applications of AI in UAV enabled IoT systems. It specifically focuses on the research in the field of convergence of three disruptive technologies namely AI, UAVs and IoT for improving the quality of life. This survey emphasizes the importance of AI in realizing autonomous and intelligent flying IoT.

Keywords: UAV, IoT, big data analytics, AI, ML

Email: mswakode@pict.edu

Vandana Mohindru, Yashwant Singh, Ravindara Bhatt and Anuj Kumar Gupta (eds.) Unmanned Aerial Vehicles for Internet of Things (IoT): Concepts, Techniques, and Applications, (193–206) © 2021 Scrivener Publishing LLC

11.1 Introduction

With the huge increase in the number and range of connected devices, IoT has become an important source of data deluge today. With ever increasing deployment of sensor nodes, IoT has a potential to support a wide range of applications in various sectors. UAVs with the characteristics of mobility and efficient deployment, further extend the delivery of IoT services. UAVs equipped with IoT devices are useful for increasing the coverage area of IoT services. The tremendous amounts of data generated and gathered by IoT devices and UAVs needs to be efficiently analysed to mine the useful information, to develop insight into the IoT data and to make real-time decisions. Big data analytics applied to IoT data brings effectiveness and efficiency in IoT applications. The combination of UAVs, IoT and big data analytics has enormous potential applications in smart cities, precision agriculture, healthcare, public safety, businesses, disaster management, mining industry, logistics and transportation and many more.

UAV-enabled IoT supports various applications in smart cities including data collection, energy efficiency, public safety, improving quality of life [1, 2]. It proves to be an effective and robust platform for disaster management such as wildfire detection and management [3]. UAVs equipped with IoT devices play a vital role in realizing intelligent applications for traffic policing and transportation systems [4, 5]. IoT and its collaboration with drones improve efficiency and information accuracy of public safety and disaster management related systems with data analytics techniques [6–10]. IoT data characteristics pose a need for algorithms to analyse variety of data in real-time, which is the case for many smart city applications [11]. Appropriate ML, DL techniques applied for analysing such data improves the performance and accuracy [12–14].

Big data analytics also helps in efficient and autonomous governance of UAVs and UAV-enabled IoT systems. These techniques play an important role in various management activities including path planning, resource management [15], security [16], navigation [17], throughput maximization [18], deployment and movement design [19]. ML techniques-based data analytics supports UAV networks optimization [20], and also multi-UAVs systems applications [21].

The convergence of big data with UAV-enabled IoT systems along with use of edge computing, fog computing and cloud computing enriches the expanded range of applications [22–24] such as air quality monitoring [25], in precision agriculture and smart farming [26, 27], public safety [28], and early forest fire detection [29].

Despite of the numerous advantages offered by big data analytics in UAV-enabled IoT systems, there are few open challenges related to the data security and privacy, variety and veracity of the data collected from heterogeneous sources, data provenance and governance issues [30, 31] which need to be addressed carefully to exploit the maximum benefits from the convergence of these disruptive technologies.

11.1.1 Related Work

Many surveys are published in the field of IoT applications for smart cities. Some of these surveys explore the collaboration of drones/UAVs with IoT for smart city applications [1–9]. Many authors have researched the opportunities for exploiting big data analytics in IoT [10, 11]. Many researchers have proposed use of machine learning techniques for analysing real-time, streaming data gathered by UAVs and IoT devices [12–14, 26–29]. Few authors have explored the application of ML, DL techniques for efficient management and governance of UAV networks and UAV-IoT collaborations [15–20]. Very few surveys exist for emphasizing the role of intelligent big data analytics in UAV-enabled IoT applications and governance both [1, 2, 20]. Some studies have proposed the use of multi-UAV systems and advanced technologies including fog computing, cloud computing, developing smart edges to perform data analytics in IoT applications [21–25]. Few researchers have proposed the big data-IoT architectures and discussed the open challenges in realizing these architectures [30, 31].

11.1.2 Contributions

This survey reviews the opportunities for using intelligent techniques in UAV-enabled IoT big data analytics with respect to the use cases in smart city applications. It also discusses the challenges and open issues in collaboration of UAVs, IoT and intelligent big data analytics.

11.1.3 Organization of the Work

Section 11.2 presents an overview of UAV-enabled IoT systems and their use in various vertical applications, especially for smart cities. Section 11.3 provides the overview of big data analytics. Section 11.4 focuses on the role of big data analytics in UAV-IoT enabled applications in smart cities and also for the governance of UAV-IoT system itself. Section 11.5 discusses the current challenges in realization of UAV enabled IoT systems. Section 11.6

presents the concluding remarks and lastly, Section 11.7 throws light on the future scope of this work.

11.2 Overview of UAV-Enabled IoT Systems

Exponentially growing IoT with billions of connected devices has potential to dramatically improve the quality of life. Numerous application domains get benefitted by ever developing IoT infrastructure and services. UAVs equipped with cameras, sensors, computing, and storage devices are efficient and economical in delivering IoT services in low accessibility areas and for temporary events. Further UAVs help in providing low-cost communication services to ground IoT deployments [20, 21]. The integration of UAVs and IoT offer support to new applications and thus widens the range of applications in different sectors including smart cities, healthcare, agriculture, supply chains, rescue operations, early detection of disasters, logistics and transportations, businesses and many more. Figure 11.1 depicts the application domains and representative applications of UAV-enabled IoT.

Despite of attractive use cases in various domains, UAV-IoT integration faces several challenges in realization. Security, data integration, establishing trust, real-time data analytics for huge volumes of data coming with high velocity are few to mention. These challenges need to be addressed for wide acceptance and adoption of UAV-IoT fusion.

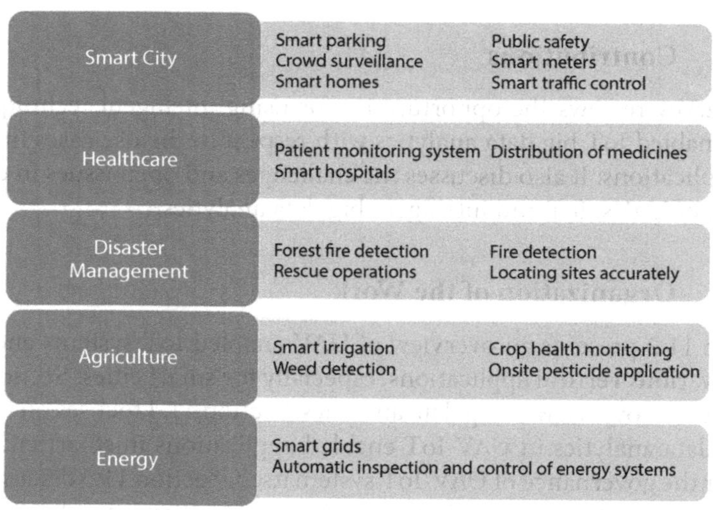

Figure 11.1 Application domains of UAV-enabled IoT.

11.2.1 UAV-Enabled IoT Systems for Smart Cities

Collaboration of individual UAVs or UAV networks with mature deployments of IoT systems target many useful applications in smart cities. The limited availability of resources and continuously increasing population density in cities calls for the efficient resource utilization and management. This requirement paves the path for adoption of technology for better governance of metro cities. The use of connected devices for remote monitoring and controlling the usage of resources become inevitable in such cases. UAV-IoT integration further extends the scope of smart city applications. Crowd surveillance, object detection, fire detection and management, smart meters, smart logistics, smart parking, smart homes and buildings, smart garbage management, public safety, urban governance and management, smart schools and offices, smart healthcare systems are few in the row [1–10]. Figure 11.2 depicts few representative applications of UAV-enabled IoT in smart cities.

11.3 Overview of Big Data Analytics

The huge amounts of data generated and collected by IoT devices and UAVs in various smart city applications need to be transformed in useful

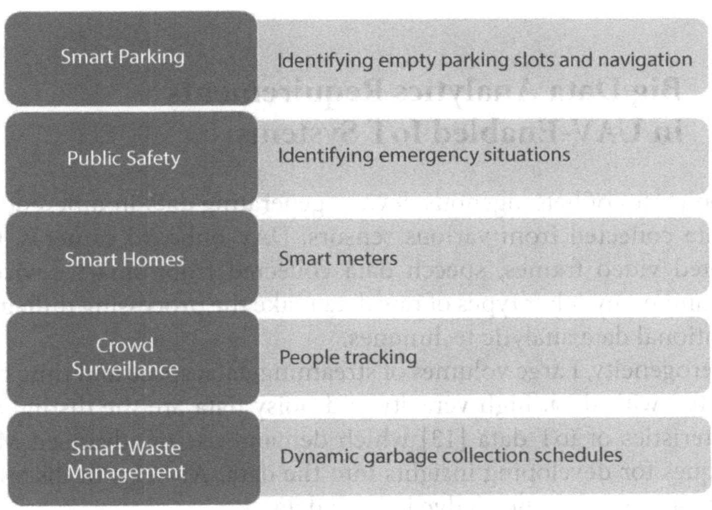

Figure 11.2 Applications of UAV-enabled IoT for smart cities.

insight which leads to efficient decision making. Further, this analysis should happen n real-time to preserve the quality of service (QoS) in most of the applications. For example, detection of fire from sensors data analysis in smart buildings and decision to start operation of anti-fire system should happen in real time. Delays in data analysis and decision making in this type of applications can result into catastrophes. Using conventional data analytics practices therefore is inappropriate in handling huge volume of miscellaneous data in different formats, coming in with high rates and demanding real time analysis. With the advancements in data analytics, it is convenient to handle IoT generated big data (large Volumes, high Velocity, high Variety—3Vs of big data) [11–14].

Real-time, offline, memory level, business intelligence level, massive level are the types of big data analytics [31]. Also, big data analytics can be classified as descriptive, predictive, prescriptive and adaptive analytics depending on whether historic data is analysed or real-time data is analyzed, whether only description of historic data is required or decisions for future events is required, whether analytic models need to adapt according to the real-time data generated by events [14].

ML, DL techniques help bring intelligence and autonomy in big data analytics. Clustering, classification, association rule mining, predictive models, neural networks play important role to bring efficiency in analyzing huge amounts of unstructured data [13].

Apache Storm, Apache Spark, Apache Hadoop and Hadoop ecosystem are popular platforms available for big data analytics [31].

11.4 Big Data Analytics Requirements in UAV-Enabled IoT Systems

IoT comprises of heterogenous devices generating data in different forms. The data collected from various sensors, UAV-onboard cameras, CCTV generated video frames, speech data collected from smart devices like Alexa, and many other types of raw data make the processing difficult with conventional data analytic techniques.

Heterogeneity, Large volumes of streaming data, space and time context associated with data, high veracity and noisy data are the distinguishing characteristics of IoT data [13] which demand use of advanced ML, DL techniques for developing insights into the data. AI helps in discovery of hidden patterns and knowledge in such data.

AI powered big data analytics has two-fold usage in UAV-enabled IoT systems:

1. For various vertical applications supported by UAV-enabled IoT systems, and
2. For efficient management and governance of UAV-enabled IoT system itself.

The following discussion explores these use cases.

11.4.1 Big Data Analytics in UAV-Enabled IoT Applications

As mentioned above various vertical applications designed over UAV-IoT systems need accurate and real-time analysis of big data generated. ML, DL techniques help to achieve this objective. Figure 11.3 depicts the layered architecture emphasizing the additional layer for data processing and big data analytics added to the traditional 3-layer architecture of IoT (Perception, communication, and application layers). Data collection happens at perception or physical layer of the architecture. This layer consists of vertical application specific IoT nodes deployment, at ground level or air

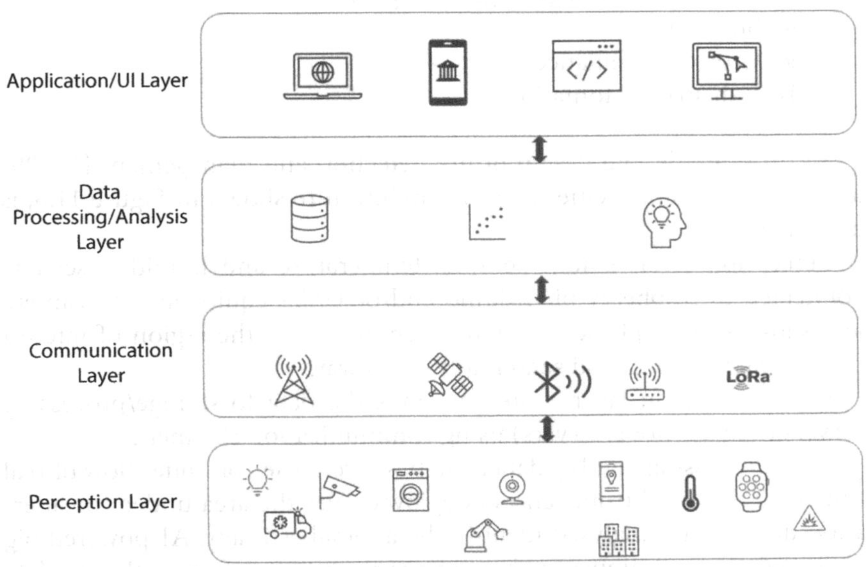

Figure 11.3 Layered architecture for UAV-enabled IoT big data analytics.

(UAVs) or combination of both for monitoring and controlling of events. The collected data after some local data conditioning travels to data storage and/or analytics servers over the communication layer which involves use of different communication technologies. The data can be stored into the proprietary databases or over cloud servers. Similarly, data analytics can be done on private servers or can be deployed on cloud servers. The data processing and big data analytics layer is responsible for performing various tasks such as data cleaning and conditioning, data pre-processing, applying analytics techniques on conditioned data and generate the analytics output. It may include the report generation, preparing graphs and charts for insights into the data, extracting hidden features from the data and identifying patterns useful for the vertical application in consideration.

Following are some representative applications requiring AI, ML, DL techniques for application specific big data.

1. Smart traffic monitoring and emergency management [4]
2. Public safety [28]
3. Disaster management [3]
4. Smart homes and buildings [13]
5. Smart parking [1]
6. Smart offices and schools
7. Smart waste and garbage management
8. Smart meters
9. Crowd surveillance
10. Industrial automation.

As an example, the design of fire detection and management [10, 29] application for smart cities over the architecture shown in Figure 11.3, is as follows:

Perception layer: smoke sensors, temperature and humidity sensors connected to raspberry pi/Arduino and/or UAVs equipped with camera and sensors. Multiple sensor nodes deployed over the region of interest collect real time data and send it to the gateway.

Communication layer: Gateway sends the data to storage/processing servers (may be cloud servers) using communication channels.

Data processing and big data analytics layer: The continues flow of real time data collected from sensors deployed over the area under consideration needs to be analysed identify the anomalies if any. AI-powered big data analytics techniques such as image processing along with text data analysis help in identifying the fire event. Notifications/warnings in such case will be sent to dashboard application.

Application layer: Dashboard application to display the data and/or notifications in case of anomalies identified. Human operator on getting notifications can take the appropriate decision and can initiate the recovery actions.

11.4.2 Big Data Analytics for Governance of UAV-Enabled IoT Systems

Along with supporting plethora of vertical applications in smart cities, UAV-enabled IoT systems should themselves be efficiently managed and governed. AI, ML and DL techniques help for various aspect of governance in such systems. For example, classification algorithms can identify the malicious UAV in the UAV enabled IoT system. ML, DL techniques enhance the security of UAV enabled applications [16]. Shifting data analytics to UAVs can reduce the latencies in decision making which would arise otherwise if data were sent to cloud servers and decision are sent back from cloud servers after big data analytics [21–25]. Use of AI and big data analytics for governance of UAV-enabled IoT systems help in realizing intelligent and autonomous flying IoT systems. Scheduling, resource management, path finding, navigation, coordination among multiple UAVs in the network are some of the tasks where ML, DL techniques are useful. Figure 11.4 describes some of the applications of AI and big data analytics for UAV-enabled IoT system governance.

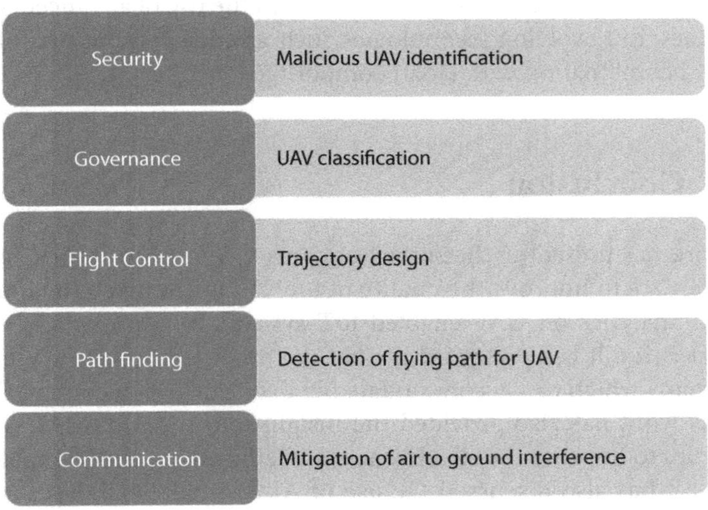

Figure 11.4 Applications of intelligent big data analytics for governance and management of UAV-enabled IoT.

11.5 Challenges

The application of intelligent techniques to big data analytics for UAV-enabled systems provides the extended support to a wide range of smart city applications. Though there many challenges in the full adoption of this triad. The major challenges are due to the resource constrained nature and heterogeneity of IoT devices, legal and regulatory norms for the use of UAVs in civilian applications and computing intensive resource demand of big data analytics techniques [32–35]. Following are the few important challenges in realization and adoption of AI powered UAV-IoT smart city applications:

1. Data security and privacy
2. Lack of trust among the various layers of UAV-enabled IoT systems
3. Latencies involved in sending data to cloud servers for analytics
4. Developing state of standards in the field of IoT and UAVs for civilian applications
5. Data integration as heterogeneous devices and multiple communication technologies are involved.

Some of these issues can be addressed with the use of advanced ML, DL techniques and evolving technologies such as edge computing, fog computing in combination with cloud computing.

11.6 Conclusion

This work has presented the survey of convergence of IoT, UAVs and big data analytics to improve the quality of life. It has discussed the impact of big data analytics on UAV-enabled IoT systems for various applications in smart cities. It has presented the layered architecture for UAV-enabled IoT systems which can accommodate big data analytics as one of the layers. This work has also provided the insight into the use of AI, ML, DL techniques to improve the effectiveness and efficiency of UAV-enabled IoT systems. It has also discussed the use of AI and data analytics for better governance of UAV-enabled IoT systems.

11.7 Future Work

The future scope of this work includes implementation of intelligent and autonomous UAV-enabled IoT systems for smart cities. It also includes to provide proof-of-concepts for the efficient use of AI and big data analytic techniques for smart city applications. Performance analysis of various intelligent big data analytics techniques for real time decision making is also the future scope of the work presented here.

References

1. Alsamhi, S.H., Ma, O., Ansari, M.S., Almalki, F.A., Survey on Collaborative smart drones and internet of things for improving smartness of smart cities. *IEEE Access*, 7, 128125, 2019.
2. Qi, F., Zhu, X., Mang, G., Kadoch, M., Li, W., UAV network and IoT in the Sky for future smart cities. *IEEE Netw.*, 33, 96, 2019.
3. Ejaz, W., Azam, M.A., Saadat, S., Iqbal, F., Hanan, A., Unmanned aerial vehicles enabled IoT platform for disaster management. *Energies*, 12, 2706, 2019.
4. Beg, A., Qureshi, A.R., Sheltami, T., Yasar, A., UAV-enabled intelligent traffic policing and emergency response handling system for the smart city. *Pers. Ubiquitous Comput.*, 25, 33, 2020.
5. Menouar, H., Guvenc, I., Akkaya, K., Uluagac, A.S., Kadri, A., Tuncer, A., UAV-Enabled intelligent transportation systems for the smart city: Applications and challenges. *IEEE Commun. Mag.*, 55, 22, 2017.
6. Alsamhi, S.H., Ma, O., Ansari, M.S., Gupta, S.K., Collaboration of Drone and internet of public safety things in smart cities: an overview of qos and network performance optimization. *Drones*, 3, 13, 2019.
7. Mehmood, Y., Ahmad, F., Yaqoob, I., Adnane, A., Imran, M., Guizani, M., Internet of Things based Smart cities: Recent Advances and challenges. *IEEE Commun. Mag.*, 55, 16, 2017.
8. Kuru, K., Planning the Future of smart cities with swarms of fully autonomous unmanned aerial vehicles using a novel framework. *IEEE Access*, 9, 6571, 2021.
9. Erdelj, M., Uk, B., Konam, D., Natalizio, E., From the Eye of the storm: An IoT ecosystem made of sensors, smartphones and UAVs. *Sensors*, 18, 3814, 2018.
10. Sharma, A., Singh, P.K., Kumar, Y., An integrated fire detection system using IoT and image processing technique for smart cities. *Sustain. Cities Soc.*, 61, 102332, 2020.
11. Cao, H., Wachowicz, M., Renso, C., Carlini, E., Analytics everywhere: generating insights from the Internet of Things. *IEEE Access*, 7, 71749, 2019.

12. Mahdavinejad, M.S., Rezvan, M., Barekatain, M., Adibi, P., Barnaghi, P., Sheth, A.P., Machine learning for Internet of Things data analysis: A survey. *Digit. Commun. Netw.*, 4, 161, 2018.
13. Mohammadi, M., Al-Fuqaha, A., Sorour, S., Guizani, M., Deep learning for IoT Big Data and streaming analytics: A Survey. *IEEE Commun. Surv. Tut.*, 20, 2923, 2018.
14. Adi, E., Anwar, A., Baig, Z., Zeadally, S., Machine learning and data analytics for the IoT. *Neural Comput. Appl.*, 32, 16205, 2020.
15. Wan, S., Lu, J., Fan, P., Letaief, K.B., Toward Big Data processing in IoT: Path planning and resource management of UAV base stations in mobile-edge computing system. *IEEE Internet Things J.*, 7, 5995, 2020.
16. Al-Garadi, M.A., Mohamed, A., Al-Ali, A., Du, X., Guizani, M.A., Survey of machine and deep learning methods for Internet of Things (IoT) security. *IEEE Communications Surveys & Tutorials*, 22, 1646, 2020.
17. Hodge, V.J., Hawkins, R., Alexander, R., Deep reinforcement learning for drone navigation using sensor data. *Neural Comput. Appl.*, 33, 2015, 2021.
18. Park, Y.M., Lee, M., Hong, C.S., Multi-UAVs collaboration system based on machine learning for throughput maximization. *20th Asia-Pacific Network Operations and Management Symposium (APNOMS)*, pp. 1–4, 2019.
19. Liu, X., Liu, Y., Chen, Y., Reinforcement learning in multiple-UAV networks: Deployment and movement design. *IEEE Trans. Veh. Technol.*, 68, 8036, 2019.
20. Bithas, P., Michailidis, E., Nomikos, N., Vouyioukas, D., Kanatas, A., A Survey on machine-learning techniques for uav-based communications. *Sensors*, 19, 5170, 2019.
21. Shakeri, R. *et al.*, Design challenges of multi-UAV systems in cyber-physical applications: A comprehensive survey and future directions. *IEEE Commun. Surv. Tutorials*, 21, 3340, 2019.
22. Khan, L.U., Yaqoob, I., Tran, N.H., Kazmi, S.M., Dang, T.N., Hong, C.S., Edge computing enabled smart cities: A comprehensive survey. *IEEE Internet Things J.*, 7, 10, 2020.
23. Zhang, W., Li, L., Zhang, N., Han, T., Wang, S., Air-ground integrated mobile edge networks: A survey. *IEEE Access*, 8, 125998, 2020.
24. Wang, X., Han, Y., Wang, C., Zhao, Q., Chen, X., Chen, M., In-edge AI: Intelligentizing mobile edge computing, caching and communication by federated learning. *IEEE Netw.*, 33, 156, 2019.
25. Hu, Z., Bai, Z., Yang, Y., Zheng, Z., Bian, K., Song, L., UAV aided aerial-ground IoT for air quality sensing in smart city: Architecture, technologies, and implementation. *IEEE Netw.*, 33, 14, 2019.
26. Tsouros, D.C., Triantafyllou, A., Bibi, S., Sarigannidis, P.G., Data acquisition and analysis methods in UAV-based applications for Precision Agriculture, in: *Proceedings of the 2019 IEEE 15th International Conference on Distributed Computing in Sensor Systems (DCOSS)*, Santorini Island, Greece, 29–31 May 2019, pp. 377–384.

27. Bah, M.D., Hafiane, A., Canals, R., Deep Learning with Unsupervised Data Labeling for Weed Detection in Line Crops in UAV Images. *Remote Sens.*, 10, 1690, 2018.
28. Zhang, Q., Sun, H., Wu, X., Zhong, H., Edge Video Analytics for Public Safety: A Review. *Proc. IEEE*, 107, 1675, 2019.
29. Ma, S., Zhang, Y., Xin, J., Yi, Y., Liu, D., Liu, H., An early forest fire detection method based on unmanned aerial vehicle vision. *Proc. Chin. Control Decis. Conf*, pp. 6344–6349, 2018.
30. Ahmed, E., Yaqoob, I., Hashem, I.A.T., Khan, I., Ahmed, A.I.A., Imran, M., Vasilakos, A.V., The role of big data analytics in Internet of Things. *Comput. Netw.*, 129, 459, 2017.
31. Marjani, M., Nasaruddin, F., Gani, A., Karim, A., Hashem, I.A.T., Siddiqa, A., Yaqoob, I., Big IoT Data Analytics: Architecture, Opportunities, and Open Research Challenges. *IEEE Access*, 5, 5247, 2017.
32. Mohindru, V., Bhatt, R., Singh, Y., Reauthentication scheme for mobile wireless sensor networks. *Sustainable Comput.: Inf. Syst.*, 23, 158–166, 2019.
33. Mohindru, V., Singh, Y., Bhatt, R., Securing wireless sensor networks from node clone attack: A lightweight message authentication algorithm. *Int. J. Inf. Comput. Secur.*, 12, 2–3, 217–233, 2020.
34. Mohindru, V. and Singla, S., A Review of Anomaly Detection Techniques Using Computer Vision, in: *The International Conference on Recent Innovations in Computing*, 2020, March, Springer, Singapore, pp. 669–677.
35. Kushawaha, D., De, D., Mohindru, V., Gupta, A.K., Sentiment analysis and mood detection on an Android platform using machine learning integrated with Internet of Things, in: *Proceedings of ICRIC 2019*, Springer, Cham, pp. 223–238, 2020.

12

Design and Development of Modular and Multifunctional UAV with Amphibious Landing, Processing and Surround Sense Module

Lakshit Kohli*, Manglesh Saurabh, Ishaan Bhatia, Nidhi Sindhwani and Manjula Vijh

Amity School of Engineering and Technology, Delhi, India

Abstract

It's been over a century to the development of the first-ever Unmanned Aerial Vehicle (UAV) built but the quest of superior design and complex application is progressing day by day at an ever-increasing pace. Nowadays even autonomous UAVs are being used at various places. Through this chapter, some of the real-life problems can be tackled and previous compromises can be reduced in UAVs. This chapter aims to follow a modular design approach to provide better functionality and a wide range of applications in all sorts of fields. While achieving advanced features like—Amphibious landing, surround sense & modularity, this approach enables UAV design to have multiple applications in real-world practice as it can be proven as a time-saving solution and used as a multifunctional UAV. This chapter also incorporates Internet of things in the UAV with all the sensor data of the surrounding environment, UAV position etc. can be transmitted to a remote server or analyzed in real-time. This approach is cost-effective, easy to use and allows for increased functionality in various fields.

***Keywords*:** UAV, modular, multifunctional, amphibious landing, surround sense, IoT

**Corresponding author*: lakshitkohli5@gmail.com

Vandana Mohindru, Yashwant Singh, Ravindara Bhatt and Anuj Kumar Gupta (eds.) Unmanned Aerial Vehicles for Internet of Things (IoT): Concepts, Techniques, and Applications, (207–230)

12.1 Introduction

Major technological advancements are happening across the globe due to the growing demand and application of UAVs in various sectors of the industry. UAVs are incorporating all the advanced technologies like auto leveling, auto flight/pilot mode, obstacle detection, long-range and bigger battery backup are getting mainstream as each passing day [1, 2]. This is a sincere effort to design and develop a smart modular Unmanned Aerial Vehicle that can come handy and can be proven effective in various situations where manpower is unreachable or difficult due to terrain and other physical hurdles while also trying to reduce cost and complexity. Studies in the field of unmanned aerial vehicles have been extensively carried out but modular functionality in UAVs is not developed yet. Modularity can introduce multi-purpose usage capabilities and can perform different tasks with different and independent interchangeable modules. There are various instances in daily life where the modular approach of the UAV can be very convenient. For example, consider a UAV primarily used for aerial photography can swap modules to have an amphibious landing and Raspberry Pi kit for real-time image recognition and can be implemented in real life for various data collection research, aerial survey or security provision in crowded places. Auto leveling feature can be used in later stages for auto take-off or maintain a certain altitude on its own in case of loss control or wind pressure in multiple directions. Due to interference, there are a good number of chances that connection between ground control and UAV can be lost and at this time UAV with this kind of feature set can come handy and can stabilize at a certain altitude level to prevent loss of property or the UAV itself. Amphibious landing modules can help land and take off the UAV on water as well as on land. It can help UAV land in low battery to the nearest water body if the land is not in proximity. Surround sense module can sense and record the environment temperatures, humidity, air pollution etc. and transmit these real-time stats to a remote server. UAVs as a combined feature set working in an integrated manner can achieve a great deal. It is also found that the development of such Unmanned Aerial Vehicles is a costly affair. Due to above-mentioned problems and scope for improvement in this field of aerial technology this research was initiated and found its motivation.

12.2 Existing System

The applications for which UAVs were developed and used in their early days have drastically changed starting from the training of the military personnels to home delivery of food and medicine. The innovations in the core electronics have leveled up and opened endless possibilities for the UAV's onboard electronic component. New designs with small & better shapes, sizes and functions were developed to be accessible to the masses. UAV advances and improvements in the creation of cheaper, lighter, more powerful electronics have improved the versatility of UAV multi-folds and enabled countless possibilities for UAVs in all types, sizes and functions to be available to the public. In the society, professional civilians and governments use different technology, ranging from micro-sized UAVs that capture aerial images during a wedding to tactical territorial monitoring through a wide range of high-altitude aircraft carrying explosive weapons UAVs aboard [3, 4]. UAVs design and production have, however, progressed but often implemented in a way that challenges its ability to work for numerous other applications. The current systems have an application-centric basic design approach that requires manufacturers to use their resources to build UAV for the specified application, which gives it an advantage for the particular requirement but restricts its capabilities in other unrelated applications. UAV use has spread across industries and there has been a lot of progress in UAV technology to increase its scope in aerial film and journalism, express shipping and distribution and gathering disaster relief information. Yet the UAVs industry is still young and evolving. Many of the technologies in the industry are continuing to innovate. However, there is still room for innovation in the modular and multipurpose UAVs market.

The network may not only be for computers, but it can also be an analogue telephone system and the interconnection of such networks is known as the Internet. The quality of life is undergoing rapid transformation and will be considerably enhanced in the future.

With the upcoming innovations like the concept, formulated as "computers everywhere" popularly known as "IoT" is in increasing demand due to its ability to develop an ecosystem of devices each connected to one another. The main aim of introducing this concept was to make the world a hyperconnected world. The term IoT was coined in 1999 by "Kevin Ashton" which was later described as a "Standardized way for computers to understand the real world" [5]. In that era, some experiments like connecting a toaster to the internet for remote on and off operation or developing the first web page or develop the Electronic Product Code or EPC, a global RFID-based item identification system intended to replace the UPC bar code made the emergence of IoT as a hope in the industry which led to various implementations of IoT. Various applications provided various solutions to extend the limits of connectivity and evolve into a world of devices connected to the internet. While it developed in Europe, the European Commission stated: "IoT is not yet a tangible reality, but rather a prospective vision of several technologies that, combined together could drastically modify the way our societies function in the next 5 to 15 years." IoT consists mainly of four independent fields of giant technologies: M2M (Machine to Machine), RFID (Radio-Frequency Identification), WSN (Wireless Sensor Networks) and SCADA (Supervisory Control and Data Acquisition) [6]. Fixed or mobile devices which are intelligent enough to communicate and exchange data automatically without human intervention via the Internet is known as IoT. Using sensors requires the collection of data and then transmitting the data over the internet for further processing. Taking a look at the present scenario, the IoT industry is in the exponentially growing phase and innovations in the sector are at the edge.

While looking onto the UAVs in the market with IoT devices installed in the UAV provides features like obstacle detection, pollution evaluation, humidity, environment, soil analyzer and many more. However, installing sensors on any device and naming it as a "Smart product" is not IoT. The IoT-based solutions require appropriate infrastructures and proper data collection and analysis systems to trigger the actions [7]. Following the proper network architectures while designing and applying algorithms that can be responsive to the inputs captured by the sensors makes it a smart product. The best example to understand the concept of smart IoT products should be the reflex action mechanism embedded in our bodies which has the ability to make decisions based on the inputs captured. For instance, upon touching a hot object the skin sensors of our body become active and transmit the data to the brain through the nervous system and then based on the decision of the brain activity is taken. To conclude, the sensors in the real-world act as the skin sensors of our body, the communication channels and the communication mediums act as the nervous system of our body and the algorithms defined in the network for decision part act as the brain. So all these components act together as a system forming an IoT.

12.3 Proposed System

The proposed system is a unique approach to design UAV while keeping the same universal fundamental design constant enabling it to be easier to understand and be adopted by other systems. The core concept of the proposed system is Modularity. It enables the system to be divided into simpler and smaller sets of function-specific components (hardware and software). Modules are independent and interchangeable such that each module contains the required components to execute a functionality individually or work in conjunction with other modules to achieve complex applications. Modules can be added, removed, or interchanged without any significant changes to the base system of the UAV. Providing this option to design and develop custom modules for various functionalities allows the system to cater the need of various functionalities and applications i.e. modularity in UAVs allows the ability to improve and expand functionalities and applications of the current system. Modularity allows for the ability to create a base system with the ability to modify and upgrade the capabilities and functionalities of the UAV by developing and utilizing different modules individually or together for different tasks. Thus, reducing cost and increasing adaptability of UAVs by not developing application-specific UAVs from scratch to just develop application-specific modules which will, in turn, reduce the time as well as the cost of design and development and also pave the way for further innovation.

The proposed system is built on the foundation of the concept of modularity and few of the modules discussed later are Base Module, Amphibious Module, On-Board Processing Module, Surround Sense Module, and IoT Module. These modules offer unique functionalities enabling the proposed system to be highly effective, cost-efficient and versatile. The base Module is chosen based on the popular Quadcopter design which is proven to be stable and efficient in various fields of use. As the base module follows the Universal fundamental design principle of the Quadcopter and allows for modularity above and beyond the basic design making it simpler and easier to adopt and build upon. Amphibious Module is the prime Module that enables the UAV to Take off and land from both Land and water increasing the potential areas of application of the drone by providing the amphibious take-off and landing functionalities.

The surround sense module allows for the integration of 2 great technologies together: IoT and UAVs. The surround sense Module consists of various sensors that can be added on to the base module along with the processing module to collect and transmit data for record and analysis of data. The main sensors of the surrounding sense module are Temperature, Humidity, Pollution, and Gas Sensors with the integration of IoT the data collected by these sensors in connection with the onboard processing module is transmitted and stored on a server for data aggregation and analysis. The surround sense module can be proven very effective in the environmental and survey applications as this allows for the added functionality to integrate such sensors and obtain data regarding various parameters very effortlessly allowing for easier and improved efficiency in data aggregation from difficult environments without affecting/altering them by the physical presence of humans.

12.4 IoT Sensors and Architecture

A framework designed to interconnect the physical devices to transfer and share data on a real-time basis by the use of the internet is known as "Internet of things (IoT)". Every node in this network is embedded with a device known as "Sensor". The function of a sensor is to collect a specific type of data, for example, a temperature sensor indicates the level of temperature. The data collected from the sensor is sent to the internet and then it is stored in the database and then analyzed for further processing. In this, a media access control address is allotted to each device and is given an ability to communicate with devices in the network [8]. The data, when received at the receiver terminal, provides valuable output statistics on higher-order analysis and processing. After the processing of data, the algorithms embedded for decision making, analyze the results, and take decisions. Automation is the process of collecting data, transmitting it, analyzing it, and acting accordingly which reduces human intervention. This network of physical devices with data collection and action taking protocols can be named as "Smart Networks" [9]. The action taking protocols are the algorithms which act as a decision-making entity in the network. The communication protocol mainly used in IoT is the TCP/IP.

12.4.1 Sensors and Theory

Sensors are devices that collect specific data from the surroundings and share the data with the corresponding processing units. The sensors are designed to measure particular parameters and transmit the values of those parameters for further usage. Sensor module serves as the key component in an IoT system. There are sensors for examining environmental parameters, for example, humidity sensor, a barometer for wind speed, air pollution sensor for measuring various pollutant gases in the atmosphere, and particulate matter like PM2.5.

The sensors used in this project are placed in the module named as the "Surround Sense Module". The surround sense module enables the UAV to gather information on its surroundings like humidity, wind speed, temperature, gaseous mixture present around the proximity, etc. [10]. Depending on the application of the UAV it can be used with different sets of sensors to serve its desired purpose, for example, there can be gyro sensors, camera sensors Temperature sensor, proximity sensor, Infrared sensor, Pressure sensor, Light sensor, Ultrasonic sensor, Smoke, Gas, or Humidity sensor, Flow and Level sensors.

12.4.2 Architectures Available

To implement the IoT network, some commonly used architectures are explained. There are two architectures which are classified based on the core mechanisms:

1. 3-Layer Architecture
2. 5-Layer Architecture.

12.4.2.1 3-Layer IoT Architecture

Figure 12.1 represents 3-layer IoT architecture. The simplest architecture to understand IoT networks is three-layer architecture [11]. The three fundamental layers in this architecture are the Perception Layer, Network Layer, and Application Layer. The perception layer consists of all the end product modules that are the sensors, actuators, triggers, or devices interacting with the environment. The Network Layer is the part that links the sensors or the end products with the client-side. It consists of the gateways which serve as the connection between the sensors data and the server.

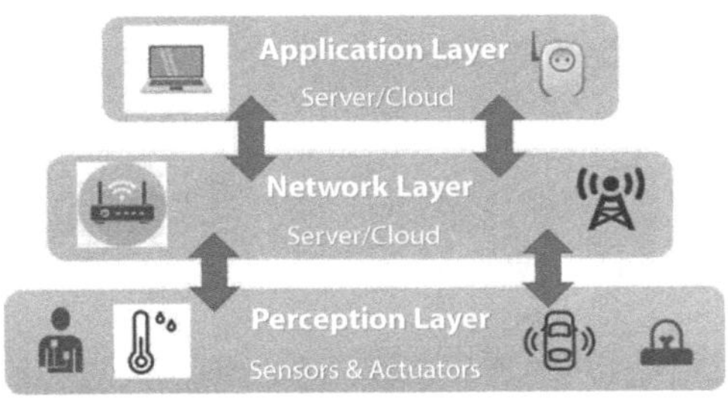

Figure 12.1 3-layer IoT architecture.

The Application Layer consists of Data processing and storage with specialized services and functionality for users. Eventually connecting these three layers, the perception layer representing the "Things" and the network layer connecting through the "Internet" and the application layer providing the user interface.

12.4.2.2 5-Layer IoT Architecture

It is an extension of the three-layer architecture which adds up two more layers to the previous architecture. The addition made to this architecture is an evolution for IoT networks as the network in this architecture is cloud-centric. All the devices in the perception layer send the data through the transport layer to the application layer like in the three-tier architecture, but after that, the data is sent to the application layer and the business layer. The layer interposed between the application layer and the transmission layer is the processing layer. Decision making and cloud computing take place in this layer. Refer to the Figure 12.2 (5-layer IoT architecture). For example, traffic data coming from a smart transport system of an urban area can be processed by the processing layer to predict traffic jams. While on the other hand the processed data can be provided by the application layer for the user end in the form of an intuitive UI dashboard. This layer can also provide interactive capabilities to users to interact with physical devices or collected data. The upper-level business layer is capable

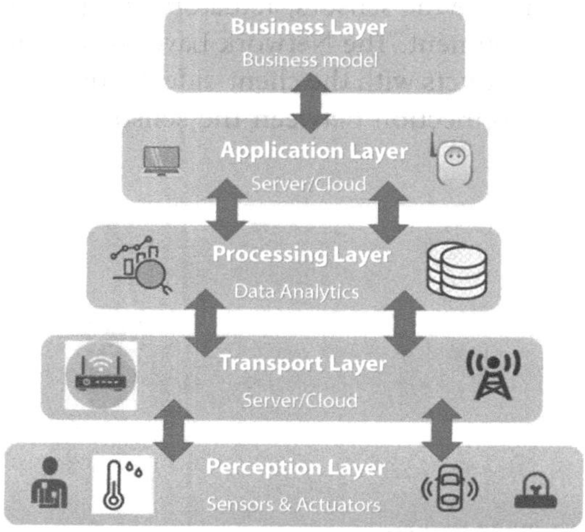

Figure 12.2 5-layer IoT architecture.

of managing the overall system [12]. It is proven time and again that it requires a sound business plan to make a technology successful.

12.4.2.3 Architecture & Supporting Modules

The architecture selected in this chapter is the five-layer architecture to design and develop the compatible modules. According to the requirement of the application, one can choose any of the architectures from the above-mentioned types. But in this chapter, we aimed to design and develop modular UAV that can be utilized for multiple applications and not just for singular applications. There are several modules that work in coordination with each other and are connected to the network. The IoT network is the network used for the communication protocols [13] of the UAV modules and the receiver side equipment. There are several technologies available to design the network, a comparison of them is shown in Table 12.1. In our case XBee technology is used. This technology is selected and used, because of its range specifications, linkage protocols, and security features. It consumes less power and is more efficient as compared to other networking technologies [14].

12.4.2.4 Integration Approach

As the UAV is designed to be modular and multifunctional, there are several modules that one can develop and use with this UAV. There are 3 modules at present, which are used to enable the modular UAV to sense the environment and evaluate the environmental parameters while sharing the data over the network in order to store, analyze and present the data on a user-friendly webpage. An integrated approach is used to maintain the flow of data from the sensors to the server. This approach explains

Table 12.1 Comparison of technologies for transmission of IoT data.

Technology	Link	Frequency	Range	Throughput
802.11a	Ground to Air	2.4 GHz	95 feet	1.4 Mb/s
802.11b/g	Air to Ground	2.4 GHz	150 feet (Max)	11–54 Mb/s
XBee-Pro	Ground to Air, Air to Ground, Air to Air	2.4 GHz	2–15 km (Depending on the antenna)	Up to 250 kb/s

the mechanisms of how all of the modules are interconnected and communicate with each other to provide the desired output. The main units present in the modules will be the microprocessors or microcontrollers which have many communication protocols and it could be used according to the sensors which generally uses the serial communication protocol. The IoT module plays a significant role in designing the mechanism of communication. The IoT module used in this project receives the data sent by the processing module and transmits it over the wireless link [15]. The IoT module used in this project works on the XBee technology which provides communication over a respectable range and provides three protocols for transmission of data (Digimesh, Zigbee, multipoint) [16]. There are multiple networking protocols supported by the IoT module, but the one used in this project is IEEE 802.15.4. This IoT module also provides the APS encryption technique which is a layer of the architecture model that will protect the transmitted data, hence providing better security features. While designing the mechanism for the integration approach, power requirements should be kept in mind, as incorporating the UAV with different kinds of modules eventually increases the power consumption.

12.4.2.5 System of Modules

In this section, the system of modules is designed, which explains the system structure or the major blocks of the system. The surround sense module senses the environment and collects the data from the sensors. A sensor is a machine that collects the information of a physical quantity from the surrounding. The measurement is in the form of the value which is then converted to the digital value or a signal to process and communicate the data to the next unit as shown in Figure 12.3. The sensor's data obtained from the sensing module is sent to the processing module. The processing module formulates and evaluates the environmental parameters required to detect the actual condition of the surroundings of the UAV. The main part of transmission which facilitates the data transmission from the UAV modules to the webpage server through gateways of networks [17]. Now the flow of data is from the data collection, data processing to the data transmission. And from the perspective of allotting the previously mentioned processes in a block unit, the flow of data will be from the surround sense module to the processing module.

These modules can also be upgraded according to one's need or according to the application. Another advantage of this is that it makes the UAV a future-ready UAV as the new inventions can be integrated with the

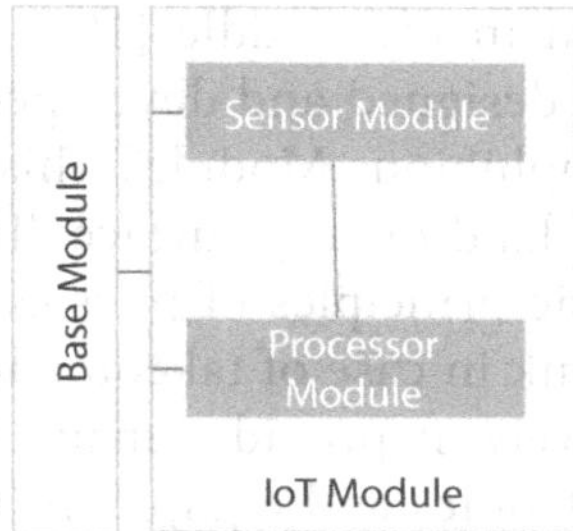

Figure 12.3 Block diagram of system of modules.

modular system easily. The architecture was chosen keeping these factors in mind and the processing module used in this UAV gives one enormous possibility of integration with the high-end upcoming technologies.

12.5 Advantages of the Proposed System

Some of the compromises present in the existing UAV systems are resolved in this chapter. This UAV is designed and developed to add even more value to the UAV industry as it would increase the capabilities and by allowing them to either improve or increase their current capabilities and applications by the utilization of the concept of modularity. The benefits of using these individual modules are the reduction of the complexity of the system. An independent module is capable of performing a specific task which reduces the cost and the time taken for the development of new functionalities as the whole system is not designed from scratch and only the module is developed. The chances of failure of the model are also reduced using the modularity as the functioning mechanism of the system of modules is not exclusively interdependent on each other. The Modular Approach to a UAV allows for the production of UAVs without any application-specific restrictions allowing much wider usage and reduced design and cost complexities. Such UAV modular capabilities allow several modules to be added or modified in considerably less time, allowing the UAV to expand its functionality depending on the module used and the task requirement.

Instead of a commercial readymade flight control system, a custom Atmega 328-based flight controller has been built and configured. The base module is made easily customizable in order to enable quick and simpler swapping of modules. The UAV base module follows the Quadcopter design of the UAV consisting of 4 propellers and motors with the weight centered in the middle [18]. The module which has an amphibious nature is designed and developed and discussed in this chapter is known as "Amphibious Module". This critical module allows the UAV to take off and land on any surface. The amphibious module is based on the very basic principles of physics that allow the UAV to float on water and not sink in case of takeoff and landing from or onto a water surface respectively. It provides many benefits because UAVs are fragile pieces of electronics and equipment that are often at risk of being destroyed by water, for example when UAVs operating over lakes, marshes, swamps or other water bodies face difficulties covering these areas. After all, there is not much land available to take off or land in case of low battery or power loss situations. In these scenarios, the UAV is vulnerable to injury. The UAV stands at a risk of getting damaged in such scenarios. Swappable modules allow the connection of the amphibious modules as per the requirement allowing to land on the water surfaces damaging the UAV components.

While usage of the Surround Sense module and the processing module enables the proposed design to interact with the environment and then process the data recorded. The surround sense module gives the user to attach multiple sensor nodes that could allow more data collection and other functionalities [19]. As the usage of those sensor nodes requires storage/transmission of data collected to the webserver/cloud. The data can be processed on the web server as well as presented on an intuitive dashboard for the user for real-time analysis. To expand the scope of the modularity of the new design approach of the UAV, this module has been developed based on the latest type of Architecture for IoT. A five-tier architecture for IoT in UAV surround sense module provides the "FUTURE-READY" capabilities to the UAV [20]. It also makes the UAV a consumer-ready product as this module also provides a business layer from the architecture which provides intuitive User Interaction/ Experience.

Many other modules, such as camera modules, computational modules containing microcontrollers or microprocessors, or various other modules for different functions, may be used for the various benefits of the proposed device by adopting the modular design methodology.

12.6 Design

There are numerous variations in the design of UAVs and different versions of them are used for different purposes. The most notable difference is seen in terms of rotor configuration like a single rotor or multi-rotor system. These configurations are chosen based on the requirement of payload carrying ability, mid-stability etc. Therefore, each type of UAV is designed with a fixed set of pre-requisites and follows these parameters to design the UAV system. But this chapter aims to reduce the requirement-based design approach as this follows a multipurpose approach and hence a stable, well maneuverable design is required to encompass all sorts of needs. Therefore, the quadcopter design has been preferred as it provides enough stability even while using heavy payloads and easy maneuverability is hence established [21]. It can move in all four directions without turning its head in the moving direction with an equal amount of thrust in all possible directions. This also helps UAV to land vertically, aim any terrain and all these advantages with simple design physics. This design methodology follows the universal quadcopter with few novel changes for modularity making it easier to adopt and use. Various modular extensions can be attached to provide extra functionalities. Modules like amphibious landing, an image processing module, sensor modules etc. can be added or removed in or out as needed with ease. The module selection is initially limited but new modules can be designed and added to the list. This can make the UAV even more useful for different tasks. All of these modules are easily added or removed when needed and have easy to use functionality for quick swap and setup.

12.6.1 System Design

One of the most important and complex components to develop for UAV to fly is the flight controller. It is the brain behind controlling UAVs position, direction and speed. Our UAV uses a custom-made flight controller programmed on an Atmega 328 microcontroller [22]. This provides an easy way for micro-adjustments and calibration for custom handling of UAV. It is done by tweaking the PID values of the flight controller algorithm [23]. This system is divided into two sections: a receiver attached on the controller board and a transmitter that controls the motion of a UAV. Multiple steps are followed sequentially to operate the UAV. It is demonstrated in the form of the block diagram below in Figure 12.4.

12.6.2 Auto-Leveling

Auto-leveling feature is used to level the UAV at a certain altitude to hover over an area and perform other tasks [24]. This feature tries to

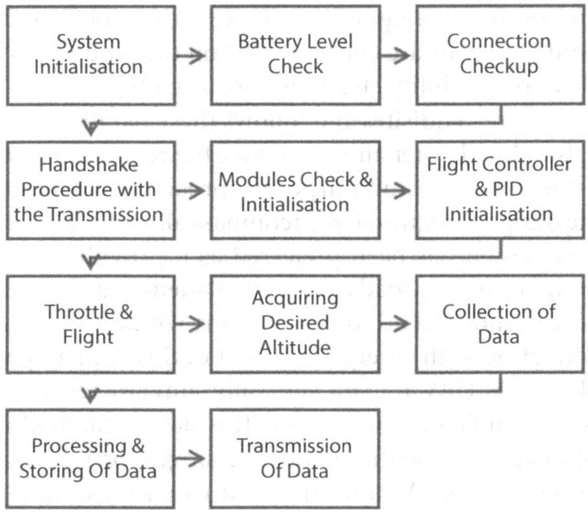

Figure 12.4 Flowchart of system design.

counteract any force exerted onto the UAVs body by wind or other means. Auto leveling is implemented by using the data that regularity comes from the gyro and accelerometer sensors. The auto-leveling feature is based on the concept of automation which is an emerging concept these days. The basic architecture of automation requires feedback linked from the output to the input. This feedback provides the decision-making algorithms to enhance the performance of the system by auditing the system constraints. There are types of algorithms which can be used in stabilizing the UAV; PID, LQR & LQR-PID [25]. The PID algorithm is used in the control system to provide this feature. When a command is transmitted by the controller to the UAVs receiver for locking the altitude, PID kicks in to stabilize the UAV and level it to the current altitude. It is also activated if there is no incoming command from the transmitter.

The mathematical expression of this algorithm is

$$u(t) = K_{\mathrm{p}} e(t) + K_{\mathrm{i}} \int_0^t e(t')\,dt' + K_{\mathrm{d}} \frac{de(t)}{dt}$$

The configurations of this algorithm are quite difficult to calculate as it is a differential equation and the exact specific configurations of the system changes as per the product's specs. The simulations to configure these are a better method for which MATLAB is used [26]. But configuring them makes it easy handling.

There are several modules that can be attached to the base module and some of them are listed below.

12.6.3 Amphibious Landing Module

This module is specifically designed for water as well as land terrain take-off and landing. It is based on the principle of buoyancy. According to Archimedes, the buoyant force is the upward thrust acting on a body that opposes the weight of a fully or partially submerged body in a liquid enabling it to float on the liquid and prevent it from drowning under some circumstances [27]. Various parameters like surface area, streamline design, material's ability to float in liquid and prevent it from sinking has been considered to design this module as seen in Figures 12.5 and 12.6. The mathematical equation for design and formation is based on the equality of these two factors. For the UAV to be capable of the amphibious ability, the buoyant force is calculated by the expression:

$$F_{Buoyant} = p\ V_f g \tag{12.1}$$

In Equation (12.1), p is the density of the liquid, V_f is the volume of the liquid displaced, g is the acceleration due to gravity.

In Equation (12.1), the known values are the acceleration due to the gravity and the density of the liquid (water). And the buoyant force can be calculated as well. Integrating the Archimedes principle and the buoyancy mechanism is necessary to completely design the module. The Archimedes principle states that the buoyant force on an object is equal to the weight of the fluid displaced by the object [28]. The mathematical expression for that is

$$W_f = F_{Buoyant} \tag{12.2}$$

In Equation (12.2), W_f is the weight of the fluid displaced. The weight of the fluid displaced is mathematically expressed as

$$W_f = m * g \tag{12.3}$$

In Equation (12.3), m is represented as the mass of the liquid.

Equations (12.2) and (12.3) will lead the derivation and understanding of the concepts on which the module will be built:

$$F_{Buoyant} = m * g \tag{12.4}$$

From Equation (12.4), the volume of the displaced liquid can be easily calculated by replacing $F_{Buoyant}$ in the equation (12.1)

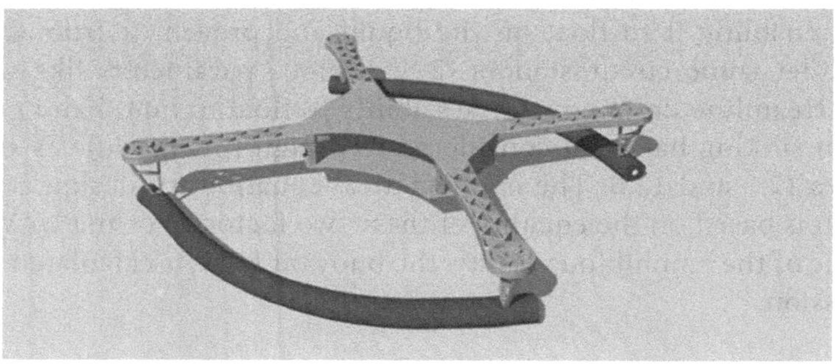

Figure 12.5 Lateral view of the 3D design of the amphibious model.

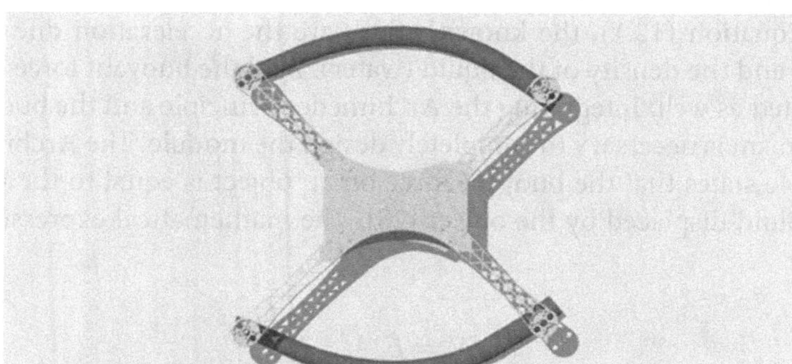

Figure 12.6 Top view of the 3D design of the amphibious model.

12.6.4 Processing Module

The processing module is designed for incorporating a processing system on the UAV for various purposes such as the use of Raspberry pi for image processing tasks, ARM-based microcontrollers for various sensor-based data collection, processing and transmission tasks etc. [29]. This module can be attached on top of the base module of the UAV as shown in Figure 12.7. This module is designed in such a way that it remains rigid and coupled on the UAV body and can handle high speed maneuver. It can be swapped when required and be avoided if not in use without affecting the UAV aerodynamics and flight stability.

12.6.5 Surround Sense Module

Surround Sense Module is designed to create a firm and stable housing for a range of sensors that are required to measure different parameters of the environment as well as the UAV itself as shown in Figure 12.8. This module can be used as a complementary module with the processing module. The sensors incorporated in this module can be arranged in the housing and later connected to the processing module for data processing and transmission to the server or remote computer.

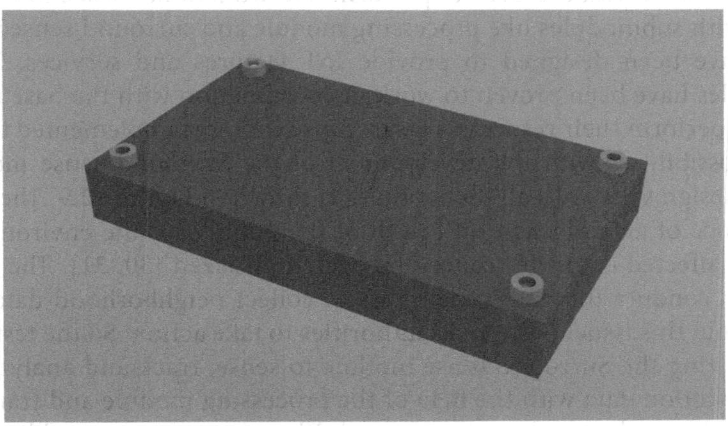

Figure 12.7 Design of processing module.

Figure 12.8 Design of surround sense module.

12.7 Results

This chapter emphasized on the modularity of the UAV and its use in everyday life. Different modules have been designed, developed and incorporated with the UAV to perform multifunctional tasks. IoT modules with submodules like processing module and surround sense module have been designed to provide IoT features and services. These modules have been proven to work in coordination with the base module to perform their respective tasks. A use case was implemented to test the possibilities with the development of the Surround sense module final design view with all the modules is shown in Figure 12.9. The consequence of air pollution on health of the public and the environment in the affected countries cannot be overemphasized [30, 31]. The main aim to conduct this experiment was to collect neighborhood data and point out this issue to the local authorities to take action. So the test case of utilizing the Surround sense module to sense, track and analyze the Air Pollution data with the help of the processing module and transmit data utilizing the transmission through Xbee thus, in turn, enabling IoT

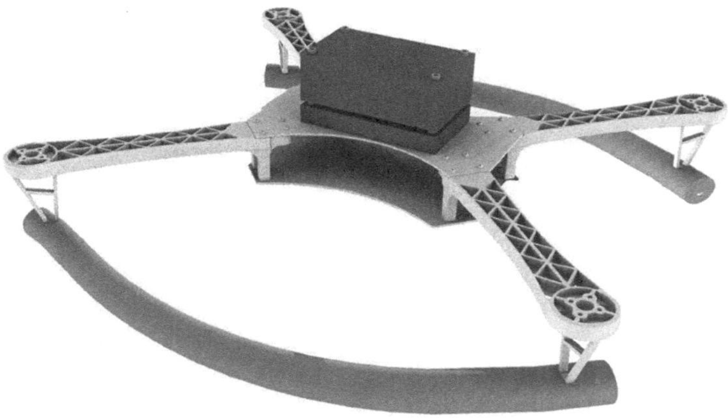

Figure 12.9 Final view of UAV with both processing and surround sense modules attached.

capabilities [32–34]. The sensors used for this purpose were Temperature, Humidity, Pollution, and Gas Sensors.

Represented in Table 12.2 and graphs in Figures 12.10 and 12.11 show different parameters of air pollution over an area. This is considerably a short amount of data to jump to a conclusion nevertheless the AQI calculated over the data set is alarming and cannot be neglected. If repeated for a longer period of time, this data can provide various insights to the pollution level like at what time of the day the AQI is highest, what constitutes the highest amount of pollution etc. By these insights' measures can be taken to reduce air pollution e.g. diverting traffic at peak hours to

Table 12.2 Data collected by surround sense module in tabular form.

Sensors	10-02-2020	11-02-2020	12-02-2020	13-02-2020
PM2.5	348	252	315	113
PM10	381	252	295	227
NO2	50	52	60	33
NH3	4	10	9	5

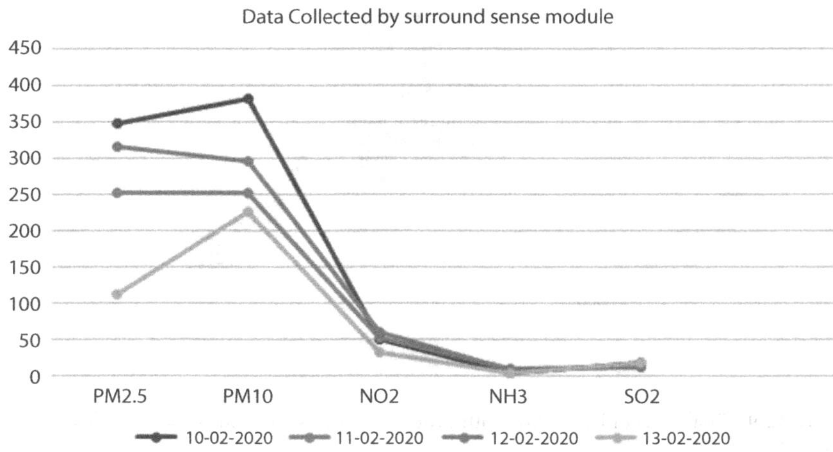

Figure 12.10 Data collected by surround sense module represented graphically.

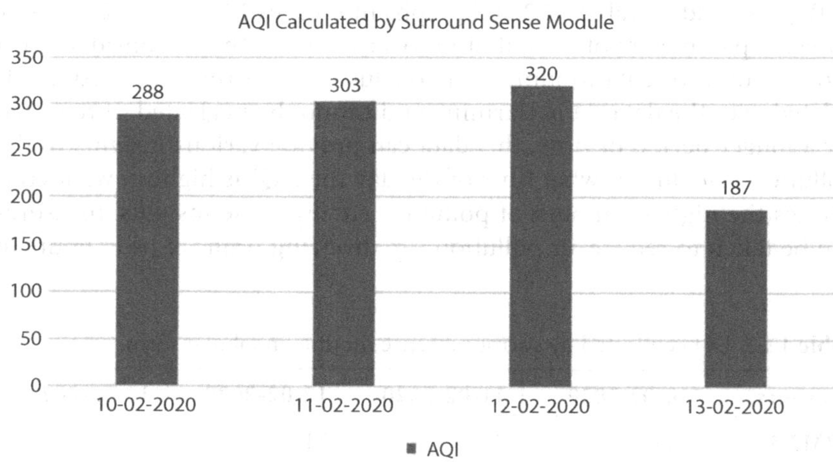

Figure 12.11 Graph of calculated AQI values by the surround sense module.

reduce traffic jams, efficiently using traffic lights, electric vehicle charging stations, pollution checks for vehicles etc. [35].

12.8 Conclusion

The UAV is designed and developed on the fundamental approach to be modular and Multifunctional. The discussed approach is found out to be effective and useful in various real-life scenarios. The proposed UAV is a modular UAV which allows for multiple modules to be developed and used for various functionalities that can be attached on to the base module (which follows the most widely used Quadcopter design). The flight controller for the base module which is responsible for the basic functionality of the UAV to fly and control. It is custom developed and has easy to calibrate controls for modules. Few modules are discussed in above section such as the Amphibious Module which allows for the functionality to allow the UAV to take off and land from both surfaces Land and water. It also allows for the UAV to float and prevents it from drowning/sinking. Other modules were developed to bring together and combine two great and upcoming technologies i.e. UAVs and IoT, as IoT has made it very simple and efficient to collect and analyze data. The proposed system can utilize this great technology to open up great possibilities of data aggregation and analysis with the help of modular IoT based UAVs. A special Module was also designed for utilization and representation of this idea. The Surround Sense Module is designed for the purpose of creating a firm and stable housing for a range of sensors that are required to measure different parameters of the environment as well as the UAV itself. This module can be used as a complementary module with the processing module to process the collected data onboard together they constitute the IoT module as the name suggests enables the ability to utilize the IoT functionality and transmit the collected data to desired server/base station. The Proposed UAV design can very easily be incorporated in multiple real-world scenarios and enable endless possibilities.

12.9 Future Scope

There is tremendous potential in the above-discussed approach for Modular multifunctional UAV and the modules. This approach can have a very broad future scope. As this approach is not limited to only the above-mentioned modules but can also be expanded by designing different sets of modules for various other functionalities and applications. Like the development of a camera module which in conjunction with the onboard processing module can enable real-time capture of images and video by the UAV. This increasing the scope of the surround senses module or completely different applications based on image processing or for recreational purposes of recording aerial footage. The possibilities of a modular approach are virtually endless and only restricted by one's imagination and creativity.

References

1. McGuire, K., de Croon, G., De Wagter, C., Tuyls, K., Kappen, H., Efficient Optical Flow And Stereo Vision For Velocity Estimation And Obstacle Avoidance On An Autonomous Pocket Drone. *IEEE J. Mag.*, 2, 2, 1070–1076, 2017.
2. Woo, C., Kang, S., Ko, H., Song, H., Kwon, J.O., Auto Charging Platform And Algorithms For Long-Distance Flight Of Drones. *IEEE Conference Publication*, 2020.
3. Ely, J.C., Graham, C., Barr, I.D., Rea, B.R., Spagnolo, M., Evans, J., Using UAV acquired photography and structure from motion techniques for studying glacier landforms: Application to the glacial flutes at Isfallsglaciären. *Earth Surf. Proc. Land.*, 42, 877–888, Wiley-Scrivener, 2017.
4. Gregory, D., From A View To A Kill: Drones And Late Modern War. *SAGE J.*, 28, 2011, 2, 2020.
5. Mohamed, K.S., The Era of Internet of Things: Towards a Smart World, in: *The Era of Internet of Things*, Springer, Cham, 2019.
6. Ding, G., Wu, Q., Zhang, L., Lin, Y., Tsiftsis, T.A., Yao, Y., An Amateur Drone Surveillance System Based on the Cognitive Internet of Things. *IEEE Commun. Mag.*, 56, 1, 29–35, Jan. 2018.
7. Shit, R.C., Sharma, S., Puthal, D., Zomaya, A.Y., Location of Things (LoT): A Review and Taxonomy of Sensors Localization in IoT Infrastructure. *IEEE Commun. Surv. Tutorials*, 20, 3, 2028–2061, 2018.
8. Fan, X., Ao, T., Xia, Z., Address Allocation Scheme Based On Local MAC Address, *Cloud Computing and Security. ICCCS, Lecture Notes in Computer Science*, 11063, 263–274, 2018.

9. Cano, J.C., Berrios, V., Garcia, B., Toh, C.K., Evolution of IoT: An Industry Perspective. *IEEE Internet Things Mag.*, 1, 2, 12–17, December 2018.
10. Environmental Monitoring Using Wireless Sensor Networks (WSN) based on IoT. *Int. Res. J. Eng. Technol.*, 04, 01, 1376, 2017.
11. Zhong, C., Zhu, Z., Huang, R., Study on the IoT Architecture and Access Technology. *2017 16th International Symposium on Distributed Computing and Applications to Business, Engineering and Science (DCABES)*, Anyang, pp. 113–116, 2017.
12. Sethi, P. and Sarangi, S., Internet of Things: Architectures, Protocols, and Applications, *Journal of Electrical and Computer Engineering*, 2017, 9324035, 25, 2017.
13. Maurya, A.K. and Ahmad, J., Iot Based Comprehensive Monitoring of Network and Related Infrastructure. *Int. J. Adv. Res. Comput. Sci., Udaipur*, 9, Special Issue 2, 181–184, Apr 2018.
14. Hilmani, A., Maizate, A., Hassouni, L., Designing and Managing a Smart Parking System Using Wireless Sensor Networks. *J. Sens. Actuator Netw.*, 7, 24, 2018.
15. Yanmaz, E., Yahyanejad, S., Rinner, B., Hellwagner, H., Bettstetter, C., Drone Networks: Communications, Coordination, And Sensing, *Ad Hoc Networks*, 68, 1–15, 2018.
16. Mondragón, L., Rodríguez, L.J., Mena, A., Rodriguez-Asomoza, J., Garcia-Juarez, A., Huerta, I., Experimental Evaluation of Transmission between Two XBee Modules Using Radio-over-Fiber Technique. *Adv. Sci. Technol. Eng. Syst. J.*, 4, 4, 2019, 10.25046/aj040415.
17. Khelifi, F., Monitoring System Based in Wireless Sensor Network for Precision Agriculture, in: *Internet of Things (IoT)*, M. Alam, K. Shakil, S. Khan, (Eds.), Springer, Cham, 2020.
18. Kumar, Bhargavapuri, M., Deshpande, A.M., Sridhar, S., Cohen, K., Kumar, M., Quaternion Feedback Based Autonomous Control of a Quadcopter UAV with Thrust Vectoring Rotors. *2020 American Control Conference (ACC)*, Denver, CO, USA, pp. 3828–3833, 2020.
19. Yang, Y., Hu, Z., Bian, K., Song, L., ImgSensingNet: UAV Vision Guided Aerial–Ground Air Quality Sensing System. *IEEE INFOCOM–IEEE Conference on Computer Communications*, Paris, France, pp. 1207–1215, 2019.
20. Fatima, Z., Bhargava, L., Kumar, A., Smart Infrastructures, in: *Internet of Things (IoT)*, M. Alam, K. Shakil, S. Khan, (Eds.), Springer, Cham, 2020.
21. Panagiotou, P., Giannakis, E., Savaidis, G., Yakinthos, K., Aerodynamic and structural design for the development of a MALE UAV. *Aircr. Eng. Aerosp. Technol.*, 90, 7, 1077–1087, 2018.
22. Ghosh, Roy, H., Dhar, S., Arduino Quadcopter—IEEExplore.ieee.org. *IEEE Conference Publication*, 2020.
23. Kuantama, E., Vesselenyi, T., Dzitac, S., Tarca, R., PID and Fuzzy-PID Control Model for Quadcopter Attitude With Disturbance Parameter, *International*

Journal of Computers Communications & Control, [S.l.], 12, 4, 519–532, 2017.
24. Farid, G., Hongwei, M., Baqar, A.H., Liwei, Q., Inverse dynamics based altitude/attitude control and stabilization of a quadrotor UAV. *9th International Conference on Modelling, Identification and Control (ICMIC)*, Kunming, pp. 675–679, 2017.
25. Argentim, L.M., Rezende, W.C., Santos, P.E., Aguiar, R.A., PID, LQR And LQR-PID On A Quadcopter Platform. *IEEE Conference Publication*, Ieeexplore.ieee.org, 2020.
26. Mohazzab, P., Archimedes' Principle Revisited. *J. Appl. Math. Phys.*, 5, 836–843, 2017.
27. Pisano, A., Boats, Balloons, and Air Bubbles: Archimedes' Principle, in: *Physics for Anesthesiologists*, Springer, Cham, 2017, https://doi.org/10.1007/978-3-319-57330-4_2.
28. Nergaard, A. and Architect, Naval & Engineer, Petroleum, The Magic of Buoyancy and Hydrostatics—Buoyancy and Effective Forces. *Mod. Appl. Sci.*, 11, 12, 78, 2017.
29. Ivković, J. and Ivković, J., Analysis of the performance of the new generation of 32-bit Microcontrollers for IoT and Big Data Application, *7th International Conference on Information Society and Technology*: ICIST 2017, 3, 2017.
30. Agarwal, A., Shukla, V., Singh, R., Gehlot, A., Garg, V., Design and Development of Air and Water Pollution Quality Monitoring Using IoT and Quadcopter, in: *Intelligent Communication, Control and Devices. Advances in Intelligent Systems and Computing*, vol. 624, R. Singh, S. Choudhury, A. Gehlot, (Eds.), Springer, Singapore, 2018.
31. Mohindru, V. and Garg, A., Security Attacks in Internet of Things: A Review, in: *The International Conference on Recent Innovations in Computing*, 2020, March, Springer, Singapore, pp. 679–693.
32. Mohindru, V., Singh, Y., Bhatt, R., Hybrid cryptography algorithm for securing wireless sensor networks from Node Clone Attack. *Recent Adv. Electr. Electron. Eng. (Formerly Recent Patents Electrical & Electronic Engineering)*, 13, 2, 251–259, 2020.
33. Mohindru, V., Bhatt, R., Singh, Y., Reauthentication scheme for mobile wireless sensor networks. *Sustainable Comput.: Inf. Syst.*, 23, 158–166, 2019.
34. Mohindru, V., Singh, Y., Bhatt, R., Securing wireless sensor networks from node clone attack: A lightweight message authentication algorithm. *Int. J. Inf. Comput. Secur.*, 12, 2–3, 217–233, 2020.
35. Mohindru, V. and Singh, Y., Node authentication algorithm for securing static wireless sensor networks from node clone attack. *Int. J. Inf. Comput. Secur.*, 10, 2–3, 129–148, 2018.

13

Mind-Controlled Unmanned Aerial Vehicle (UAV) Using Brain–Computer Interface (BCI)

Prasath M.S.*, Naveen R. and Sivaraj G.

Aeronautical Engineering, Bannari Amman Institute of Technology, Erode, Tamilnadu, India

Abstract

In today's world drones are playing a vital role in all the fields. The drone controlling needs some precession skills and they can be controlled by skilled persons. In recent days, wireless applications are widely extended in the scientific, educational, and hobbyist communities. Brain-computer interface (BCI) is a connection between the human brain and computers. The scope is concentrated on the development boards which permit wireless communications. The neurons of our brains are capable of producing waves with certain frequencies. The frequency of the waves depends on our thought and actions performed by the brain. In present world, some hardware devices are available to sense the brain waves and process them. One such is the EEG (Electroencephalography) device; the EEG registers the ionic current flows within the neurons of the human brain along the surface of the head (scalp). The electrical signals generated in the brain are captured by the mind wave sensor and further the waves are processed with the BCI. The BCI gives commands microcontroller board and the pre-programmed microcontroller board sends the commands to the transmitter device of the drone. Based on the frequency of the wave produced by the neurons of the brain, the transmitter of the drone is controlled. And finally, the transmitter transmits signals to the receiver which is placed in the drone, thus controlling the actions of the drone. By implementing this type of EEG technique along with the BCI, even the professional drones can also be controlled by a common person with a few training in controlling the brain. The paper deals with the integration of BCI technology with unmanned aerial vehicles.

**Corresponding author*: prasathms90@gmail.com

Vandana Mohindru, Yashwant Singh, Ravindara Bhatt and Anuj Kumar Gupta (eds.) Unmanned Aerial Vehicles for Internet of Things (IoT): Concepts, Techniques, and Applications, (231–246) © 2021 Scrivener Publishing LLC

***Keywords*:** Drone, BCI technology, neurons, mind wave sensor, EEG technology

13.1 Introduction

An Unmanned Aerial Vehicle (UAV) is an aircraft that can be operated from ground and it can fly without the crew members to control in it. It is commonly known as drones. From the past decade, the Unmanned Aerial Vehicles (UAVs) have become a part of society. They play major roles in many areas and their service is unmatchable in major areas. Initially, they were used as surveillance drones in the military and later depending upon the size, their area of application expanded rapidly to scientific, commercial, agricultural and the other areas such as aerial photography, delivering online products, inspections and even used in drone racing competitions. Even in this pandemic situation, the drones are used to spray the sanitizers at hotspots.

13.1.1 Classification of UAVs

Unmanned Aerial Vehicles can be classified broadly depending upon their functions and sizes. Their functions include the role in different areas like defense, photography, agriculture and other hobby purposes.

Classification based on their size determines their area of application. So the classification of the unmanned aerial vehicle based on the size plays an important role. Depending on the size, the UAV we can be classified as Micro Air Vehicle, Medium Air Vehicle and Small Air Vehicle. And depending upon the type of wings and rotors used, the UAV can be classified as fixed-wing, rotor copters and flapping wing UAVs. These are the classifications of the UAVs based on their size and rotors used.

13.1.2 Drone Controlling

The drones may have a wide range of applications but operating a drone for a specific purpose is not an easy job. We require some serious skills to operate a drone. Sometimes we need to practice in flying the drone using some simulation software which is similar to the flight simulators. Building a drone takes high cost because of the components used in it. So it should be operated carefully and precisely. The idea behind this chapter is what if we have a technology for controlling the drones effectively? What if a drone that can fly and respond to whatever we think in our mind? It would be easier for everyone to operate the drone according to their purpose. Actually, it is possible to operate the drones with the help of our mind. It is possible with the emerging technologies and it is called the Brain–Computer Interface (BCI) [1]. This BCI technology enables a connection between the human brain and the drone with some hardware and software integration which helps in controlling the drones effectively [2].

13.2 Mind-Controlled UAV With BCI Technology

The Brain–Computer Interface (BCI) technology translates the signals produced in the neurons of the brain and commands the computer to work according to it. It is an integrated system of both hardware and software to work together in controlling the drone [3].

BCI Technology provides a new way of communication between the human and the machine. Initially, it was used as a system for physically challenged people. Many researchers have tried this BCI technology to help physically challenged people [4].

Whenever an action is done by the human brain it emits some electrical signals. A sensor (mind wave) is used to pick these signals. This sensor is based on Electron Encephalography (EEG) technology [5]. The collected signals are amplified and sent to the computer and it translates to specific commands. These commands were sent to microcontroller and finally the microcontroller commands to the transmitter which is already programmed with suitable commands. The receiver in the drone receives the signal and works accordingly. This is a brief intro about this BCI technology [6].

For every action performed in the face, the neurons of the brain will react to it and emit in the form of signals with definite wavelengths. The wavelengths of these signals are based on the type of action performed. The wave type with wavelengths and mental states are given in Table 13.1 [7].

The objective of BCI technology is to help the physically challenged or disabled people to interact with the help of computers [8]. The famous scientist Stephen Hawking used a BCI technology-enabled device as a voice synthesizer for him. It converts the brain signals to voice outputs. Similarly, it can be used in many forms. Many researchers used BCI technology and developed a wheelchair for disabled people [9]. Even some BCI enabled wheelchairs are commercially available in the market. The mind waves sensor picks the signals and BCI technology-enabled wheelchair will according to the user's mind wave signal [10]. The BCI for drone controlling was adapted from the BCI for the wheelchair and it helps in controlling the drone precisely and effectively [11].

Table 13.1 Brain waves and its frequency ranges.

Brain wave type	Frequency range	Mental state and conditions
Delta	0.1 to 3 Hz	Deep sleep, dreamless sleep, on REM sleep, unconscious
Theta	4 to 7 Hz	Intuitive, creative, recall, imaginary, dream
Alpha	8 to 12 Hz	Relaxed (but not drowsy) tranquil, conscious
Low Beta	12 to 15 Hz	Formerly SMR, relaxed yet focused, integrated
Mid-range Beta	16 to 20 Hz	Thinking, aware of self and surroundings
High Beta	21 to 30 Hz	Alertness, agitation

Many researchers have been started to use this BCI technology to focus on flying the drones. These drones come under the category of semi-autonomous drones. Some researchers are even focusing on controlling the drone with the blinking of an eye [12]. The blinking of the eye also creates signals in the brain and the EEG picks these signals to control the drone. It is possible to control the Drone in three-dimensional space with eight different directions using the blinks. The same mind wave sensor can also be used to pick the blink signals to control the drone are whatever device connected [13].

In coming to the drones for controlling with BCI, quadcopter comes to handy with this technology. The quadcopters have six degrees of freedom when comparing to other unmanned aerial vehicles. More degrees of freedom mean more controllability of the drone. So the quadcopters are the best choice for using this BCI technology and it has a wide range of applications in agricultural aerial photography military and other purposes [14].

13.3 Layout and Architecture of BCI Technology

BCI technology uses a wide variety of hardware and software components. The interactions and connectivity of these components are responsible for BCI technology [15].

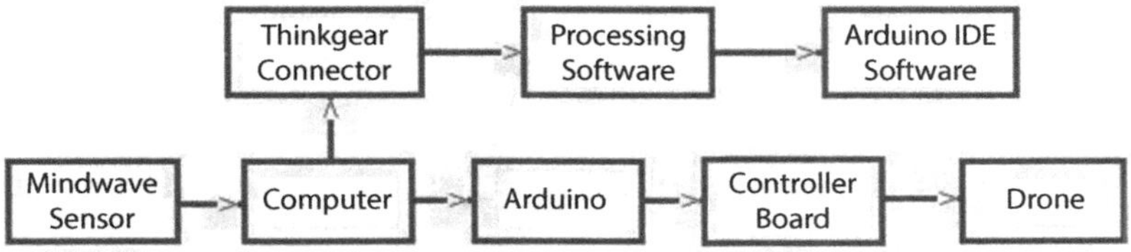

Figure 13.1 Layout of BCI technology.

The above Figure 13.1 is the layout for the BCI technology-enabled drone. This shows how the BCI technology works between the hardware and software components of the system to help the drone to control with human brain signals [16].

13.4 Hardware Components

For establishing this BCI technology, we need several numbers of hardware components and software components. The hardware components play a major role in establishing the BCI Technology. The sum of the hardware components are given as follows,

(a) NeuroSky mind wave headset
(b) Microcontroller board—Arduino
(c) Computer
(d) Drone (Quadcopter).

13.4.1 Neurosky Mindwave Headset

This BCI technology utilizes Electron Encephalography (EEG) to pick the neuron signals with the help of a mind wave sensor. These mind waves sensors are commercially available in markets and are ready to use with the given driver CD. Many manufacturing companies make these sensors with 80 to 90% of accuracy in reading the signals that are produced by the neurones. Any mind wave EEG headset can be used to pick up these signals. Some of the choices are NeuroSky mind wave headset, Emotive EEG headset and Emotive Insight headset.

The mind wave headset can capture the brain waves and easy to fit on the head and ear. The EEG technology is used in this headset and it reduces wire connections [17]. This device consists of a headset equipped with their sensor arm and an ear clip. This sensor uses dry electrodes

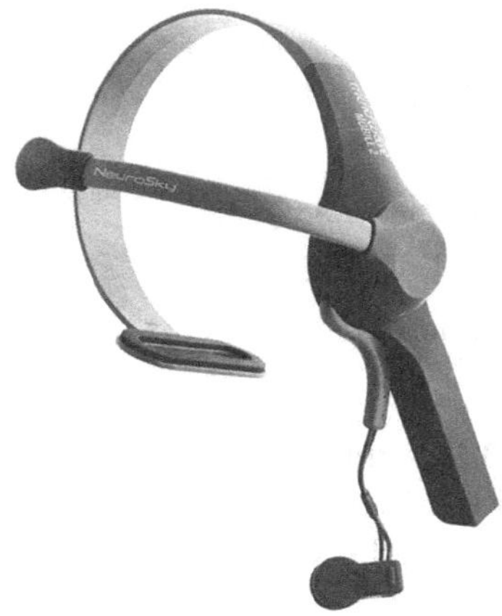

Figure 13.2 Neurosky mindwave headset.

which can measure the brain waves directly from the scalp and can be easily worn over the head. Hence this sensor safely measures the signals from the human brain. Neurosky mind wave sensor is the choice of EEG headset [18] shown in Figure 13.2. This sensor is comparatively smaller in size than other sensors and the frequency range is between 2.420 and 2.471 GHz RF. It can be easily connected to computers and tablet computers via Bluetooth or Wi-Fi connection. Hence it can be easily paired with Android, iOS and Windows operating systems. It is powered by two AA-size batteries to power the device. It can measure a variety of signals from the brain like raw signals, mental comments, facial expressions and even the eye blinks. It measures the brain activities based on attention, concentration, stress and relaxation.

13.4.2 Microcontroller Board—Arduino

The Arduino board is a small microcontroller board and it is like a miniature computer. It can perform the entire task similar to a computer. It has open-source hardware and software and helps to do many DIY projects. Additionally, these boards were supported by many user communities which helps in the design and manufacture of interactive devices. This board is highly customizable and uses the programming language based on C and C++. This board includes Li-Po charging circuits which allow the usage of Li-Po batteries as power supply.

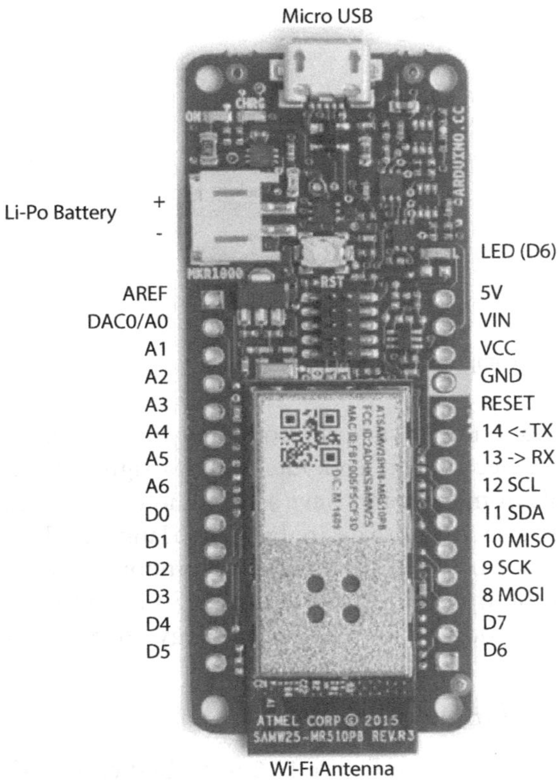

Figure 13.3 Arduino MKR 1000.

The Arduino MKR 1000 shown in Figure 13.3 is a powerful microcontroller board that combines the functionality of Arduino board with Wi-Fi shield. It is designed to offer the Arduino zero board with Wi-Fi compatibility. It has a USB port for power supply. The processing speed of this board is 2.4 Hz with 32-bit low power ARM MCU [19]. It makes the perfect choice of the microcontroller for this BCI-enabled drone.

13.4.3 A Computer

A computer or a laptop shown in Figure 13.4 is used to run the programs of Arduino and mind wave headset which are necessary to establish the BCI connection. We need a computer which can run the software components that are compatible with the BCI.

Figure 13.4 Laptop computer.

The configuration of OS and the computer must be minimum enough to run the BCI. Because the computer plays a significant role in receiving EEG signals from the mind wave sensor and the software components must translate those signals to desired machine language. Further, it should create an interface between the hardware components to give necessary commands to the transmitter of the drone. So a computer with a good configuration is important for a BCI technology-enabled drone.

13.4.4 Drone for Quadcopter

The quadcopter as shown in Figure 13.5 is the best choice of drone for the BCI technology for the drone. It has a higher number of degrees of freedom than other types of UAVs. Also, it is easy to operate and can do complex operations more efficiently. It has a wide area of applications. Hence the quadcopter are the best choice of drone for BCI-enabled drone [20].

Figure 13.5 Quadcopter drone.

Nowadays the quadcopter drones are easily available in markets with good configuration. So it would be easier to get a good quadcopter at a cost-effective price. And that can be easily or readily used for acquiring this BCI technology [21]. By applying this BCI technology to a quadcopter may create new areas of application to the drones and even a physically challenged person can also operate at severe conditions.

13.5 Software Components

Similar to the hardware components the software components of the BCI also determines the interaction between the human and drones. The following are the necessary software components for this technology.

(a) Processing P3 software
(b) Arduino IDE software
(c) Thinkgear connector software

13.5.1 Processing P3 Software

The Processing P3 shown in Figure 13.6 is an open-source software for the computer language development. It is used to write the program for

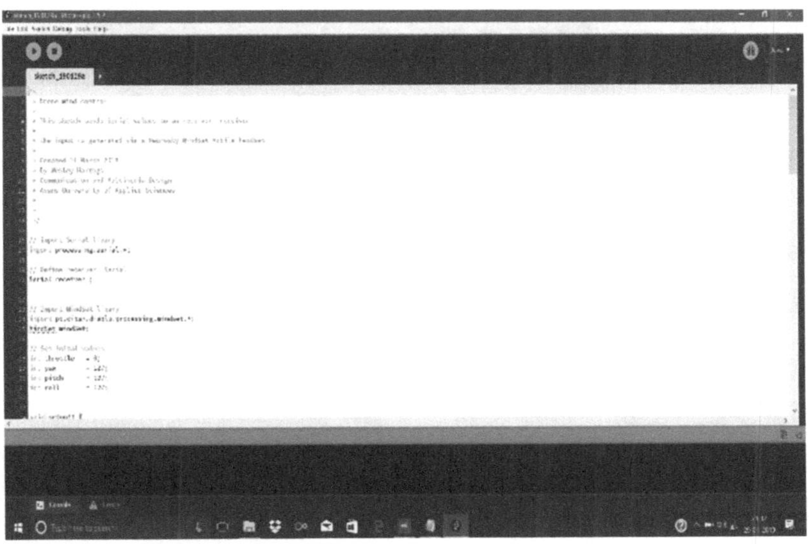

Figure 13.6 Processing P3 Software Window.

computers [22]. It uses the Java-based language to write the programs. It is flexible software to learn the coding. It establishes the communication between the computer and the Arduino board. According to the program it is further transferred to Arduino to process the program for commands given.

13.5.2 Arduino IDE Software

The Arduino IDE shown in Figure 13.7 is an open-source software product by Arduino and it is available in many online platforms. It is used for writing and compiling the codes into the Arduino board [23]. The Arduino IDE is available for operating systems like Windows Mac and LINUX which makes it very versatile to use with a wide range of operating systems.

Arduino IDE is based on Java language and which helps to embed the code written to the Arduino module. It also supports languages like C and C++ for coding. It is used to upload the coding commands to the microcontroller Arduino MKR 1000 and this makes the module to work according to our commands. This Arduino IDE plays an important role in establishing the BCI for uploading the command to the microcontroller.

13.5.3 ThinkGear Connector

The ThinkGear connector is a program that connects between the mind wave headset and computer via Bluetooth or Wi-Fi technology. It receives

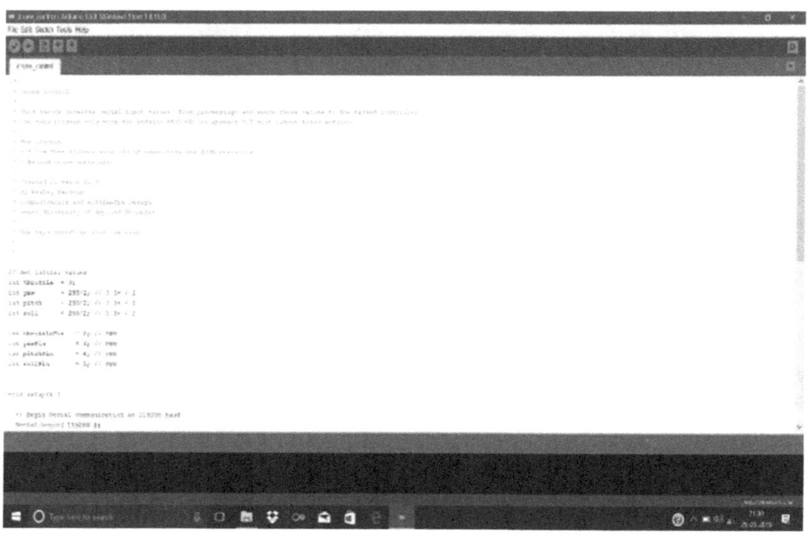

Figure 13.7 Arduino IDE Software Window.

the signals that are sent by the headset. It is connected serially with the processing P3 software and it is compatible with Windows Mac and LINUX operating system.

The ThinkGear connector runs in the background of the computer. It allows our mind wave signals to process in it and sends us feedback commands to order no ID. The ThinkGear connector should be running at the background before paring the headset with the computer.

13.6 Hardware and Software Integration

The most important part of BCI technology is hardware and software integration. This integration of hardware and software establishes the connection between the human brain and the drone [24]. The hardware integration is given in Figure 13.8.

First, all the necessary software should be installed on the computer. The ThinkGear connector receives the signal from the brain via NeuroSky

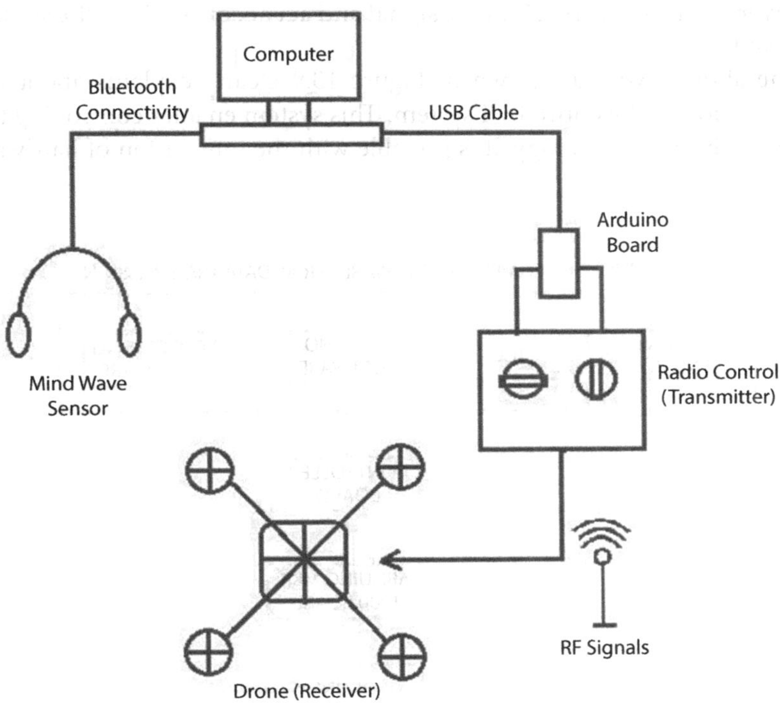

Figure 13.8 Hardware connectivity diagram.

mind wave headset. Then the Processing P3 software has to be installed for or writing the required coding. Later that coding has to be used in Arduino IDE software to upload the coding in Arduino module. Now all the software has been configured with the necessary coding and integrated with the computer. The necessary hardware connections have to be performed.

NeuroSky mind wave headset Arduino MKR 1000 board and drone are the major hardware components that are needed for establishing the BCI technology-enabled drone. Apart from the major hardware components, there are some minor components like a breadboard, jump clips, resistors, capacitors, and wirings are there to connect the Arduino board with the transmitter.

This BCI technology does not control the drone directly. It only controls the transmitter of the drone. Depending upon the signal sent by the transmitter, the drone responds. This is how the BCI controls the drone. For controlling the drone a circuit is designed with the minor components to power the transmitter. The Arduino board and the transmitter are connected into the breadboard. So, the command from the Arduino is transferred to the transmitter to control the drone. The receiver in the drone receives the signal and act accordingly to the signals received [25].

The above layout as shown in Figure 13.9 clearly explains about the transmission of the entire BCI system. This system enables controlling the drone with BCI technology. It is possible with the integration of hardware

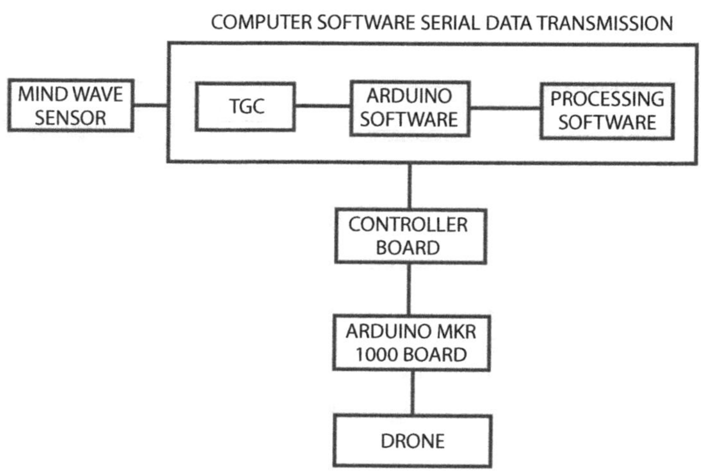

Figure 13.9 Data transmission diagram.

and software components. When an action is performed in the brain, the neurons create some EEG signal in it and the NeuroSky mind wave headset picks up those EEG signals and sends them to the computer via Bluetooth or Wi-Fi connectivity [26].

The ThinkGear connector software reads the received signals and processes them according to the wavelength of the received signal. Then the processed signals are sent to the Arduino board. The Arduino board which was already loaded with the commands from the Arduino IDE software receive the signals in analogue form. Along with other minor components in the breadboard reads and send signals to the transmitter of the drone.

The transmitter is the remote control of the drone. Each drone has specifically configured with a transmitter and receiver combo. The transmitter receives the signals from the breadboard and it transmits the signals to the receiver. These signals were RF signals which determine the throttle, pitch, roll and yawing movements of the drones. The 4 channel RF drone is the basic drone configuration and depending upon the area of application the number of channels may vary. The headsets may be configured according to the number of channels used in the drone [27]. The entire BCI technology works to control the transmitter of the drone to control the drone. This makes drone controlling a much easier task.

The connections between the headset and the computer are established with Bluetooth or Wi-Fi. The Arduino board is connected with the breadboard and then it is connected to the computer with a USB cable. The breadboard is also connected with the transmitter of the drone to control the drone. The data transmission is initially from the brain signals picked by the headset and the headset sends these signals via Bluetooth connectivity to the computer. The ThinkGear processes it and sends them to the Arduino board. Further, it acts according to the signal and commands and sends feedback to the transmitter. The transmitter transmits the RF signal to the drone depending upon the signal it has received. This is the entire data flow or data transmission between all the components (both hardware and software) of the BCI system [28].

13.7 Conclusion

The concept of controlling the drone using mind waves is emerging and it leads to many new areas of applications with less skill in drone controlling. Implementation of EEG in drone technology is an emerging field in drone controlling and it enhances the drone controlling with the help of simple EEG sensors [29]. The functionality of drones can be altered or reprogrammed according to the application area and also the area of application can be extended. This system can also help the people who suffer from physical disability e can also interact with the drone.

As similar to the application of normal drones the BCI technology-enabled drones can be used in all the fields [30]. The drone controlling needs some serious skill and BCI enabled drones doesn't need that. Even a person with less knowledge in drone controlling can also control the drones effectively [31–33].

References

1. Chiuzbaian, A., Jakobsen, J., Puthusserypady, S., Mind Controlled Drone: An Innovative Multiclass SSVEP based Brain Computer Interface. *2019 7th International Winter Conference on Brain-Computer Interface (BCI).*
2. Lin, J.-S. and Jiang, Z.Y., Implementing remote presence using quadcopter control by a non-invasive BCI device. *Comput. Sci. Inf. Technol.*, 3, 4, 122–126, May 2015.
3. Cheng, C.H., Li, S., Kadry, S., Mind wave-controlled robot: An Arduino Robot simulating the wheelchair for paralyzed patients. *IJRC*, 1, 3–15, Jun 2018.
4. Vidya, G., Vipitha, E., Hridya, S., Brain controlled home automation system. *IRJET*, 5, 4, 166–168, Apr 2018.
5. Mehendale, A. and Mehta, S., Mind Controlled Quadcopter. *Int. Res. J. Eng. Technol. (IRJET)*, 6, 6, 2114–2119, 2019.
6. Nourmohammadi, A., Jafari, M., Zander, T.O., A Survey on Unmanned Aerial Vehicle Remote Control Using Brain-Computer Interface. *IEEE Trans. Hum.-Mach. Syst.*, 48, 4, 337–348, May 2018.
7. Lin, H. and Li, Y., Chapter 25, in: *Using EEG Data Analytics to Measure Meditation*, Springer Science and Business Media LLC, New York, United States, 2017.
8. Kumar, R. and Paul, N., A review on EEG control smart wheel chair. *IJARC*, 8, 9, 1–2, Dec 2017.
9. Yu, Y., He, D., Hua, W., Li, S., Qi, Y., Wang, Y. *et al.*, Flyingbuddy2: A brain-controlled assistant for the handicapped. *Proceedings of the 2012 ACM Conference on Ubiquitous Computing*, 05–08 September, pp. 669–670, 2012.
10. Philips, J., Millan, J.R., Vanacker, G., Lew, E., Galan, F., Ferrez, P.W. *et al.*, Adaptive Shared Control of a Brain-Actuated Simulated Wheelchair. *Proceedings of the IEEE 10th International Conference on Rehabilitation Robotics*, 13–15 June 2007.
11. Diez, P.F., Muller, S.M.T., Mut, V.A., Laciar, E., Avila, E., B.-Filho, T.F. *et al.*, Commanding a robotic wheelchair with a high-frequency steady-state visual

evoked potential based brain–computer interface. *Med. Eng. Phys.*, 35, 8, 1155–1164, August 2013.

12. LaFleur, K., Cassady, K., Doud, A., Shades, K., Rogin, E., He, B., Quadcopter control in three-dimensional space using a noninvasive motor imagery-based brain–computer interface. *J. Neural Eng.*, 10, 4, 1–15, June 2013.
13. Kosmyna, N., Bernard, F.T., Rivet, B., Towards Brain-Computer Interfaces for Recreational Activities: Piloting a Drone. *Proceedings of the 15th International Federation for Information Processing Part I*, September 14–18, pp. 506–522, 2015.
14. *Mind-Controlled Drones: Not as far away as you think*, https://www.forbes.com/sites/kristykiernan/2019/04/03/mind-controlled-drones-not-as-far-away-as-you-think/?sh=7dd3bd6a190f
15. https://www.kickstarter.com/projects/bci/make-100-create-your-own-brain-computer-interface
16. Mandel, C., Luth, T., Laue, T., Rofer, T., Graser, A., K-Bruckner, B., Navigating a Smart Wheelchair with a Brain–Computer Interface Interpreting Steady-State Visual Evoked Potentials. *Proceedings of the International Conference on Intelligent Robots and Systems*, 10–15 October 2009.
17. Raja, R., Debb, S., Bhattacharyac, P., Brain-Computer Interfaced Single Key Omni Directional Pointing and Command System: A Screen Pointing Interface for Differently-abled Person, RoSMa2018. *Procedia Comput. Sci.*, 133, 161–168, 2018.
18. Tiwari, K. and Saini, S.P.S., Brain Controlled Robot Using Neurosky Mindwave. *JTASR*, Nov, 2015.
19. Arduino MKR 1000, https://store.arduino.cc/usa/arduino-mkr1000.
20. Raheja, O., Pawar, K., Saraf, M., Maiti, S., Mind Controlled Assistive Quadrotor Drone. *Int. J. Adv. Res. Comput. Commun. Eng.*, 7, 3, 341–345, 2018.
21. Vincenzi, D.A., Terwilliger, B.A., Ison, D.C., Unmanned aerial system (UAS) human–machine interfaces: New paradigms in command and control. *6th International Conference on Applied Human Factors and Ergonomics (AHFE 2015) and the Affiliated Conferences*, AHFE, 2015.
22. *Processing P3 software*, https://www.dcu.ie/iss/software/Processing-P3.shtml.
23. *Arduino IDE software*, https://www.arduino.cc/en/guide/environment.
24. Rosca, S., Leba, M., Ionica, A., Gamulescu, O., Quadcopter control using a BCI. *IOP Conf. Series: Materials Science and Engineering*, 2017.
25. Vishwanath, R.M., Kumaar, S., Omkar, S.N., *A Real-time Control Approach for Unmanned Aerial Vehicles using Brain–Computer Interface*, Arxiv, New York, 2018.
26. Vijayendra, A., Kumaar Saksena, S., Vishwanath, R.M., Omkar, S.N., A Performance Study of 14-Channel and 5-Channel EEG Systems for Real-Time Control of Unmanned Aerial Vehicles (UAVs), in: *2018 Second IEEE International Conference on Robotic Computing (IRC)*, IEEE, pp. 183–188, 2018.

27. Duan, X., Xie, S., Xie, X., Meng, Y., Xu, Z., Quadcopter Flight Control Using a Non-invasive Multi-Modal Brain–Computer Interface. *Front. Neurorobot.* 3, 1–11, 31, May 2019.
28. Sancripstopal, E. and Ruiz, E., *Wireless development boards to connect the world*, pp. 20–27, Springer International, Cham, Switzerland, Aug 2018.
29. *EEG technology*, https://en.wikipedia.org/wiki/Electroencephalography.
30. *BCI enabled drone*, https://www.hackster.io/WesleyCMD/mind-control-drone-c8b28a.
31. *Brain controlled drone*, https://futurism.com/the-byte/mind-controlled-drone-kickstarter.
32. Kushawaha, D., De, D., Mohindru, V., Gupta, A.K., Sentiment analysis and mood detection on an Android platform using machine learning integrated with Internet of Things, in: *Proceedings of ICRIC 2019*, Springer, Cham, pp. 223–238.
33. Mohindru, V. and Singla, S., A Review of Anomaly Detection Techniques Using Computer Vision, in: *The International Conference on Recent Innovations in Computing*, Springer, Singapore, pp. 669–677, March 2020.

14

Precision Agriculture With Technologies for Smart Farming Towards Agriculture 5.0

Dhirendra Siddharth[1], Dilip Kumar Saini[1]* and Ajay Kumar[2]

[1]*Department of Computer Science & Engineering, RAMA University, Kanpur, Uttar Pradesh, India*
[2]*Department of Biotechnology, RAMA University, Uttar Pradesh, India*

Abstract
This chapter looks at the role UAVs play in precision farming and the Internet of Things. It also analyzes scenarios for UAV implementations in a precision agriculture. IoT technology core principles are described, including smart sensors, networks and protocols used in agriculture, as well as IoT applications and smart farm solutions. It also analyzes the use of UAV systems in diverse agricultural ecosystems. UAV innovations are helping to improvethe farming exponentially. By the use of agriculture data and robotic solutions that integrate artificial-intelligent strategies, lays the groundwork for future sustainable agriculture. By revisiting each critical phase, this chapter analyzes the new era of farming system and role of UAV technologies which is help to improve the agriculture area, so that farmers can enable totake decisions to save cost of farming when preserving ecosystem and changing how food is generated.

Keywords: Unmanned aerial vehicles, agriculture 5.0, Internet of Things, smart farming

14.1 Introduction

Accuracy Agriculture is the third stage of the new agrarian revolution, Agri-tech expert states [1]. In October 2016, the U.S. Department of Agriculture

**Corresponding author*: dilipsaini@gmail.com

Vandana Mohindru, Yashwant Singh, Ravindara Bhatt and Anuj Kumar Gupta (eds.) Unmanned Aerial Vehicles for Internet of Things (IoT): Concepts, Techniques, and Applications, (247–276) © 2021 Scrivener Publishing LLC

reported the net returns and operating income for Precision Agricultural developments [2]. In embracing such technology, though, there is ambiguity and trade-offs involved. To ensure the sustainability of agricultural production, it is necessary to take the environment into account. The factors that will promote the implementation of sustainable farming technology, according to a market study, include better education and training for farmers. Farms which strive to be powered technologically in some way have great advantages, such as saving time and energy. However, introducing these advantages to the farm will rely on farmers' ability to incorporate new innovations into their fields [3]. The USDA stated that Precision Agriculture adopters' operating benefit for maize farms was $163 per hectare greater than that of non-adopters on average [2]. Increased use of precision farming resources is not just important for improving financial performance for a farm [4].

This post discusses important steps in information-based farming and focuses on data analytics. It discusses novel applications unique to individually critical process, from information and data collection in agricultural area to activities related to variable rate equipment. It examines that by the help of new technologies, the agriculture can aid in a balanced supervisory process.

14.2 Drone Technology as an Instrument for Increasing Farm Productivity

Agriculture is not an exclusive field. The productivity of field Laboure's has been greatly increased by the progressive robotics of agricultural systems. The only viable solution must come from the technology industry to this pressing need for agricultural productivity. Advanced processing of image data and drone technologies are capable of being core elements of a technologies combination that will fill the resource void. It will help satisfy existing agricultural demand and the requirements of the forthcoming [5].

For mobile, sophisticated image data acquisition, most applications rely on drones as an aerial medium. Drones may be rendered with a range of sensors, based on particular project specifications, for data such as image type. Analyzing crop plant health is the most advanced science, focused on drone image data. The Normalized Vegetation Difference Index (NDVI) will be established by a drone platform equipped with infrared cameras. Drone technology has taken the planning for the NDVI control to a whole new level of precision. This degree of knowledge encourages bugs, pathogens and plagues to be identified early [5]. Drone technology is increasingly used in coverage today and farm entitlements administration is main applications today. Every animal has a different heat mark with high-resolution infrared cameras that allow greater accuracy to be counted when opposed to conventional methods. With a variety of sensors, drone vehicles may be used in the entire production process [3, 5].

The drone technology industry and the processing of data and photographs are all in a continuous state of transition and development. Agricultural business operations are expected to fully exploit the potential of the drone technology. The successful processing of image images and the integration of drone-borne imagery and analysis into existing agricultural processes are a major challenge. For the agriculture industry, drone technology and expert approaches for analyzing image evidence are of considerable significance. The right combination of technology is needed to maximize yields and to reduce yields in agriculture. UAV technology used in a variety of applications during agricultural process, detailed mapping for forecasting drives, to effective field spraying, to field and plant condition assessment. The workload and hence the cost of materials will be of vital value in the Asia-Pacific region. The optimum capacity of the system is open for use, and improved performance [2, 5].

14.3 Mapping and Tracking of Rice Farm Areas With Information and Communication Technology (ICT) and Remote Sensing Technology

The IRRI launched a programme called Remote Sensing Based Knowledge and Crop Insurance in Developing Economies (RIICE) in 2012. This Development and Cooperation program has sponsored by the Swiss Organization [6, 8] (Figure 14.1).

In 2014, the Republic of the Philippines introduced and sponsored a new organization named the Philippines Rice Information System (PRISM). In the Kingdom of Thailand, the field scope was extended during Phase II (2015–2017) [7].

Satellite-based rice monitoring (SRM) systems cover crop modeling, remote sensing, and ICT software. RIICE technology is able to provide reliable, timely information at the village level on areas planted with rice. Approximately 24 million hectares of rice are tracked in 2016 with precision over 85% [8].

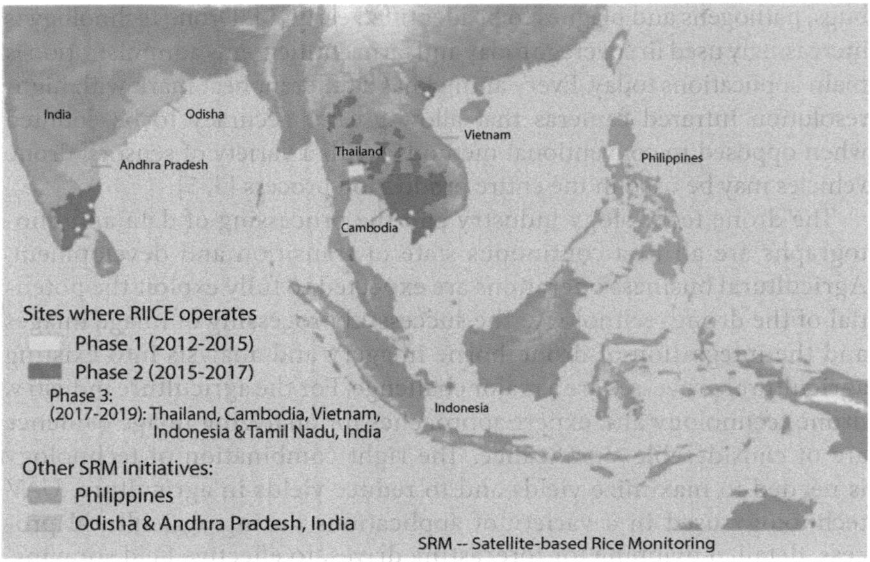

Figure 14.1 Rice monitoring with the help of satellite.

Above everything, the Satellite based Rice Monitoring (SRM) approach is focused on the introduction of emerging technology. This rice management system assists stakeholders in the rice industry. The information provided will also help supply chain players and governments to better manage and recognise any risks associated with rice production. In addition, high-quality data produced by RIICE technology can be used to make crop insurance products more affordable and transparent [11]. Plans for mapping and monitoring satellite-based rice crops already rolled out in good practice. Added Combined Remote Sensing and Agronomy ICT's. The ICTs have been used for earth observation with advanced remote sensing, seed propagation and interpretation applications [9].

14.3.1 Methodology and Development of ICT

Three software modules are deployed on the satellite rice monitoring device. Rice Yield Estimation System (Rice-YES) ORYZA Crop Growth

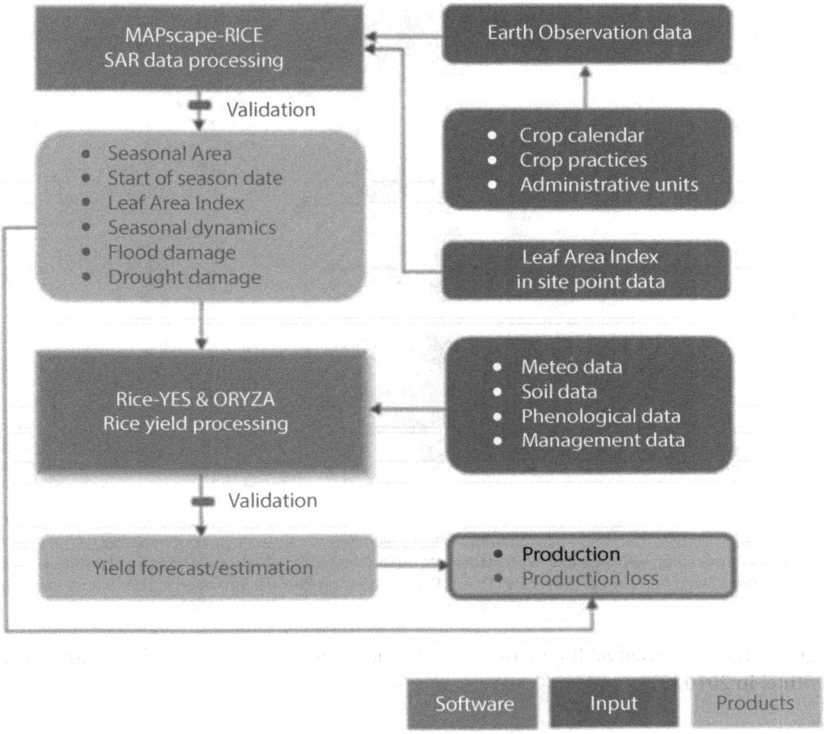

Figure 14.2 MAPscape-Rice Rice processing of SAR raw data [36].

Model and MAPscape-Rice are used (Figure 14.2). Rice-YES combines remote sensing info with soil, climate and agronomical administration info to put on rice crop. Maps were created for the rice region of the Mekong Delta and for the start of the season (SoS) (Winter Spring) [9].

Throughout the times of natural calamities including drought and earthquakes, the system provides a map of the impacted area. When contrasted with typical flood region.

Rice area and ground details were complete timely and accurate to farmers with a degree of accuracy exceeding 85%. A field and soil and water evaluation system observing the health condition of rice crops is also included in the process [9].

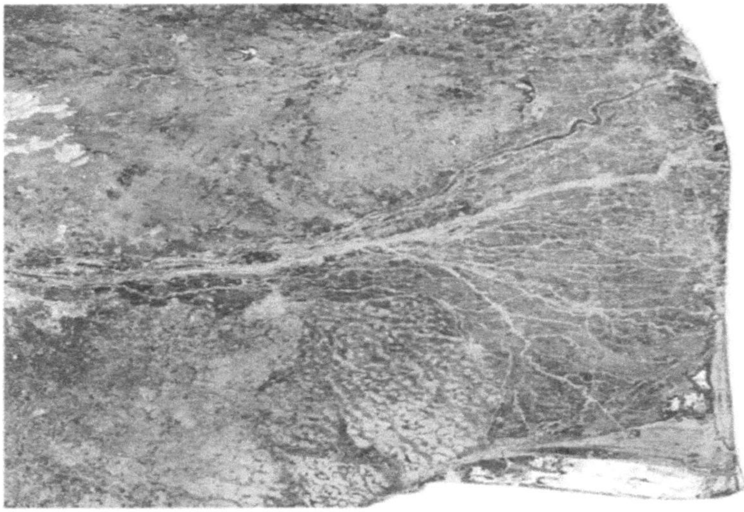

Note: Light blue to magenta colours indicate cultivated rice fields whereas light to dark green represent forests. Information derived from these data contributes in acceleration of insurance pay out impacting more than 200 000 rice farmers who were not able to plant their rice during the Samba 2016 season because of insufficient water. Credits: Tamil Nadu Agricultural University (TNAU). Remote Sensing-based information and insurance for Crops in Emerging Economies (RICE), European Space Agency (ESA).

Figure 14.3 Processed SAR data over Tamil Naidu, India in Cauvery Delta region form Sentinel in 2016 [37].

14.4 Strong Intelligence From UAV to the Agricultural Sector

Throughout the last three years, the application of drones to farming has grown in amazing ways, says SAP. HANA by SAP and Leonardo [10].

We will discuss the recent past of drones related to agricultural problems in this chapter. The emphasis will be on the technical benefits provided to the Agri-sector by the analysis of drone existing data output software. We'll present two examples of using SAP drone tech to solve real-world farming issues (Figure 14.3).

14.4.1 Latest Agricultural Drone History

Drone technology attracted the interest of both growers, developers and entrepreneurs. 'Precision farming' is the new agricultural technique which aims to make production more effective.

The drone dedication centered not only on the production of drone-captured images needed. The startups that elevated funds divided broadly

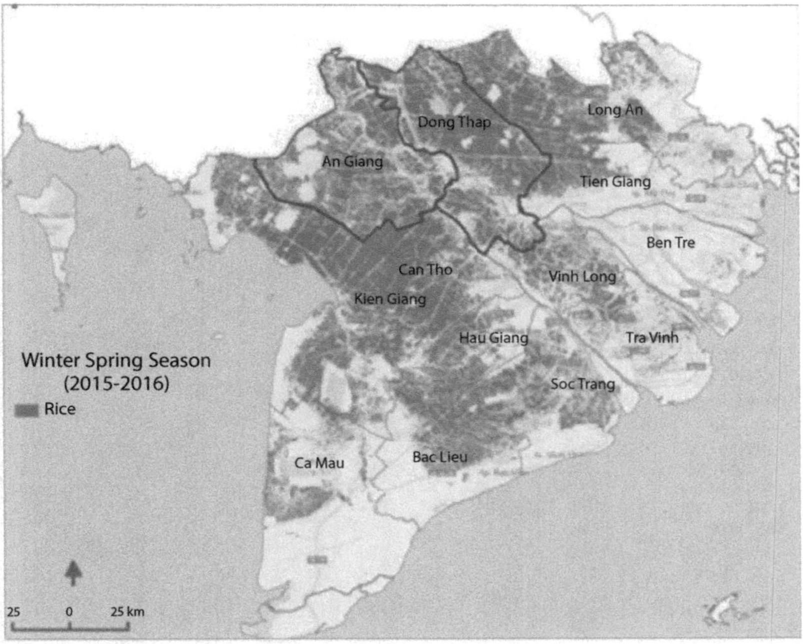

Figure 14.4 Rice area for Mekong Delta, Viet Nam for Winter Spring season 2015–2016 derived from SAR Sentinel-1 data and *in situ* information [37].

into two groups. First one is providing some analysis of the images obtained and the manufacturers of unmanned aerial vehicles (UAV) and second is drone software platforms mapping flights. Some have done so. In this chapter the focus will be on analyzing the pictures got [11].

There were signs it toward the end of 2015 whereby expectations may well have been inflated for the technology in agriculture (Figure 14.4). One potential sign of this may be the fall of 64% compared to 2015 in capital for drone start-ups and applications. More notably, however, the signals have appeared in the agricultural community [12]. Farmers were able to fly over their farms even more than they wanted in the early days to detect problems including drainage leakage. But the detail wasn't enough fast and farmers protested that the images had very little value. It became clear however by time, the images up-to-date them. This has still tardily to rectify issues.

Agriculturalists quickly required more out of their photographs besides the term "acting intellect" became popular with startups and investors focused on technology. The first move in presenting this actionable information was to establish crop health maps that would classify areas with

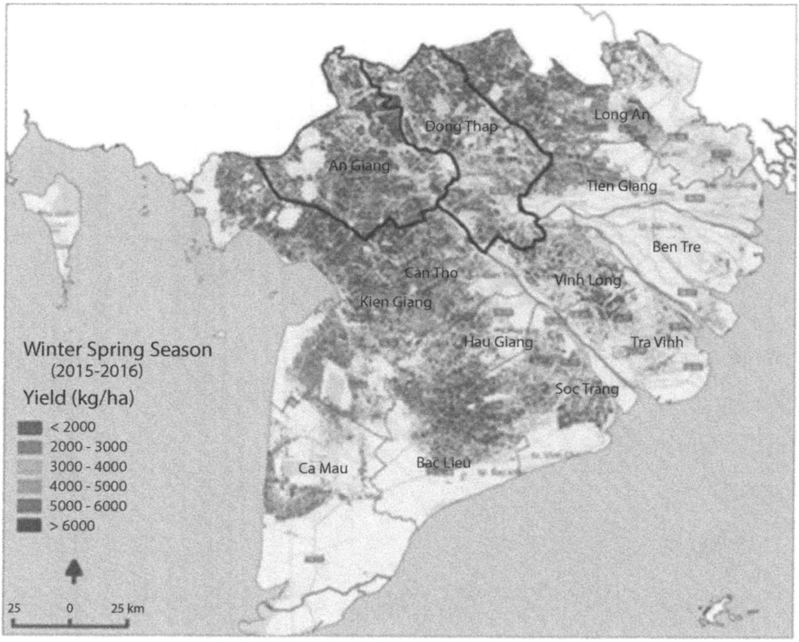

Credits: RIICE, European Space Agency-ESA.

Figure 14.5 Yield map for Mekong Delta, Viet Nam for winter spring season 2015-2016 derived from SAR Sentinel-1 data and *in situ* information [37].

possible yield losses for farmers (Figures 14.5 and 14.6). Using Near-Infrared (NIR) sensors, it's done through calculating the live green plants in harvests. These maps show crop health by color, ranging from dark blue/green for most vegetable areas to red for less protected areas (see Figure 14.7) [13].

14.4.2 The Challenges

Drone farming technologies focused on image sharing for processing into the cloud. Farmers and agronomists, however, have reported that this can become a hard job. Without real-time, actionable observational knowledge, many believe that their costs are not worth the technology.

14.4.3 SAP's Next Wave of Drone Technologies

The standardization of drones has made the actual flying entity not as much of significant. SAP Released SAP Leonardo in 2016 to address this

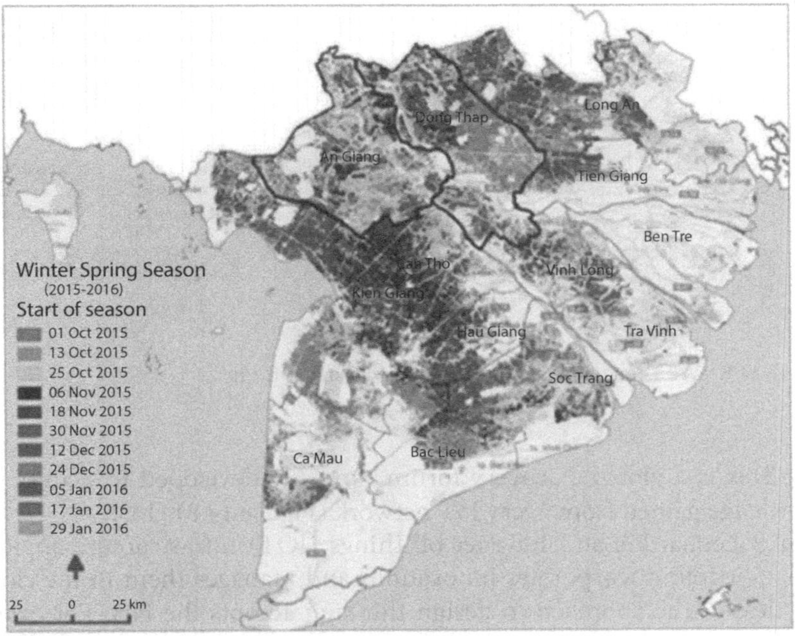

Credits: RIICE, European Space Agency-ESA.

Figure 14.6 Start of season map for Mekong Delta, Viet Nam for winter spring season [38].

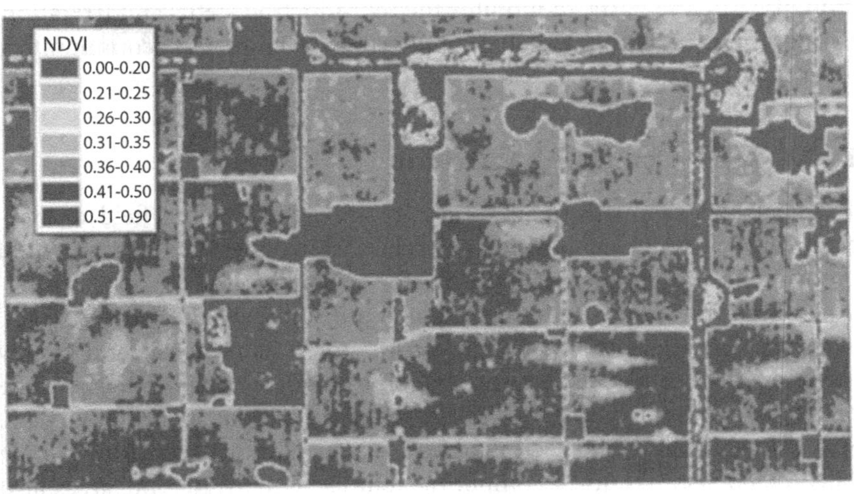

Source: DroneDeploy (no date)

Figure 14.7 An example of an NDVI map depicting crop health.

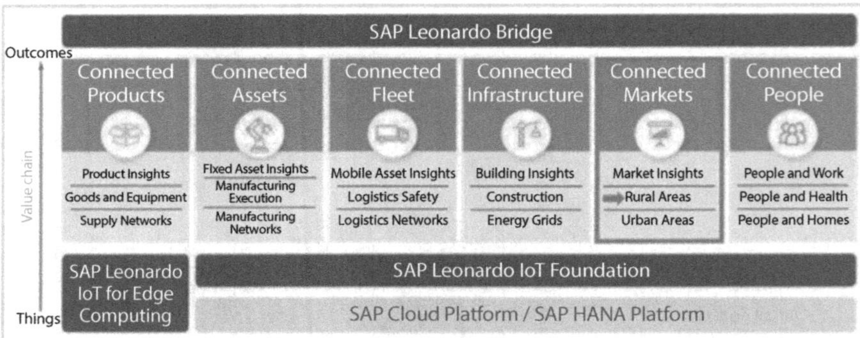

Figure 14.8 SAP Leonardo—a digital modernization platform.

call. This is a global discovery forum expressly developed to deliver the knowledge gained from every IoT network (Figure 14.8) [14].

SAP Leonardo's and Internet of Things (IOT) infrastructure applications portfolio incorporates innovations and manages them in the cloud seamlessly. The approach to design thinking accepts the fact. For example, drone may be integrated all data in a typical fashion into a device. Design Thinking provides a simple approach to plan and test solid ideas easily, using exclusive Leonardo app modules [14]. The agriculture area is the pre-renowned commercial drone use area. Drones are used to detect crop diseases and pests, to monitor the reproduction status and irrigation. Farmers connect with the global supply chain, even in rural communities, via mobile devices.

14.4.4 SAP Connected Agriculture

The goal of UAV platform is to support creativity in the field of agribusiness with a modern business model. This involves the development of innovations and the current strategies for optimization.

A significant feature of the app is that it utilises HANA Cloud on the IoT platform. The amount of data that can be stored is immense, and greatly beats most cost-effective conventional on the spot storing. Farming drone carried five sensors for instance will generate the alike of 50,000 GB of data. Such as using the cloud technologies to conveniently access and handle data, Cloud also has quick computing abilities. Finally, Remote areas also lack access to stream the data into the cloud from the drone sensor. There are distinct developments in software and hardware components that solve this problem [15].

- Solar cell charged will power the local Wi-Fi receiving stations.
- Smart intelligence adjusts the task workload on acquiring drone receivers.
- Pre-processing on-farm data would diminish the volume of data to be transmitted to the cloud.
- A local Wi-Fi service to access that information can be collected easily
- Processing on drone would be required for retrieving the data after flight.

We need to collect data not only from drones but from all available sources of information to create actionable intelligence at decision level. It's clear that data gathered by drones only won't give us a full image of the issue. Drone data can be used along with GIS data, data to predict, as well as other information sources. This is what IoT framework Leonardo Uses Related Agriculture uses to promote collaboration through open interfaces and standardization through the Leonardo Foundation Technological Tools [16].

IoT applications offered by the SAP Cloud Platform could be used to connect the devices. The interaction may be bidirectional, linking to remote devices, but also transmitting commands and receiving system data to remote devices.

14.4.5 Cases of Real-World Use

There are practical real-world instances of linking drones from SAP's Leonardo Linked Farming suite offering useful lessons for innovative solutions to vastly distinct agricultural problems.

14.4.5.1 Crop Surveying

Several yields can emerge as of drone monitoring to increase viability and harvest performance. For e.g., bananas, cotton, grapes.

The Leonardo Related Farming Suite was introduced to display prototypes/ideas for each sector. A record of a yield tree will be given:

- Summary of entirely agricultural steps useful to tree/bush cash crop
- Full proof that yield originates from region of farming developed

- List of the trees affected by the pest or blights
- A log of tree inputs, e.g. fertilizer/manpower/insecticide
- Benefit and Loss information at bush/tree level
- Data of seeds collected from the plants and ties to novel arboreal seedlings
- Study of the yields and steps for increasing crop quantities and quality.

Yields are really a major concern with all farmers with cash crops. Increased yields are vital to fulfilling demands for food as the population of the world has grown.

Holding the size of the challenge in mind here is important. Growers must also improve their operation if plantations are to thrive commercially. 2000 acres of banana plantains are common, and the survey of such a large area requires an efficient thinking. A variety of hypotheses had been brainstormed in a Design Thinking class. While Internet of Things sensors are affordable and usable, the absolute number needed to tag each. The solution chosen was drone overflying of plants/fields/forestry combined with GIS data and advance analysis and has been introduced in the project. Related Agriculture makes use of applied technology to obtain actionable perspectives [17].

14.4.5.2 Capture the Plantation

In standard grid pattern even, the plantations are well laid with the leaves. This makes it possible to map large plantation areas easily for human-controlled or autonomous UAVs. At various angles, a sequence of smooth, two-dimensional images is taken, using GPS coordinates to record the location of the images [18].

14.4.5.3 Image Processing

To ensure quick durability, the lots of pictures collected by the UAV are processed in HANA. To assemble millions of images into three-dimensional (3-D) geographical info, OpenDroneMap is used.

The next move is to use Pix4D (Pix4D, no date), another image processing method. This is a solution based on advanced automated aerial triangulation to transform the 3D point cloud into 3D surface models. This method is focused solely on quality of the picture and special techniques of optimization. The result of approach is a GeoTIFF file. It is a metadata standard for the public domain that enables the embedding of geo-referencing information inside a TIFF file. Additional knowledge includes the probability, ellipsoids, teamwork mechanisms, map projection data [18].

14.4.5.4 Working to Create GeoTiles and an Image Pyramid

It is possible to merge GIS-layer data into GeoTIFF. The SAP Item store applies yields, records of fertilizers, and records of harvests to all historical data gathered for each tree. The SAP Geo Services layer essentially creates a picture pyramid by which the user can dig up and down a stack, down to a single branch [19].

Linked Agriculture can produce multiple attributes to track all of the events applied to the plant over time, including down to the tree level.

A farmer could use the Linked Farming crossing point to repeat time and monitor whether the plant evolved and established over 25 years, as per SAP Proof of Concept. In Related Agriculture, HANA Analytics can be used to comprehend the influence of actions. For e.g.,

How has the harvesting capability affected the rainy season? Costly fertilizer proved beneficial in the yields?

An advanced device makes survey of the drones. Drones are now becoming commodity products and, for a few hundred bucks, you can purchase really capable units. SAP Proof of Concept threads the images together, making them into clouds of objects. Scenario experiments using

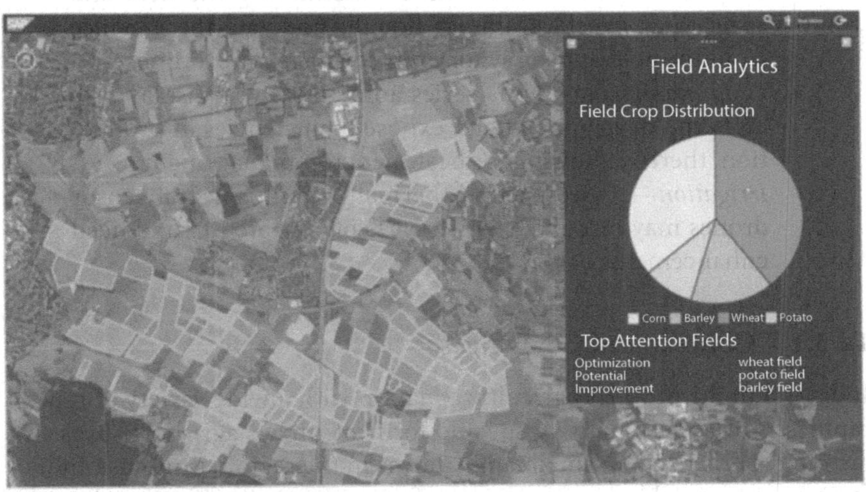

Figure 14.9 Linked interface for agriculture [39].

the Leonardo Machine Learning (Artificial Intelligence) framework is some of the most powerful approaches to valuable information.

The machine learning model of linked agriculture remotely models a farm and offers insight into future outcomes. In the course of time the Leonardo ML Engine is tailored to an individual plantation. When comparing forecasts to real effects, a surprising precision was found. The data is in digital form, it is possible to incorporate a whole variety of technology to collect useful information (Figure 14.9) [19].

14.5 Drones-Based Sensor Platforms

It is estimated that the global population will reach 9 billion by 2050 and that food production will grow by 70%. Unmanned use of aerial vehicles in agriculture paves the way for real-time viewing of field information. Theoretically, PwC predicts the need for drone-powered agricultural solutions to be USD 32.4 billion [20]. It's used at different stages and during entire harvesting cycle:

- *Analysis of field and soil*—Subsequently detailed 3D maps for soil can be planted for further operations the expected and nutrient status will be evaluated.
- *Planting*—Unmanned aerial systems shoot nutrient seeds in the soil for reducing planting costs.
- *Crop spray*—The drones will be monitoring the field and sprig the correct volume of liquid, modulate the distance from the field and spray for even coverage in real time.
- *Crop monitoring*—Time series animations will display precise crop development and expose inefficiencies in production, thereby allowing for healthier crop management.
- *Irrigation*—Hyperspectral, thermal or multispectral sensor drones may recognize which parts of area are dry and need enhancements.

14.5.1 Context and Challenges

India is a multi-product agricultural nation with a wide variety of topographies, soil and climate. A specific form of mixed agri-horti-livestock farming is practised on small family farms in the region. Multitask Indian farmers, and quickly turn from crop farming to animal husbandry. The Indian agriculture sector has improved over and through this flexibility.

Despite the transition, there are still a range of factors restricting Indian agriculture, including erratic weather, dispersed and limited land holdings, unscientific farming, slow technological adoption. It suggests a desperate need for technical change inside the system. Agriculture needs to be more based on instantaneous knowledge so farmers can [20]. In the agricultural background there are many problems relating to the introduction of UAVs:

- *Quality software*—Technology plays a key role in the technology's applicability from flight path planning through to final image processing.
- *Legal issues*—The respective nations have their own legislative system for the application.
- *Acceptability*—Technical unconsciousness can be an obstacle to its saturation.
- *Flight range and time*—Many UAV have small ranges to flight that narrow area that they can reach.
- *Initialization development costs*—Drones are very expensive and have features ideal for use in agriculture.
- *Airspace disturbance*—Drones share the same airspace as manually controlled planes.
- *Accessibility*—Farmlands do not have sufficient access, for the most part. Farmers need to invest in networking processes.
- *Wetter reliance*—Drones' procedures are heavily climate-based Word, thereby restricting their use.

14.5.2 Stakeholder and End Consumer Benefits

This is a ground-breaking invention that generates immense benefit over the entire value of the product.

Farmers—Farmers have access to data about their farms in real time, and thus are capable of making educated decisions. They are able to schedule their entire crop cycle, maximise and make full profit from farm operations. Which results in an increase in the net income of farmers from their farms.

Input partners—Optimization of farm activities and a data-driven approach will assist corporations to prepare their supplies ahead of time.

Credit and insurance firms—Credit and insurance providers also profit, as they simplify business processes. Insurance companies can disburse the cash pay-out effectively based on real-time field results. A Digitalized

Farm, Similarly, a farmer's credit-worthiness on a digitized farm could be better justified.

Mechanization Industry Farm—Machinery farm activities can be made more effective, thereby growing resource use.

Supply chain intermediaries—Using indicators of crop yields and expected harvesting will benefit aggregators.

Food manufacturing industry—Institutions of food processing can also plan and aggregate procurement using farm info. Farm data include information on location, acreage, yield, and time of harvest [21].

14.5.3 The Technology

TCS has developed and produced in-house, fully autonomous multirotor drones. It uses advanced technology, and multi-security structural health tracking. This UAV has a lengthy range with heavy payload and high strength capabilities. Multi payloads are configurable; there are thermal cameras and multi-spectral. It is available with payload and internet frequencies in a customizable range. It is suitable for various applications such as protection of the environment, forestry, livestock and structure review [22, 23].

14.5.3.1 Provisions of the Unmanned Aerial Vehicles

1. Quad-rotor (4-rotor helicopter) [22] (Figure 14.10)
2. Payload: Camera for monitoring crop health
3. Size: 2.5 feet length × 2.5 feet width × 2 feet height)

Figure 14.10 TCS Quad-rotor drone.

4. Geo-fence, home return feature in case emergency like low battery (height set at 60 m)
5. Weight: 4.5 kg
6. Power: Battery powered electric motors

14.6 Jobs of Space Technology in Crop Insurance

The most important predictors for evaluating insurance claims in the Government of India's Pradhan Mantri Fasal Bima Yojna (PMFBY) crop insurance scheme are crop yield forecasts at the lowest defined administrative level. To estimate crop yields, the well-established crop cutting experiment (CCE) technique was used. The design and calculation of CCE plots is focused on observational evidence and on the use of random numbers in current methods of yield estimation. CCEs as required further down the new harvest insurance policy may not be taken into account in the crop situation of the new year (area sown and crop condition) [23].

Using remote sensor data from satellites the CCE locations need to be calibrated. A great deal of pilot experiments was performed in different parts of the world. The pilot experiments have been carried out in the districts of Karnataka, Haryana, and Madhya Pradesh. In each province, two Districts were designated during the 2015–2016 winter season. During the winter season, study was performed in one block of a selected state. The blocks mentioned for examination were respectively FatehabadRatiya (Haryana), YadgirShorapur (Karnataka), HoshangabadBabai (Madhya Pradesh), and Solapur Karmala district (Mahar Maharashtra) [23].

Based on remote sensing, high resolution satellite data is used to calculate vegetation indices. These indices show crop vigor and crop water status, respectively. The district as a whole is divided into 4 groups/strata dependent on these two indices—Very Fair (A), Fair (B), Rational (C) and Poor (D) (Figure 14.11).

In addition to geographic location and field photographs (Figure 14.12), ISRO has developed an Android app to collect Crop Cutting Experiment data.

All of the CCE data collected via smartphones is submitted in live data to ISRO's Bhuvan geoportal. The planning of CCE using Remote Sensing indices is statistically effective and thus will improve the CCE quantity. The state government of Karnataka used this strategy during the 2016 monsoon season for operational CCE preparation and the government of the state of Odisha for the 2017 rainy season (Figure 14.13) [24].

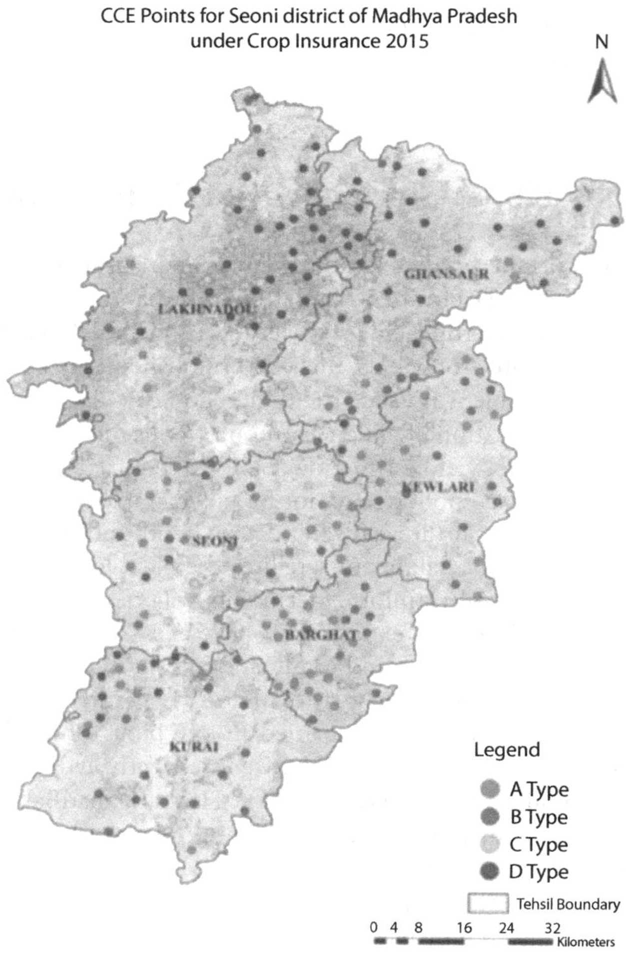

Figure 14.11 Crop cutting experiment (CCE) sites.

The beneficiary of this invention will be the State Agriculture departments and the insurance agencies. However, the farmers will benefit indirectly from this technology, as it guarantees.

Various factors helped to make this work a success:

- A compelling need to improve/rationalize the CCE
- Long experience with the use of data from satellites
- Wide range of high-resolution data available from satellites

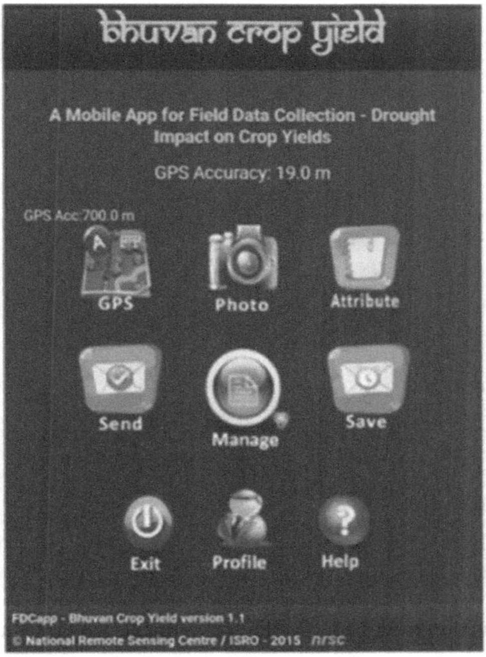

Figure 14.12 Android app being used for Crop Cutting Experiment data collection using smartphones.

- Smartphones are now easy to access throughout the country.
- Bhuvan portal's availability for regional data storage
- Daily capacity-building by MNCFC for smartphone-based data collection of State agricultural department officials
- The presentation of this technology in different fora—lectures, conferences, training etc.

Nevertheless, the use of that strategy also has many drawbacks.

- Eight crops (sugarcane, wheat, rice, potato, rapeseed, mustard, sorghum, jute and cotton) are currently being operationally calculated using satellite data. The approach to CCE preparation focused on remote sensing is restricted to those eight crops.
- Even among the eight crops listed above, the relationship between crop yield and remote sensing-based index is comparatively poor for some crops (other than cereals). In such

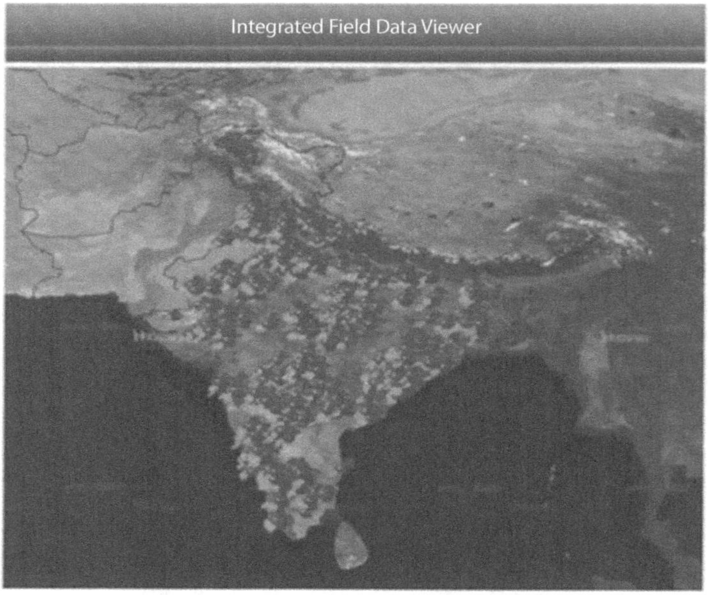

Figure 14.13 Information from Crop Cutting Experiments submitted to ISRO's Bhuvan platform.

situations, the CCE preparation based on remote sensing could not be statistically viable.

- Only until the maximum vegetative stage of a crop is reached can remote sensing-based CCE plans be made. Therefore, it offers very short lead time for implementation in this market.
- Due to the constant cloud cover during the rainy season, it is difficult to obtain cloud-free optical data for most monsoon season crops. Which limits the implementation of CCE planning based on remote sensing.
- While the country's smartphone use has increased immensely, many field officials have no access to smartphones. They have trouble collecting smartphone-based data.

Below are different lessons learned through the pilot studies and the development process:

- Required to implement officials gave an unprecedented response to recent technology learning
- Yield values were statistically quite close to those of a significant number of conventionally acquired

- Many new insights could be obtained from data collection on smartphones.
- Higher resolution satellite data is needed to make crop classification more accurate
- Remote sensing indices, such as soil, should be paired with other yield management parameters.

Given the gradual increase in the performance of satellite info collected and the rapid development of numerous other associated technologies, this strategy can also be further strengthened. The pilot studies for various crops were performed in different Argo-climatic regions of the world. In the states of Odisha and Karnataka, the approach has also been implemented operationally [24].

14.7 The Institutionalization of Drone Imaging Technologies in Agriculture for Disaster Managing Risk

Myanmar is an ethnically mixed country with a population of approximately 52 million. In rural areas, more than 70% of the population lives. Agriculture, cattle, forestry, aquaculture and other natural resource industries constitute more than 60% of the country's employment. Myanmar is one of the countries with the greatest chance of natural hazards in Southeast Asia. Among the main threats are earthquakes, flooding, hurricanes, droughts and tsunamis. Increased risks from climate change are also vulnerable to the region [25].

Subsequently, farming was the sector most impacted by tragedies, responsible fordeaths. The problems need more comprehensive techniques based on an extensive examination of hazards. In 2016, Myanmar has stepped up to farming sector to handle disaster by the help of disaster risk reduction (DRR) and adaptation to improve government agencies in the agriculture sector [25].

14.7.1 A Modern Working

The World emphasized the necessity to move from reactive management of disasters to constructive risk reduction. It is not possible to isolate the solution to the crisis from efforts to adapt to broader development and climate change. Modern methods of operating have been seen as the cornerstone to creating stability and reducing environmental disasters and the challenge and threat of climate change.

The FAO started collaborating with Myanmar Aerospace Engineering University (MAEU) in September 2016 to study the use of UAV. This led to technology institutionalization within Agriculture Ministry, Livestock. The MOALI Drone Mapping Team has extremely country-specific drones and technological experience. FAO is recognised as the world's first catastrophe risk management agency (DRM) drone to be used in agriculture [25].

14.7.2 Discovering Drone Mapping Technology

The first series of drone mapping missions to kick off the FAO's emergency response and resilience-building programmes were carried out.

The FAO and the MAEU also undertaken a number of field testing and airlifts tests. FAO also offered practical guidance on methodologies for quickin-flight evaluation.

Using UAVs established by the FAO and the Department of Agriculture (DoA), quick plotting assignments were undertaken to notify community assessments and summarizing, and to identify beneficiaries. Data obtained from outputs of drone flights, such as high-resolution flood-affected images.

It identified mapping sites based on:

1. Evidence of standing crops and destruction from the Agriculture Department
2. Consultation with officials at MOALI
3. Advising city and rural officials
4. logistics/Safety/Access Ease.

Any positive impacts have arisen from this pilot project and the recognition that the system is really useful. The data obtained from the drone also helps to address concerns about recipient prioritization at field level. Irrigation schemes and other water supplies can also be examined; collected data can be used for forthcoming danger valuation and backup preparation. When required government entry points are taped, the pilot project will proceed.

14.7.3 From Lowland to Uplands, Drone Mapping Technology

Torrential rains and cyclone Komen caused extreme floods and landslides in rural west Chin State in July 2015. Thousands of inhabitants were expelled, and half of the region's agriculture was washed out [25]. The applicability and technological validity of drone mapping innovations in upland farming has been demonstrated by FAO experts. The mapping exercises allowed experts from the government and FAO to powerfully validate the pertinency of UAV technology.

14.7.4 Institutionalization of Drone Monitoring Systems and Farming Capability

FAO continued working with MAEU to develop capabilities related to the use of technology by drones within MOALI. The FAO has shown the value of capacity development to expand technology such as mapping systems to all regions of the DRR [25].

The Government has formed the MOALI Drone Team with technical assistance from the FAO. The UAV mapping team comprises of 30 comprehensivespecialists in numerousuniversities. Research is a joint collaboration of two Chinese universities. It is the first of its kind to settle in the world. The drone mapping team has a responsibility to use this revolutionary geospatial technology to enhance tragedy readiness and reply operations for MOALI, include:

- Engage in training activities relating to drone actions, servicing in addition data processing in agriculture for enhanced DRR
- Routine flight flights to carry out
- Carry out flight missions assessing damage as required
- Daily servicing of drones and other flight equipment.

The FAO, MOALI and MAEU have arranged a training course for DRR in agriculture on drone mapping operations and research applications [27].

The development and supply of aerial mapping systems and instruments has been funded by the FAO. Drone fleet consists of 2 hex copters and 2 UAVs with fixed wing. The recent experience of FAO-MAE has taught the drone architecture and instrumentation. Equipment and software for data analysis were also supplied [25].

14.8 Usage of Internet of Things in Agriculture and Use of Unmanned Aerial Vehicles

To help growers, improve efficiency and reduce running costs, the Internet of Things (IoT) has been used. However, in most agricultural areas, prohibit the use of IoT in agriculture because of no WIFI or resources. In this chapter a Wireless Sensor Network (WSN) system based on Unmanned Aerial Vehicle (UAV) will be established [26].

The position of investigation in farming is highly promising, such as in the prevention of organic tragedies. The shortage of Wi-Fi stations and resources is a significant impediment to the introduction of tracking systems. An alternative approach is to use UAV for real-time data collection and analytics in wide areas [26].

14.8.1 System and Application Based on UAV-WSN

Systems based on UAV-WSN have been developed in many farms and adopted in the People's Republic of China.

The following Collaborators funded this project:

- Shenzhen Agriculture Technology Research Centre
- Shenzhen Nopoison Agrochemicals Co., Ltd., the largest fertilizer provider in the country
- D-Tech (Xintai) Technology Co. Ltd., Xintai County, Taian City, Shandong Province
- Shenzhen Economy and Trade Information Committee, funding provider.

The original condition with the farms' surveillance that there was no Wi-Fi system and no base station, so there are signals were too weak and we are facing difficulty in connection. Agriculturalists wanted a considerable amount of time to compile data on the farm. The new technology consists of using mobile communications such as GPRS of portable communications (3G or 4G). There was less resources on the farmland, or very bad and unreliable signals. Data gathered was difficult to transmit to the farmers' control center [26, 28–30]. This smart network system uses Wireless Sensor Network (WSN) mesh technology, which is 3G or 4G cell networking, GPS, 3D GIS [26, 31–34].

14.8.2 Using a Complex Comprehensive System

The wireless sensor network Unmanned Aerial Vehicle contains one detailed, complex framework that closely combines the above techniques. Figure 14.14 shows the acquired data through serial port communication with the Unmanned Aerial Vehicles. It was saved to contact through a serial port on an SD card after the data was acquired.

Figure 14.14 describes the Unmanned Aerial Vehicle—wireless sensor network system diagram. There are networks of wireless sensor networks that integrate hundreds of Zigbee nodes linked to sensor modules. It then integrates with these networks [27, 35].

Zigbee node will span a land radius of anywhere 200 and 500 m. Around 1,000 to 2,000 acres of farmland will theoretically be covered by hundreds of nodes. Up to ten sensors are made up of each sensor module such as soil humidity, sunlight intensity, soil pH value, CO2, wind intensity, soil fertilizer, soil temperature, rain intensity. The acquired data would then be moved from the supervisor inside the wireless sensor network to the Unmanned Aerial Vehicle side for data collection (Figure 14.15).

14.8.3 Benefits Assessment of Conventional System and the UAV-Based System

IoT infrastructure expenses with 100-acre area: CNY 100,000. Annual operational and maintenance expenses for the system: CNY 12,000.

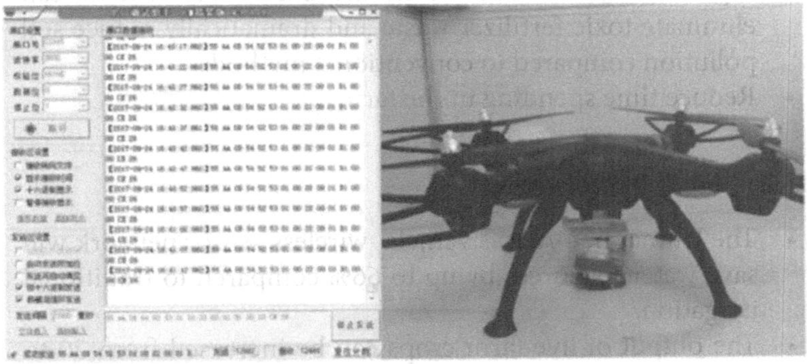

Figure 14.14 Data acquired with UAV.

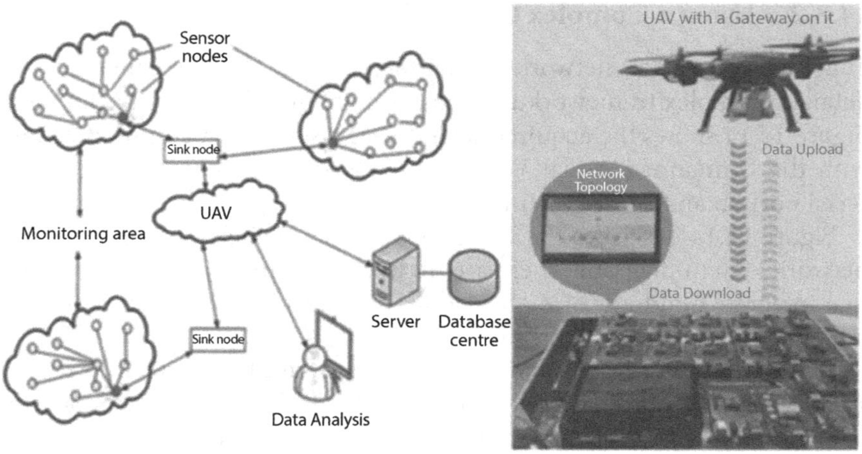

Figure 14.15 UAV-WSN system.

14.8.3.1 *Merit*

- Water supplies can be saved significantly by accurate irrigation by calculating relevant parameters by the UAV-WSN scheme.
- Savings in spending on human resources, i.e., reduction in employees by one manager and one staff.
- Improves production quality and raises farm live.
- By more precisely measuring the mixing rate of pesticides, organic fertilizers and water, the UAV-WSN scheme can eliminate toxic fertilizer waste and dramatically reduce soil pollution compared to conventional methods.
- Reduce time spending in the farm.

14.8.3.2 *Saving Expenses*

- The Unmanned Aerial Vehicle–wireless sensor network will save water resources by up to 66% compared to traditional irrigation.
- The output of live farm crops can be increased from 20 to 80%, the period of growth decreased by up to 30% and the amount of production increased two times.
- Get the investment back from the UAV-WSN and receive income in one year.

14.8.3.3 *Traditional Agriculture*

- Restricted information on the agriculture is mainly obtained by the farmer by the senses. Broad manufacturing capability is limited and it's a shortage of uniform guidelines and actions.

14.8.3.4 *UAV-WSN System-Based Agriculture*

- With a high degree of accuracy, farmers can collect data on the farmland ecosystem in real time. Knowledge is sent to the UAV within a control centre for further analysis. Study should be broad-based [27].

14.9 Conclusion

Farm data should be managed by agricultural management systems so that findings are coordinated to resolve tailored strategies for each farm. The transformation to Agriculture 5.0 is on the initiative of most main equipment manufacturers for the next decade, so manufacturers of off-road equipment can play a significant role in this process. It appears to be the perfect time to step into a modern and sustainable agriculture that can demonstrate the full potential of information management to overcome the problems of agricultural production in the 21st century.Millions of farmers would benefit from the input they get from the field in real time. But the UAV-WSN platform is still not mature enough to be used on a large scale. To develop applications for fishing, poultry and livestock, more research and development work is needed.

References

1. Zhang, Y., The Role of Precision Agriculture. *Resource*, 19, 9, 2019.
2. Schimmelpfennig, D., Farm Profits and Adoption of Precision Agriculture, ERR-217, U.S. Department of Agriculture, Economic Research Service, October 2016.
3. Díez, C., Hacia una agriculturainteligente (Towards and intelligent Agriculture), in: *Cuaderno de Campo*, vol. 60, pp. 4–11, 2017.
4. Rose, D.C. and Chilvers, J., Agriculture 4.0: Broadening responsible innovation in an era of smart farming. *Front. Sustain. Food Syst.*, 2, 87, 2018.
5. Laksham, K.B., Unmanned aerial vehicle (drones) in public health: A SWOT analysis. *J. Family Med. Prim. Care*, 8, 2, 342–346, 2019.

6. Frantz, D., Schug, F., Okujeni, A., Navacchi, C., Wagner, W., van der Linden, S., Hostert, P., National-scale mapping of building height using Sentinel-1 and Sentinel-2 time series. *Remote Sens. Environ.*, 252, 112128, 2021.
7. Nelson, A., Setiyono, T., Rala, A.B., Quicho, E.D., Raviz, J.V., Abonete, P.J., Maunahan, A.A., Garcia, C.A., Bhatti, H.Z.M., Villano, L.S. *et al.*, Toward an operational SAR-based rice monitoring system in Asia: Examples from 13 demonstration sites across Asia in the RIICE project. *Remote Sens.*, 6, 10773–10812, 2014.
8. Gille, S., Parzhanivelan, S., Yadav, M., RIICE remote sensing-based flood assessment helps Government of Tamil Nadu, India in directing flood relief measures, in: *ASEAN Sustainable Agrifood Systems*, 9 February 2016, [online]. [Cited 14 August 2017]. https://www.asean-agrifood.org/rice-remotesensing-based-flood-assessment-helps-government-of-tamil-nadu-india-in-quickly-directing-floodrelief-measures/).
9. Setiyono, T.D., Quicho, E.D., Romuga, G.C., *Rice Yield Estimation System (Rice-YES) User Manual*, International Rice Research Institute, Los Baños, Philippines, 2017.
10. Burwood-Taylor, L., The next generation of drone technologies for agriculture, Agfunder News, 16 March 2017 [online]. [Cited 22 July 2017]. https://agfundernews.com/the-next-generation-of-dronetechnologies-for-agriculture.html.
11. DroneDeploy, No date. Plant health [online]. [Cited 12 August 2017]. https://support.dronedeploy.com/ v1.0/docs/plant-health.
12. Klerkx, L., Jakku, E., Labarthe, P., A review of social science on digital agriculture, smart farming and agriculture 4.0: New contributions and a future research agenda. *NJAS - Wageningen Journal of Life Sciences*, 90–91, 100315, 2019.
13. Helwatkar, A., Riordan, D., Walsh, J., Sensor technology for animal health monitoring. *Proceedings of the 8th International Conference on Sensing Technology*, Liverpool, UK, Sep. 2–4, 2014, [online]. [Cited 13 July 2017].
14. METOS, *Integration with SAP Leonardo brings precision agriculture to a new level*, [online]. [Cited 13 August 2017]. http:/metos.at/home/integration-with-sap-leonardo-brings-precision-agricultureto-a-new-level/.
15. SAP, a. *Design Thinking with SAP*, [online]. [Cited 28 July 2017]. https://designthinkingwithsap.com/ en/.
16. SAP, b. Solution explorer, in: *Connected agriculture*, [online]. [Cited 24 August 2017]. https://solutionexplorer.sap.com/solexp/ui/vlm/is_cp_agriculture/vlm/is_cp_agriculture-ind-is_cp_agriculture/ is_cp_agriculture-bpr-479,is_cp_agriculture-e2e-1461,is_cp_agriculture-ist-4537.
17. Holme, A.McR., Burnside, D.G., Mitchell, A.A., The development of a system for monitoring trend in range condition in the arid shrublands of Western Australia. *Aust. Rangel. J.*, 9, 14–20, 1987.
18. Eisaian, A., *Tansformational power of digital agriculture–why now?*, 2017, [online]. [Cited 17 September 2017]. https://www.intelinair.com/transformational-power-of-digital-agriculture-why-now/.

19. OpenDroneMap, *OpenDroneMap: What is it?*, [online]. [Cited 14 July 2017]. http://opendronemap.Org.
20. Statistics Times, *Sector-wise contribution of GDP of India*, 2017, [online]. [Cited 12 August 2017]. http:// statisticstimes.com/economy/sectorwise-gdp-contribution-of-india.php.
21. Singh, D., Srinivasan, K., Nar, S., Piplani, D., Food Traceability and Safety: From Farm to Fork – A Case Study of Pesticide Traceability in Grapes. *J. Adv. Agric. Technol.*, 4, 40–47, 2017.
22. Kandaswamy, G., Senior Scientist at TCS Research and Innovation gopi.kandaswamy@tcs.com.
23. Government of India, *Crop Insurance*, [online]. [Cited 22 August 2017]. http://agri-insurance. gov.in/Pmfby.aspx.
24. Ray, S.S. and Dubey, S.K., Assistant Director Mahalanobis National Crop Forecast Centre Department of Agriculture, Cooperation & Farmers Welfare Ministry of Agriculture & Farmers Welfare, Government of India ncfc@gov.in.
25. Sandoval, R., Disaster Risk Reduction/Climate Change Specialist FAO Myanmar roberto.sandoval@fao.org.
26. Verdouw, C., Wolfert, S., Tekinerdogan, B., Internet of Things in agriculture. *CAB Rev.*, 11, 1–12, 2016.
27. Yin, W., Zhang, J., Ma, L., Yu, Y., Shenzhen Wissea Technology Co., Ltd. yinwu@wissea.com; zhangjinna@wissea.com; malu@wissea.com; yuyanping@wissea.com.
28. Mohindru, V. and Garg, A., Security Attacks in Internet of Things: A Review, in: *The International Conference on Recent Innovations in Computing*, 2020, March, Springer, Singapore, pp. 679–693.
29. Mohindru, V., Singh, Y., Bhatt, R., Hybrid cryptography algorithm for securing wireless sensor networks from Node Clone Attack. *Recent Adv. Electr. Electron. Eng. (Formerly Recent Patents Electrical & Electronic Engineering)*, 13, 2, 251–259, 2020.
30. Mohindru, V., Singh, Y., Bhatt, R., A Review on Lightweight Node Authentication Algorithms in Wireless Sensor Networks, in: *2018 Fifth International Conference on Parallel, Distributed and Grid Computing (PDGC)*, 2018, December, IEEE, pp. 517–521.
31. Mohindru, V. and Singh, Y., Node authentication algorithm for securing static wireless sensor networks from node clone attack. *Int. J. Inf. Comput. Secur.*, 10, 2–3, 129–148, 2018.
32. Mohindru, V. and Singh, Y., Performance analysis of message authentication algorithms in wireless sensor networks, in: *2017 4th International Conference on Signal Processing, Computing and Control (ISPCC)*, 2017, September, IEEE, pp. 468–472.
33. Mohindru, V., Bhatt, R., Singh, Y., Reauthentication scheme for mobile wireless sensor networks. *Sustainable Comput.: Inf. Syst.*, 23, 158–166, 2019.

34. Mohindru, V., Singh, Y., Bhatt, R., Securing wireless sensor networks from node clone attack: A lightweight message authentication algorithm. *Int. J. Inf. Comput. Secur.*, 12, 2–3, 217–233, 2020.
35. Mohindru, V. and Singh, Y., Efficient approach for securing message communication in wireless sensor networks from node clone attack, 2016.
36. Setiyono, T., Quicho, E., Gatti, L., Campos-Taberner, M., Busetto, L., Collivignarelli, F., Haro, F., Boschetti, M., Khan, N., Holecz, F., Spatial Rice Yield Estimation Based on MODIS and Sentinel-1 SAR Data and ORYZA Crop Growth Model. *Remote Sens.*, 10, 2, 2018.
37. Gnanachandrasamy, G., Ramkumar, T., Senapathi, V., Chung, S.Y., Vasudevan, S., Identification of saline water intrusion in part of Cauvery deltaic region, Tamil Nadu, Southern India: Using GIS and VES methods. Mar. Geophys. Res., 37, 2, 2016.
38. Phan, H., Le Toan, T., Bouvet, A., Lam, N., Duy, T., Zribi, M., Mapping of Rice Varieties and Sowing Date Using X-Band SAR Data. *Sensors*, 18, 316, 2018.
39. Bollini, L., Caccamo, A., Martino, C., Interfaces of the Agriculture 4.0, pp. 273–280, 2019.

15

IoT-Based UAV Platform Revolutionized in Smart Healthcare

Umesh Kumar Gera, Dilip Kumar Saini*, Preeti Singh and Dhirendra Siddharth

Department of Computer Science & Engineering, RAMA University, Kanpur, Uttar Pradesh, India

Abstract

Urgent nursing is a serious part in treatment where time, affordability, and precision of qualitative knowledge jeopardize performance. In addition, the feasibility of emergency care is dependent proceeding the consistency and precision of the info acknowledged in the urgent demand and the information obtained through the process of urgency transport. The progress of an addition surgical operation in an intensive care unit also depends on data gathered at the two stages: ambulance call and shift. However, much of the data obtained during an ambulance call is inaccurate and the tedious and time-consuming process of capturing, storing, sorting, and removing data persists during emergency transport. From a collection of facts gathered, as well as data given by the sick person or sick person family, urgency doctors mostly neglect the health condition of the patient and critical medical facilities. The mobile phone industry and the Internet of Technology (IoT) networks make robust data collection possible and are rapidly being used in health tools and software. It includes addresses an Internet of Things technology to procure emergency care services focused on patient-centric information. A car collision case is based on the investigation. It explores the consequences of experiments carried out.

Keywords: Unmanned Aerial Vehicle (UAV), Internet of Things (IoT), artificial intelligence, healthcare, ubiquitous computing

**Corresponding author*: dilipsaini@gmail.com

Vandana Mohindru, Yashwant Singh, Ravindara Bhatt and Anuj Kumar Gupta (eds.) Unmanned Aerial Vehicles for Internet of Things (IoT): Concepts, Techniques, and Applications, (277–294) © 2021 Scrivener Publishing LLC

15.1 Introduction

Thanks to the announcement by Amazon that it plans to use UAV to send orders to consumers, use of such UAV for viable motives has seen a lot of press late. This is a really interesting and revolutionary project through various expected and unexpected impacts. The future use of UAV is very hoped in healthcare, too. In order to improve care prevention and transmission, can the sector make better use of this technology? UAV have also tested to provide diet relief and healthcare stuff send to earthquake-ravaged nations, to begin with [1]. Accelerated distribution right to the source of drugs, medications and supplies It is possible to suppress eruptions of dangerous infectious illnesses. The detailed list of what could be transported rapidly to areas where terrestrial or conventional air traffic will be stopped by critical damage to infrastructure is comprised of communication devices, mobile technologies and portable shelters. Drones help provide people from a distance or from a distance for more successful care. While handheld, tiny indoor drones may carry medication to the bedside of a bed in the future. A clinic participant, thereby avoiding such human movements. This would result in smoother and less vulnerable to mistake in the administration of drugs.

UAV may offer patients with treatment and equipment to be cared for—a hospital-based climate instead of inside the home. More can be seen in the future. In the hospital, treatment program and residence therapy seem to be provided. Drone technology is going to make those conditions better and safer. There will be a smoother delivery of this home-based care [2]. It is easy to take the patient's blood and send it straight to the laboratory with the UAV for testing while a provider is running at home. It is necessary to recommend drugs, antibiotics and treatments performed by a doctor. To be delivered to the building by UAV.

An individual from a certain area would no longer have to collect AEDs, which can easily be difficult to find. By pushing a button or a smart smartphone programmed, just called the automated external defibrillators (AED). Mobile innovations are now being implemented by healthcare companies to resolve some of the challenges in the field today. Healthcare is evolving with intelligent devices, handheld electronics, remote surveillance, telemedicine and knowledge sharing networks. Drones, robotics and artificial intelligence are expected to take on some healthcare activities undertaken by humans in the near future to eliminate uncertainty, costs and errors [3].

Today, a healthcare provider may appear on a screen remotely and most frequently have a fair diagnosis and have ample guidance to review available studies. It has become unimportant to distance. Geography was, essentially, history! In truly remote areas, though, having medicines, vaccines, blood or even collecting biological samples available for study is a major limitation [4]. In healthcare today, drones are rapidly being used to target the unreached and create relative, not complete, isolation. In a time of technological change, we are alive. It is well known, however, that healthcare providers are traditional worldwide. In a recent report, Goldman Sachs forecasts that over the next five years, overall global drone investments will amount to approximately US$110 billion. Drones were widely used by the military in wartime. With the assistance of an onboard camera, many drone systems provide surveillance. Environmental surveillance, crop spraying, beach shark surveillance, habitat protection control, fire surveillance, police and government unrest and international border control, recreation, documentaries, coverage of accidents, television coverage, disaster relief situations for humanitarian assistance, and scientific study and discovery are the various use cases. Amazon Prime Air is a leader of drone shipping to areas up to 30 min away, with items as large as five pounds. Pizzas are supplied nowadays by drones.

Supplying societies with critical health services is no easy feat. The Medical the Medical Professionals from the third world's first services and aid staff to in big hospitals, time-stressed staff face a number of concerns. Day-challenges that can aid in overcoming unmanned or UAS aircraft systems. Drones enable the delivery to remote locations of serum, birth control, vaccines, blood and other remedial provisions and potential to enter people seeking emergency medical treatment in few times [5].

15.2 IoT-Based UAV Platform for Emergency Services

Gadgets and utilities built on the Internet of Things (IoT) are quickly becoming ubiquitous in our lives, cultures, and economies. In connectivity, power, fitness, home and other industries, high-performance mobile networking, elevated computer usage, connected products and IoT networks are now offering affordable Internet connection solutions. In the other hand, the web of Things (WoT) is seen as an extension of the IoT and aims to resolve ambiguity in IoT environments [6]. RESTful Online Services [7] have become the default way of using IoT computers to provide customer services. There has been a lot of success and advances in having UAVs a realistic alternative in tandem with the IoT revolution in situations such as search & rescue, solar panel & wind turbine monitoring, rapid scouting, farm surveillance, etc. UAVs are paired today with a common resource assessment and maintenance software system. New companies have been developed by Intel aerial data suppliers and Airbus Aerial.

In chapter, we concentrated on WoT and IoT to create a focused UAV computing infrastructure. The Interface needs UAV planning and monitoring of entry requirements, equipment and personnel. The past likewise enables UAV operatives to rapidly organize UAV navies with different applications in Smart and Digital Communities to map and respond to any emergency scenarios. Civil UAVs are an important platform for urban emergency operations and prevention. In order to respond to the sight of a collision and then determine the situation, emergency responders are usually likely to find congested highways [8]. It is also hard to understand why human beings are stuck anywhere if there is fire and smoke in the region. In such cases. Our first UAV concept experiment was performed to help emergency responders achieve these objectives [9].

For first call, the ambulance procedure begins at the urgency organization station. At this period, vital information is presented by the call centre staff about the time pressure situation. Many callers, however, do not record the incident accurately and give information around the careful location of crash. In Ref. [10], the experts presented a smart IoT-based expertise that can conveniently include additional information to address the complexities of emergency calls. The specifics will be fixed in infected people information in the emergency call. Such an arrangement can improve reply to an emergency and save time and reduce the risk of death. In Ref. [11], there is a lengthy article by scientists on the therapeutic use of IoT. In terms of using semantics and ontology to share a vast volume of medical data as well as data processing, methods for dealing with emergency medical services have been developed. To ensure that the findings are available, so-called indirect emergency health facilities are also provided in the study. info obtainability needs info analysis on preceding level. These could appear by means of a medical record. A health management system that needs remote medical advice is also covered in the report.

Because of the number of artefacts that may be involved in an IoT device and the scale of the network that can pose security issues, the IoT faces many problems, such as interoperability, anonymity, authenticity, etc. In Ref. [12], the authors present a definition to fix the interoperability problems in IoT systems in an experiment. Interoperability can be a problem in emergency care and, in practice, a significant concern. China's IoT system for emergency situations is applied in Ref. [13]. The experts describe a blood donation control framework based on IoT. It would also be useful to set up private patient files using this tool. Similar to that mentioned in Ref. [14], a remote control and management system for healthcare specifics is described in Ref. [16]. This method highlights the potential of WSN for use in healthcare (IoT).

15.3 Healthcare Internet of Things: Technologies, Advantages

There is a great state of despair in the healthcare industry. Health services are more expensive than ever, the population of the world is declining, and the number of chronic ailments is growing. What we are approaching is a world in which most people have good insurance care out of control, a substantial portion of the population would be unproductive because of old age, and people would be more vulnerable to chronic disease. Is it not the end of the planet that we suspected it was? The growth of IoT tech is at your rescue, no matter what. While technology won't rescue the planet from ageing or eradicate chronic ailments at once, it will make it easy to at least access healthcare in a pocket [17].

Medical diagnosis absorbs a large amount of healthcare costs. Software can switch routines for medical review from a clinic to the sick person home. The analysis would thus reduce the essential to be seen. In this modern example, referred to as the IOT, takes broad pertinence in many sectors, plus health attention. In the healthcare industry, complete implementation of this model is a common dream, as it allows hospital facilities to run more capably and sick person to access well handling [18]. There are unprecedented advantages of the usage of this technology-based healthcare system that will maximize the quality and reliability of therapies and eventually enhance patients' health.

15.3.1 Advantage

15.3.1.1 Concurrent Surveillance and Tracking

In the case of a medical emergency, actual period nursing of smart strategies will safe life, including heart disease, diabetes, etc. By using a mobile remedial expedient linked to a mobile application, linked smartphones will gather medicinal and further necessary well-being info to track situation in place in real time and use the handset's network connectivity to pass the information gathered to a doctor. The Focus for Similar Well-being Policy released a learning showed that due to remote patient control of patients with heart disease. This information is processed in the AI model and may be exchanged by an approved individual who, irrespective of their location, time or computer, may be a doctor, an insurance agent, a participating healthcare organization, or an external consultant to help them access the data obtained.

15.3.1.2 From End-To-End Networking and Availability

Through assistance of healthcare smartphone apps and novel skills, Internet of Things will ease the patient safety process. Inter dependent, M-to-M connectivity, info sharing and info suffer are enabled by Healthcare IoT, which makes healthcare networks efficient for delivery. Connection protocols: Wi-Fi, Z-wave, Bluetooth LE, ZigBee, and additional new software can reinforce the method pathogens and diseases are diagnosed by sick person and can even invent innovative care approaches [20]. As a result, the technology-driven configuration eliminates costs by eliminating needless trips, leveraging higher quality services and maximizing allocation and planning.

15.3.1.3 Information and Review Assortment

Due to real-time use, if cloud storage is unavailable, Big data transmitted by a healthcare tools in limited period is difficult to store and manage. It is also a tough gamble for healthcare professionals to collect and manually translate data from multiple sensors and networks. Internet of Things tools can capture, analyses and report information in actual-period and decrease the essential to stock data. With experts receiving entree to last diagram analysis, much of this would be over-clouded [21]. Healthcare activities also enable organizations to acquire critical healthcare analysis and info flow understandings that accelerate forecasting and are fewer reactive decision-making.

15.3.1.4 Warnings and Recording

In the case of life-threatening situations, on time warnings are important. Medical IoT systems capture crucial data and relay the data for real-time monitoring to physicians, while alerting consumers to essential components from smartphone apps and other linked devices. Reports and warnings give a straightforward picture, regardless of location and period, of a patient's condition. It also allows well-versed tests to be made and on-time care. IoT then entails alerting, tracking and reporting in real time, encouraging hands-on procedures, enhancing accuracy, prompt provider intervention, and improving the effects of full implementation of healthcare.

15.3.1.5 Wellbeing Remote Assistance

In the event of an emergency, patients can use smart smartphone apps to contact a doctor who is several miles away. Medics will check patients for mobility options for healthcare quickly and recognize the signs on-the-go. Several healthcare supply chains are now aiming to develop robots that will, on the basis of patient prescription and ailment-related data, deliver medications accessible by connected devices [21]. In the hospital, IoT will improve patient safety. This, in essence, would decrease the increase in health insurance for people.

15.3.1.6 Research

For testing purposes, IoT for healthcare may also be used. That's how IoT helps us to generate a large array of data on patient disorders that would have taken several years if we manually compiled it. For statistical research that would help medical science, the data thus obtained may be used. Thus, not only the IoT, but our computational tools will save time. Therefore, in the field of medical science, IoT has a major impact [21]. It causes the implementation of therapeutic therapies that are broader and prolonged. IoT is used in a variety of devices to improve the efficiency of patients' healthcare facilities.

15.3.2 Complications

15.3.2.1 Privacy and Data Security

Data security & privacy is one of the most critical concerns faced by the IoT. In real-time, IoT systems record and relay data. The bulk of IoT devices, however, lack data protocols and specifications. Furthermore, there is considerable uncertainty about compliance with data rights. These two things make data particularly vulnerable to cyber hackers that can break into the system and threaten patients and physicians with personal health information (PHI). Cybercriminals will exploit patient information to purchase medications and medical devices that they can market later, and build false Ides [22]. In the name of the patient, hackers could even make a false argument for defense.

15.3.2.2 Integration: Various Protocols and Services

Multi-device convergence is also slowing the implementation of IoT in the healthcare industry. The explanation for this impediment is that the suppliers of electronics have not reached an agreement on contact specifications and criteria. Therefore, although the array of devices is related, the disparity in their communication protocol complicates and hinders the data aggregation process. This non-uniformity of the related system protocols slows down the whole mechanism and limits the reach of IoT scalability for healthcare [22].

15.3.2.3 Overload and Accuracy of Data

Due to the use of multiple communication protocols & specifications, data aggregation is complicated, as discussed earlier. IoT programmers, though, do collect a lot of details. To obtain important insights, the information obtained by IoT devices is used. However, the volume of information is so large that it is becoming extremely impossible for doctors to collect proof from it, which ultimately impacts the accuracy of decision-making. In addition, this concern is growing as more sensors that gather more and more data are associated [23].

15.3.2.4 Expenditure

Surprised to see cost variables in the parts of the challenge? Some of you, I realize, would be; but the bottom line is: for the common guy, IoT has not yet made healthcare affordable. The boom in healthcare costs is a worrying sign for all, particularly developed nations. The situation is such that 'Medical Tourism' has been developed in which patients with chronic diseases have access in developing countries to healthcare facilities that cost less than a tenth. The principle of IoT in the healthcare field is a fascinating and promising idea. As of now, though, it has not addressed the cost considerations. The stakeholders must make it cost-effective in order to effectively execute the production of IoT apps and to achieve its optimum optimization, or it will still stay beyond the control of all but high-class individuals [23].

15.4 Healthcare's IoT Applications: Surgical and Medical Applications of Drones

Due to its distinct variety of usage in numerous sectors, the rise of the IoT is thrilling for everybody. It has many uses in nursing. In nursing aids IoT with:

- Decreasing the waiting time for emergency departments
- Patient, employees, and merchandise control
- Strengthening distribution of medications
- Ensuring critical hardware distribution

Several wearables & accessories have already been introduced by IoT that have made patients' lives comfortably. The following ones are these units.

15.4.1 Hearables

Hearables are new-age hearing aids that have completely transformed the relationship of people who have suffered hearing loss with the environment. Often, listeners are compliant with Bluetooth, synchronizing the mobile with it.

It lets you filter sounds from the natural world, equalize and blend layered components. Doppler Labs is the most fitting example of this [24].

15.4.2 Ingestible Sensors

Ingestible sensors are, technically, a new technological wonder. They are pill-sized sensors that track our body's medicine and warn us if any anomalies are sensed by our body. As they help to curb complications and provide an early warning for diseases, these sensors can be a blessing for a diabetic patient. One such example is Proteus Digital Wellness.

15.4.3 Moodables

Moodables are devices which enrich the environment, helping to fuel our enjoyment of the day. It may sound like science fiction, but it is not far from reality. Thync and Halo Neurosciences are now focused on it and it has taken huge strides. Moodables are head mounted wearables that boost our mood by delivering a low-intensity current to the brain [24].

15.4.4 Technology of Computer Vision

Along with AI, computer vision technology has given rise to drone technology that seeks to simulate visual reality and thus make decisions on given parameter in optimal solution. To sense obstacles and fly over them, drones such as Skydio use machine vision technology. In order to enable visually disabled persons to maneuver comfortably, this technology can also be used [24].

15.4.5 Charting for Healthcare

IoT applications such as Audemix reduce the amount of manual work a doctor needs to perform during patient mapping. It is run by voice commands and input is received by the user. It makes the patient's details conveniently available for examination. This saves 15 h for doctors operating with them [25].

15.5 Drones That Will Revolutionize Healthcare

The medical device industry has seen many advances in healthcare being developed and introduced. It's all pale relative to the importance that IoT would offer to healthcare. Here are a handful of special places where the most leverage would be on smart and wired networks. Patients and healthcare providers alike are seeking to reduce costs and find treatment methodologies that are more effective. The Internet of Things (IoT) could provide the fastest way to accomplish such aims, in addition to other technical developments [28].

15.5.1 Integrated Enhancement in Efficiency

A patient relations professional, points out that healthcare facilities face various organizational difficulties as they aim to manage stock inventories, monitor human property, and maintain surgical instruments. The IoT would reinforce the way the supply chain is handled by hospitals, clinics, and other suppliers.

In addition to helping healthcare facilities to keep track of current inventory, technology such as wireless RFID sensors and cloud-based information systems would also help them to forecast potential needs. Big Data analytics can help physicians and administrators perform statistical research and reduce overstocking-related costs [28]. Furthermore, they would be able to build personnel schedules dependent on previous information and collect real-time details on shipments and other facets of the supply chain.

15.5.2 Offering Personalized Healthcare

Wearable technology is in its infancy right now, but over the next five years, it will revolutionize the way physicians practice personalized medicine. As with all technology, wearable equipment can become more affordable, making it available to clients at all income levels. In addition, groundbreaking opportunities can be found by physicians and scientists to adapt wearable technologies to clinical decision making [29].

Modern wearable devices, for instance, allow physicians to remotely track vital signs, asthma symptoms, diabetic data, and other critical details. They will get more detailed and much smaller within the next five years, just as today's smartphones have more computing capacity than the monolithic computer terminals of the 1980s.

The IoT would allow doctors to remotely treat patients as well. A patient may be able to connect with a doctor using a computer, tablet, or mobile to explain symptoms rather than entering an office. To explain the symptoms, a patient may be able to connect with a specialist using a TV, tablet or mobile phone. This monumental improvement in the care site would increase the usability of the facility significantly. Sensor technology is now getting more reliable, allowing clinicians to determine specific knowledge about the needs and skills of a patient [29].

15.5.3 The Big Data Manipulation

In the healthcare sector, Big Data provides a variety of opportunities. A day in the U.S. Around 20 TB (terabytes) of data is generated by the Department of Commerce, while the Harvard Business Review reports that all industries generated 2.5 quintillion TB of data in 2012. Since the data is already being generated by companies, governments, and healthcare facilities, the challenge lies in analysis and integration.

15.5.4 Safety and Privacy Optimization

Healthcare IT News identifies protection and privacy as the primary IoT barriers to healthcare. Instead of trying to retrofit devices with security features, manufacturers and developers will focus from the start on developing stable devices for the next five years. In order to avoid obtaining information that can compromise a person's wellbeing, they can also find ways to limit their information intake [30].

It is likely that policymakers will find ways to codify and mandate privacy in the IoT market. Businesses and healthcare services will take the lead by then when securing patient records and using data ethically. Those who fail will, in this respect, suffer from negative reputations and public outcry.

15.5.5 Enabling M2M Communication

Not only is the Internet of Things consisting of many devices that are different. To allow Bluetooth-enabled devices to "talk" to one another, it relies on machine-to-machine (M2M) connectivity. If a patient wears a monitor that alerts him or her to physical changes such as blood pressure or heart rate, via Bluetooth technology, the same device can pass information to a doctor's office device or home computer [30–33].

Over the next five years, contact with M2M will increase in prevalence. Not only can patient-centered devices connect with the devices of healthcare providers, but healthcare equipment will communicate via Wi-Fi interchangeably. Venues such as imaging centers and Cath laboratories which have facilities that can interact to improve accuracy and decrease the potential for human error during procedures.

15.6 Healthcare Revolutionizing Drones

The drone era has come and today both robotic driving and autonomous flight are increasingly becoming a reality. Businesses are competing for a piece of the sky from new start-ups to existing firms such as Google and Amazon, aiming for the right ways to implement drones into our lifestyle.

Here is a complete list of the most exciting drones capable of revolutionizing healthcare in the near future [31, 34, 35].

15.6.1 Google Drones

Google has already filed a patent on a drone that can give people in need emergency assistance. The drone can arrive at the scene before an ambulance can get there, as in the previous case. To help you pick the type of emergency and also explain the drone's ETA, a computer (or a prospective app) was also included in the patent [31].

15.6.2 Healthcare Integrated Rescue Operations (HiRO)

In order to better deal with the effects of natural disasters on US soil, Subbarao of Hattiesburg, Mississippi, needs a telemedicine drone to be supplied. After recent tornadoes that left individuals stranded, unreachable by ambulances, and ready to drop off equipment that is critical to the emergency situation, he finds his drone to be powered by GPS [31].

15.6.3 EHang

EHang has signed an agreement with Lung Biotechnology PBC in the US to build up to 1,100 units of its 185 drones, the world's first human-carrying autonomous drone. The aim is to automate the transfer of people to emergency conditions in the field of donated organs [31].

15.6.4 TU Delft

As a project that incorporates a cardiac defibrillator and a 2-way touch radio + camera into the drone, the TU Delft Emergency Drone has been developed. The ambulance services will send the drone to the patient in the case of cardiac arrest, where bystanders will be told how to administer CPR and proceed with the automatic defibrillator until the emergency services take over [31].

15.6.5 Project Wing

Google's parent corporation, Alphabet, has also been working on Project Wing to use food, clean water and other medical supplies for disaster relief and distribution. In both the United States (partially) and Queensland, Australia, the project has been successfully tested. The Federal Aviation Administration (FAA) received final clearance last month in order to undergo full-scale checks at one of the locations licensed by the FAA [31].

15.6.6 Flirtey

With drone delivery of first aid kits and emergency medicine, Flirtey has made its own separate delivery of food, water and a first aid package, as the Nevada-based start-up is approaching one step closer [31].

15.6.7 Seattle's VillageReach

This Seattle-based international nonprofit corporation has collaborated with Matter Net, a drone company focusing on autonomous transport in the Silicon Valley. The goal of the current research project is to move blood samples to the main hospital in Lilongwe, the country's capital, from remote community clinics [31].

15.6.8 ZipLine

A UAV start-up based in San Francisco reached an agreement earlier this year with the Rwandan government to try to supply blood to the world for transfusion [31].

15.7 Conclusion

Earlier study has established to the healthcare is enormously expanded by the usage of the IoT technique and the definition of health safety coverage. IoT systems such as IoT and WSN are used for patient-centered data dispensation, preservation and retrieval, a systematic literature review has shown. Data mining takes full advantage of IoT networks, where information is stored autonomously and continuously. For fast decision-making, Fog/edge computing helps process the collected data locally. With regard to the period that is a critical stage in the implementation of healthcare, fast decision-making is a big concern. This discussion an Internet of things allowed urgency medicinal service distribution scheme that deals by sick person around info from various sources, including bionic info, that is not widely measured in medicinal care for reason behind lot of cost spending in bionic problems. So, the IoT help to support this type of problem in healthcare in minimum cost which is highly useful for society.

References

1. Perrier, E., *Positive Disruption: Healthcare, Ageing & Participation in the Age of Technology*, The McKell Institute, Australia, 2015.
2. Zhu, N., Diethe, T., Camplani, M., Tao, L., Burrows, A., Twomey, N., Kaleshi, D., Mirmehdi, M., Flach, P., Craddock, I., Bridging e-Health and the Internet of Things: The SPHERE Project. *IEEE Intell. Syst.*, 30, 4, 39–46, 2015.

3. Sarkar, S. and Misra, S., From Micro to Nano: The Evolution of Wireless Sensor-Based Healthcare. *IEEE Pulse*, 7, 1, 21–25, 2016.
4. Seera, M., Lim, C.P., Liew, W.S., Lim, E. and Loo, C.K. Classification of electrocardiogram and auscultatory blood pressure signals using machine learning models. *Expert Systems with Applications*, 42, 7, 3643–3652, 2015.
5. Ozcan, K., Velipasalar, S., Varshney, P.K., Autonomous Fall Detection With Wearable Cameras by Using Relative Entropy Distance Measure. *IEEE Trans. Hum.-Mach. Syst.*, 47, 1, 31–39, 2017.
6. Datta, S.K., Bonnet, C., Costa, R.P.F.D., Harri, J., Datatweet: An architecture enabling data-centric iot services, in: *2016 IEEE Region 10 Symposium (TENSYMP)*, May 2016, pp. 343–348.
7. Datta, S.K., Bonnet, C., Nikaein, N., An IoT gateway centric architecture to provide novel M2M services, in: *2014 IEEE World Forum on Internet of Things (WF-IoT)*, March 2014, pp. 514–519.
8. Choi, S., Sung, N., Park, J., Ahn, I., Kim, J., Enabling drone as a service: One M2M-based UAV/drone management system, in: *2017 Ninth International Conference on Ubiquitous and Future Networks (ICUFN)*, pp. 18–20, 2017.
9. Matos, J. and Postolache, O., Iot enabled aquatic drone for environmental monitoring, in: *2016 International Conference and Exposition on Electrical and Power Engineering (EPE)*, Oct 2016, pp. 598–603.
10. Seiber, C., Nowlin, D., Landowski, B., Tolentino, M.E., Tracking hazardous aerial plumes using IoT-enabled drone swarms, in: *2018 IEEE 4th World Forum on Internet of Things (WF-IoT)*, Feb 2018, pp. 377–382.
11. Datta, S.K., Khan, M.I., Codeca, L., Denis, B., Harri, J., Bonnet, C., Iot and microservices based testbed for connected car services, in: *2018 IEEE 19th International Symposium on "A World of Wireless, Mobile and Multimedia Networks" (WoWMoM)*, June 2018, pp. 14–19.
12. Aziz, M.V.G., Hindersah, H., Prihatmanto, A.S., Implementation of vehicle detection algorithm for self-driving car on toll road cipularang using Python language, in: *2017 4th International Conference on Electric Vehicular Technology (ICEVT)*, Oct 2017, pp. 149–153.
13. Ali, Z.H., Ali, H.A., Badawy, M.M., Intenet of Things (IoT): Definitions, challenges and recent research directions. *Int. J. Comput. Appl.*, 128, 1, 37–47, 2015.
14. HaddadPajouh, H., Dehghantanha, A., Parizi, R.M., Aledhari, M., Karimipour, H., A survey on Internet of Things security: Requirements, challenges, and solutions. *Internet Things*, 100129, 2019.
15. da Costa, C.A., Pasluosta, C.F., Eskofier, B., da Silva, D.B., da Rosa Righi, R., Internet of Health Things: Toward intelligent vital signs monitoring in hospital wards. *Artificial Intelligence in Medicine*, 89, 61–69, 2018.
16. Islam, S.R., Kwak, D., Kabir, M.H., Hossain, M., Kwak, K.-S., The Internet of Things for healthcare: a comprehensive survey. *IEEE Access*, 3, 678–708, 2015.

17. Li, J., Ma, Q., Alan H.S., Chan, S.S., Man. Health monitoring through wearable technologies for older adults: Smart wearables acceptance model, *Applied Ergonomics*, 75, 162–169, 2019.
18. Zhu, N. *et al.*, 'Bridging e-health and the Internet of Things: The SPHERE project. *IEEE Intell. Syst.*, 30, 4, 39–46, Jul./Aug. 2015.
19. Chang, S.-H., Chiang, R.-D., Wu, S.-J., Chang, W.-T., A contextaware, interactive M-health system for diabetics. *IT Prof.*, 18, 3, 14–22, May/Jun. 2016.
20. Pasluosta, C.F., Gassner, H., Winkler, J., Klucken, J., Eskofier, B.M., An emerging era in the management of Parkinson's disease: Wearable technologies and the Internet of Things. *IEEE J. Biomed. Health Inform.*, 19, 6, 1873–1881, Nov. 2015.
21. Fan, Y.J., Yin, Y.H., Xu, L.D., Zeng, Y., Wu, F., IoT-based smart rehabilitation system. *IEEE Trans. Ind. Informat.*, 10, 2, 1568–1577, May 2014.
22. Sarkar, S. and Misra, S., From micro to nano: The evolution of wireless sensor-based healthcare. *IEEE Pulse*, 7, 1, 21–25, Jan./Feb. 2016.
23. Tokognon, C.A., Gao, B., Tian, G., Yan, Y., Structural health monitoring framework based on Internet of Things: A survey. *IEEE Internet Things J.*, 4, 3, 619–635, Jun. 2017.
24. Alam, K.M., Saini, M., Saddik, A.E., Toward social Internet of vehicles: Concept, architecture, and applications. *IEEE Access*, 3, 343–357, Mar. 2015.
25. *Unmanned Aircraft Systems (UAS): Frequently Asked Questions*, Federal Aviation Administration, Washington. DC, 2017, Available at Accessed November 12, 2017.
26. Alves, R.C.A., Gabriel, L.B., Oliveira, B.T.D., Margi, C.B., Santos, F.C.L.D., Assisting physical (hydro)therapy with wireless sensors networks. *IEEE Internet Things J.*, 2, 2, 113–120, Apr. 2015.
27. Xu, B., Xu, L.D., Cai, H., Xie, C., Hu, J., Bu, F., Ubiquitous data accessing method in IoT-based information system for emergency medical services. *IEEE Trans. Ind. Informat.*, 10, 2, 1578–1586, May 2014.
28. Olaronke, I. and Oluwaseun, O., Big data in healthcare: Prospects, challenges and resolutions, in: *Proc. Future Technol. Conf. (FTC)*, Dec. 2016, pp. 1152–1157.
29. YIN, Y., Zeng, Y., Chen, X. and Fan, Y. The internet of things in healthcare: An overview. *Journal of Industrial Information Integration*, 1, 3–13, 2016.
30. Caro, F. and Sadr, R. The Internet of Things (IoT) in retail: Bridging supply and demand. *Business Horizons*. 62, 1, 47–54, 2019.
31. https://doctorpreneurs.com/9-drones-that-will-revolutionise-healthcare/
32. Mohindru, V., Bhatt, R., Singh, Y., Reauthentication scheme for mobile wireless sensor networks. *Sustainable Comput.: Inf. Syst.*, 23, 158–166, 2019.
33. Mohindru, V., Singh, Y., Bhatt, R., Hybrid cryptography algorithm for securing wireless sensor networks from Node Clone Attack. *Recent Adv. Electr. Electron. Eng. (Formerly Recent Patents Electrical & Electronic Engineering)*, 13, 2, 251–259, 2020.

34. Mohindru, V., Singh, Y., Bhatt, R., A Review on Lightweight Node Authentication Algorithms in Wireless Sensor Networks, in: *2018 Fifth International Conference on Parallel, Distributed and Grid Computing (PDGC)*, 2018, December, IEEE, pp. 517–521.
35. Mohindru, V. and Garg, A., Security Attacks in Internet of Things: A Review, in: *The International Conference on Recent Innovations in Computing*, 2020, March, Springer, Singapore, pp. 679–693.

Index

Printed in the USA/Agawam, MA
September 16, 2026

910661.011